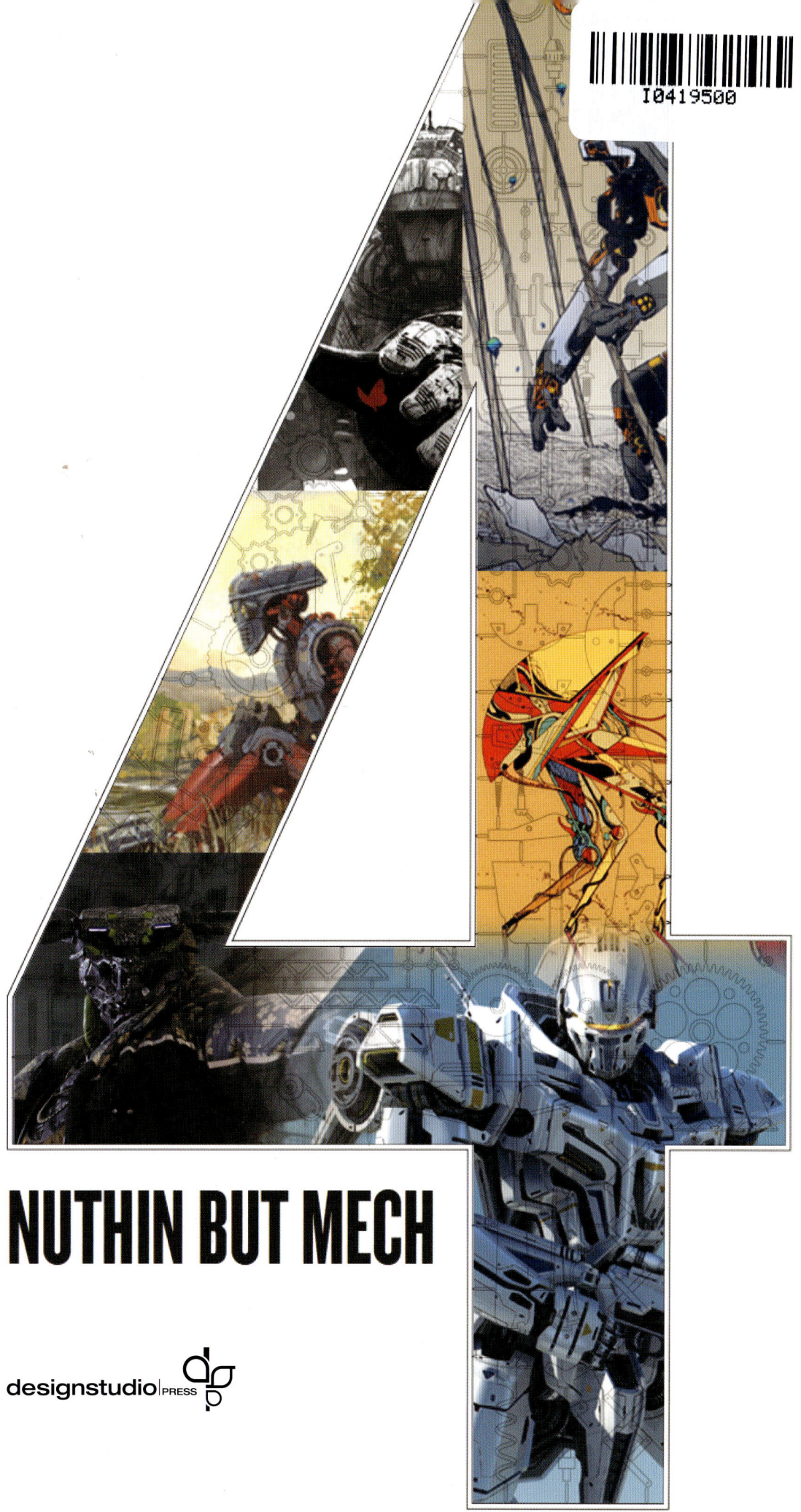

NUTHIN BUT MECH

designstudio|PRESS

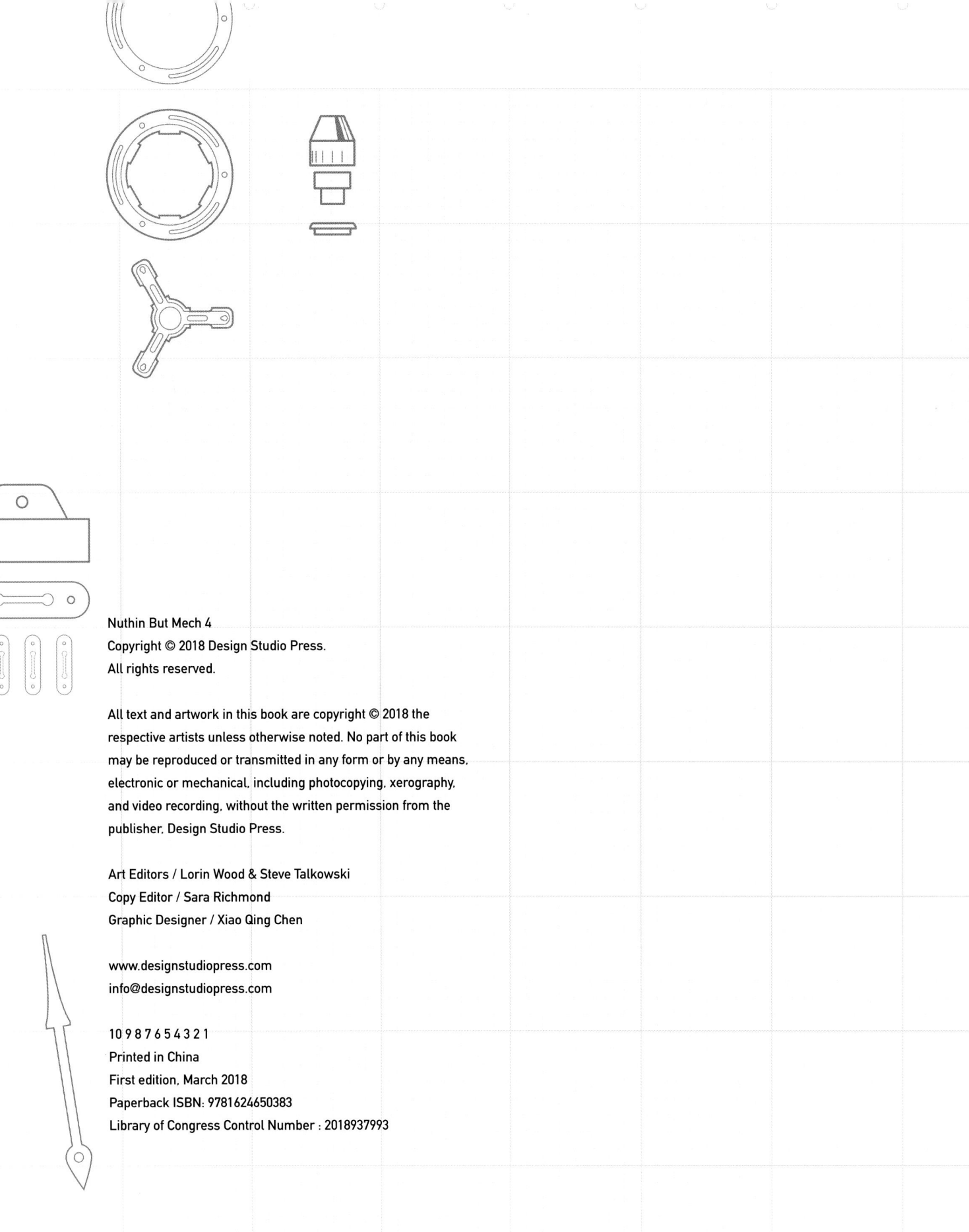

Nuthin But Mech 4

Art Editors / Lorin Wood & Steve Talkowski
Copy Editor / Sara Richmond
Graphic Designer / Xiao Qing Chen

www.designstudiopress.com
info@designstudiopress.com

10 9 8 7 6 5 4 3 2 1
Printed in China
First edition, March 2018
Paperback ISBN: 9781624650383
Library of Congress Control Number : 2018937993

TABLE OF CONTENTS

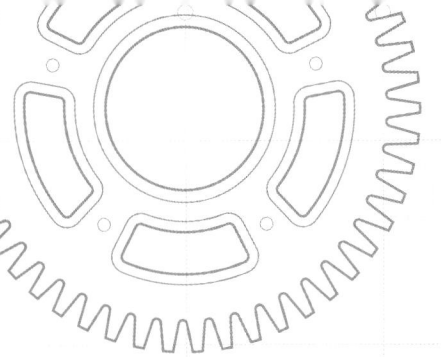
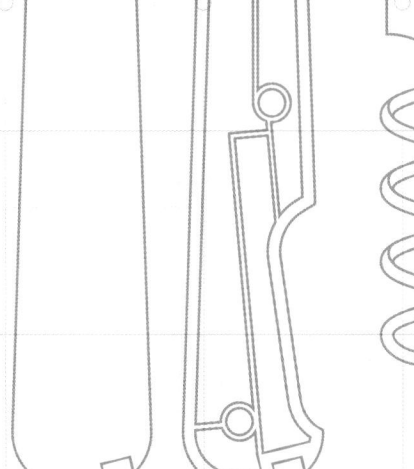

FOREWORD

Every big project needs a champion—that certain someone who cares enough about realizing a vision to help all involved rise up and overcome the challenges along the road of completion. In the *Nuthin' But Mech* series of books this has been Lorin Wood. Without Lorin there may have been one book in this series, maybe, but no way would there have been four. The world needs more people like Lorin: people who care about pursuits outside of their day jobs and daily routines, sticking with a self-imposed task for the love of it and not for a paycheck.

Lorin has now built the world's finest collection of original mech-related art done by the world's most talented mech artists/designers. This collection will now conclude with this fourth and final book in the series, *Nuthin' But Mech 4*.

I know fans of this series will appreciate the dedication and effort needed to create the art for these books by all the contributing authors. But I also hope readers recognize that the greater pursuit of doing something well for the sake of practicing one's craft, exercising imagination and honing skills, is something we can all be inspired to do for ourselves, just for the joy of doing.

When we endeavor into the unknown we can make our greatest discoveries about what we have to share with others through whatever our medium of communication might be. For many of us it's a blank piece of paper waiting for that first mark to be put upon it to lead us down the path of visual discovery. For others it's picking up a lump of clay and starting to form it into something new and never before seen.

Whatever your medium is, I strongly encourage you to press forward in these pursuits and believe they are worthy of your time. Forget the pressures and responsibilities of your real-world demands for a moment, and let your imagination run, just for you, just for the hell of it. Create, discover, learn, and grow as an individual, and then share your discoveries with others. Maybe someday you can bridge the gap of doing great things not only for yourself, but also for others, by championing a collective project. Just as Lorin has done for all of us: the benefactors of his selfless efforts in the realm of *Nuthin' But Mech*.

Thank you, Lorin.

Scott Robertson

Los Angeles, CA
February 12, 2018

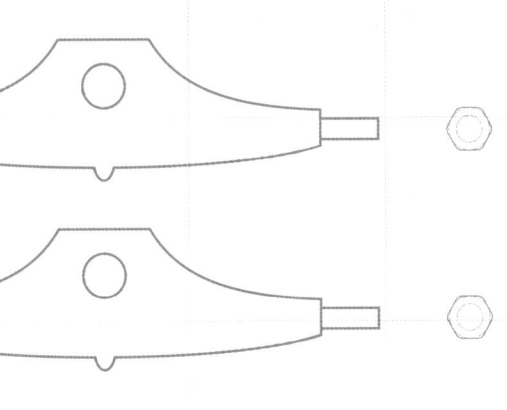

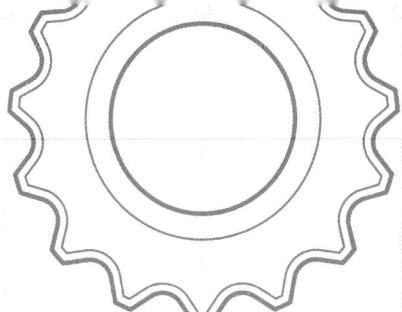

INTRODUCTION

We knew that this day would come. Our journey has reached its end—on this road, at least. To say that this book series has been a journey would be an understatement. It started with a blog (nuthinbutmech.blogspot.com; shameless plug), which I started back in 2009. The initial inhabitants were primarily friends I had made over the years to populate our nook of cyberspace with quality robot designs and illustrations. It turned out to be pretty successful.

The idea for a printed companion to the blog was proposed to me by, I think it was, Thom Tenery, who suggested that I run the idea past Scott Robertson; he had recently joined the blog. Scott agreed and thought it would be a fun idea.

When he asked me in 2012 to take the reigns of the first book, I was both excited and flattered by the challenge. This was a learning opportunity for sure, as I had never tackled a publication of this caliber and scope before, let alone with Design Studio Press. Some of the best and most talented artists from around the world needed to be organized and shepherded along a relatively tight delivery schedule. That was one obstacle.

I also needed them to deliver high-quality work, despite their other professional and personal obligations (trust me; they were busy). Not surprisingly, each of them delivered above and beyond what I was expecting. When the work began to steadily trickle in, it was like Christmas morning for about a month straight. I honestly felt like the winner.

New and original art from designers, illustrators, and 3D artists that I admired was filling up my inbox, but the cherry on top was that the artists deferred any individual payment to a charity of our choosing. When no one jumped ship at this request, that admiration and respect was solidified even more so. It spoke volumes to both their character and passion to their craft.

After four volumes, though, it has come time to close this chapter of the *Nuthin' But Mech* book series, and its intentionally poorly spelled title. I cannot express my gratitude enough to Scott Robertson and the staff at Design Studio Press: Tinti, Victor, Teena, and the others working behind the scenes. Thank you for letting us obsess on robots for the past five years and carrying us on through to the finish line, despite the various bumps inherent on the road of publication. I also have to express a huge thank you to the artists of these past four books (I will not name you individually here because we need to keep the page count down). You generously donated your time and immense talents to this wonderfully niche subject and did so while thanking me in the process! I'm still puzzled by this….

Let me finally express my personal gratitude to you, the readers. Thank you for the encouraging notes and emails (or just for buying the books), which kept this series going. All artists enjoy validation and appreciation of their work, but beyond this, if you were inspired by the work published in these books, that is the highest compliment an artist can receive.

Welcome back to the final outing into the world of *Nuthin' But Mech*!

Lorin Wood
Dallas, Texas
2017

AARON BECK

Aaron draws robots. At least until robots draw robots. Then we're all out of a job.

www.aaronbeck.com

ALEX JAY BRADY

Alex is a designer in the UK, working in games and movies as a concept artist, who also enjoys taking time to paint as a hobby.

www.artstation.com/artist/boac

ALEX FIGINI

Born in London, England, now living in Canada. Alex has been a concept artist in the entertainment industry since 2006, working on AAA games for Sony and EA. He has also worked in film and been published in a number of books and magazines. Originally a 2D artist sticking primarily to Photoshop, over the past several years he's been using ZBrush, Marvelous Designer, and KeyShot in his workflow, all of which have yielded great results and proved to be incredibly valuable for production. In addition, Alex is an Instructor with Learn Squared and has just released an online course, "Concepting in ZBrush," which takes students through his design and thought process when using these digital tools, explains his workflow, and tries to distill 10 years of experience into four, easy-to-follow lessons. Sign up for the course at www.learnsquared.com.

www.artstation.com/artist/alexfigini

AMIN AKHSHI

Amin is a freelance concept designer, currently focusing on futuristic design for movies and video game cinematics in both fields (hard-surface and organic) as well as developing designs from concept through manufacturing production to create innovative products in medical, electronics, industrial, and other product categories.

www.amin.artstation.com

ANDREA MANCARELLA

Andrea is an Italian concept artist with a passion for story-driven designs and cinematic storytelling. He is currently working as a freelance artist for the entertainment industry.

www.andreamancarella.com

ARA KERMANIKIAN

Ara is a designer focused on sophisticated, futuristic vehicle, character, and set design for film, games, television, VR worlds, and collectibles. He is particularly fond of designing mechs and cybernetic-enhanced creatures and robots. Also an educator at the ArtCenter College of Design and Otis College of Art and Design, Ara is currently writing his second book, Polysculpting, which is his strategic approach to creating 3D models for film, games, television, ads, VR worlds, and 3D-printed collectibles, using a hybrid of polygonal modeling and digital sculpting. In addition, he has written master classes for 3D Artist magazine and various online publications, and has been showcased in several books and magazines, including editions of Nuthin' But Mech, Mastering Maya, and Introducing ZBrush.

Ara primarily designs digitally in 3D using digital-content creation software such as ZBrush, Maya, Photoshop, and KeyShot, among many other digital tools. Results can be used in motion graphics for film, TV, or VR, and can be printed in 2D in multiple compositions, using multiple vantage points and colorways. Using 3D-printing technology, they can also be printed as physical, articulated statues. Ara's approach allows for rapid prototyping and iterative design exploration to get the most compelling, desired result.

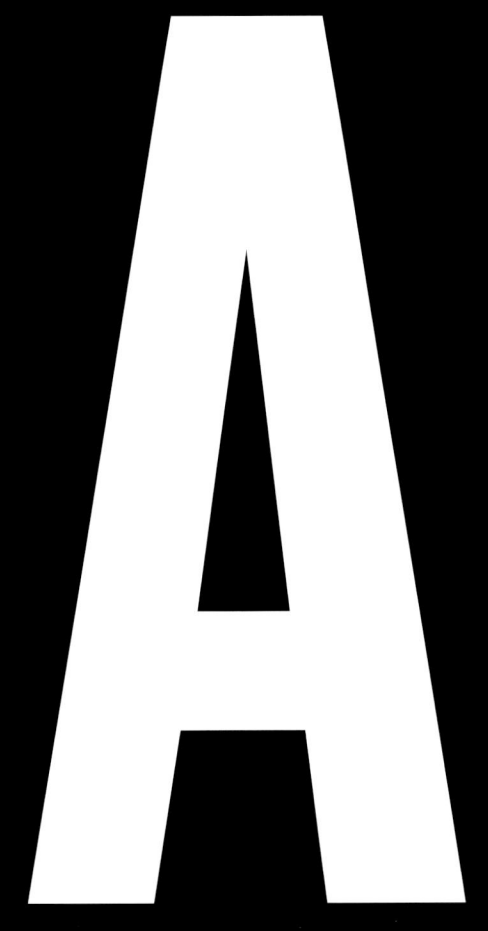

Aaron Beck

Alex Jay Brady

Alex Figini

Amin Akhshi

Andrea Mancarella

Ara Kermanikian

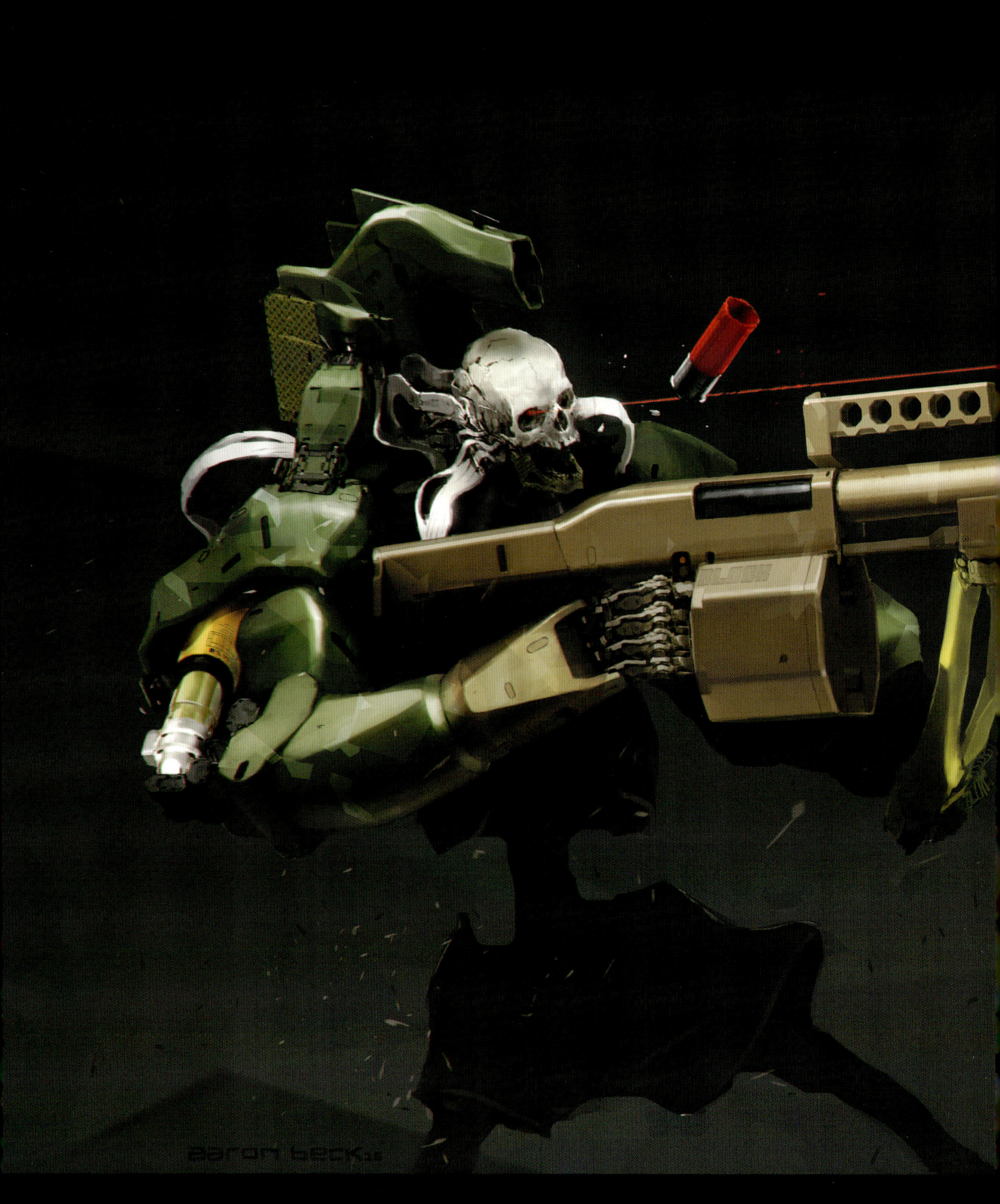

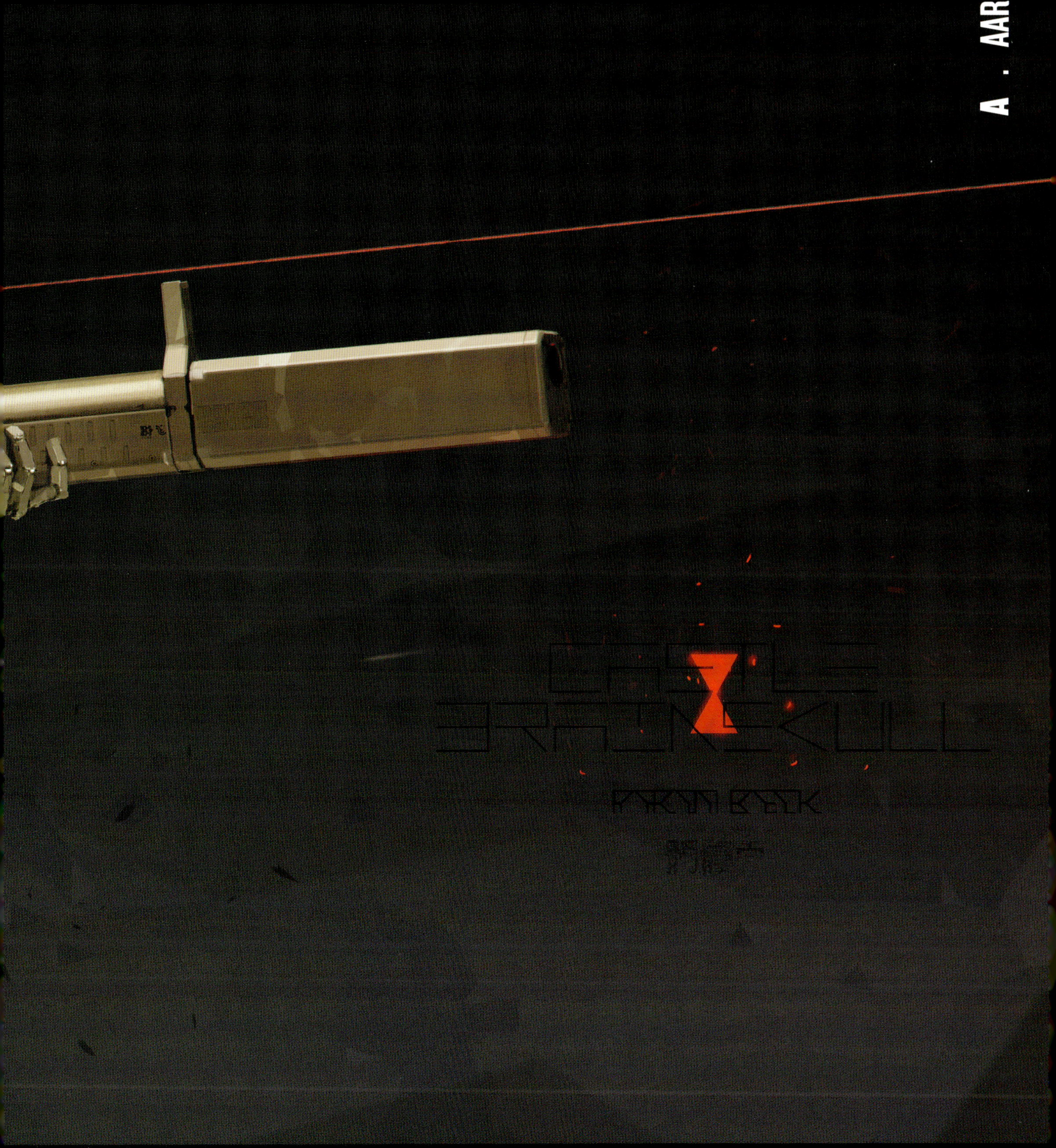

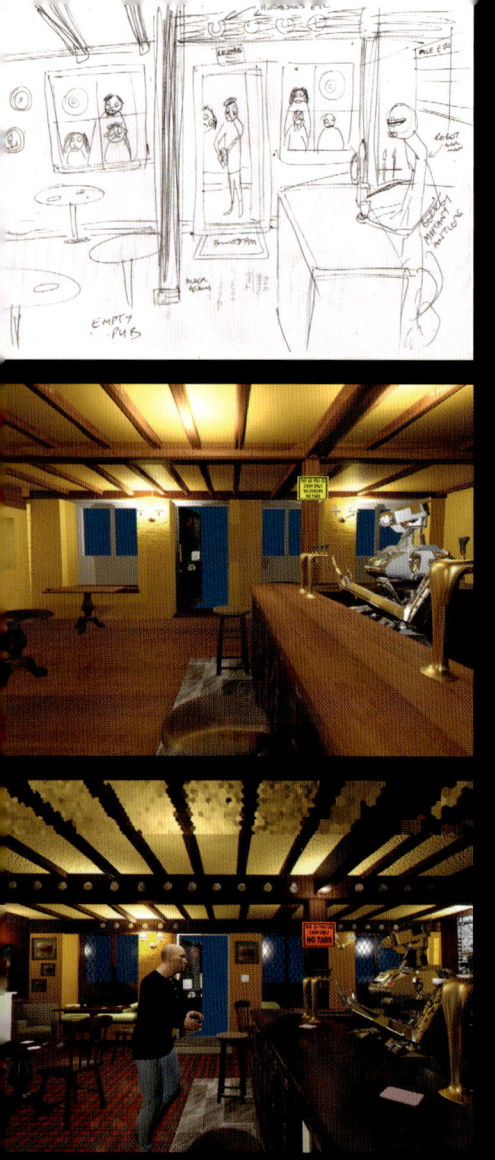

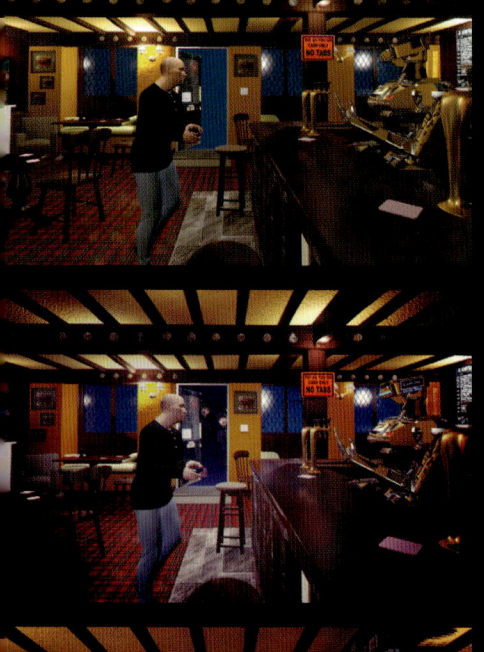

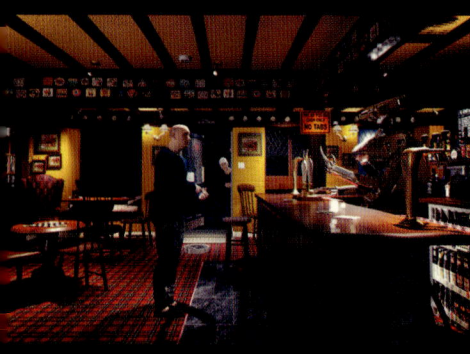

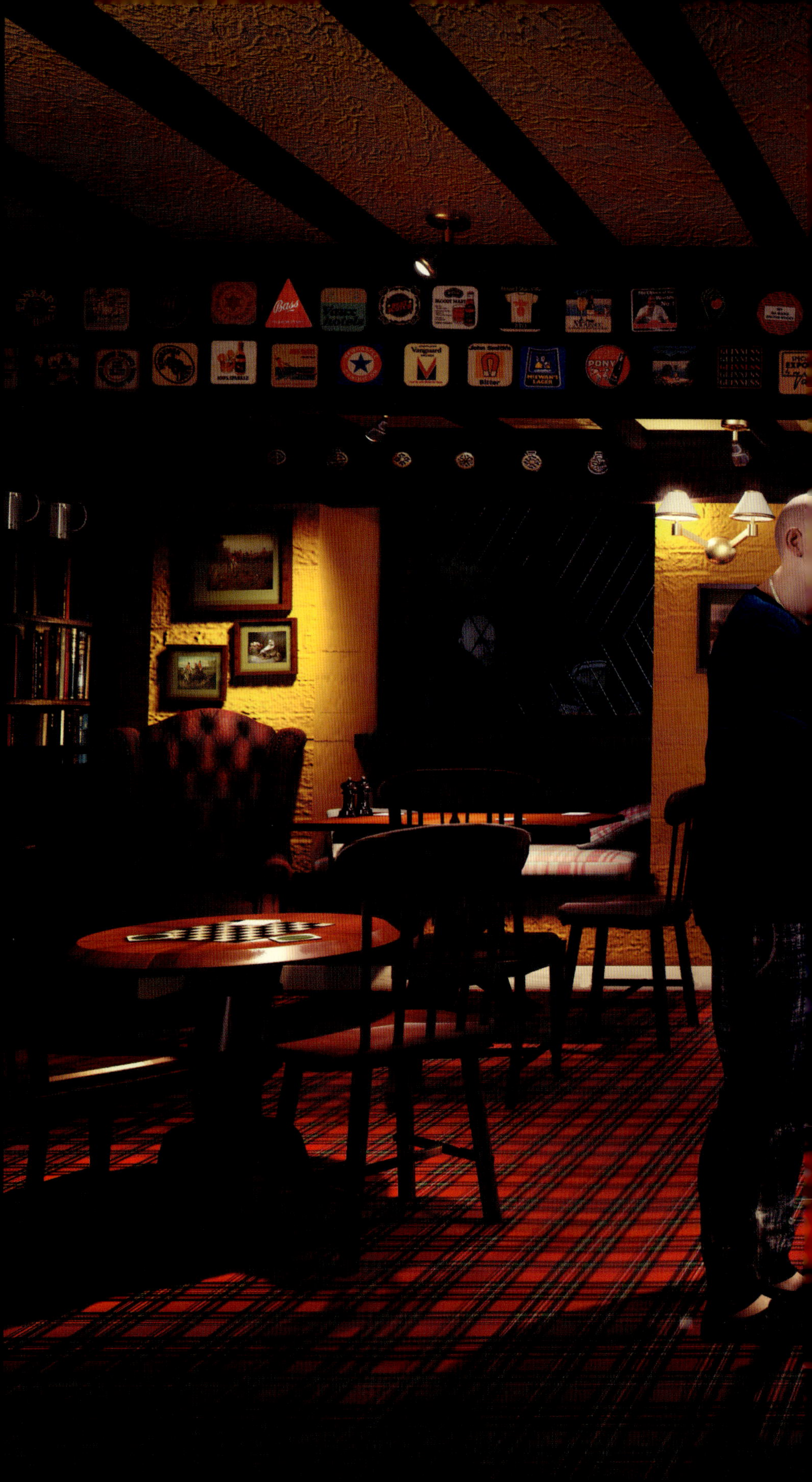

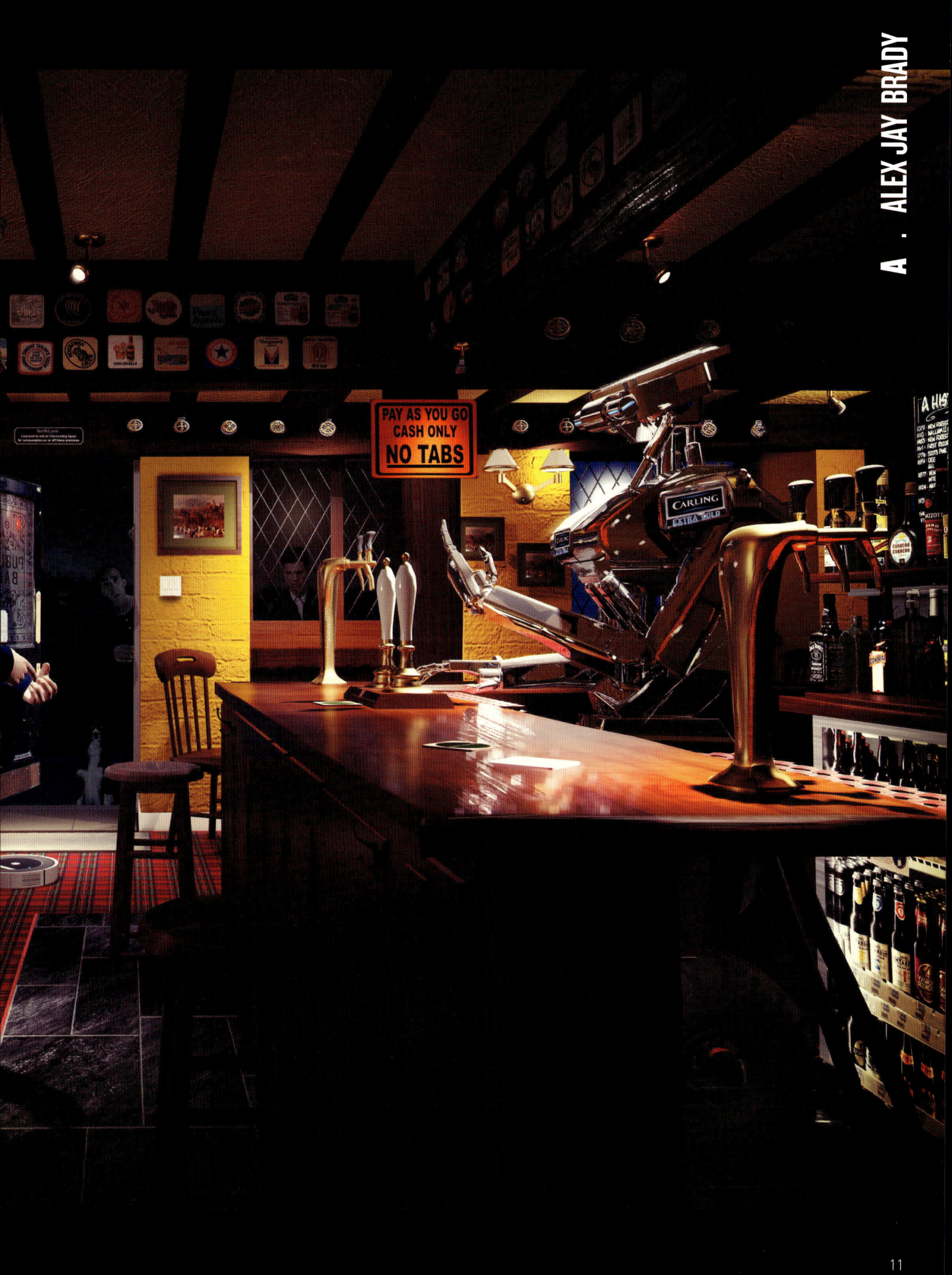

PAY AS YOU GO
CASH ONLY
NO TABS

CARLING
EXTRA COLD

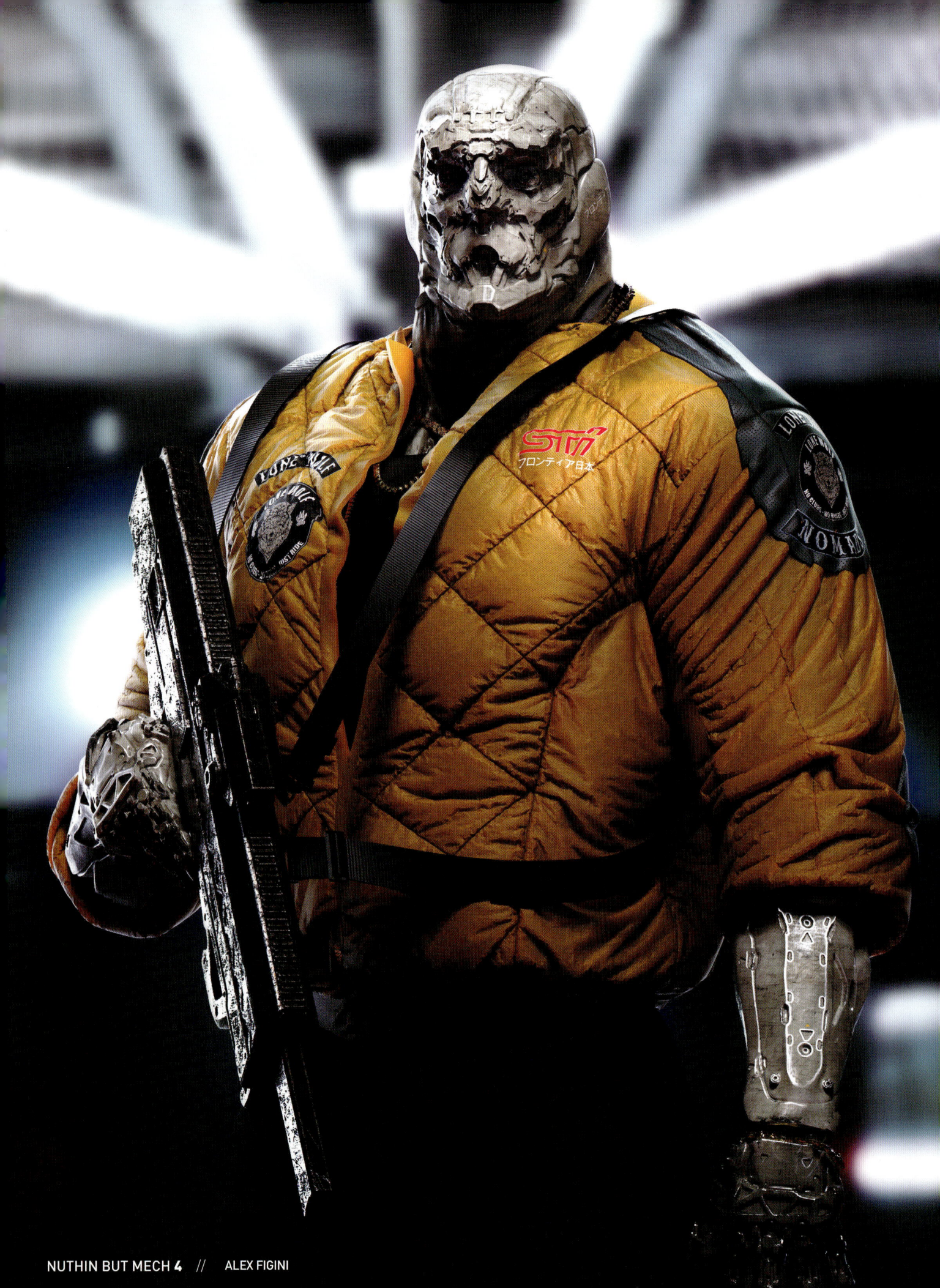

A . ALEX FIGINI

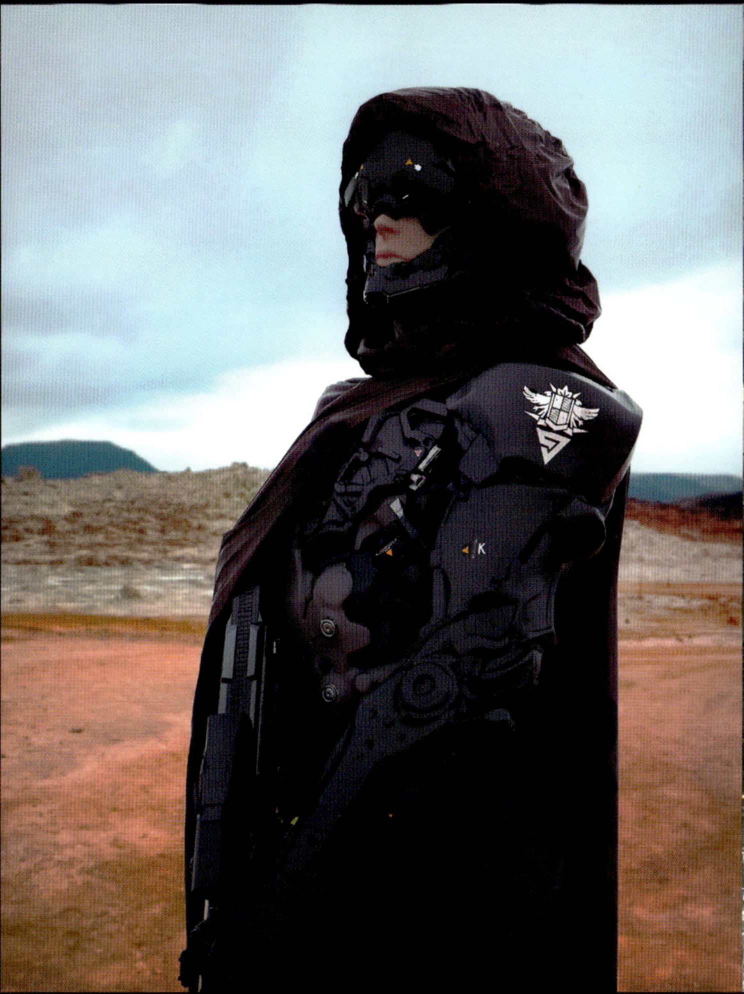

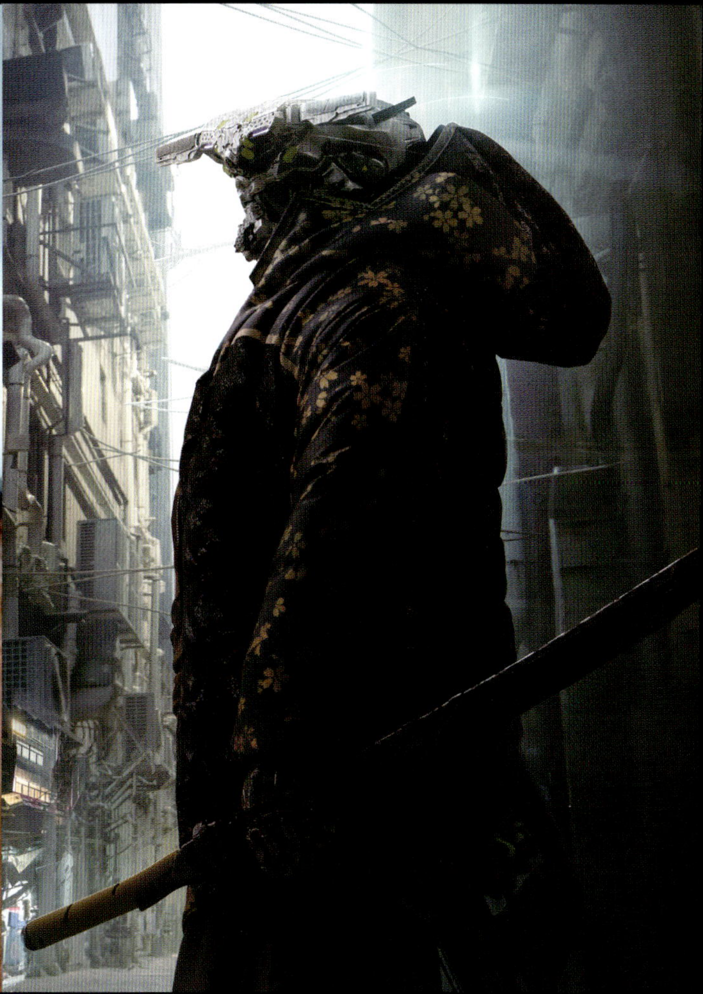

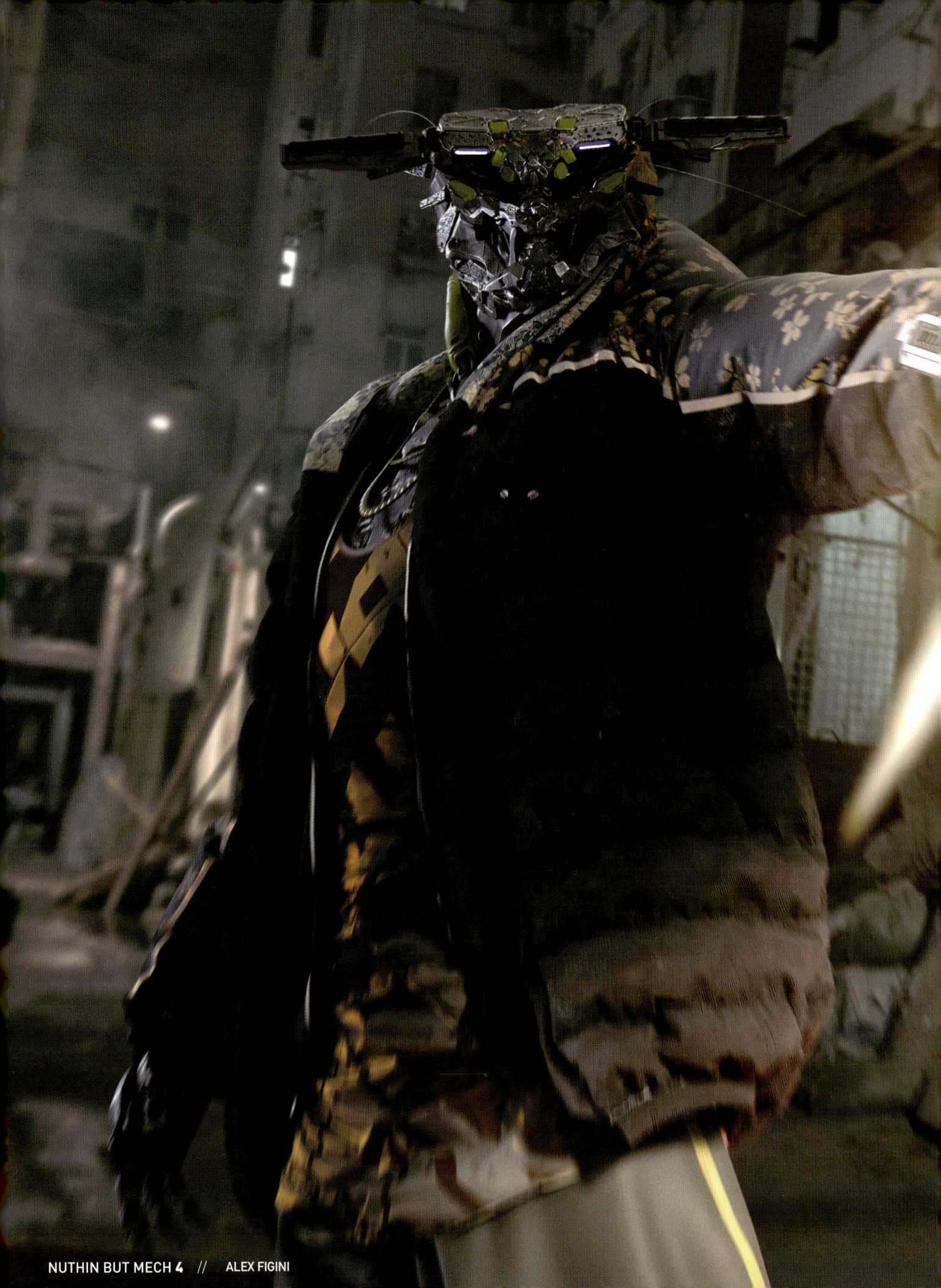

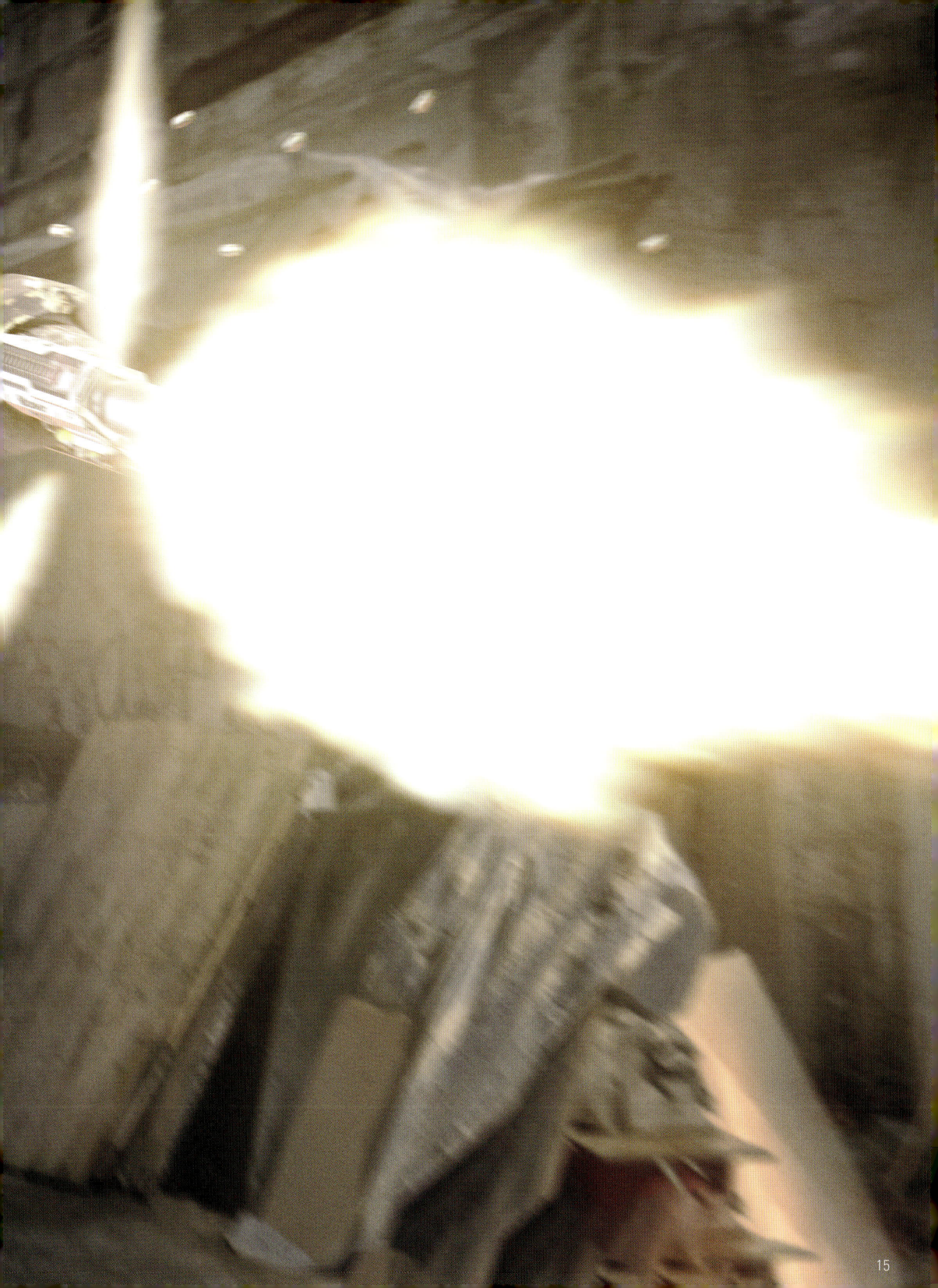

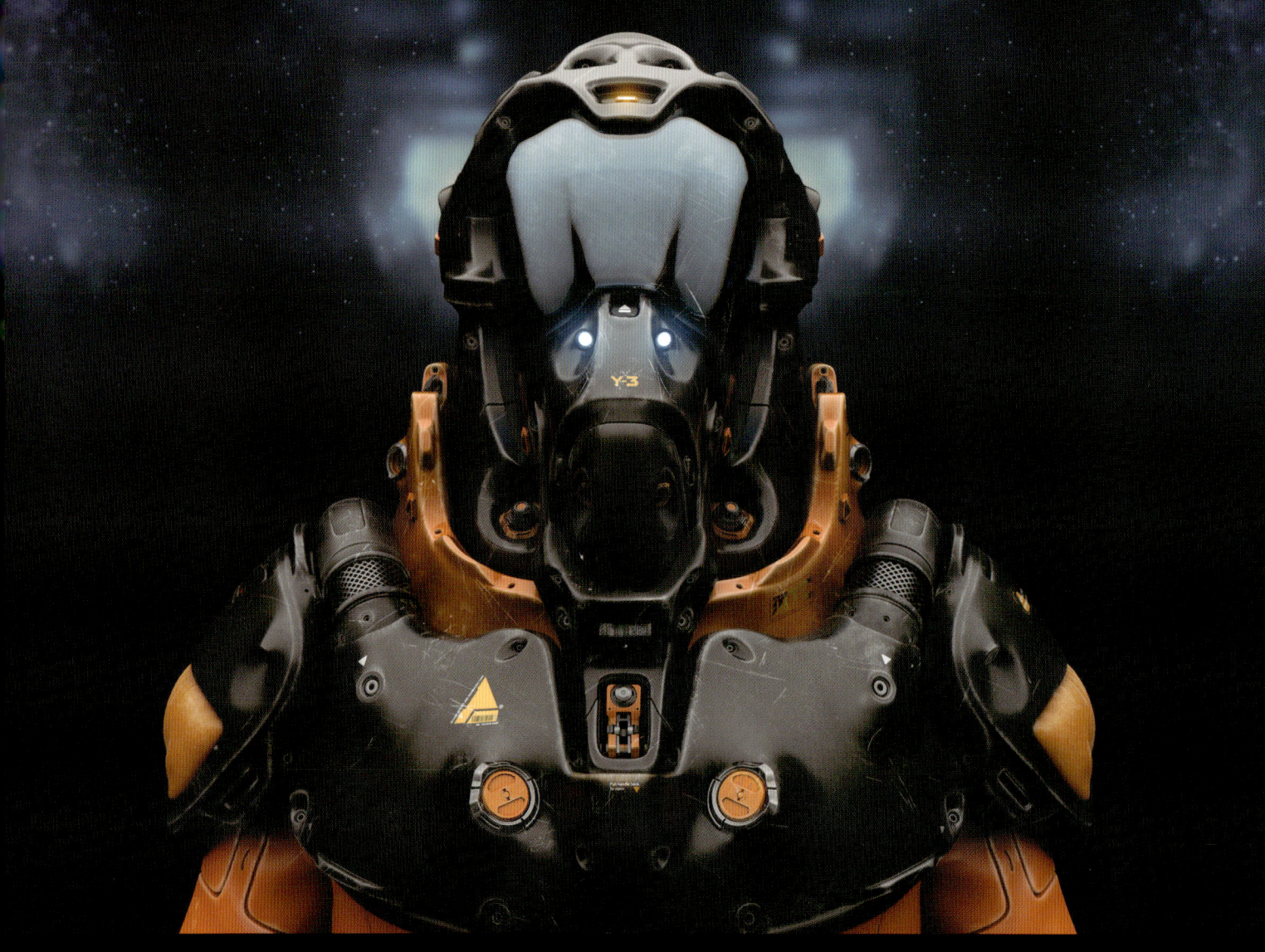

U.S.B.W.L.

(U.S. Army Biological Warfare Laboratories) The idea was to design a suit for scientists who are working in military laboratory research to develop biological weapons.

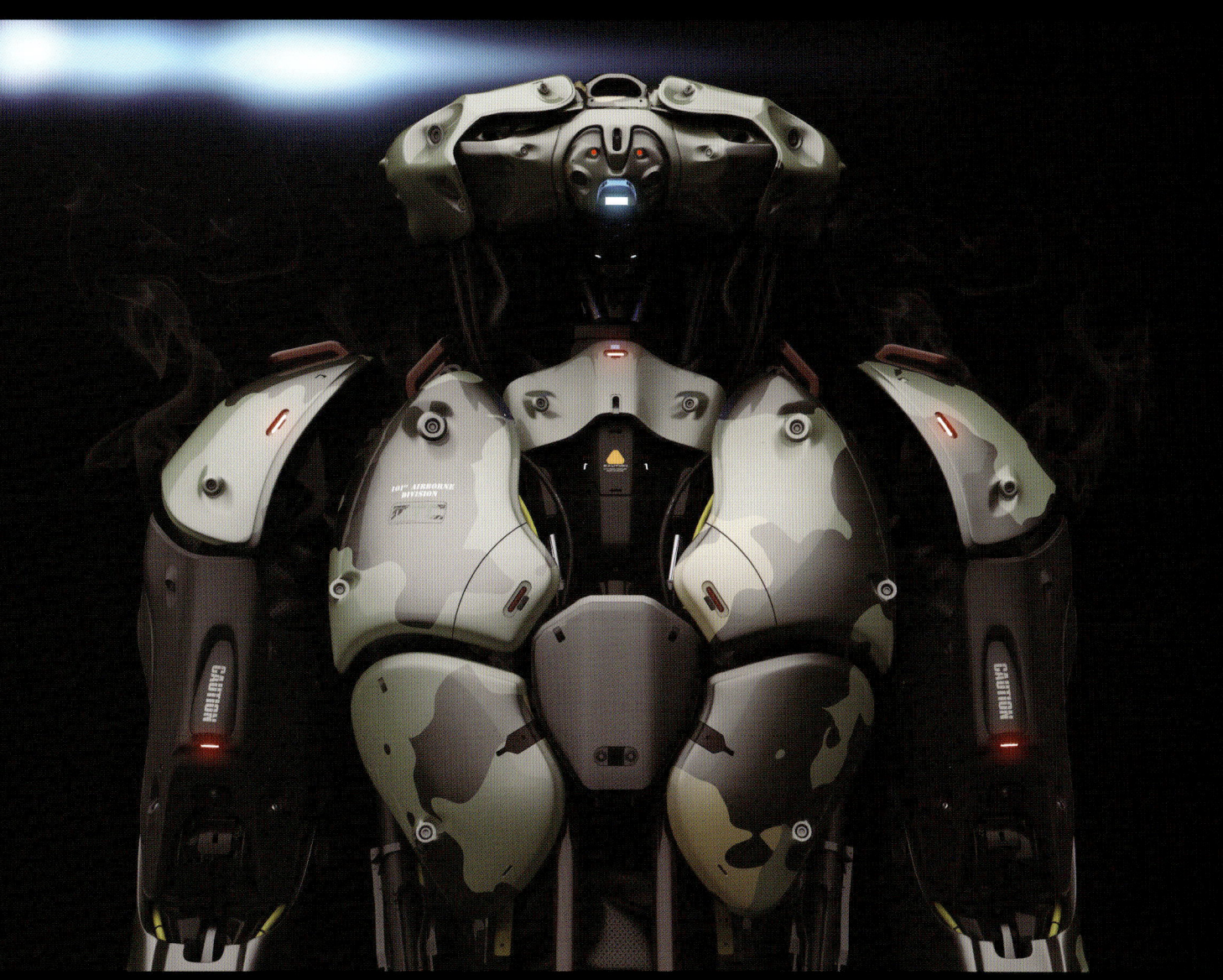

Strike Force

A concept for future military soldiers, they deploy rapidly worldwide by air, land, or sea, and, on order, conduct air assault or ground operations to destroy enemy forces, seize key terrain or facilities, and control specific land areas.

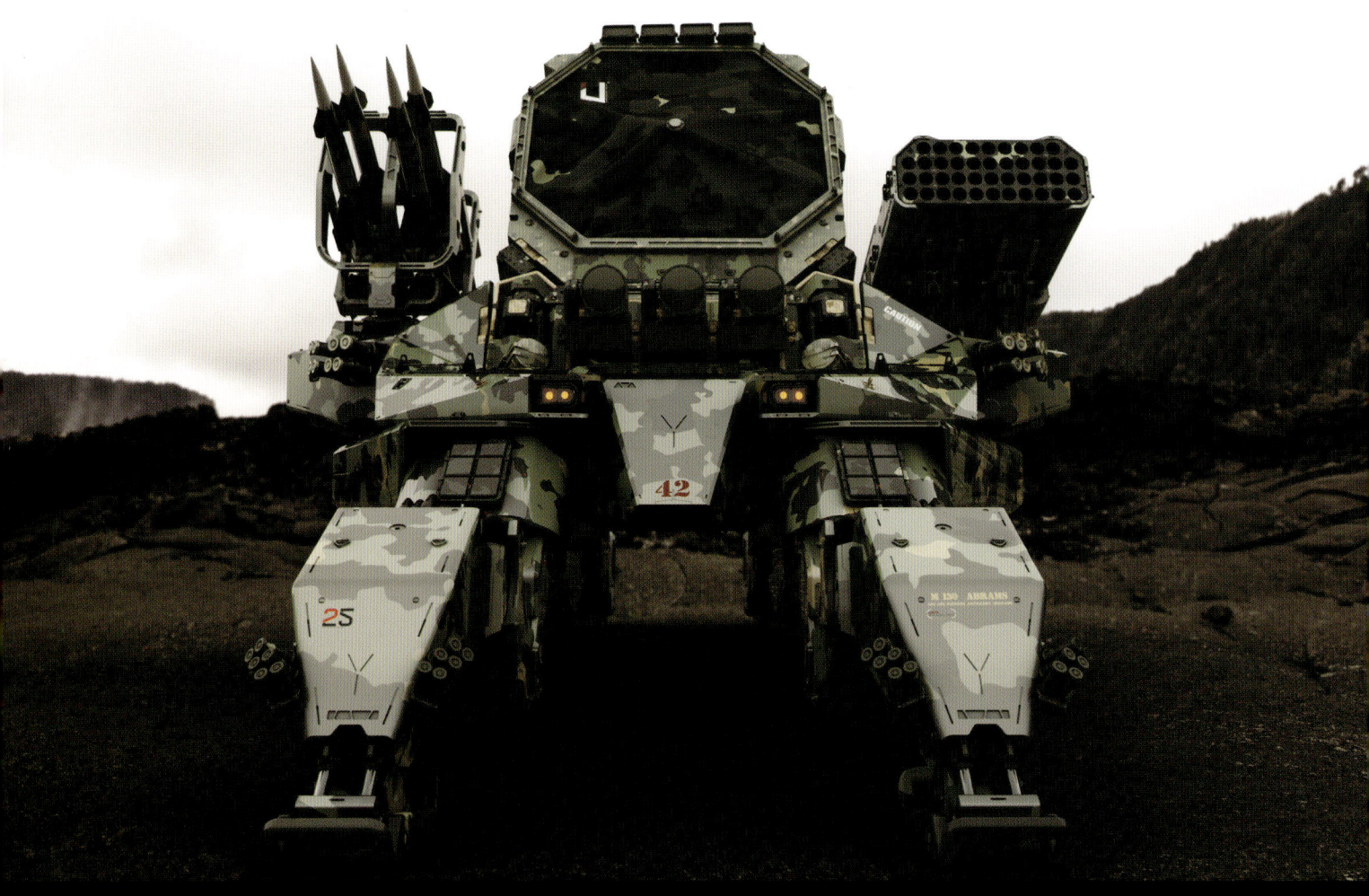

M130 Abrams, 108th Air Defense Artillery Brigade

I was looking for some military vehicles and an idea crossed my mind: design a mech for artillery division that can track any aircraft and bring it down! This mech also has the ability to stand over uneven ground and balance for firing.

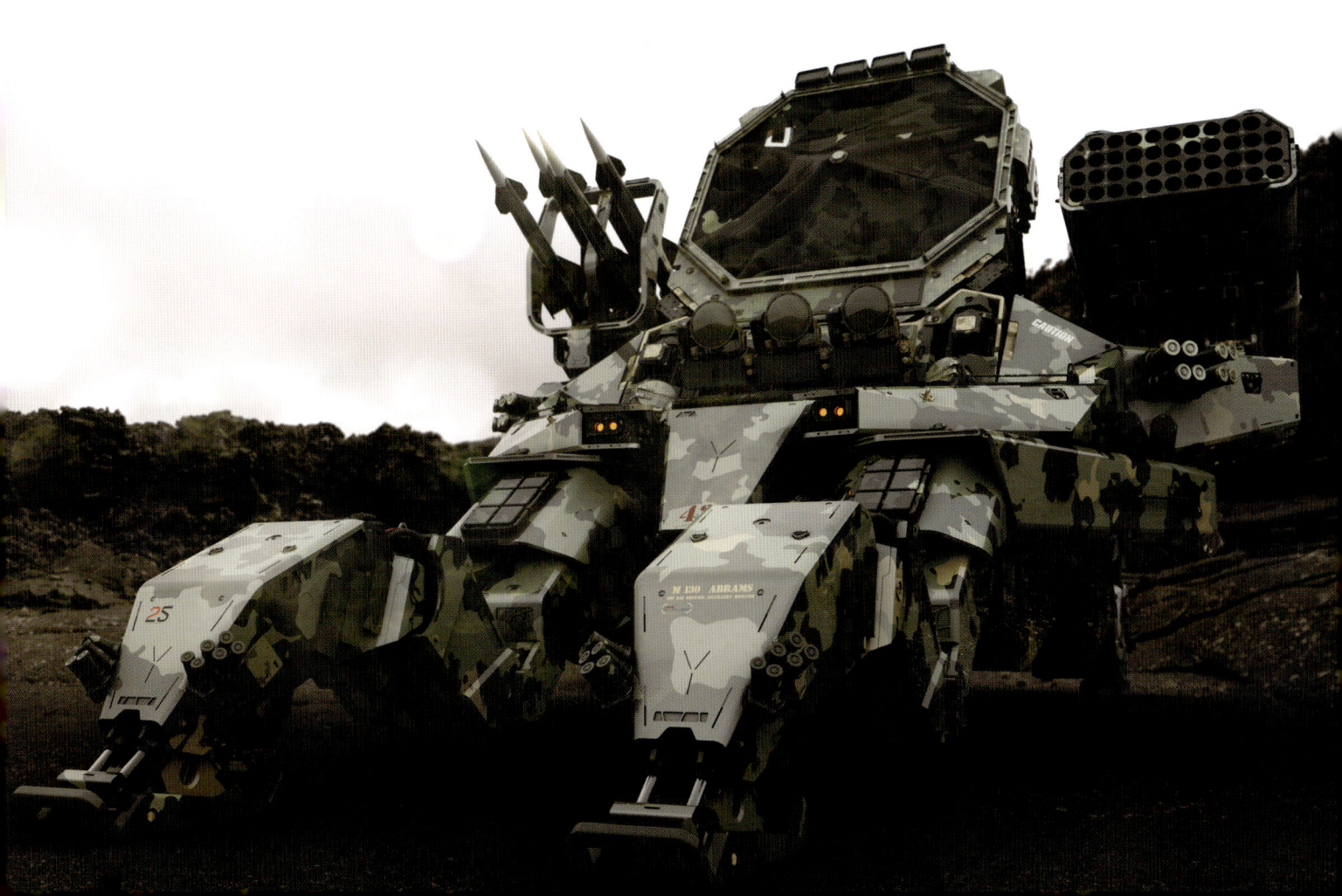

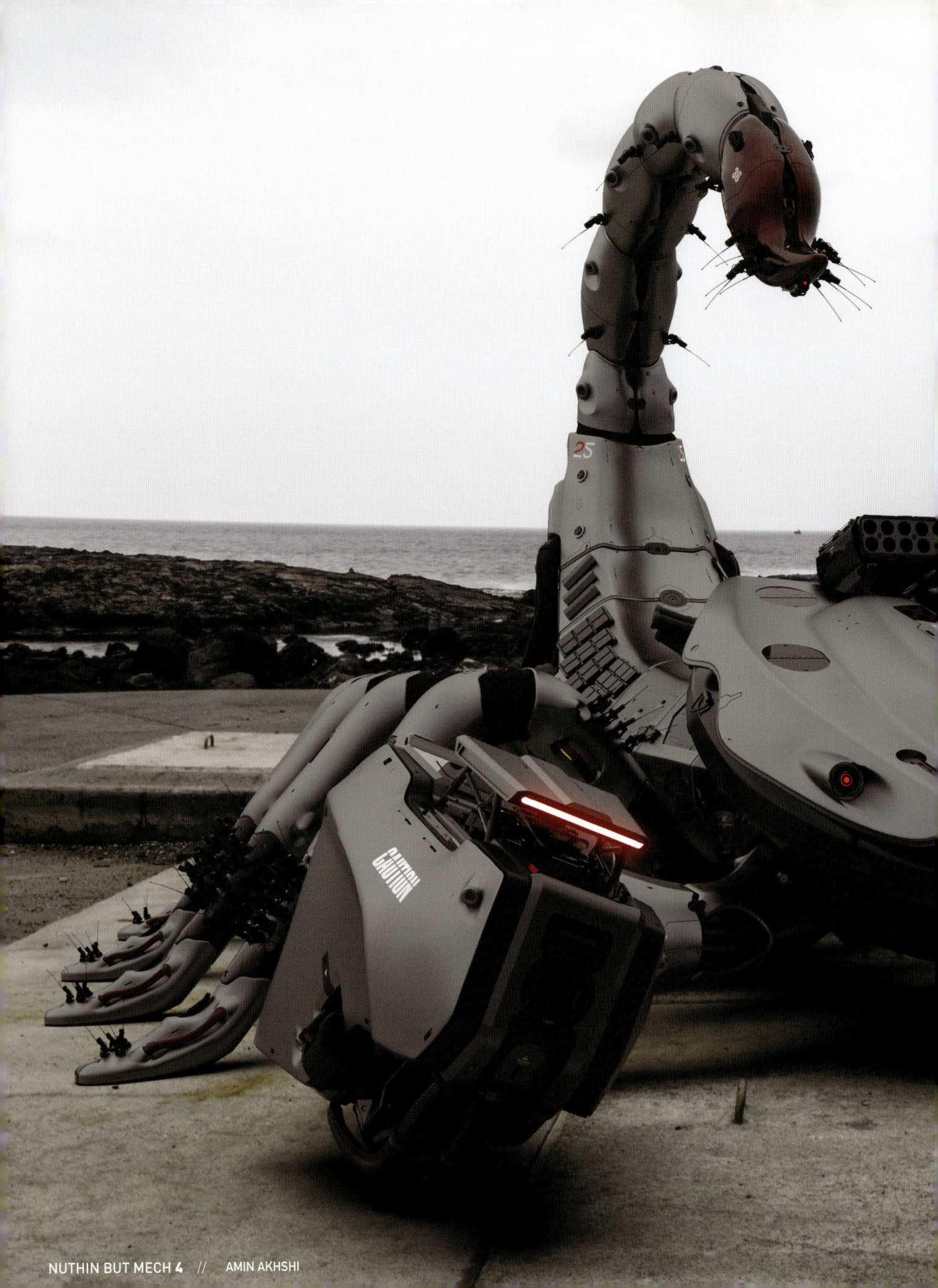

Deathstalker

I was highly inspired by Vitaly Bulgarov and the amazing Black Phoenix Project to design a killer machine in the shape of the most dangerous species of scorpion.

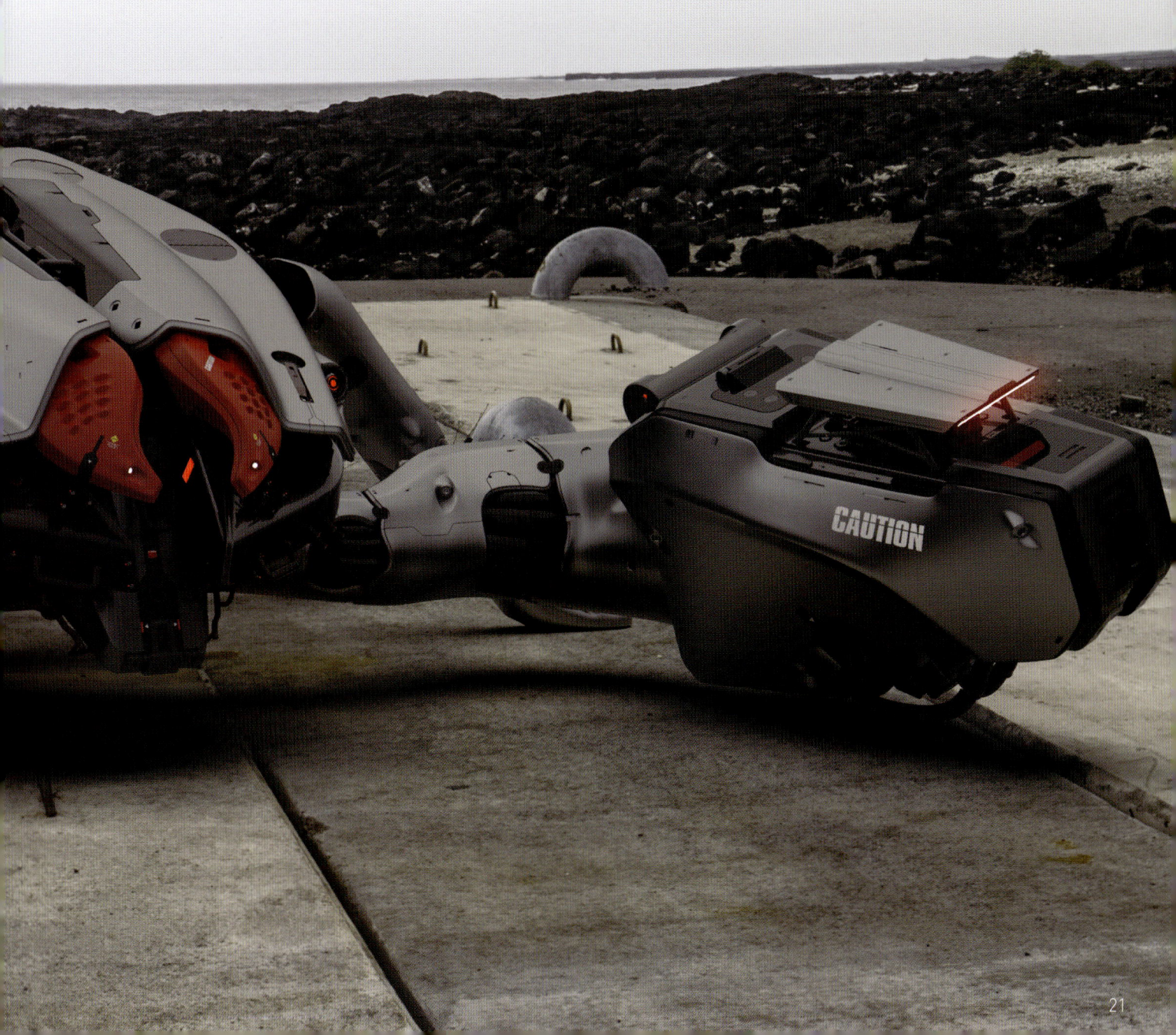

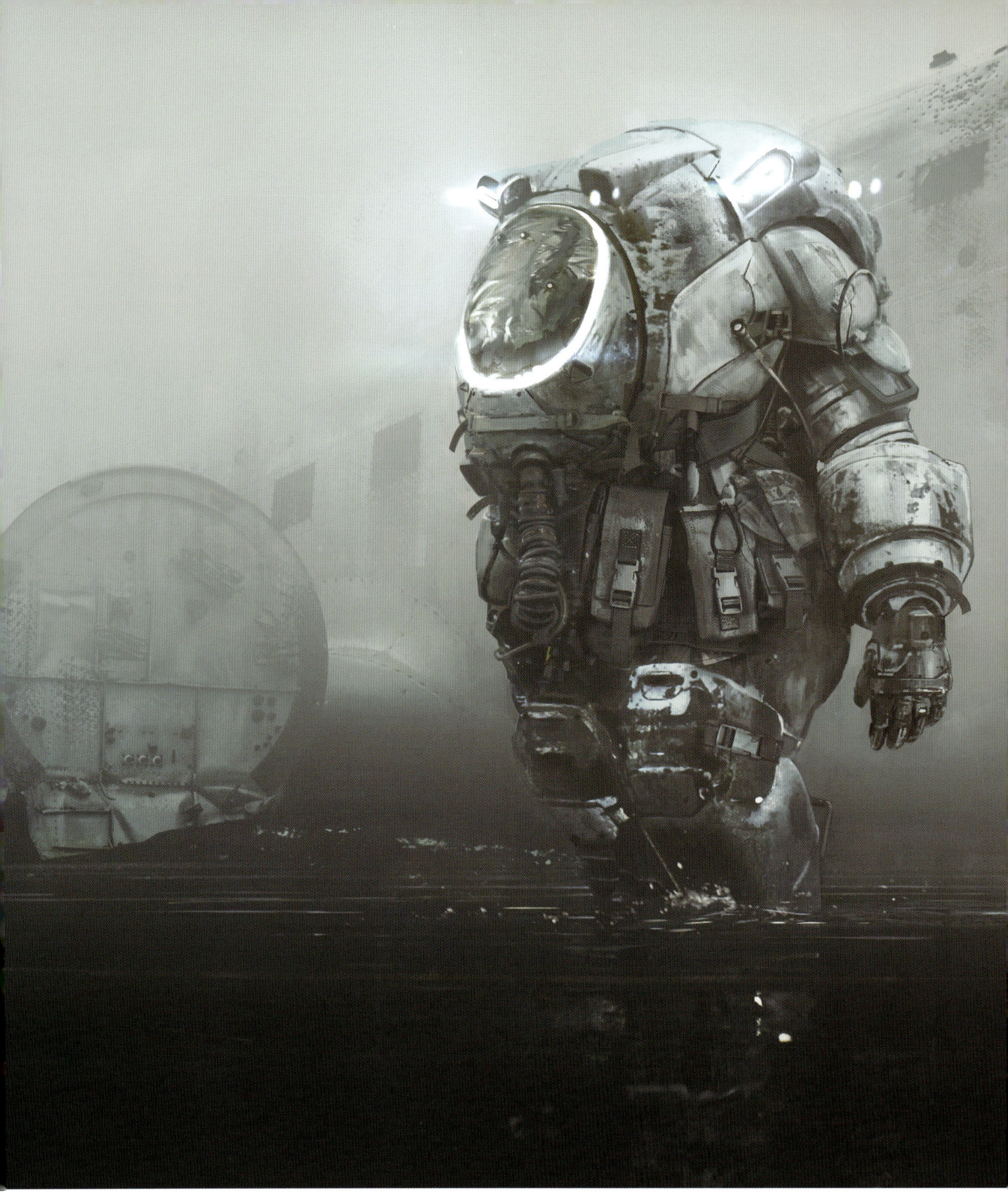

Life Ahead

Key frame shot.

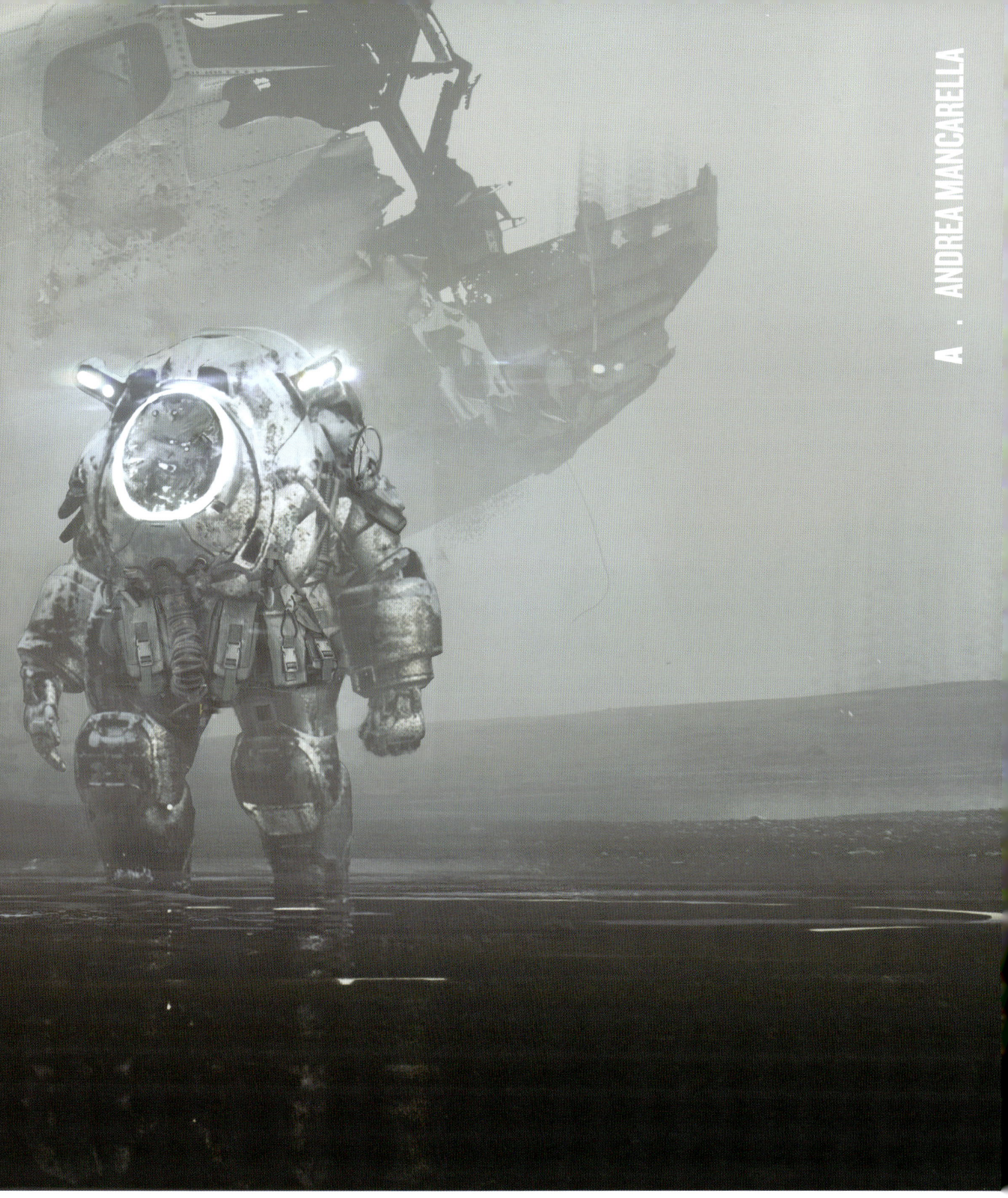

Two operators survived a landing crash while approaching a planet. The scope of the mission was to collect samples of alien life discovered via deep space network recordings.

There is nothing I love more than to project my concepts into a cinematic composition. My interest always arises from stories. Design, light, and composition are all tools that help me build my narratives. It is pretty much like blending ingredients for a recipe. I always try to keep them talking to each other, like they are glued together by the instant they have been captured in.

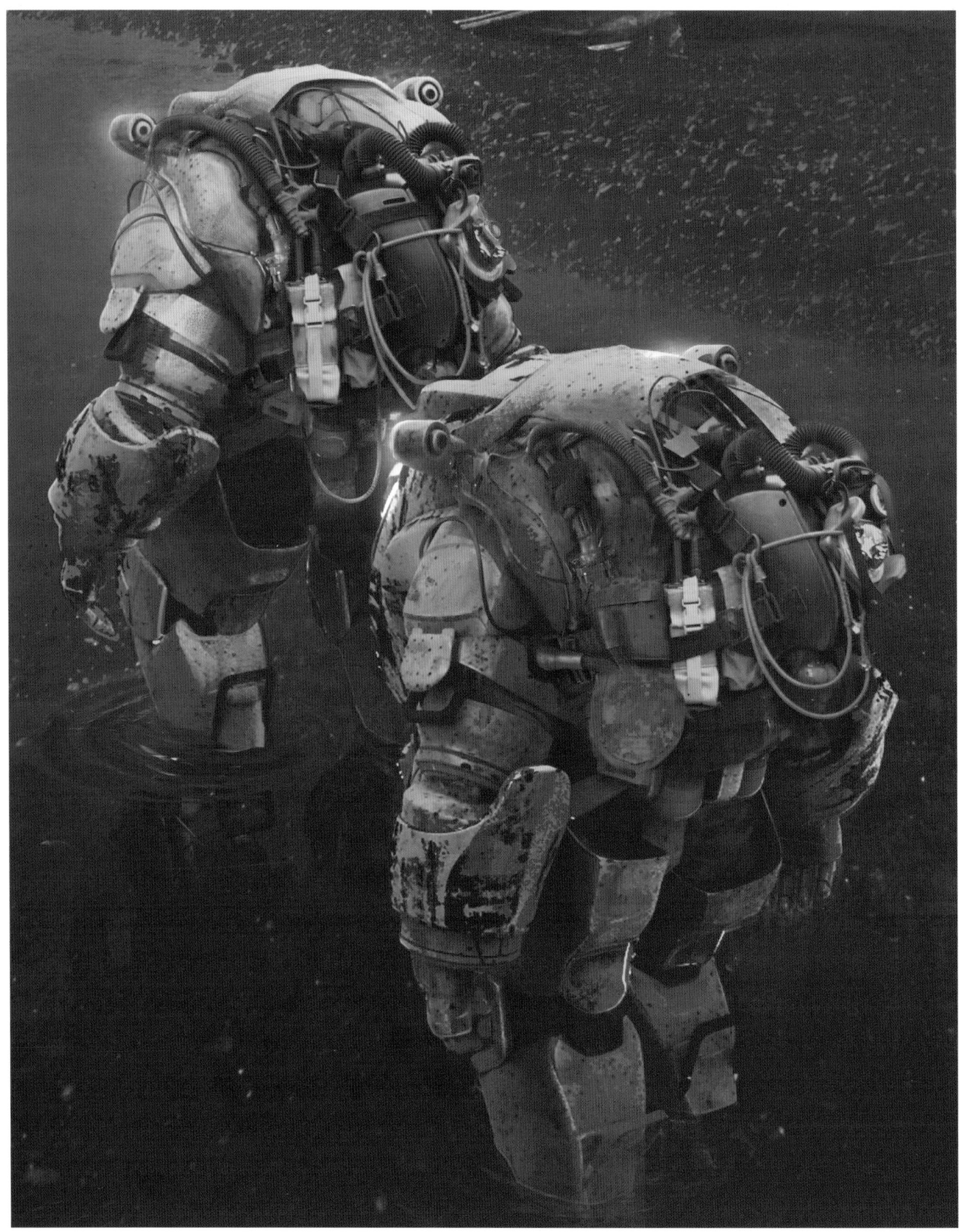

Life Ahead, Team.

Back of the operator suit with additional
survival elements.

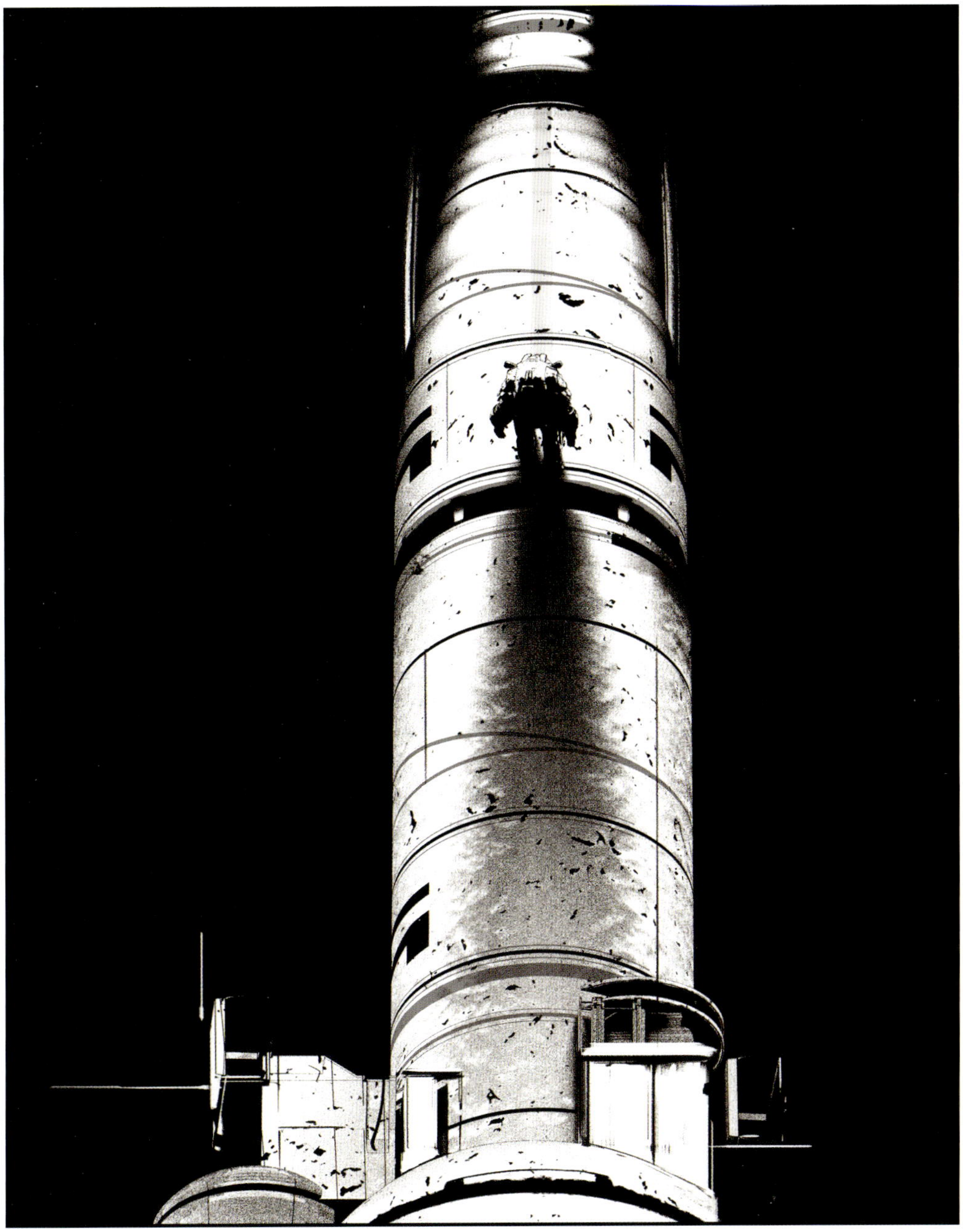

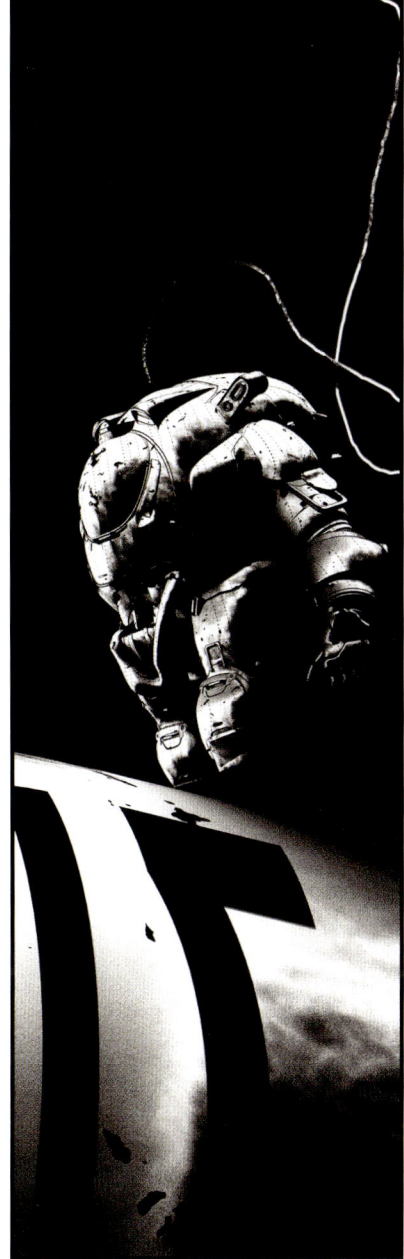

Working in black and white always helps me understand my focal points, as well as letting the light portray the story without worrying about unnecessary details. A two-tone composition is pretty much the core of an image, and is all we need to make it memorable.

Above: Ship walk.
Operator checking for ship malfunctions.

Below: Silhouettes of the suit design.

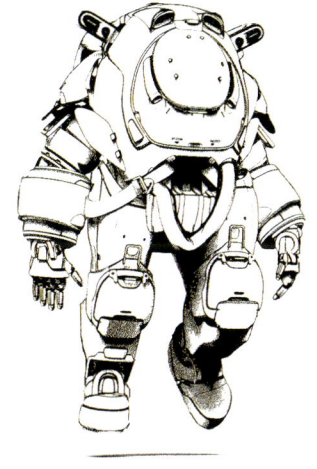
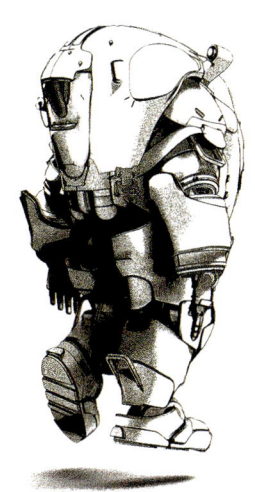
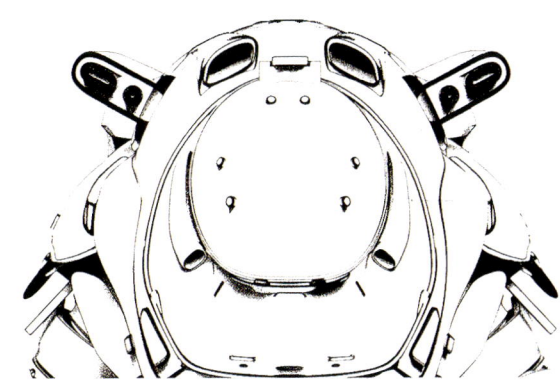

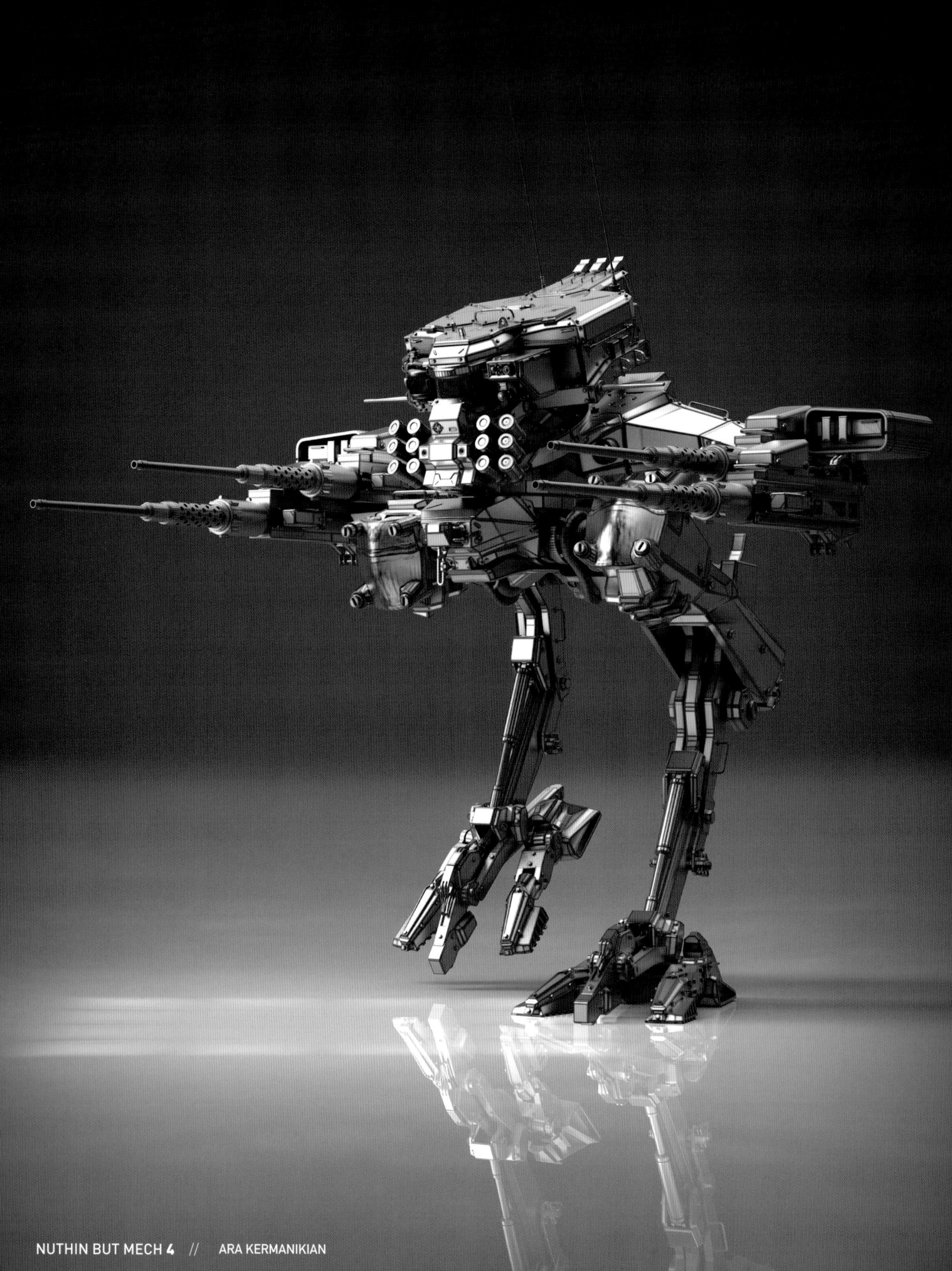

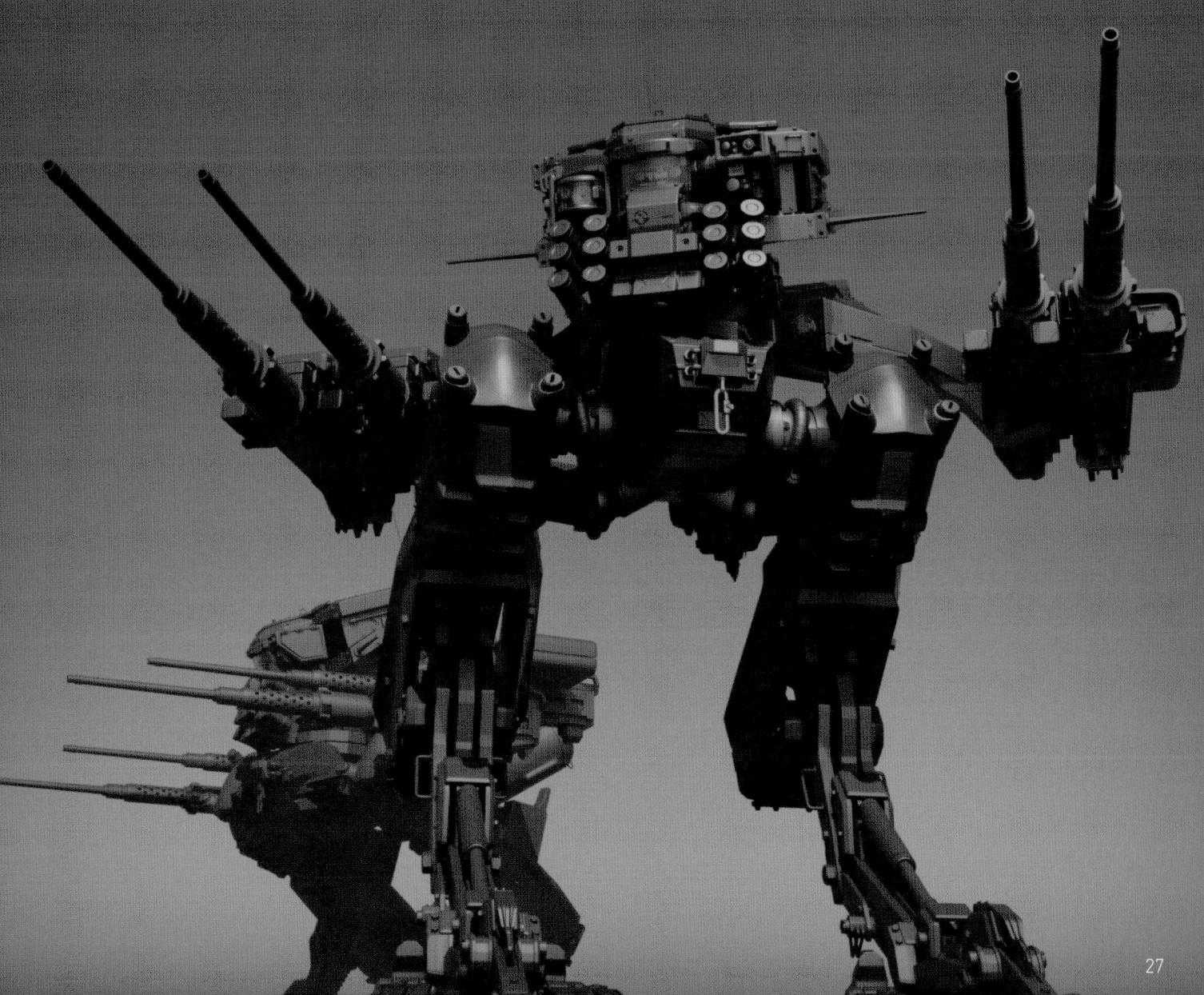

BEN PROCTER

Ben has been designing places and thingies for film since 2001 . . . the year, not the movie. He lives in Los Angeles with his wife, son, and way too many pets. Ben is currently in production designing the Avatar sequels with the incomparable Dylan Cole.
www.benprocter.com

BENJAMIN LOUIS

Benjamin is a French creative designer at Faurecia and a worldwide automotive interior supplier, living in Detroit, Michigan. Responsible for the General Motors design account, he works on the production of car interiors as well as internal research and innovation projects, forecasting two to five years in the future. His daily job consists of managing challenging ergonomics, kinematics, costs, and quality and manufacturability constraints while applying proper brand styling to the design.

Benjamin was awarded with a First Class special distinction in 2007 for his master's in transportation design and management at France's International School of Design, not only for his car designs, but also for a 30-foot-long yacht (in production since 2007 and sold worldwide), motorcycles, quads, and many more projects.

During his free time, and by being highly curious and a constant self-improver, Benjamin likes to step aside from today's reality and unleash his growing creativity on personal projects, such as spaceships, cars, concept arts, and, obviously, last but not the least, mechs.
www.asphaaalt.com

BRYAN REPKA

Bryan received his bachelor's degree in visual effects from Savannah College of Art and Design, on the East Coast. Upon completing his degree, he went to Los Angeles to get his feet wet in the industry as a 3D modeler.

Throughout the years, he has aided in the making of many films and games, working at studios such as Industrial Light & Magic, Blizzard Entertainment, Method Studios, Mirada Studios, and Prologue Films. His most recent work can be seen in *Pacific Rim, Transformers: The Last Knight, Doctor Strange, Ant-Man, San Andreas, Destiny, World of Warcraft,* and *Overwatch.* Currently, Bryan resides with his wife and two little girls in Redmond, Washington, and is employed at Microsoft 343 Industries as a senior character artist.
www.artstation.com/artist/brepka

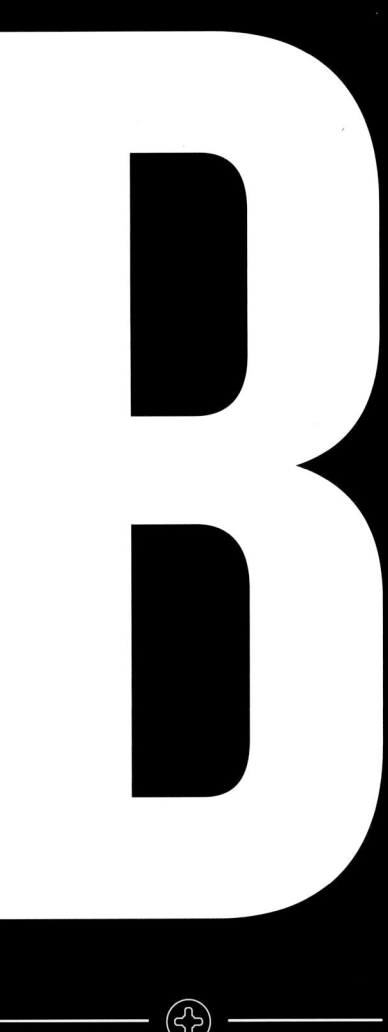

Ben Procter

Benjamin Louis

Bryan Repka

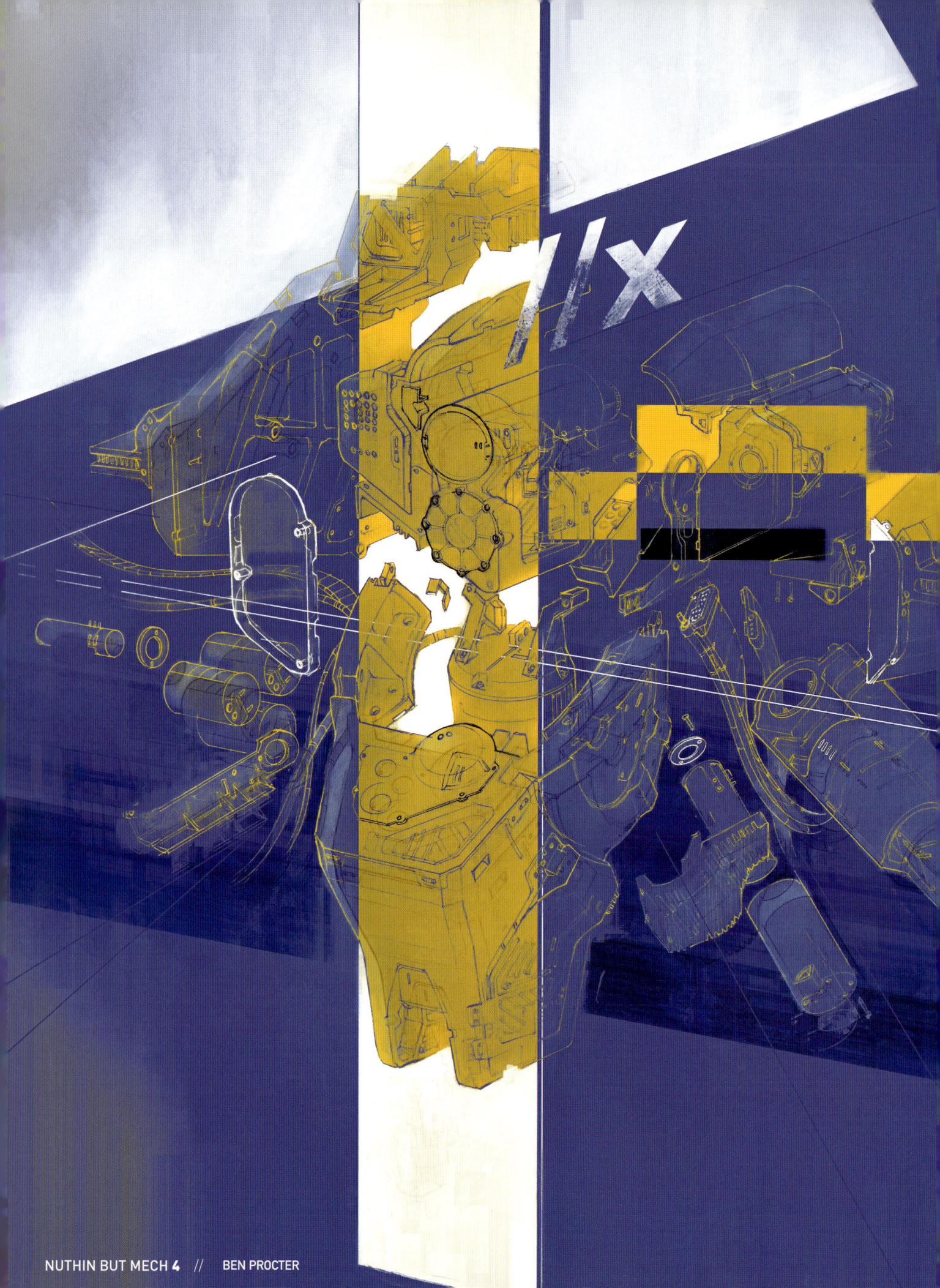

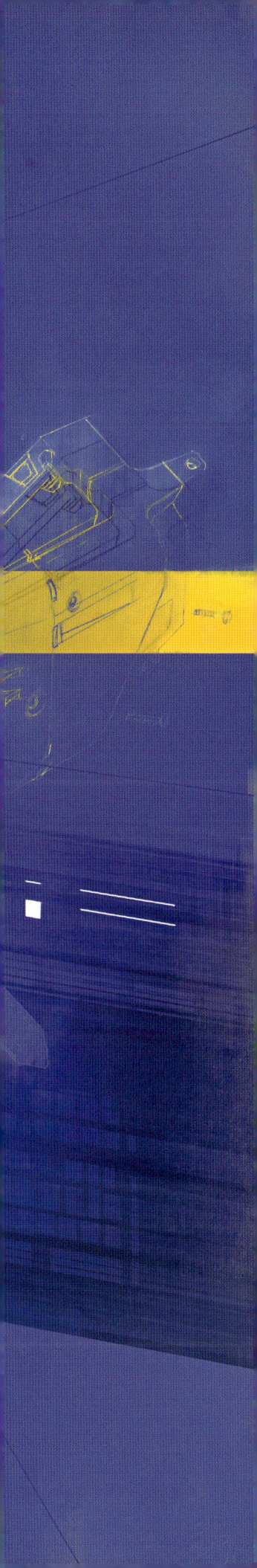

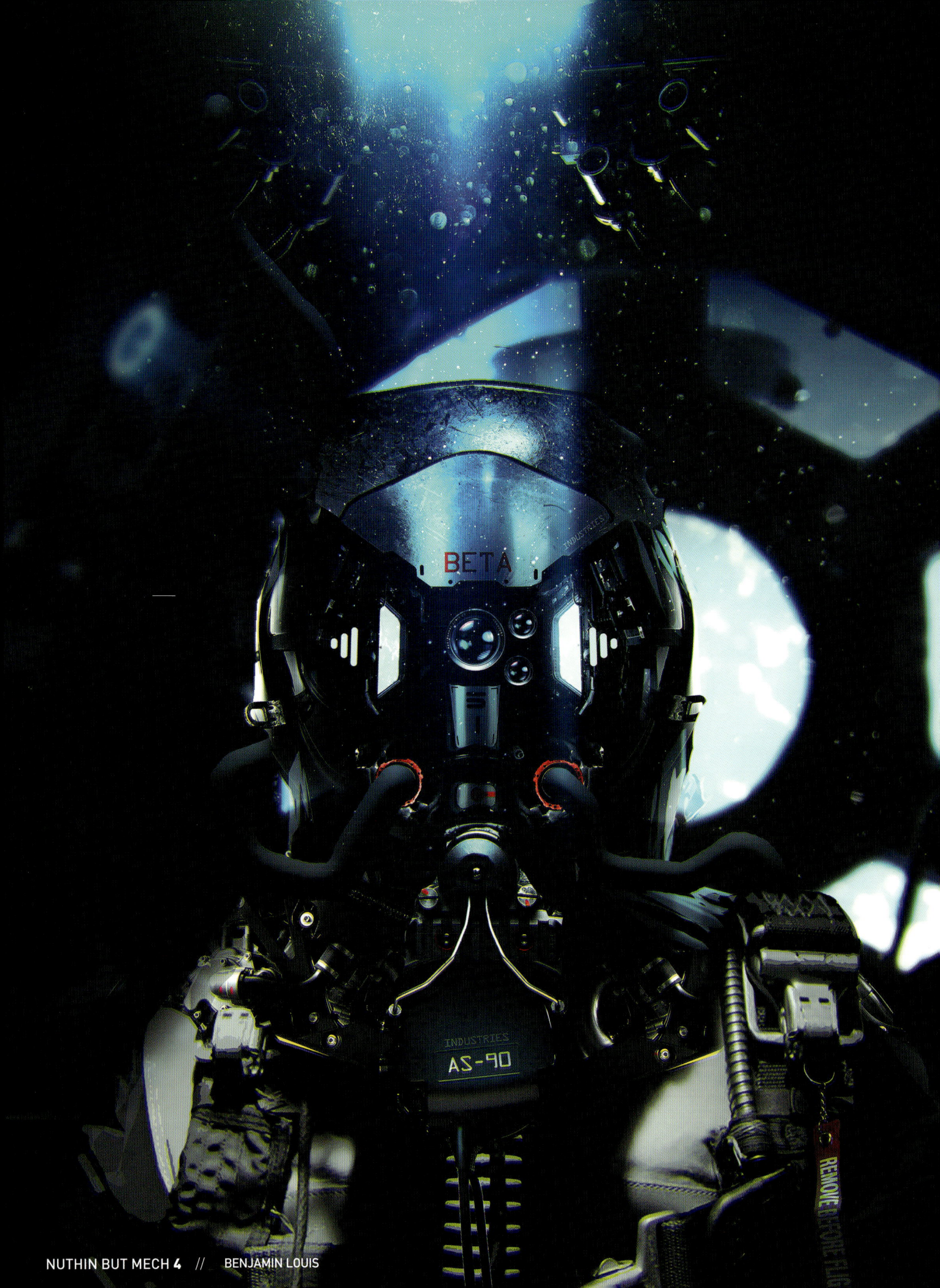

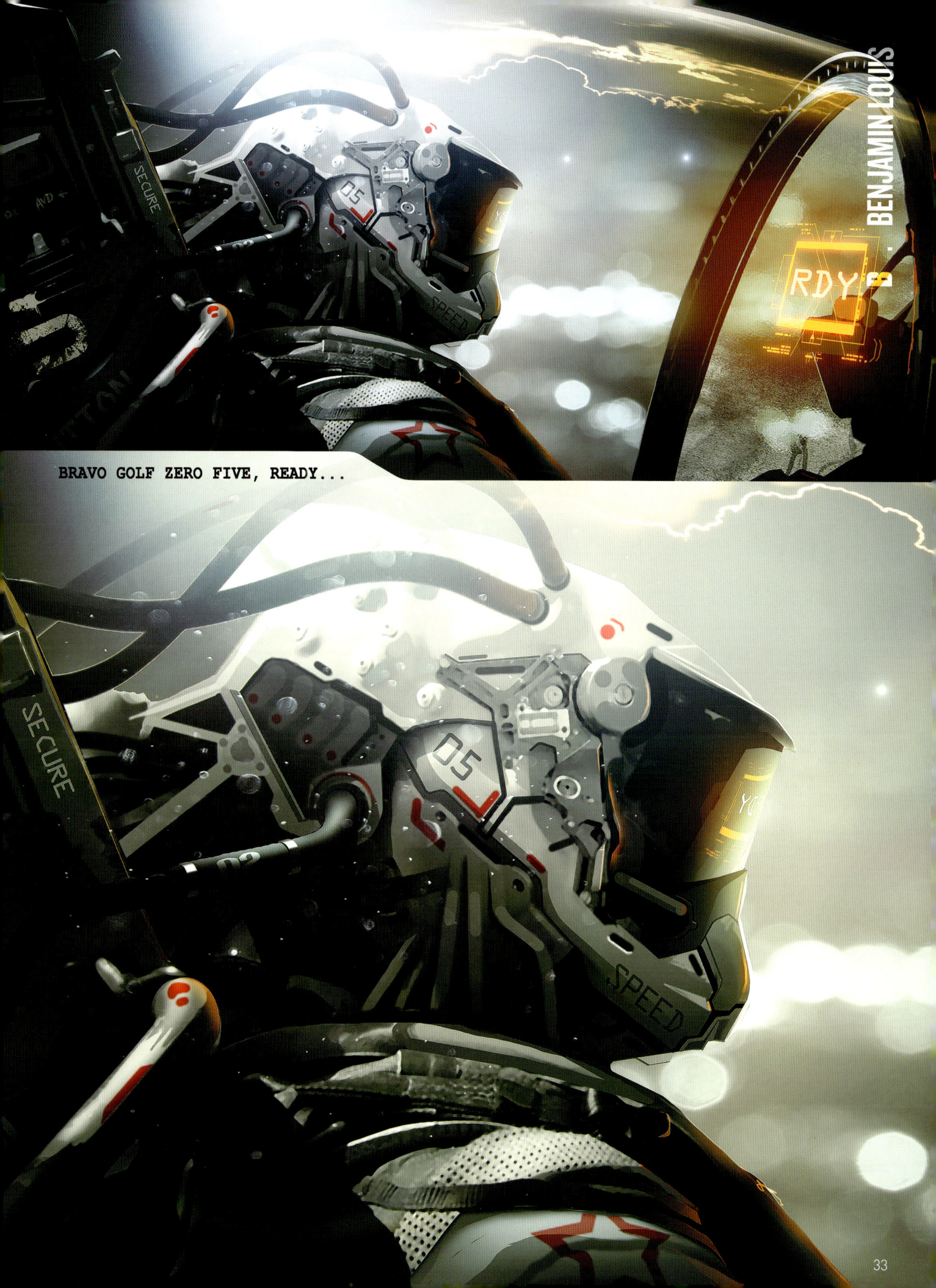

BRAVO GOLF ZERO FIVE, READY...

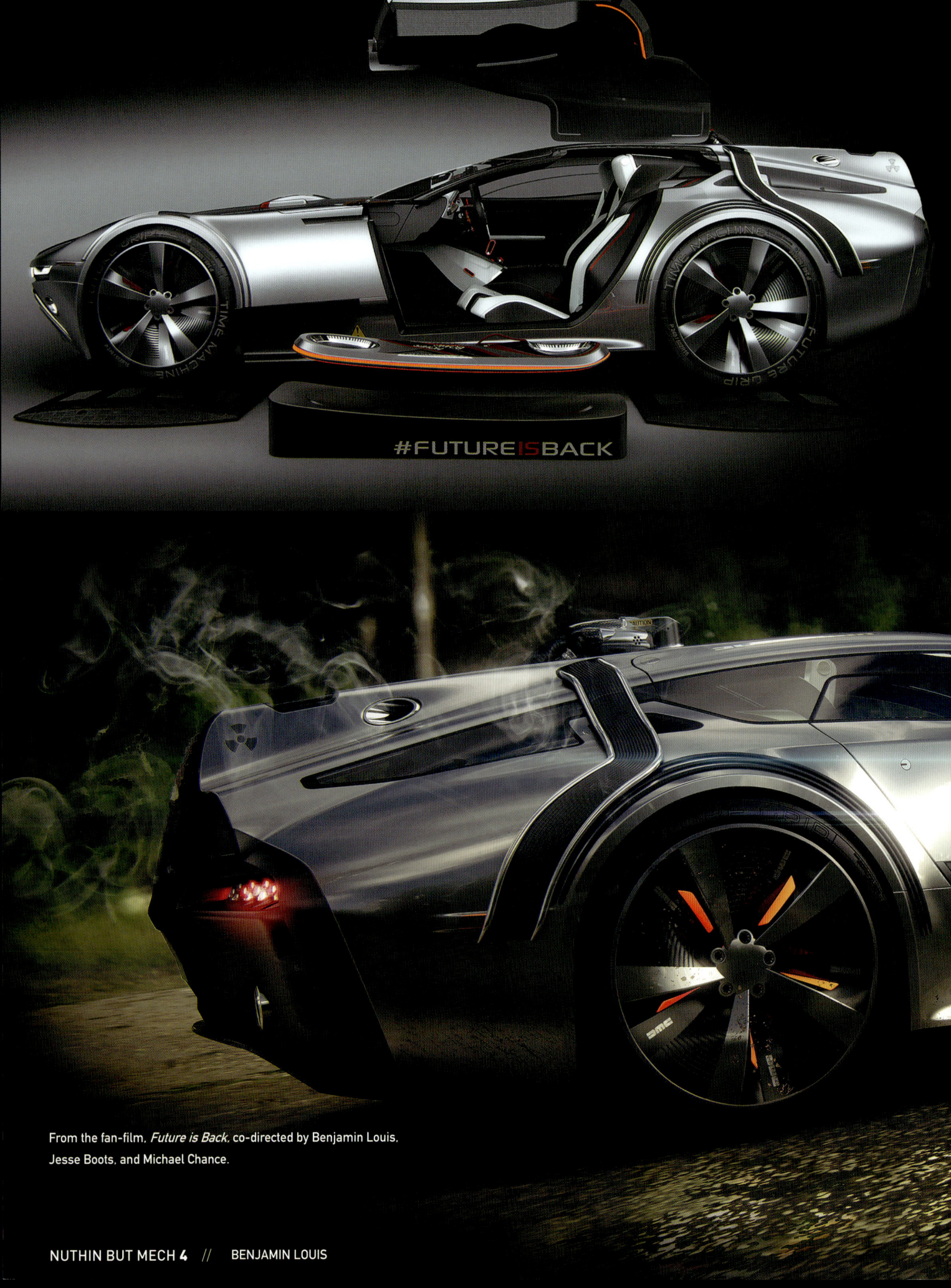

#FUTUREISBACK

From the fan-film, *Future is Back*, co-directed by Benjamin Louis,
Jesse Boots, and Michael Chance.

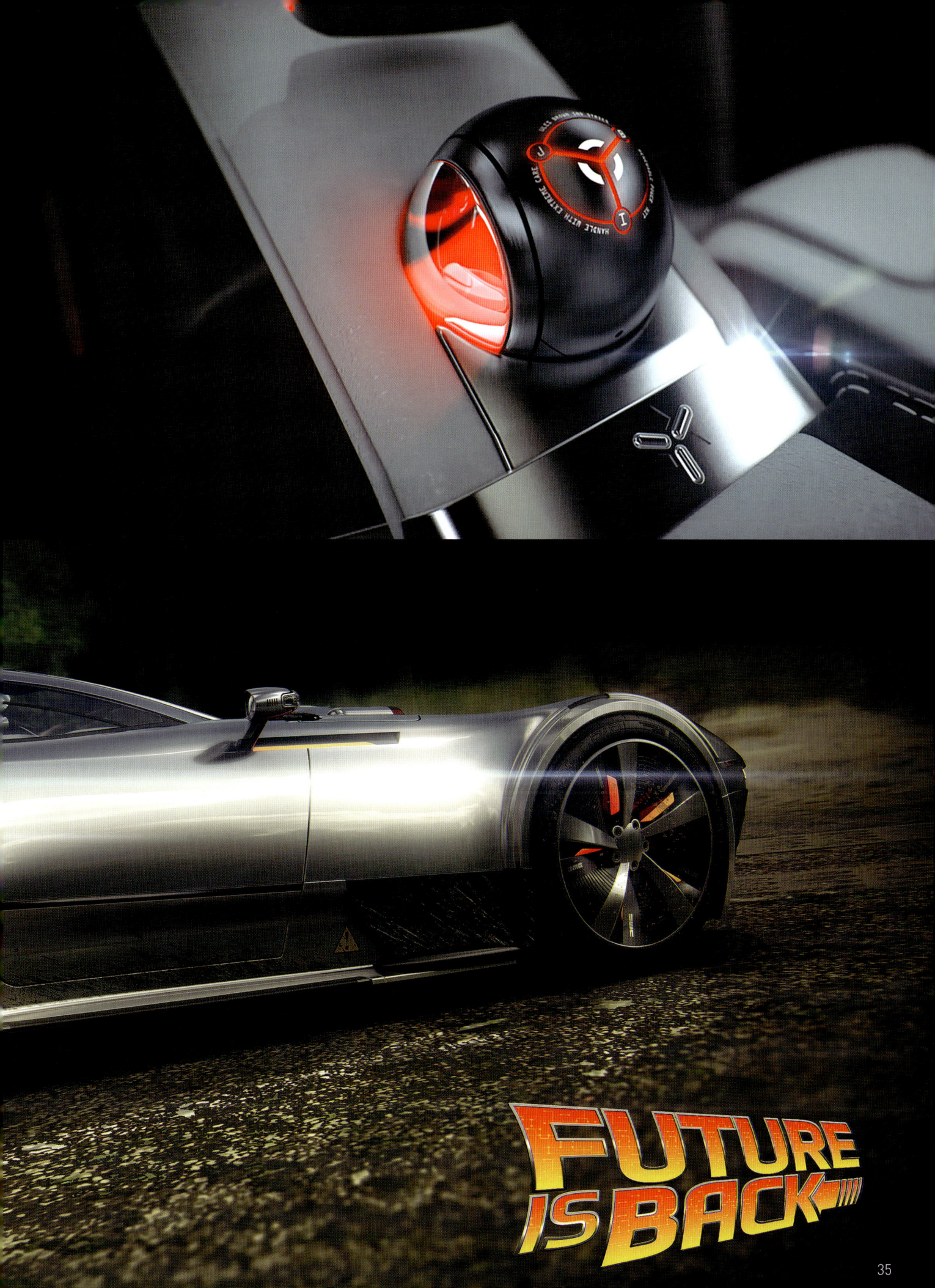

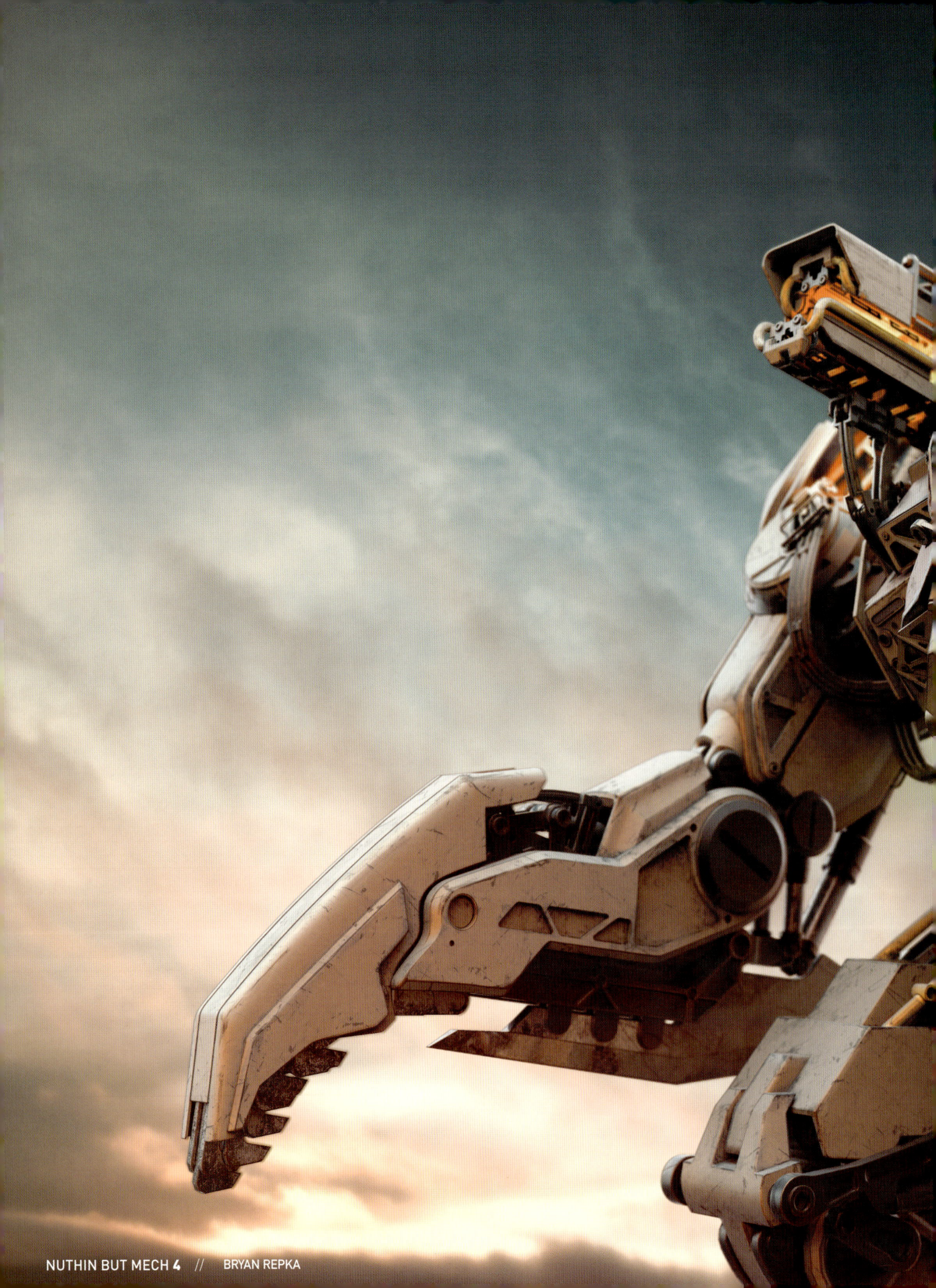

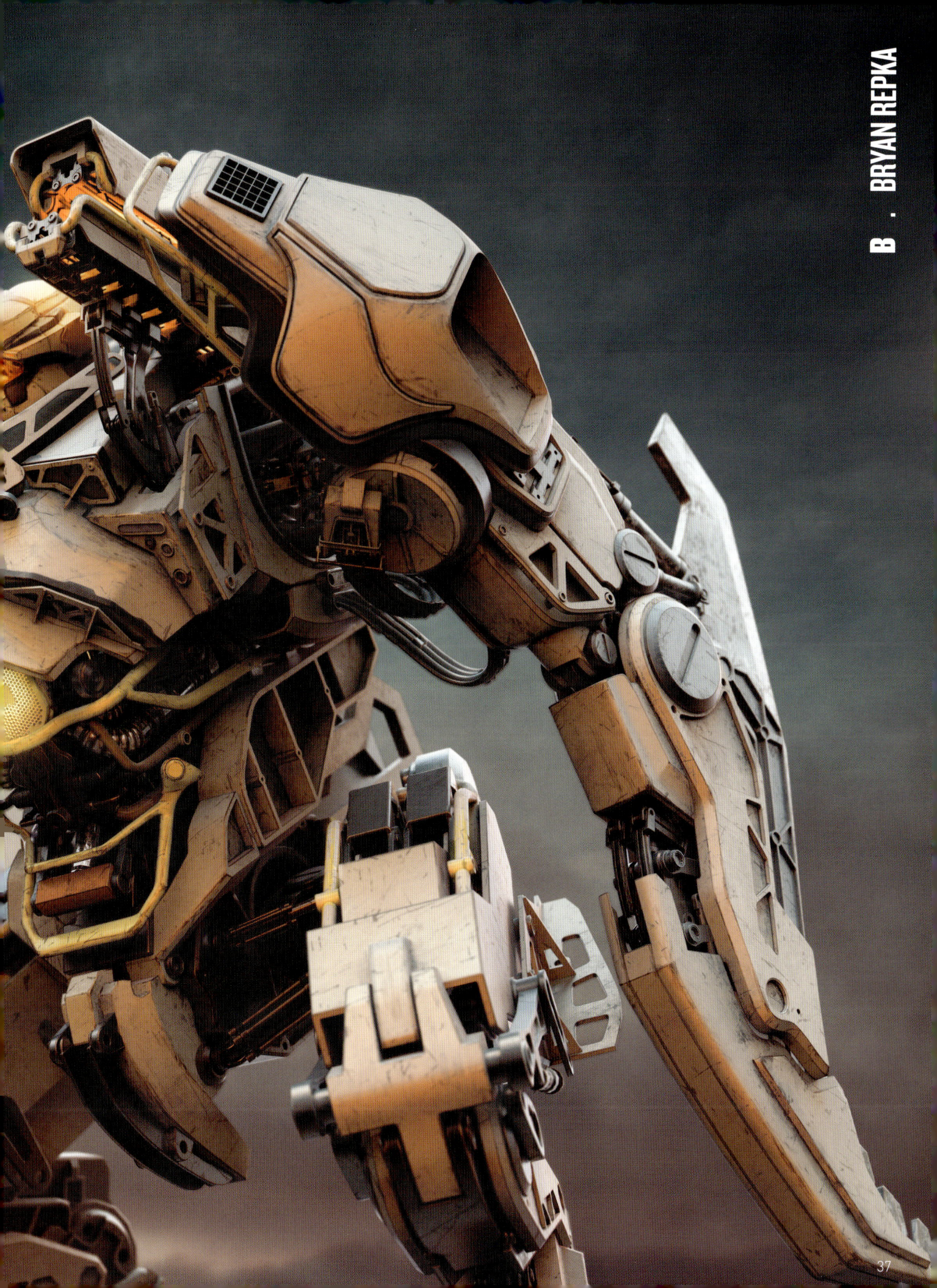

CALUM WATT

Calum is a freelance storyboard and concept artist and illustrator working in the entertainment industry. He has created artwork for Neill Blomkamp, Lucasfilm, Disney, Sega, DC Entertainment, and Framestore. He lives and works in the United Kingdom, somewhere near the sea.

www.calumalexanderwatt.com

CHRIS ROSEWARNE

Chris is a British concept artist and illustrator working in the film and television industry. His fast cinematic renderings and industrial prop designs have led him to projects internationally, from studios in Los Angeles to London and across Europe. Born in 1978 to artist parents, Chris grew up in London and studied art at St. Martin's College before graduating with a BA (Hons) in model making for design and media at Arts University Bournemouth. In 2003, he was employed as a freelance model maker by Artem, where he worked on the films *Reign of Fire* and Terry Gilliam's *The Brothers Grimm*.

After four years as an industry prop maker, Chris turned his attention to the art department and began work on the sci-fi, cult game *Doom*, applying his hands-on knowledge of machining, materials, and workshop processes to the design of props and set dressing. He has since worked on a wide range of productions, from making high-tech designs and atmospheric key frames for George Lucas's *Star Wars TV* series to intricately detailed matte paintings for the BBC's documentary series *Planet Dinosaur*.

Chris's most recent projects include *Artemis Fowl*, Tim Burton's *Dumbo*, *Star Wars VIII*, the sci-fi horror *LIFE* and the award winning *Guardians Of The Galaxy*. In 2012, Chris received an Emmy nomination for his work with Jellyfish Pictures for Outstanding Special Visual Effects on the series *Inside the Human Body*.

www.chrisrosewarne.com

CHRIS STOSKI

In his 19 years of working in the entertainment industry, Chris has worn many hats. As a concept artist and visual designer, he has worked at Google, Industrial Light & Magic, and Electronic Arts (EA), to name a few. His project experience ranges from art directing on Hollywood blockbusters, such as *Star Trek*, to concept design on AAA game titles, like *Battlefield* and EA's *Star Wars* game. His recent move into the augmented reality and mobile gaming worlds allowed him to try his hand at many other aspects of design, including UX, UI, and real-time concept development in game engines. He now works at Niantic Labs where, after their launch of *Pokémon Go*, they are hard at work on cool, new things that you might love on your phone.

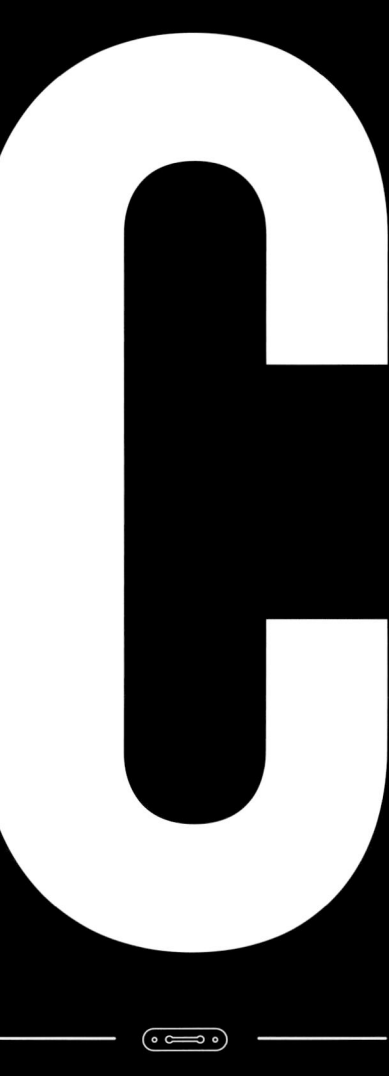

C

Calum Watt

Chris Rosewarne

Chris Stoski

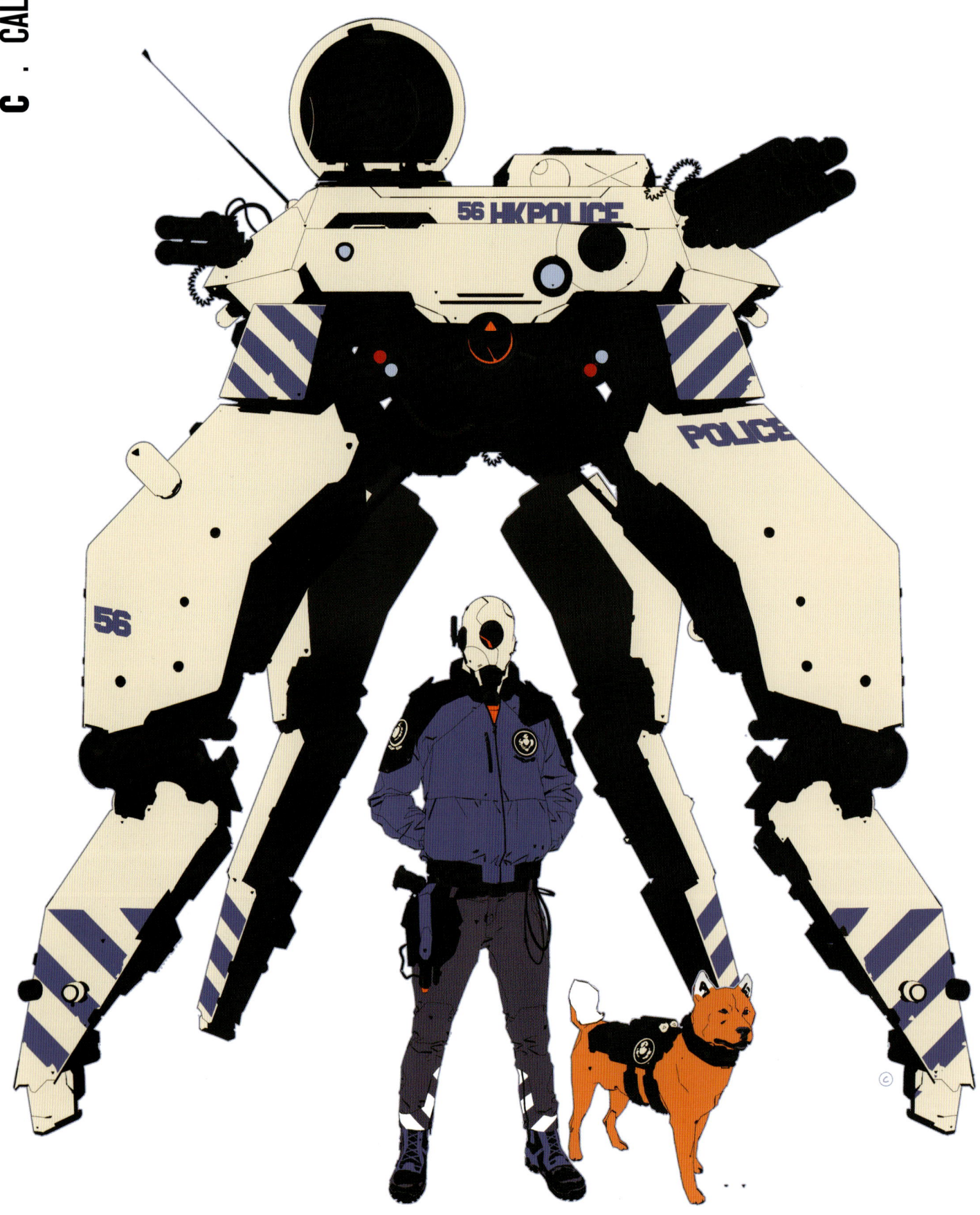

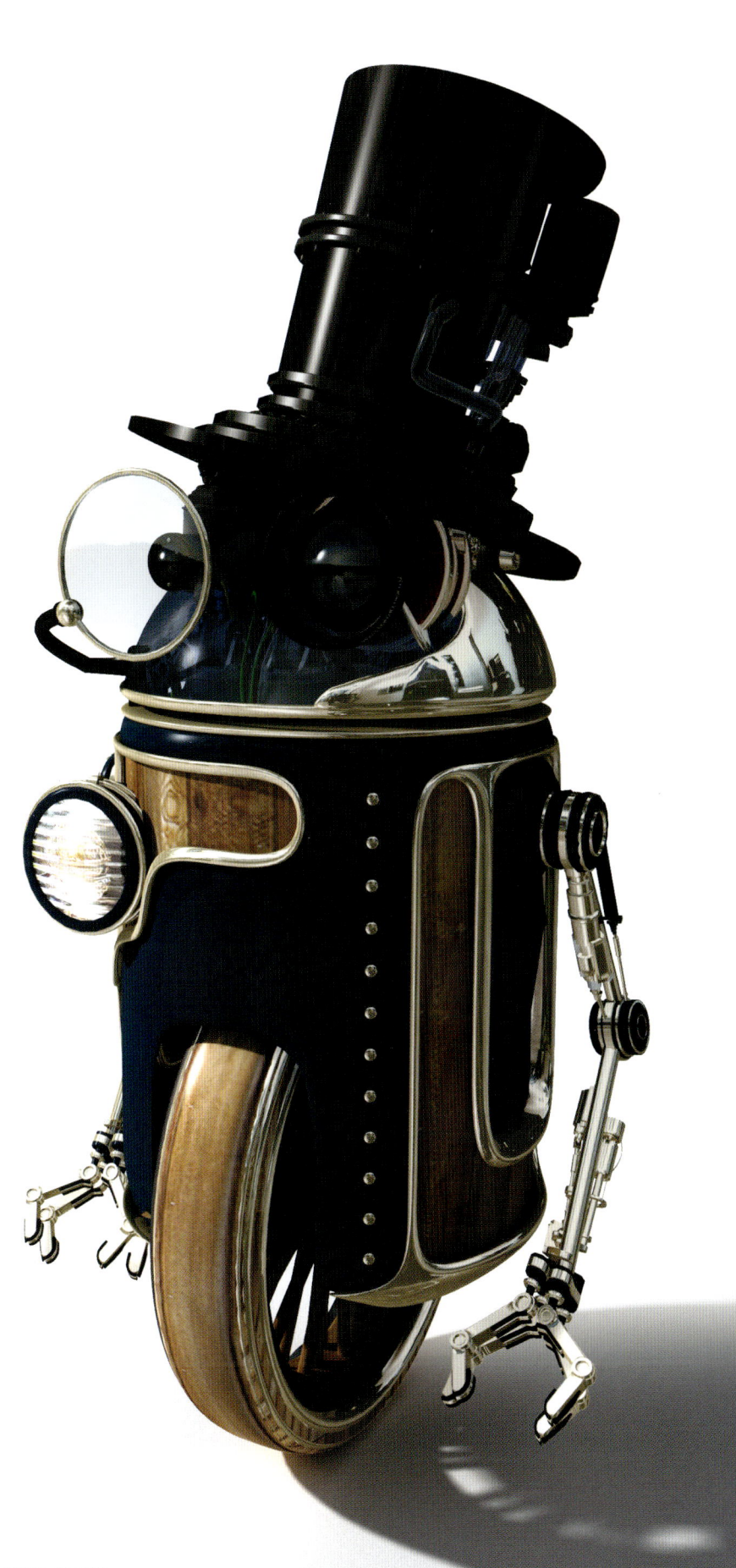

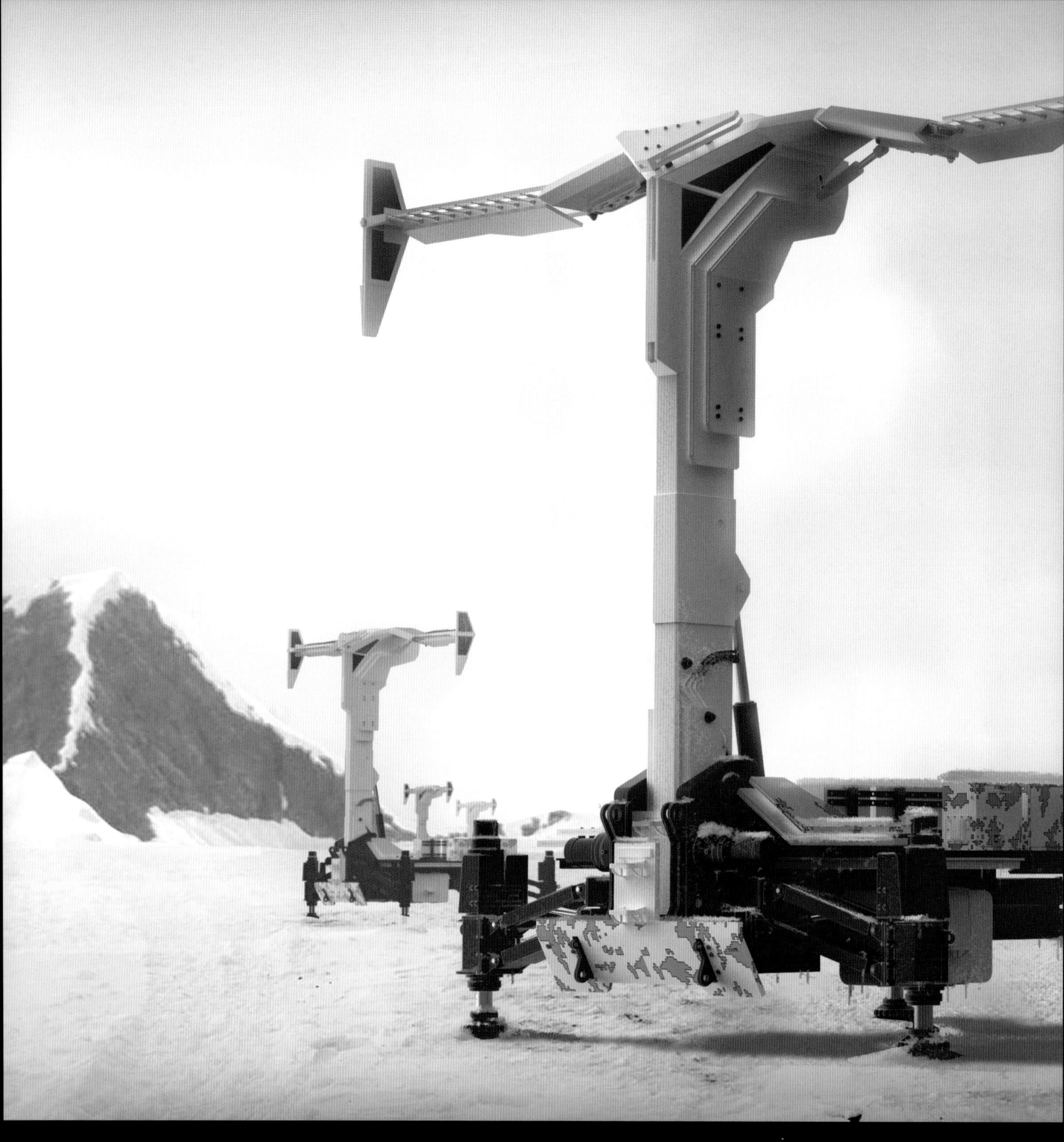

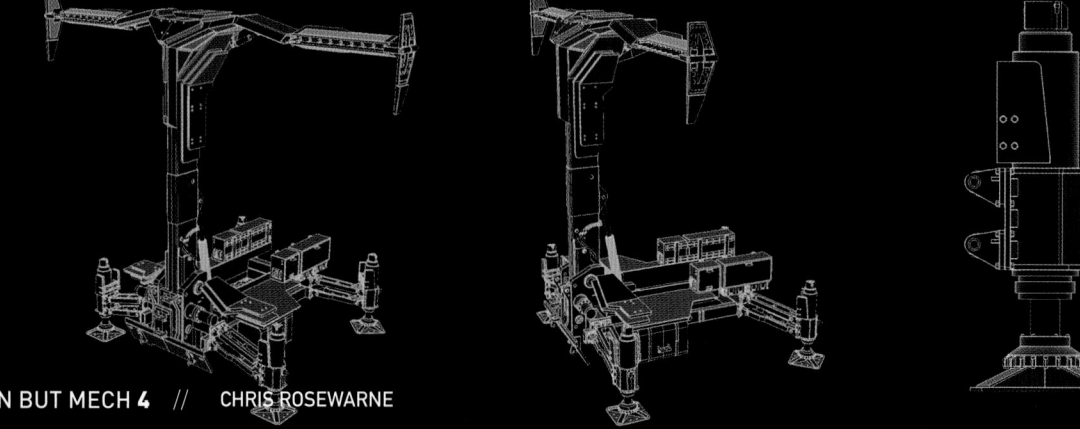

NUTHIN BUT MECH **4**   //   CHRIS ROSEWARNE

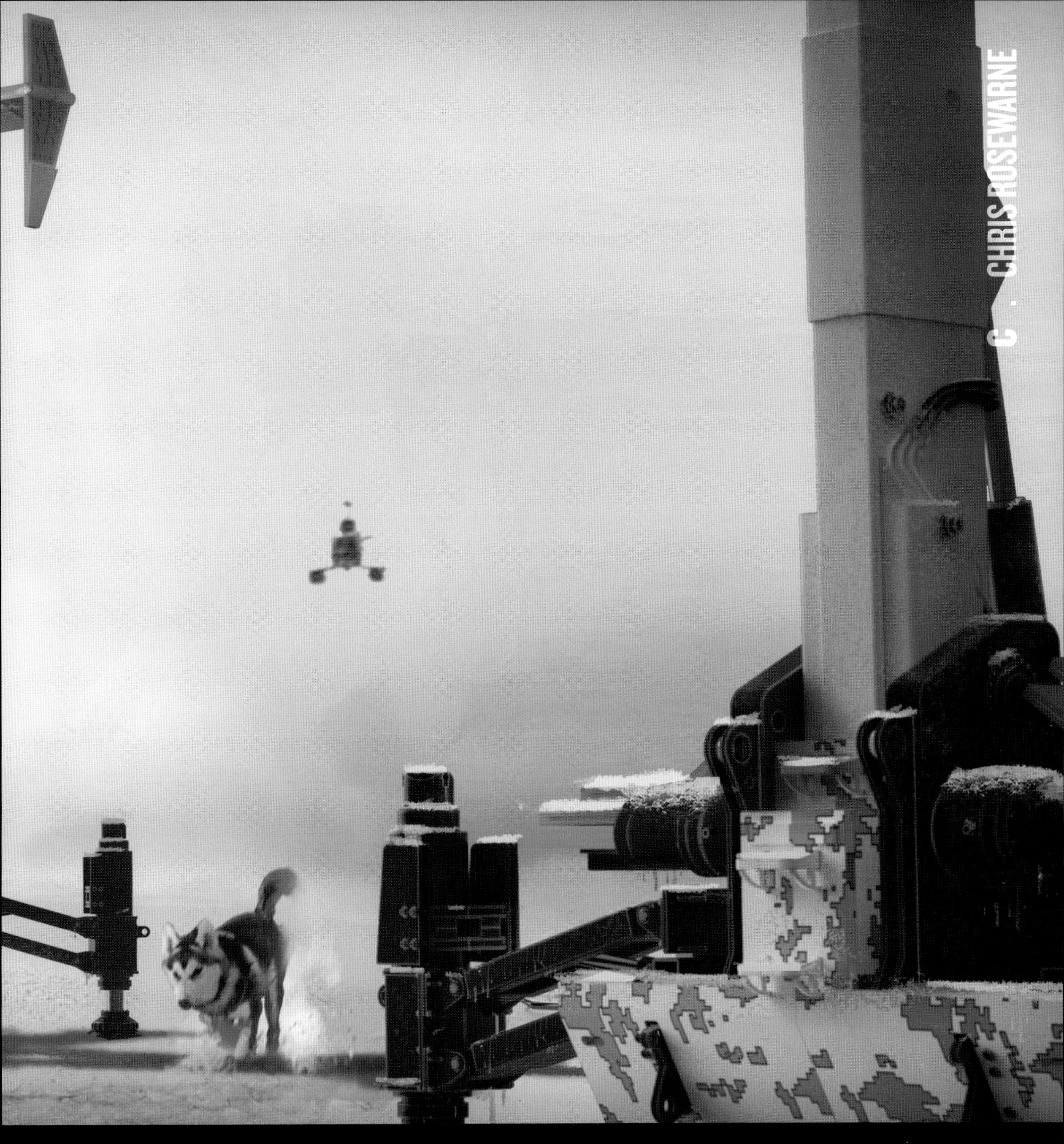

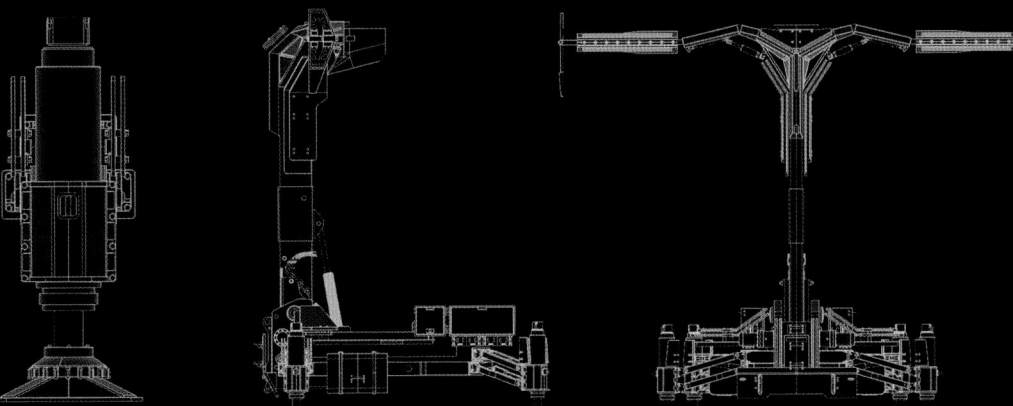

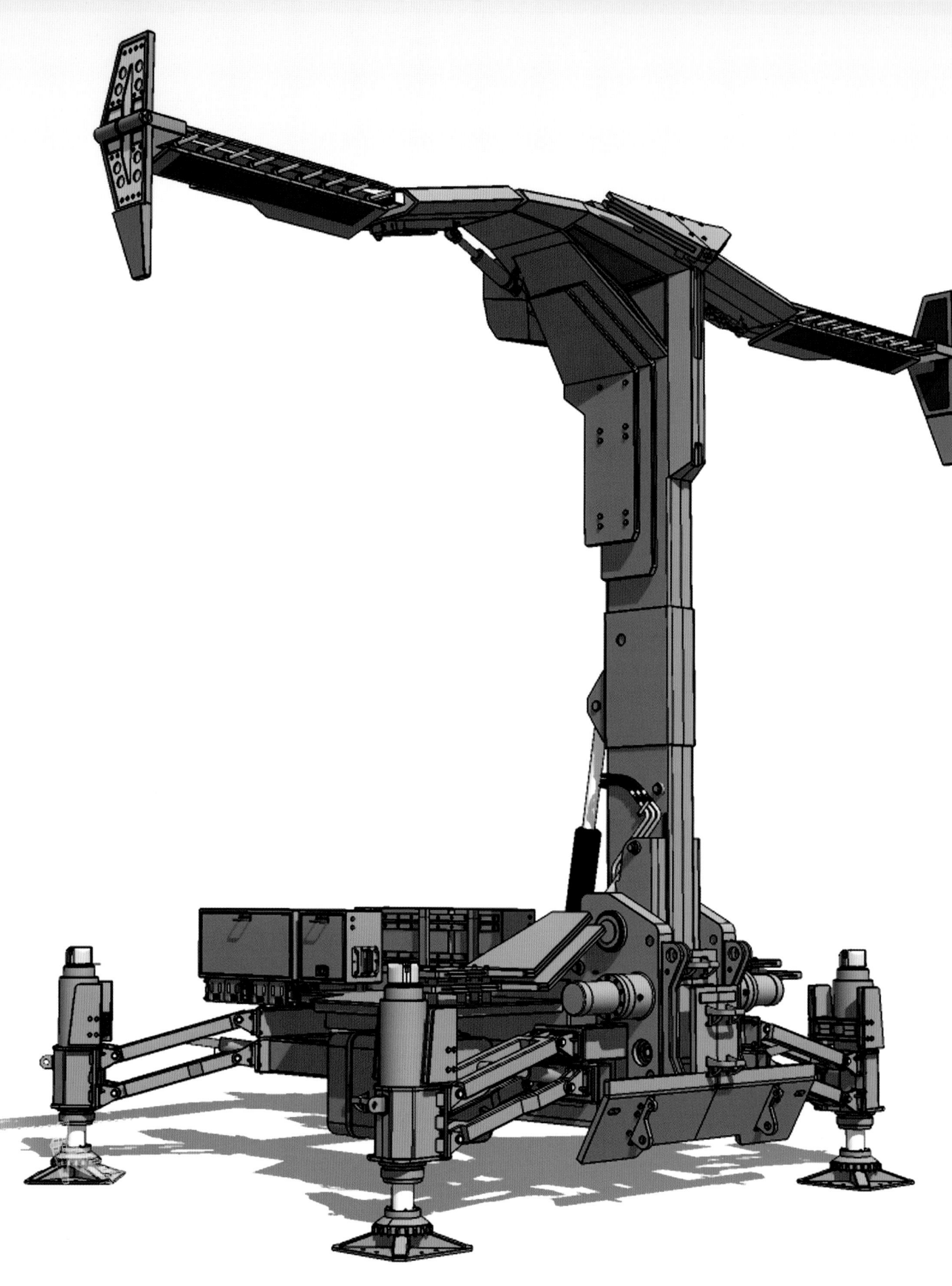

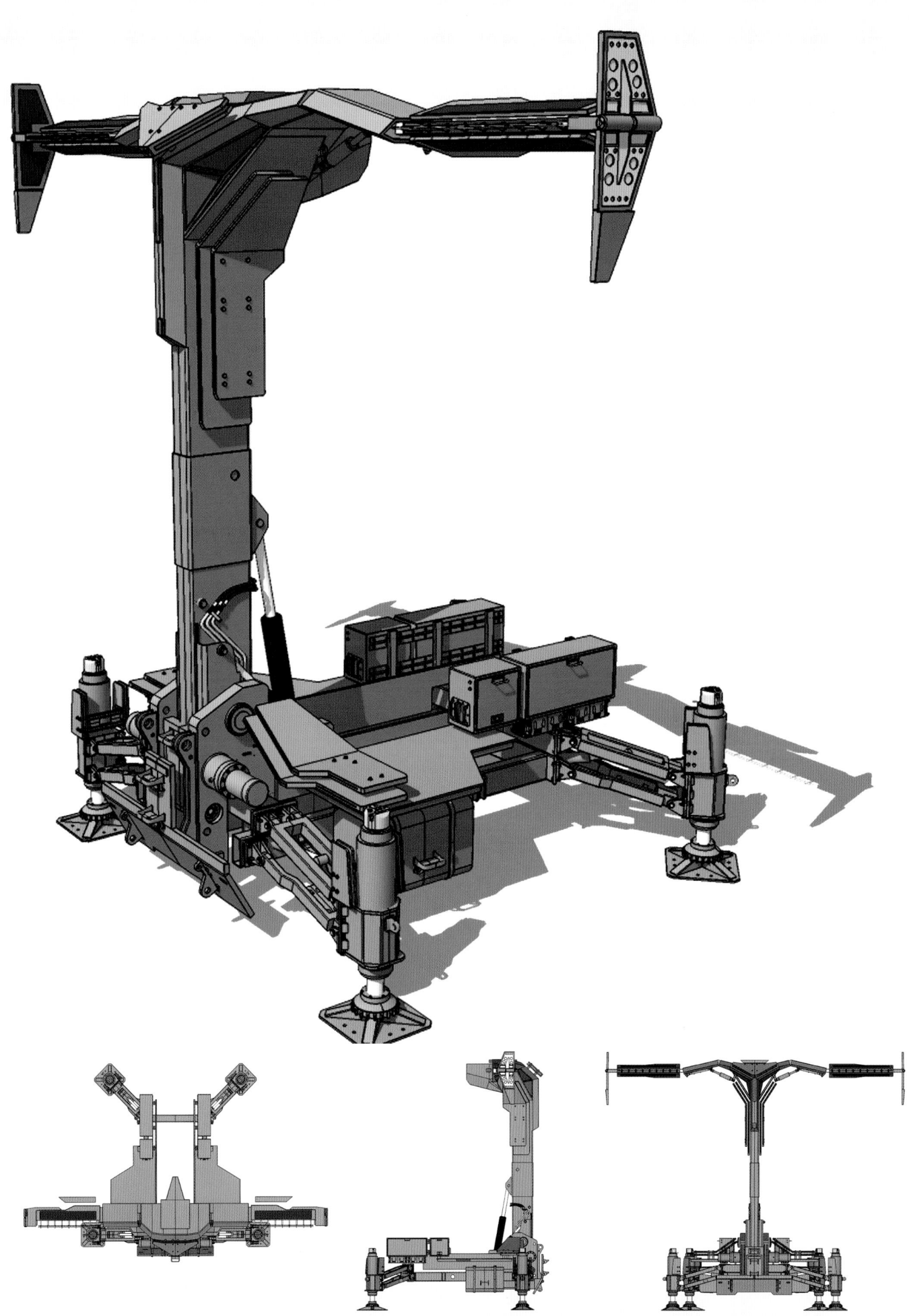

DANNY GARDNER

From the beginning, Danny has had a passion for art and design. Born in 1989, he grew up in a family of creatives and has been drawing since age three. He took figure drawing, painting, and animation classes in high school, along with product and transportation design classes through ArtCenter College of Design's Saturday High program. Danny had always dreamed of attending ArtCenter to major in transportation design. But after a year at Pasadena City College, when he was ready to apply, he became aware of a new major starting at ArtCenter: entertainment design. Having immediately fallen in love with the diversity and creative process of concept art, he changed his focus. However, cars are still, and will always be, one of his greatest life passions. After attending ArtCenter, Danny worked as a freelance artist for film and TV until landing a position at Sony Santa Monica. He worked there for three years and is now at Respawn Entertainment, working on *Titanfall* for the past three years and counting. With a rapidly growing interest in product design, he looks forward to bringing his ideas into the real world and exploring many different creative outlets.

www.dannydraws.com

DARREN BACON

Darren is a concept artist who has contributed to the development of video games, film, and animation at Bungie, Walt Disney Television Animation, ImageMovers Digital, and Electronic Arts. He is currently living in Seattle, Washington, and working at Microsoft's 343 Industries. His most recent work can be seen on *Halo 5: Guardians*.

www.darrenbacon.com

EDON GURAZIU

During childhood Edon was always drawing and making stuff, so when he finished high school he already knew what route he would take. At Graphic Lyceum in Utrecht, Netherlands, he learned the fundamentals of 3D and game asset production. After two years, Edon left school to get closer to his goal by devoting all his time to the fundamentals of design. While building up his portfolio from scratch, he got his first little gigs that consisted of short films and small indie games. Specializing in concept design for film, games, robotics, firearms, and products, Edon has been working with such clients as 20th Century Fox, NVIDIA Corporation, MPC, and many more.

www.artstation.com/artist/guraziu

ERIC LLOYD BROWN

Eric is a concept designer living in Los Angeles and has worked in animation, games, and live action films. Currently he is a vehicle and prop designer for *Transformers: Robots in Disguise* at Hasbro Studios.

www.ericlloydbrown.com

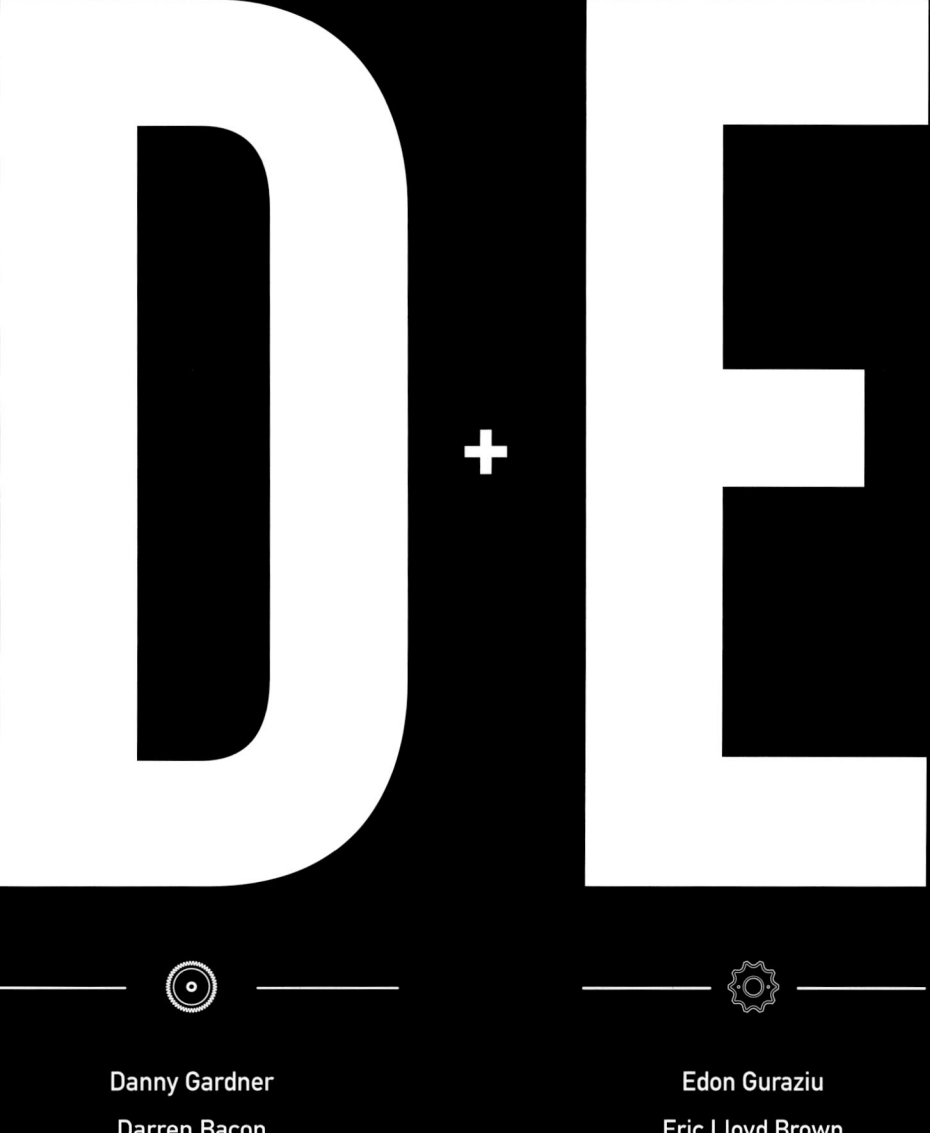

D + E

Danny Gardner

Darren Bacon

Edon Guraziu

Eric Lloyd Brown

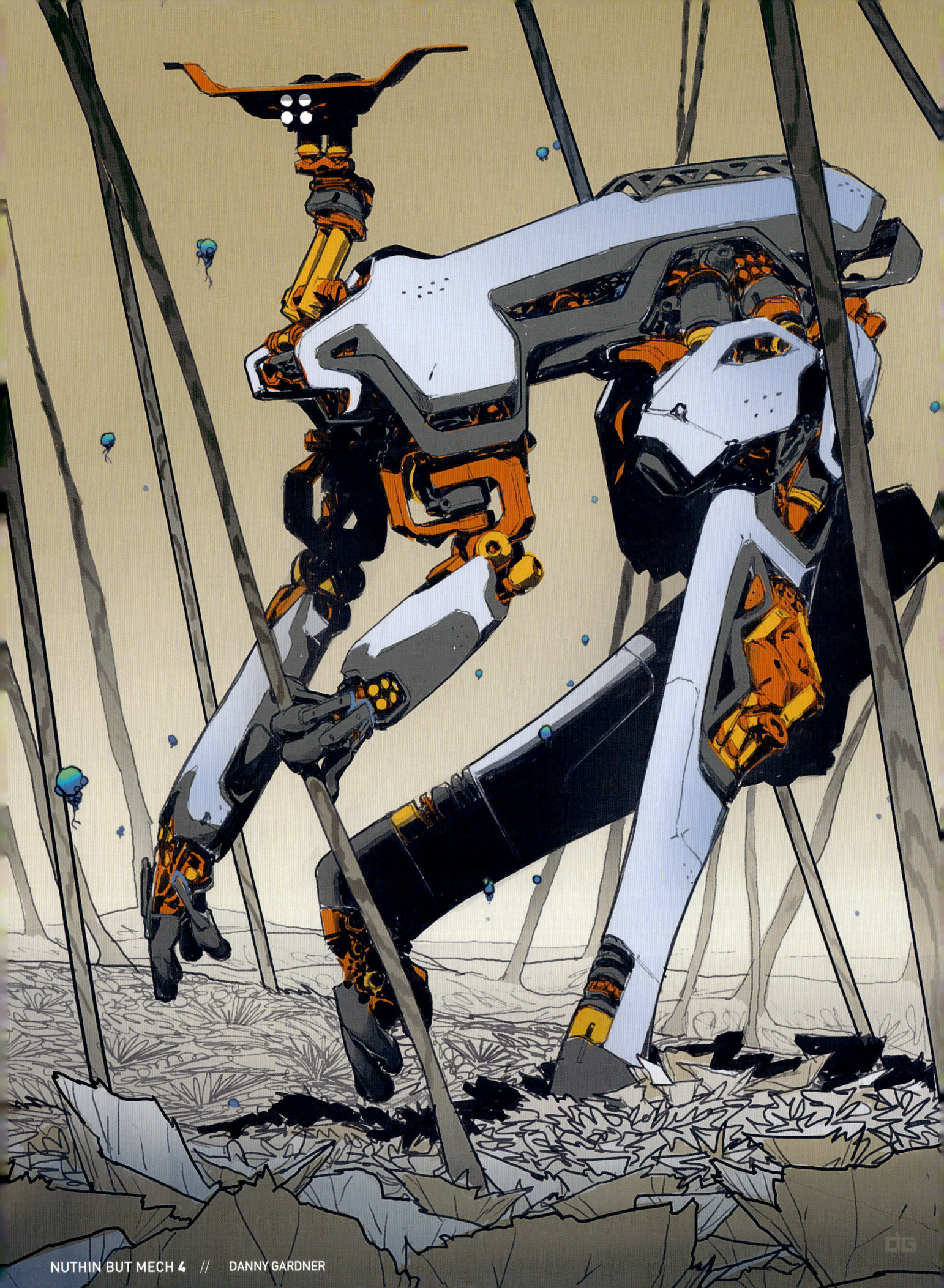

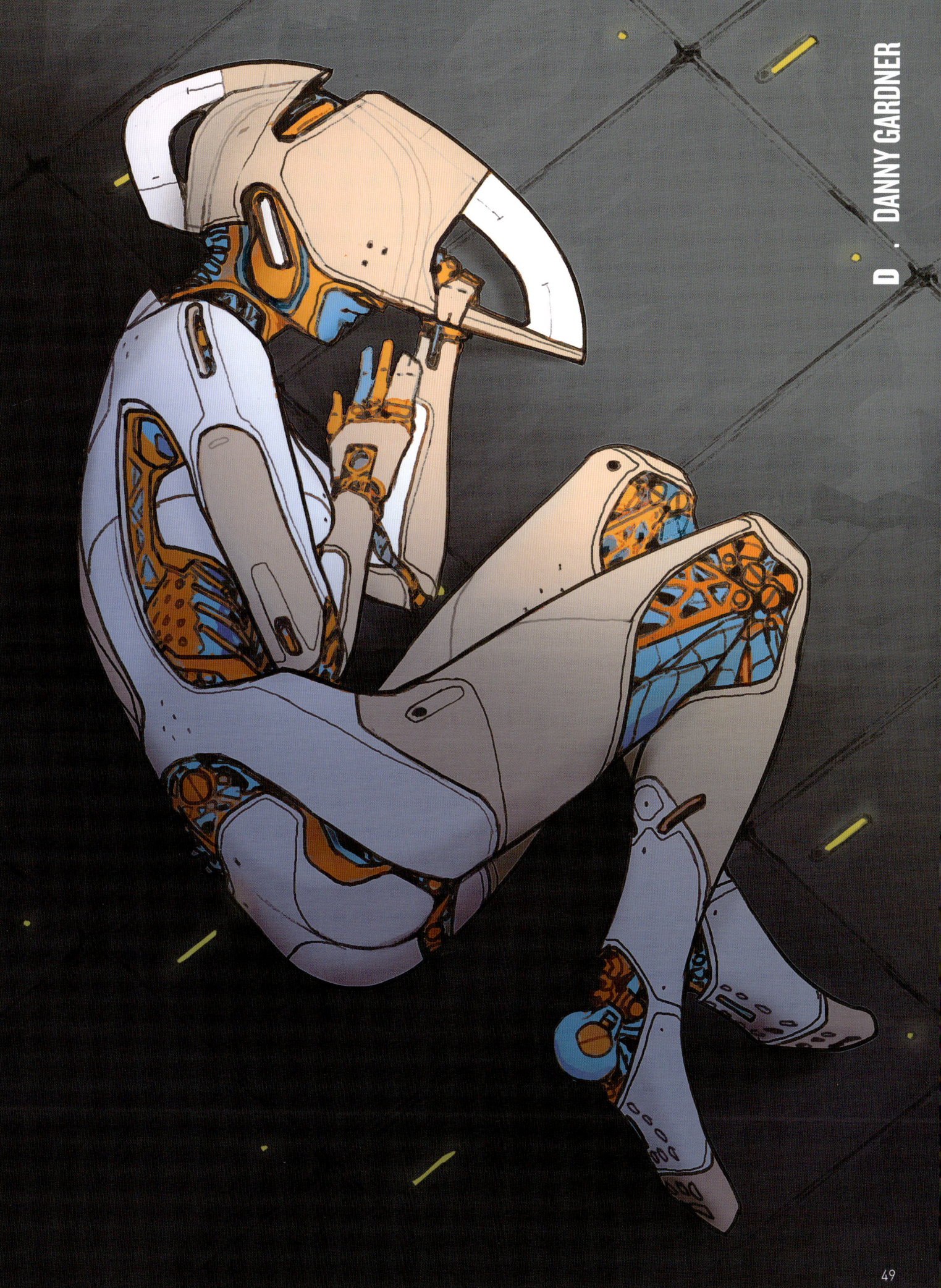

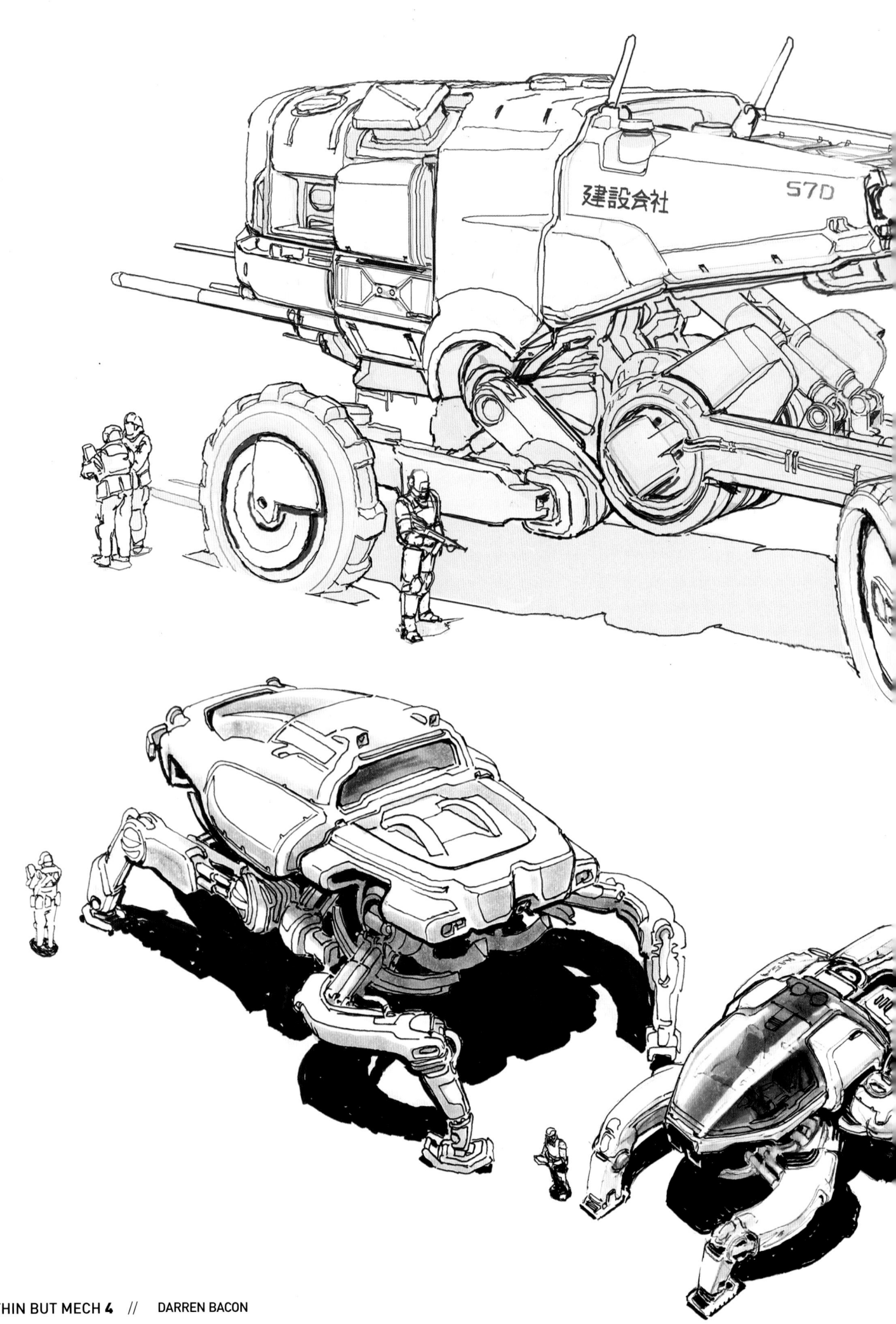

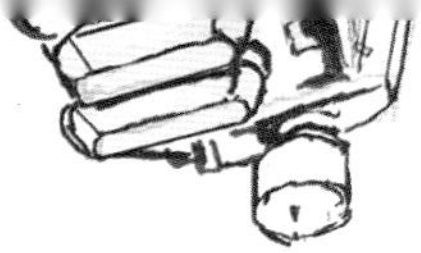

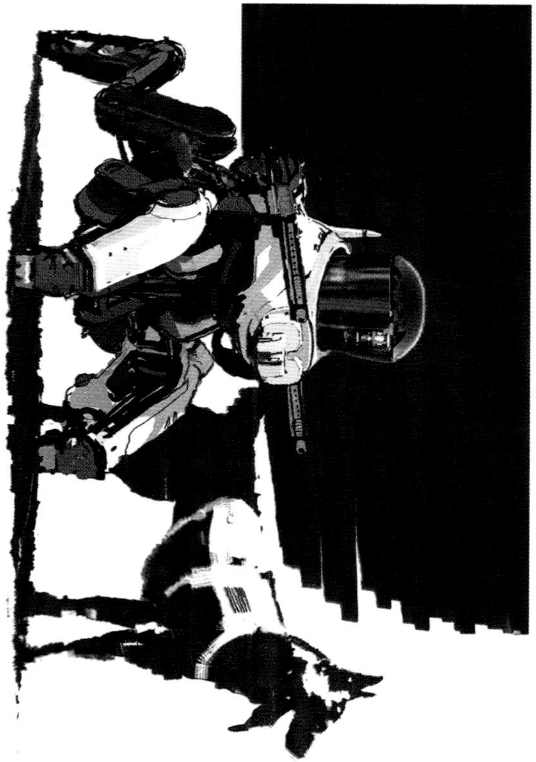

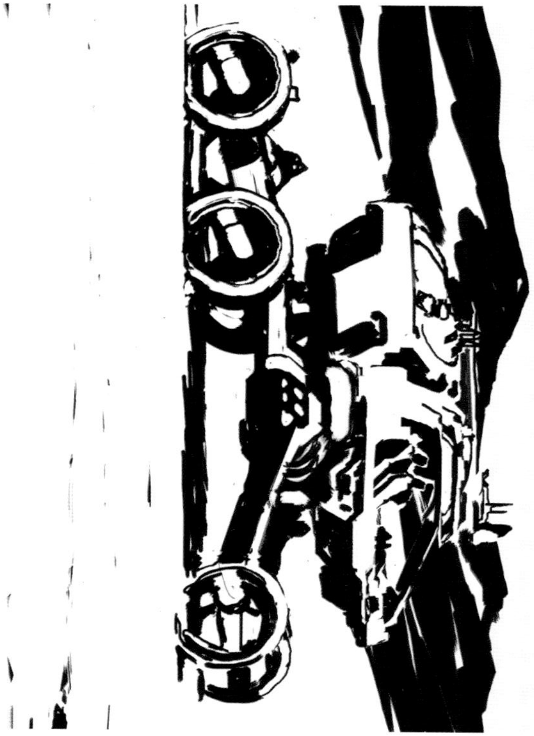

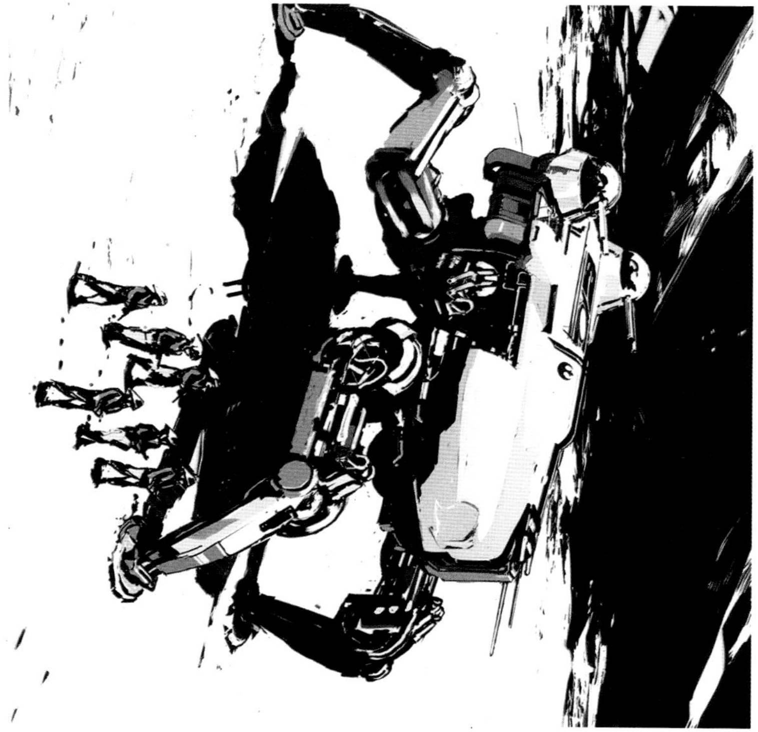

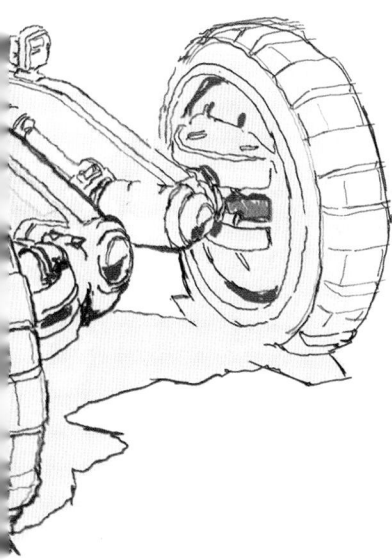

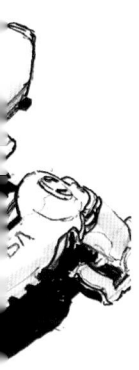

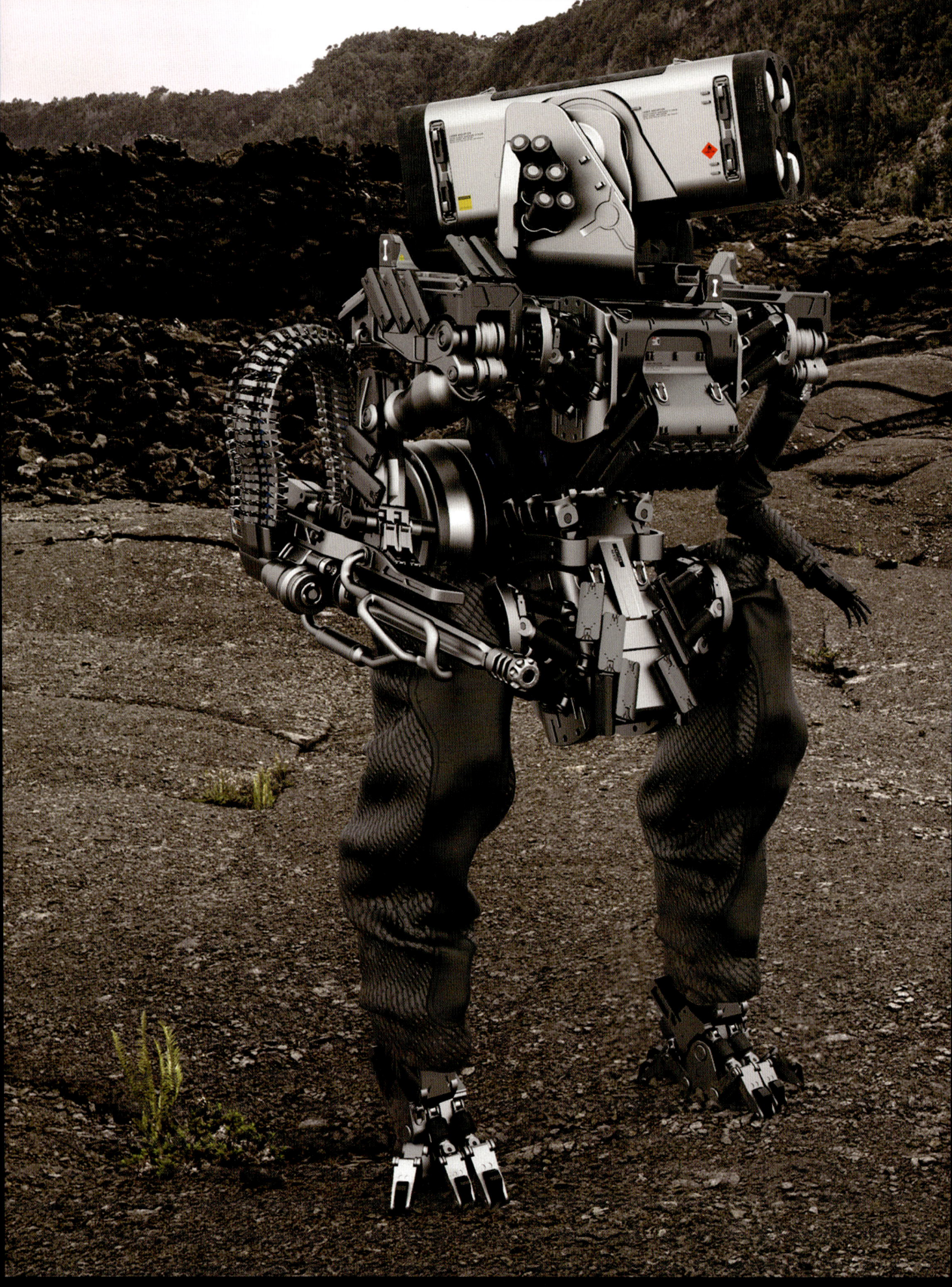

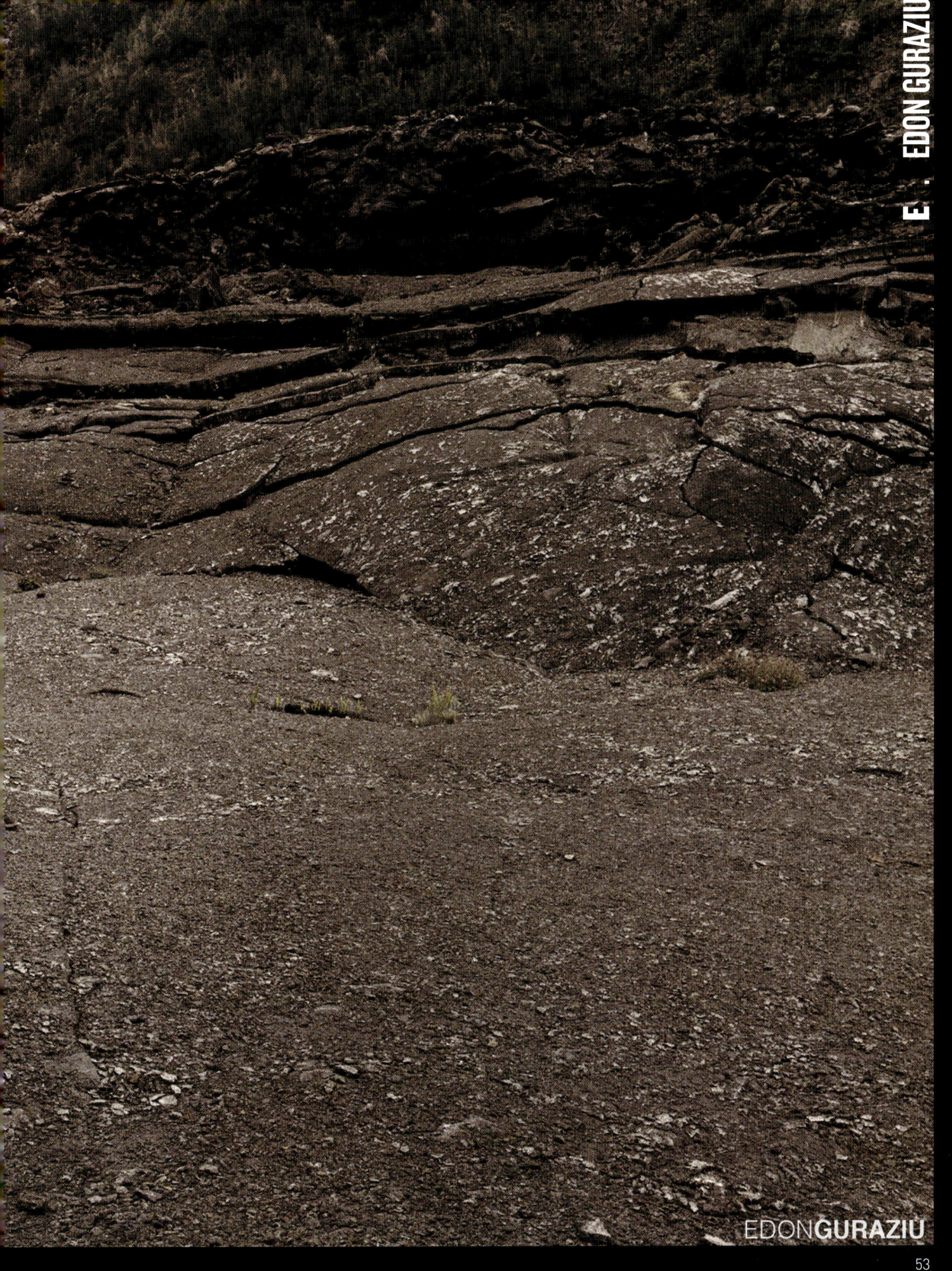

EDON**GURAZIU**

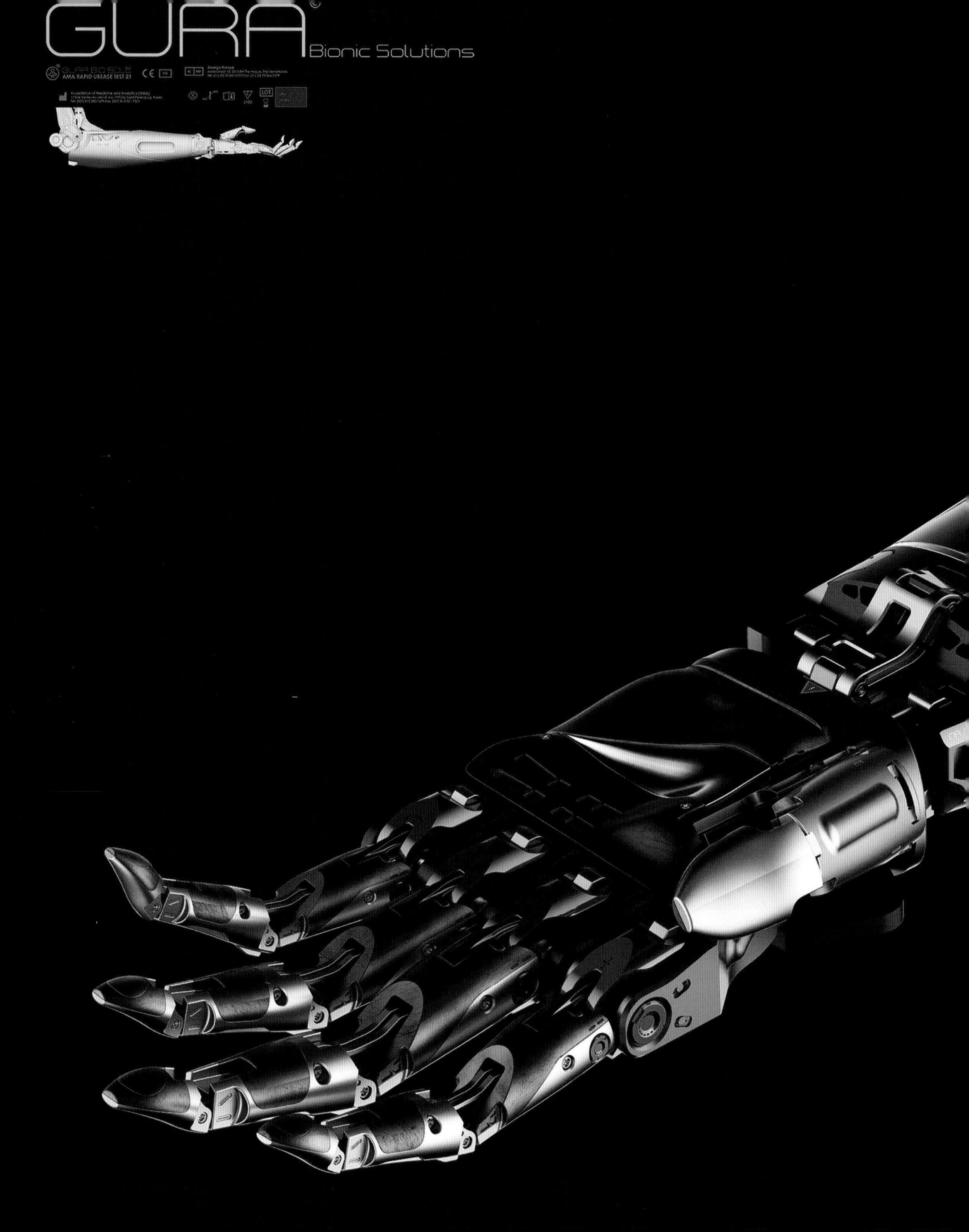

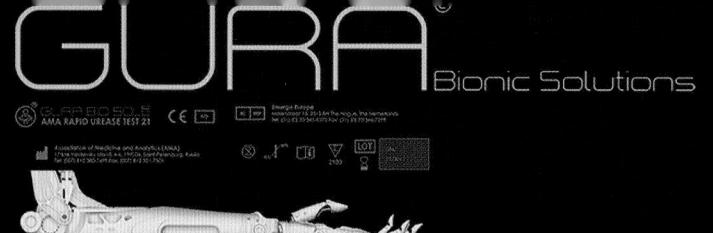

GURA®
Bionic Solutions

GURA BIO SOL 5
AMA RAPID UREASE TEST 21

A subsidiary of Medicine and Analytics (AMA)
Nevsky prospekt 54, 190000 Saint-Petersburg, Russia
Tel: (007) 812 380-7495 Fax: (007) 812 50-7504

Emergo Europe
Molendoorf 15, 2513 AH The Hague, the Netherlands
Tel: (31) 0 70 345-8570 Fax: (31) 70 346-7299

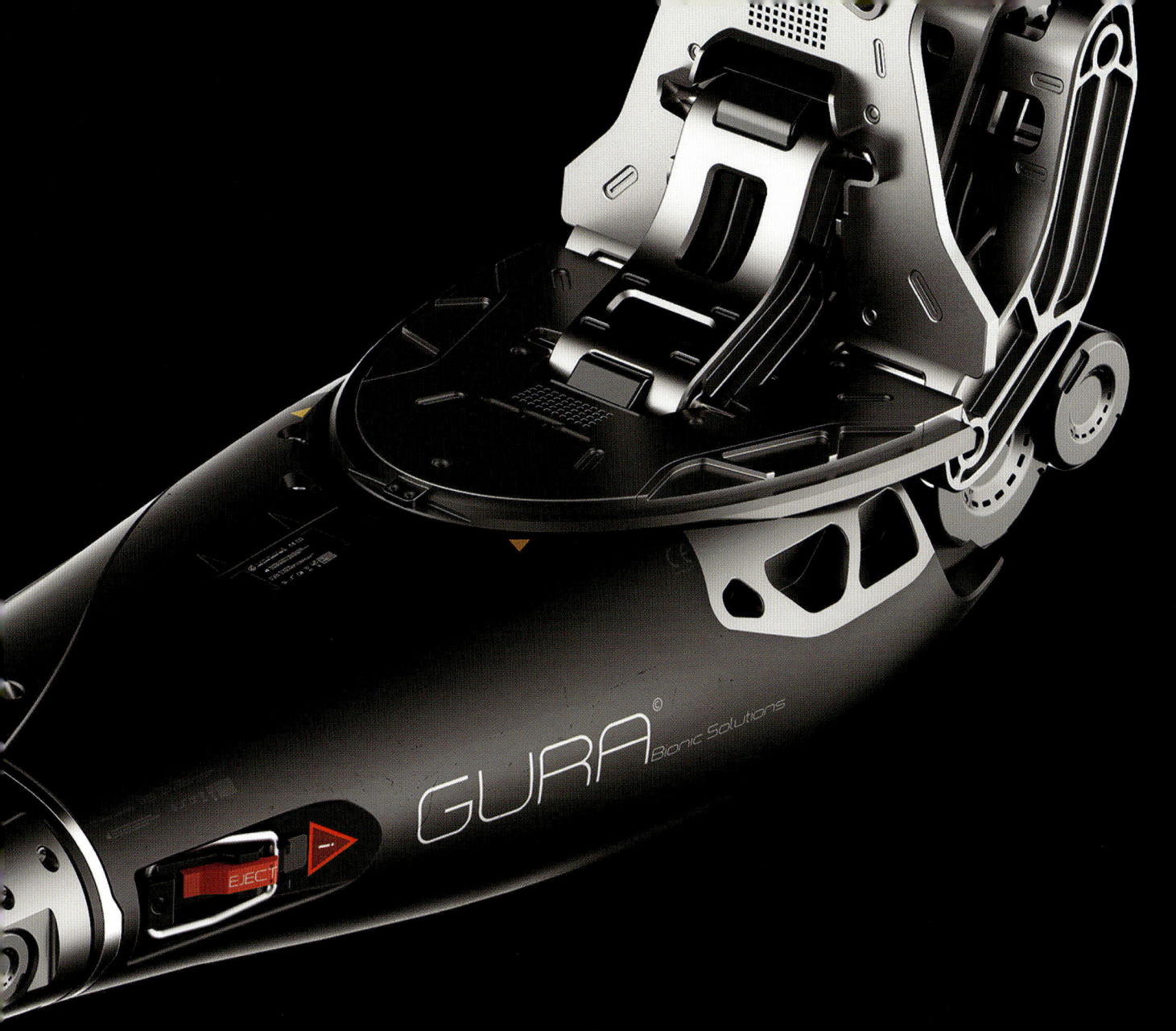

GURA© Bionic Solutions

EJECT

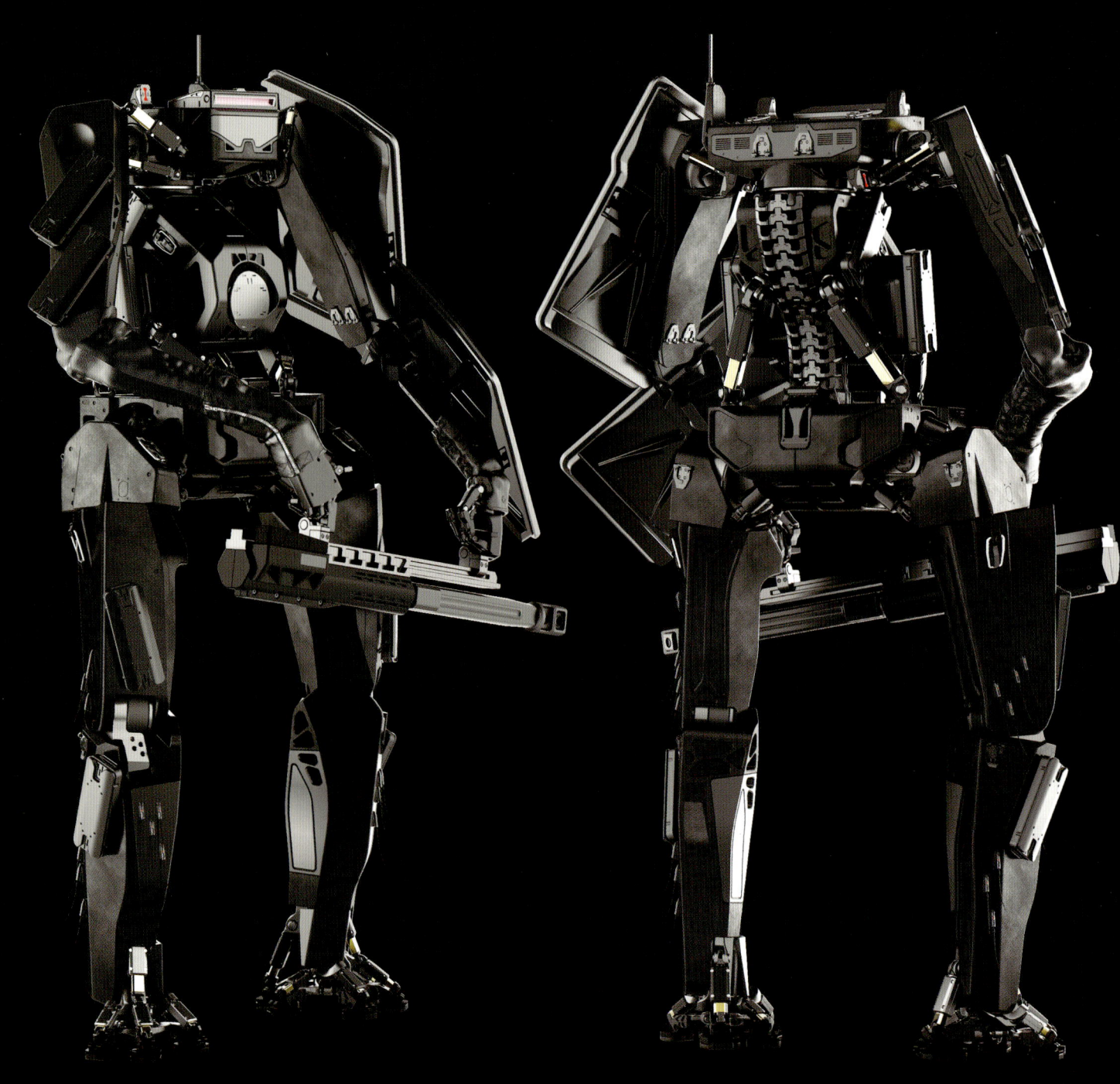

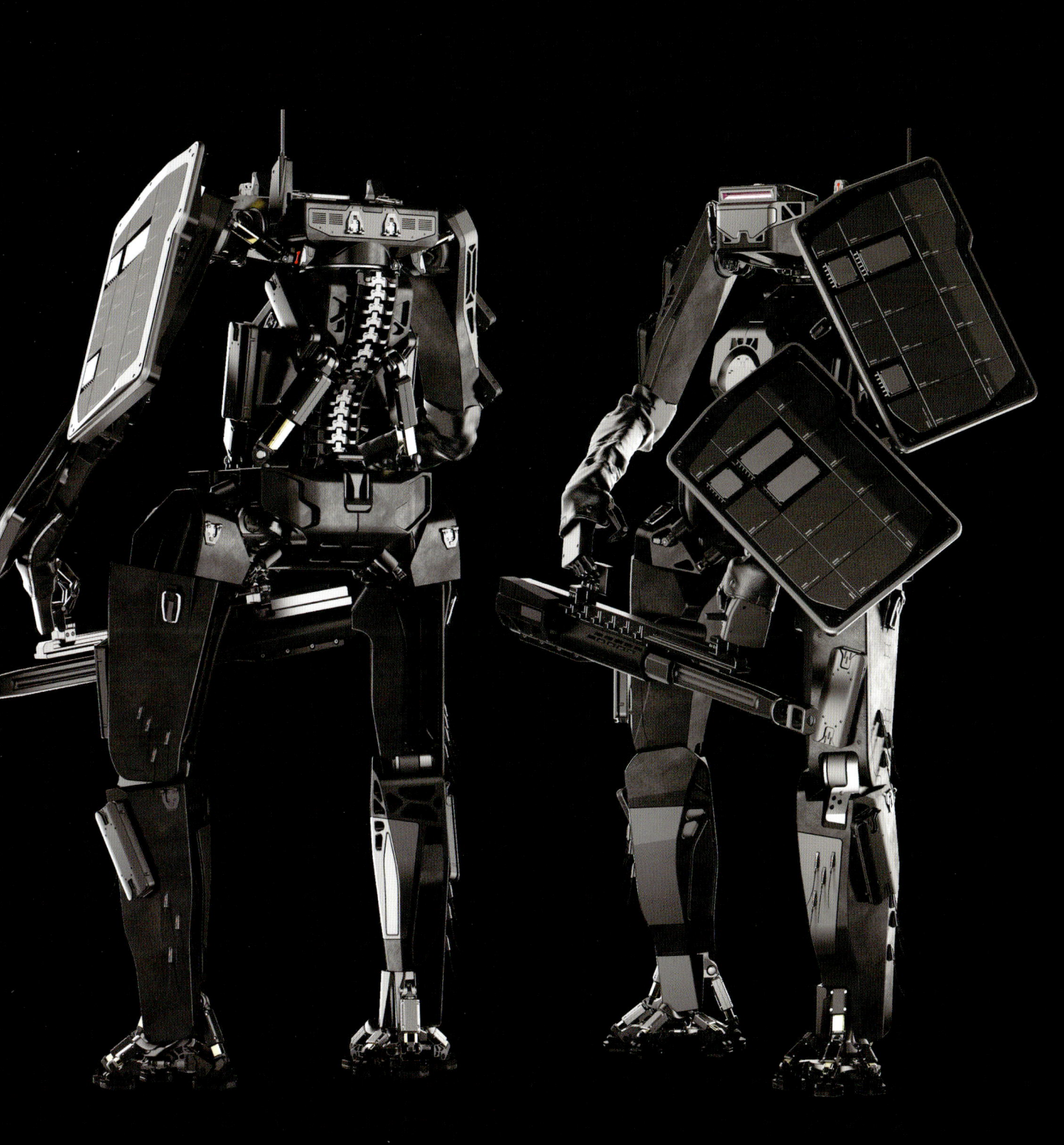

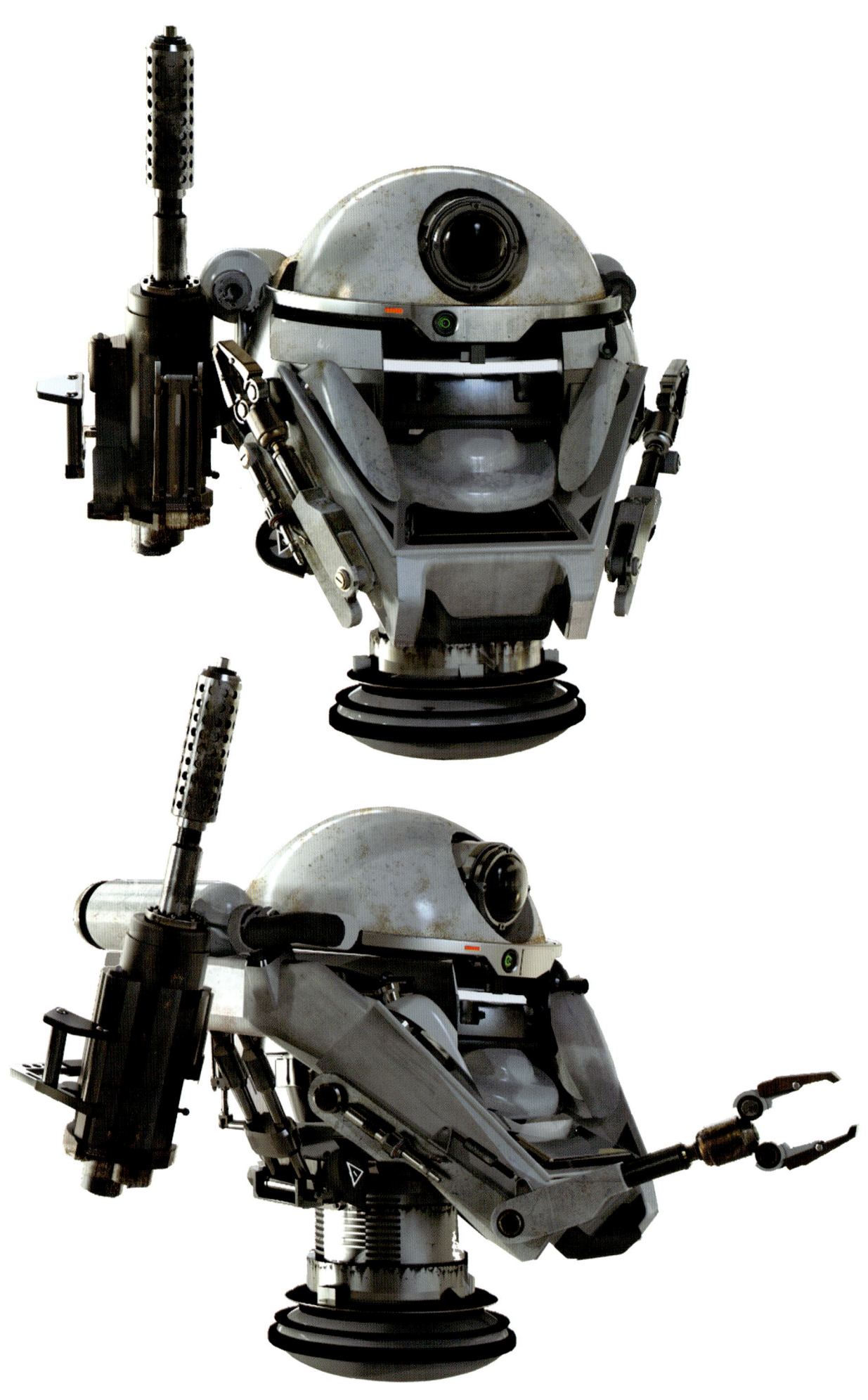

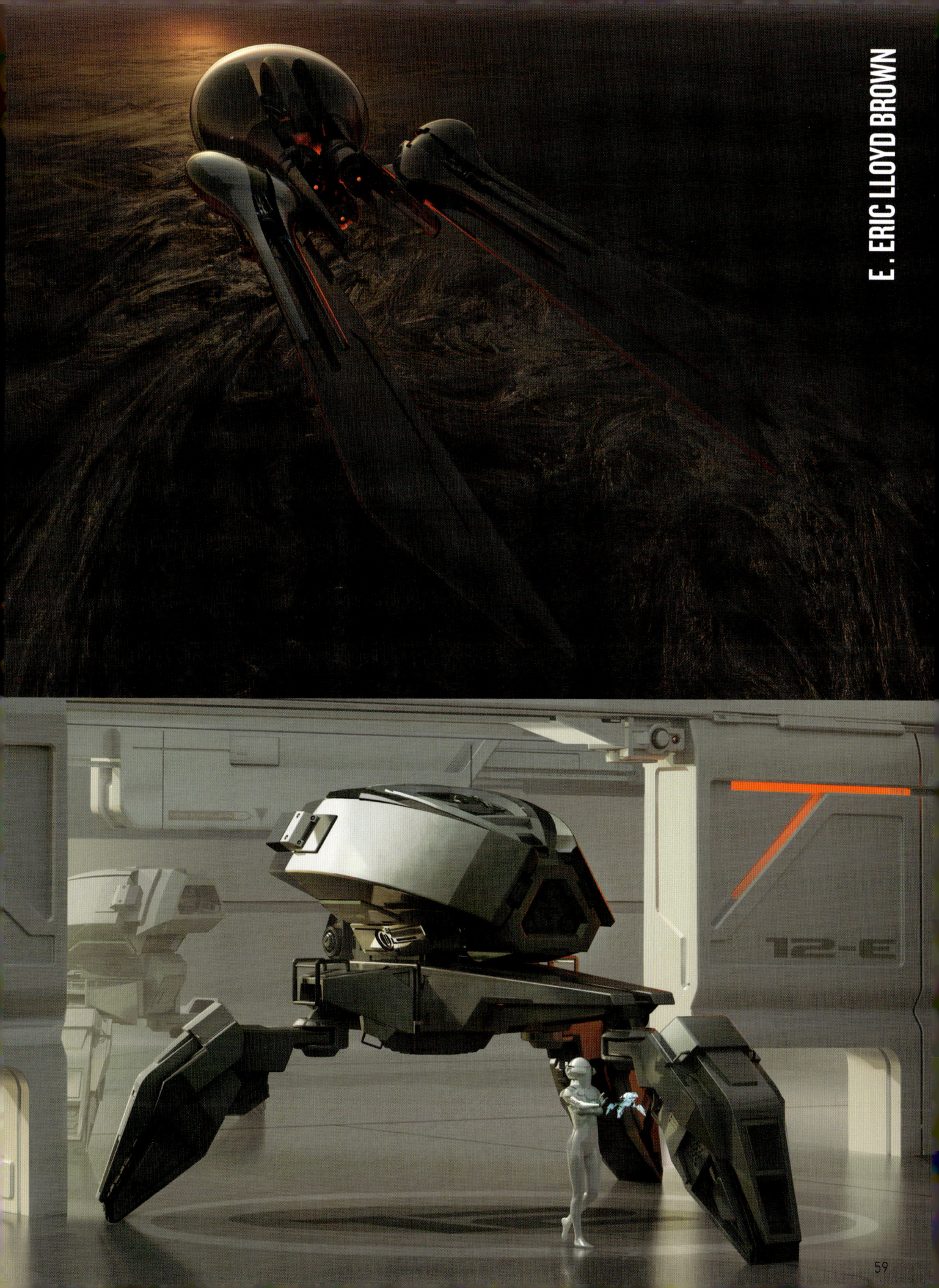

59

Gus lives in Seattle with his wife Kelley and their dog Mina, and he continues to work with filmmakers, game studios, and production designers, helping them bring their stories to life.

www.brushonfire.com

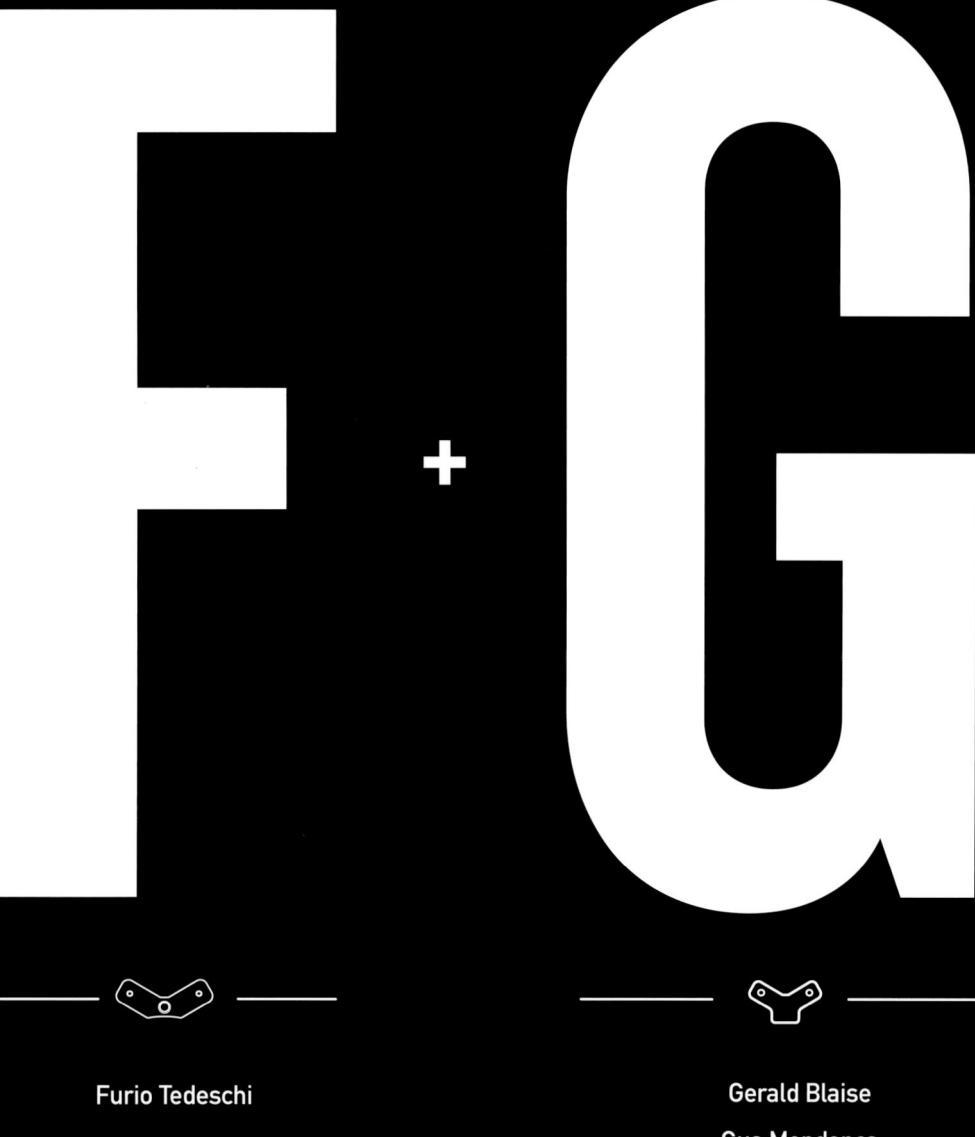

F + G

Furio Tedeschi

Gerald Blaise

Gus Mendonca

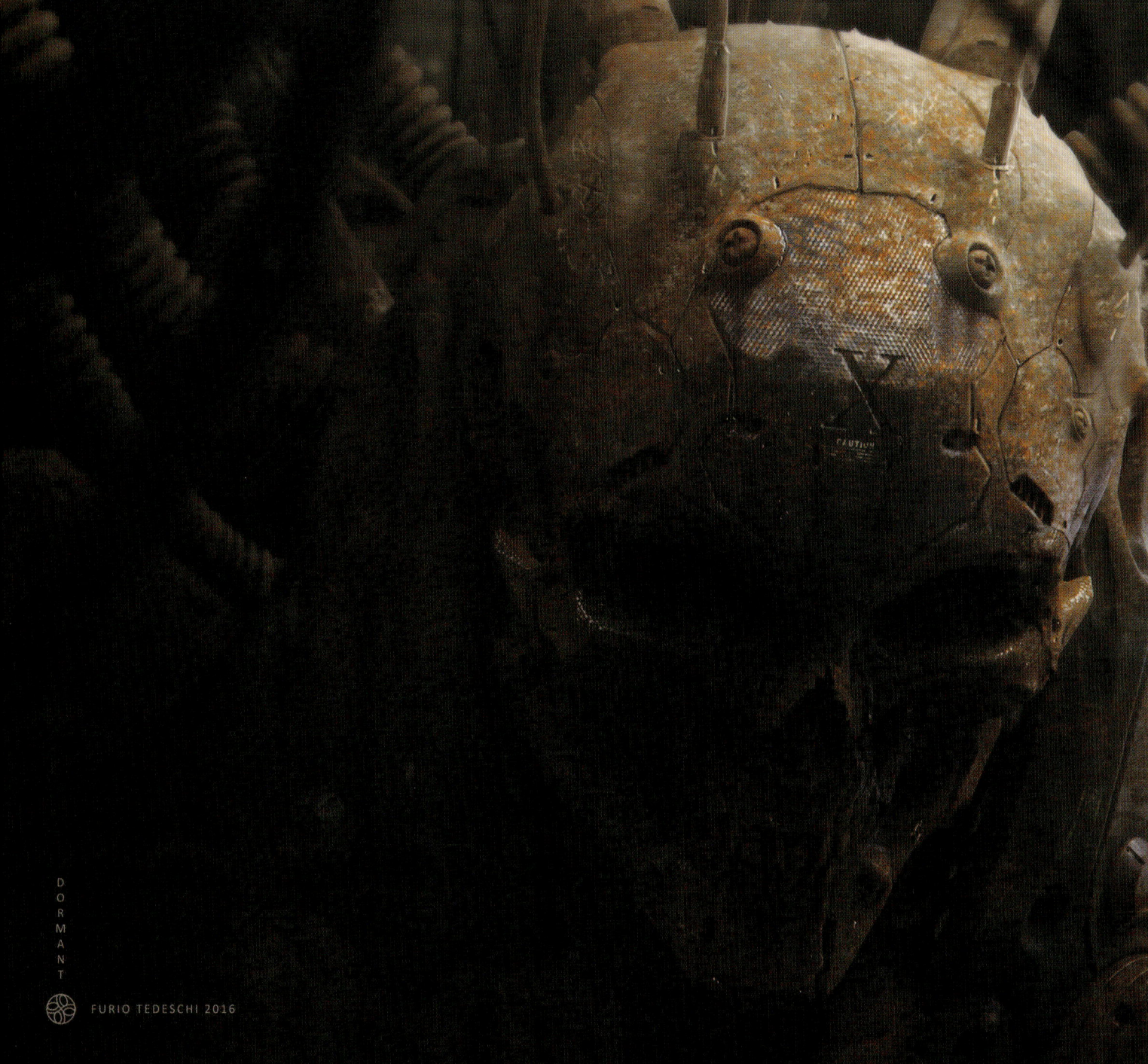

DORMANT

FURIO TEDESCHI 2016

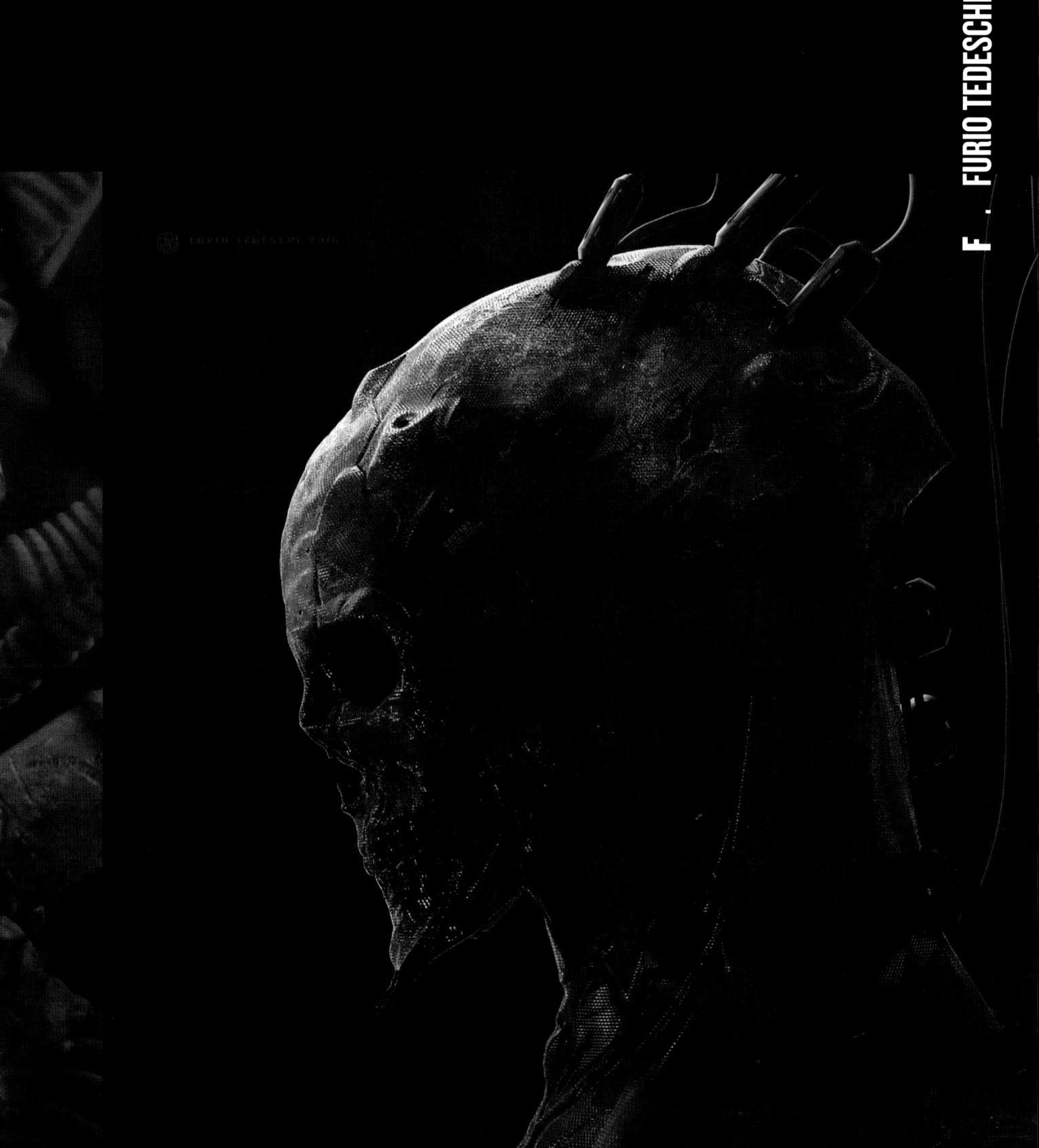

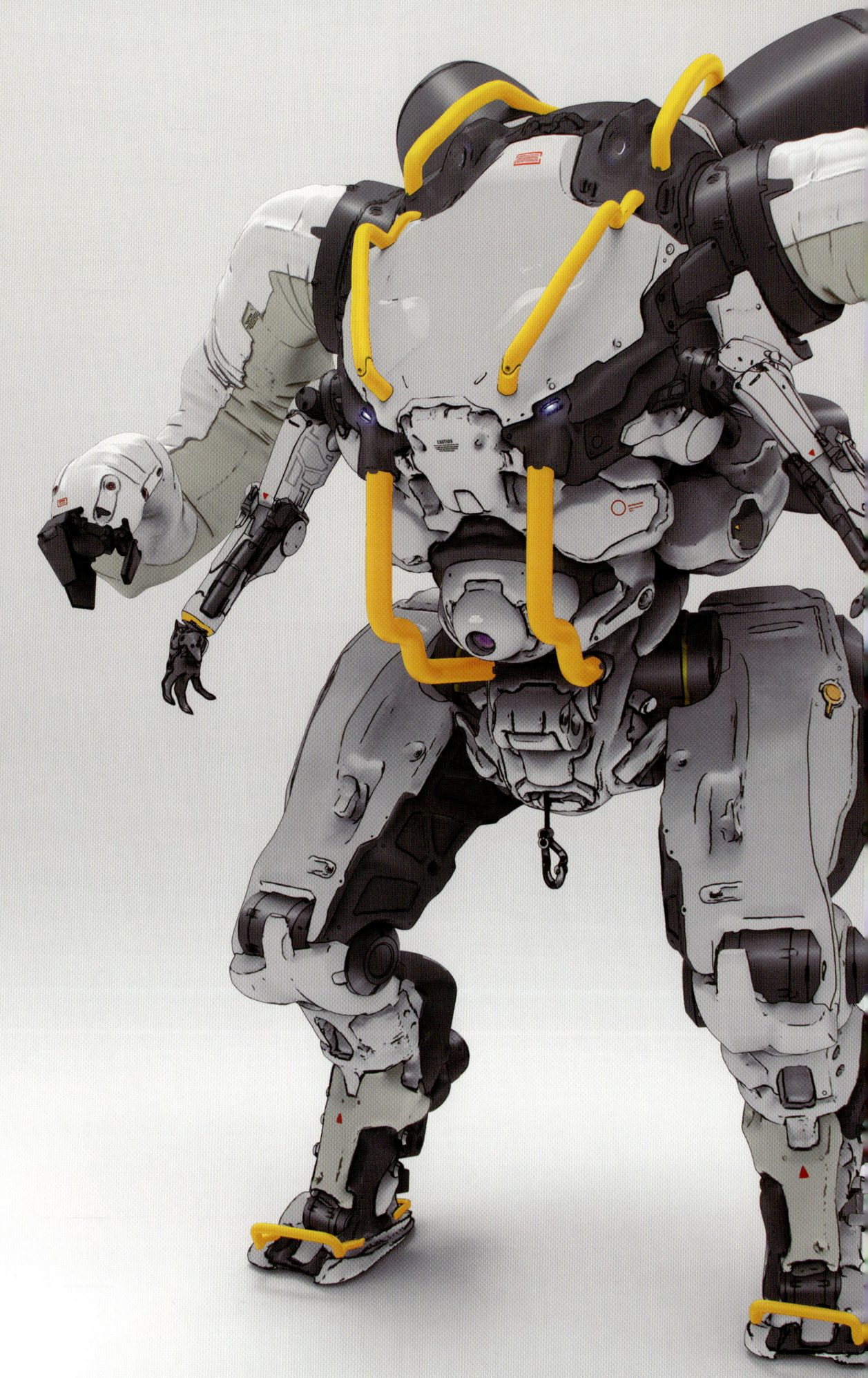

FURIO TEDESCHI 2016

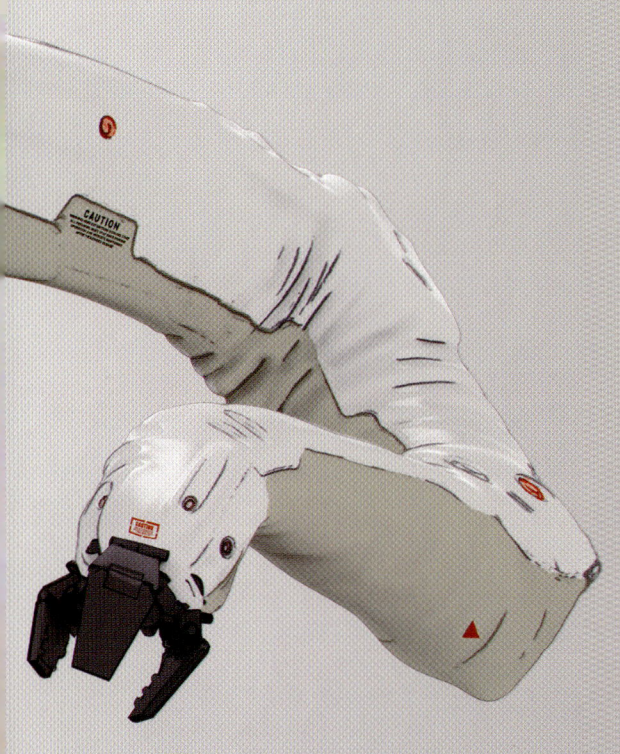

O.R.U
ORBITAL REPAIR UNIT

FURIO TEDESCHI 2014

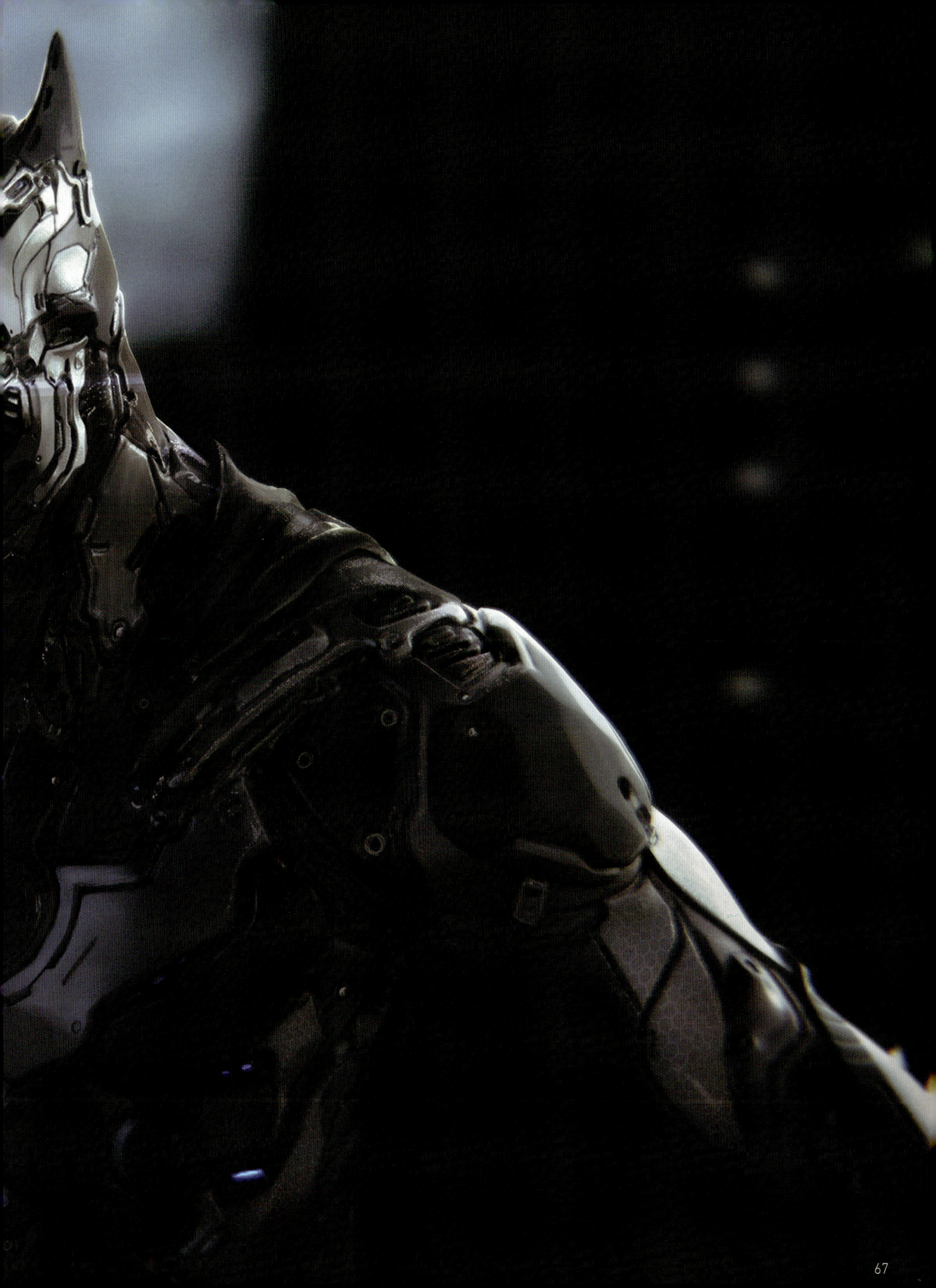

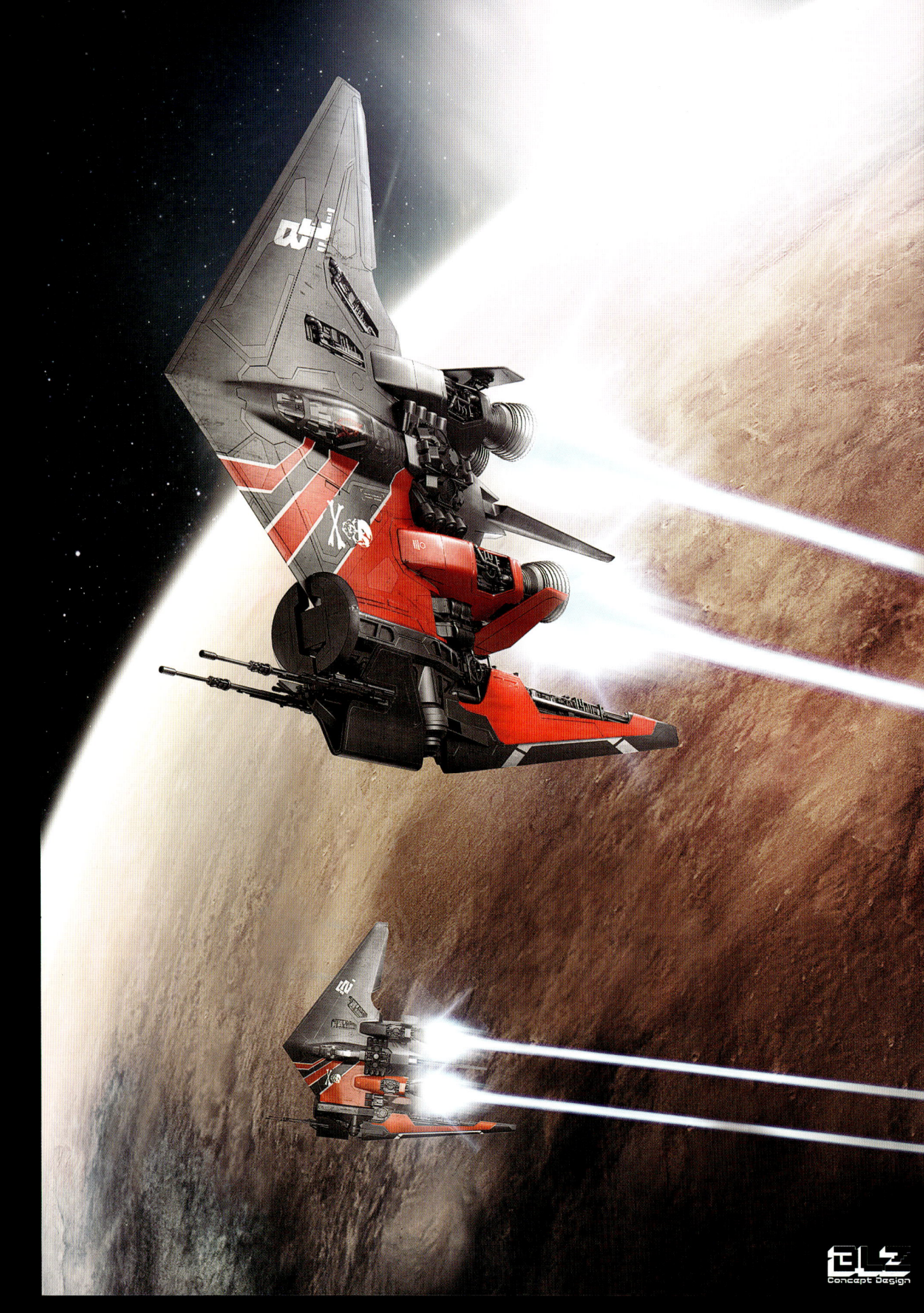

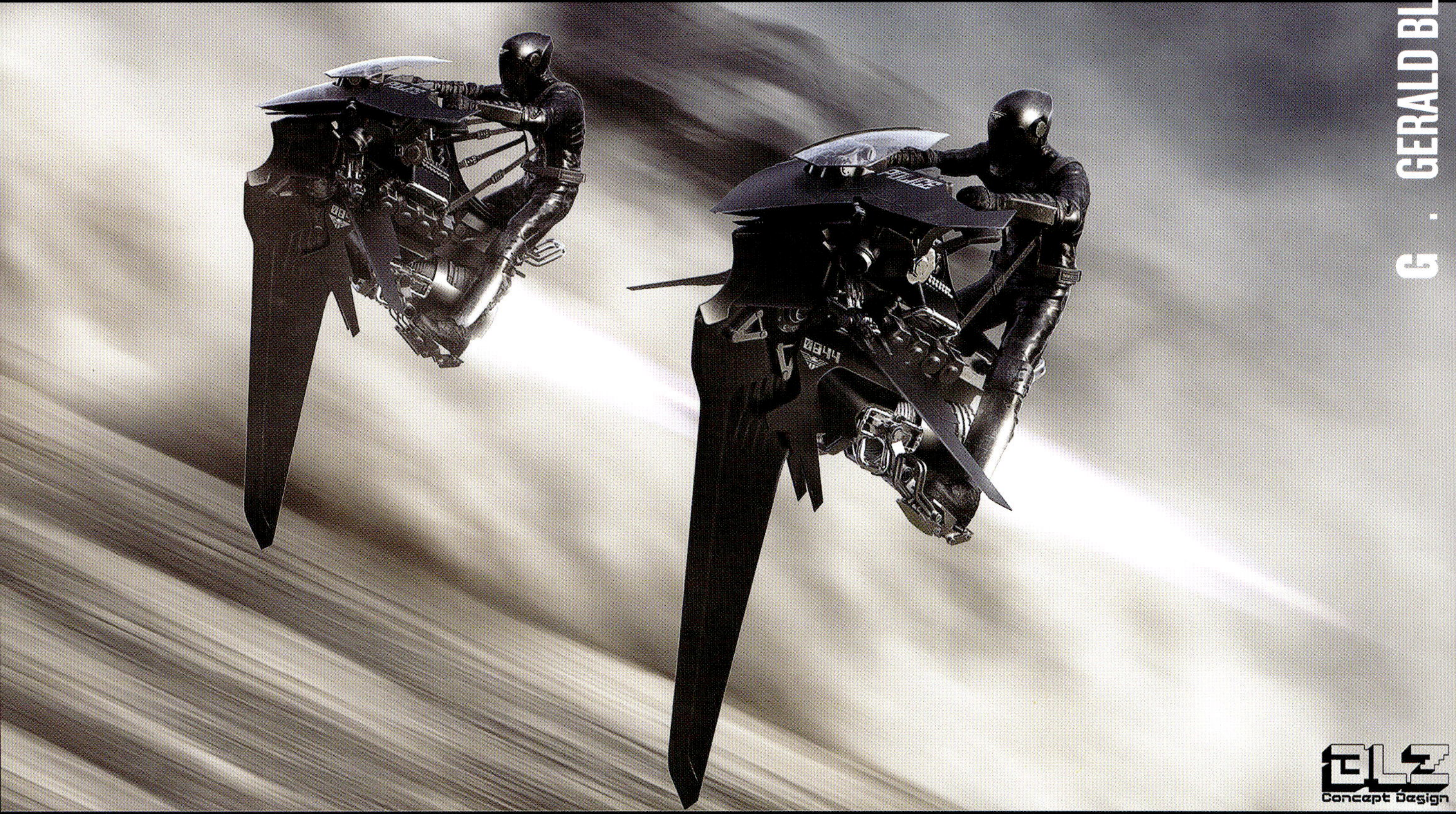
0844
BLZ
Concept Design

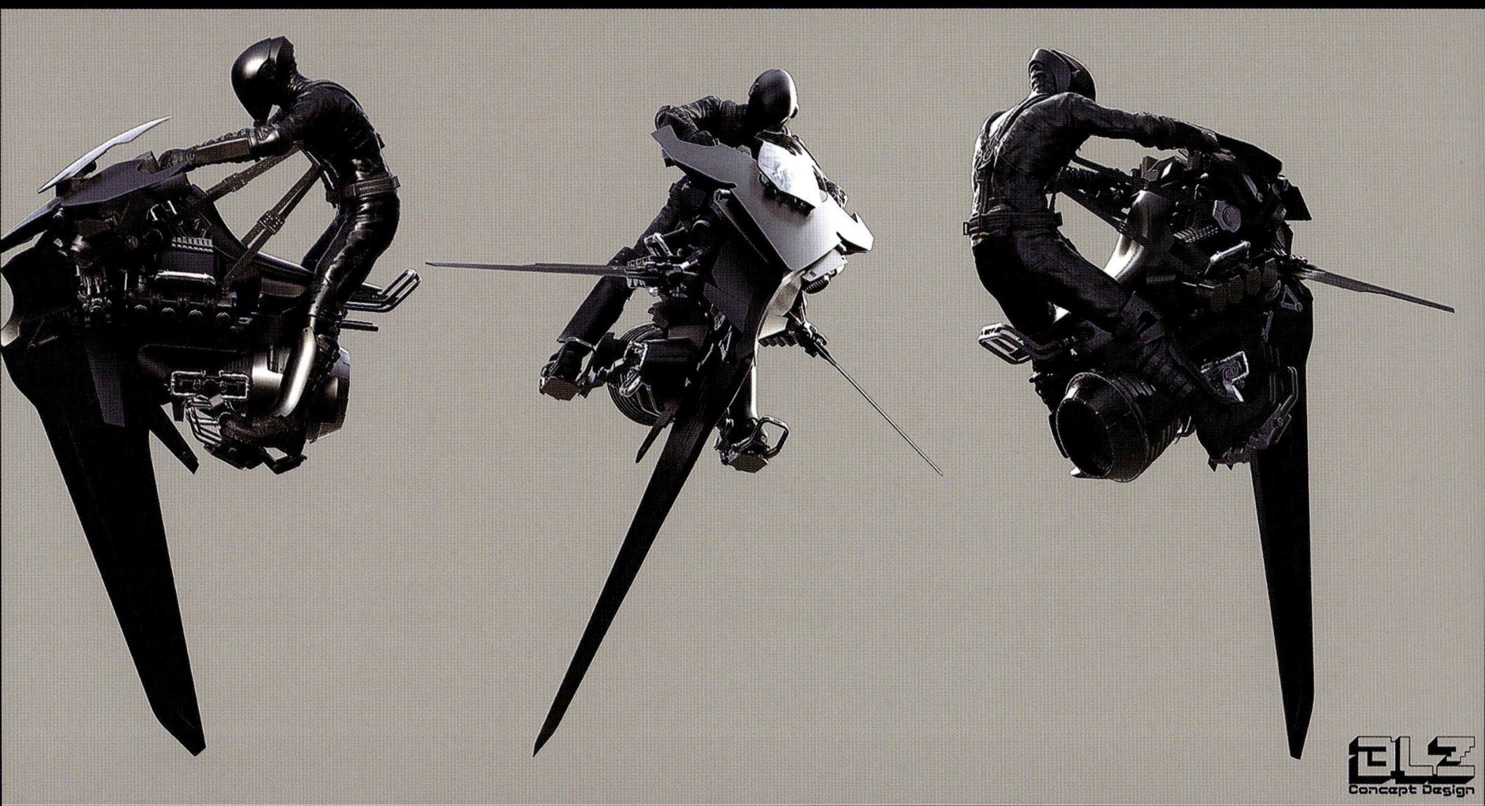
BLZ
Concept Design

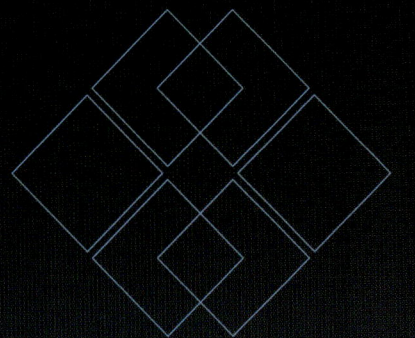

BOOMER

BLACK & WHITE EDITION

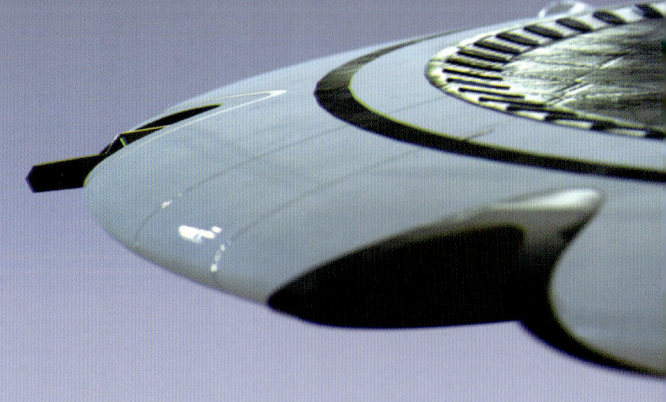

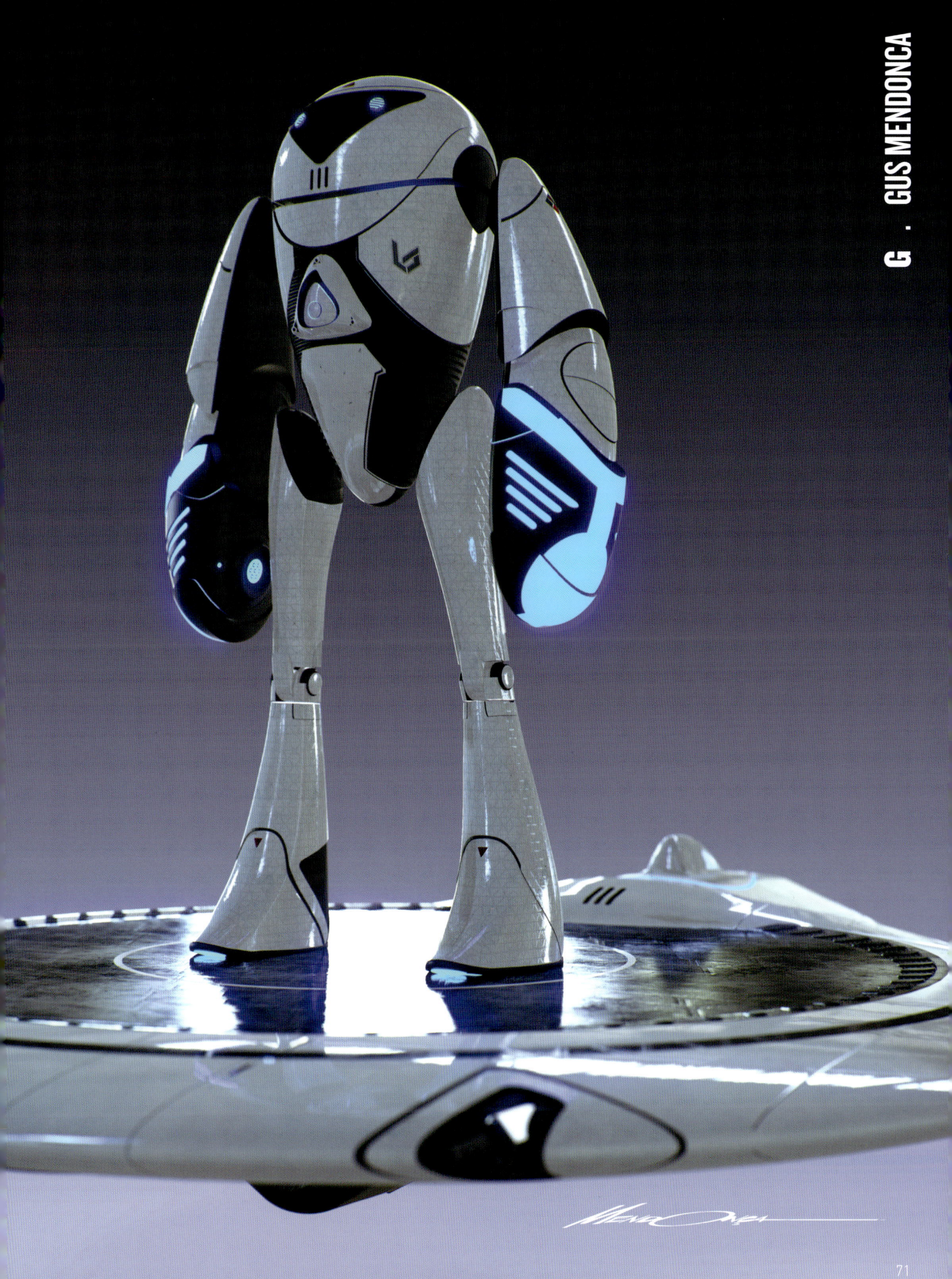

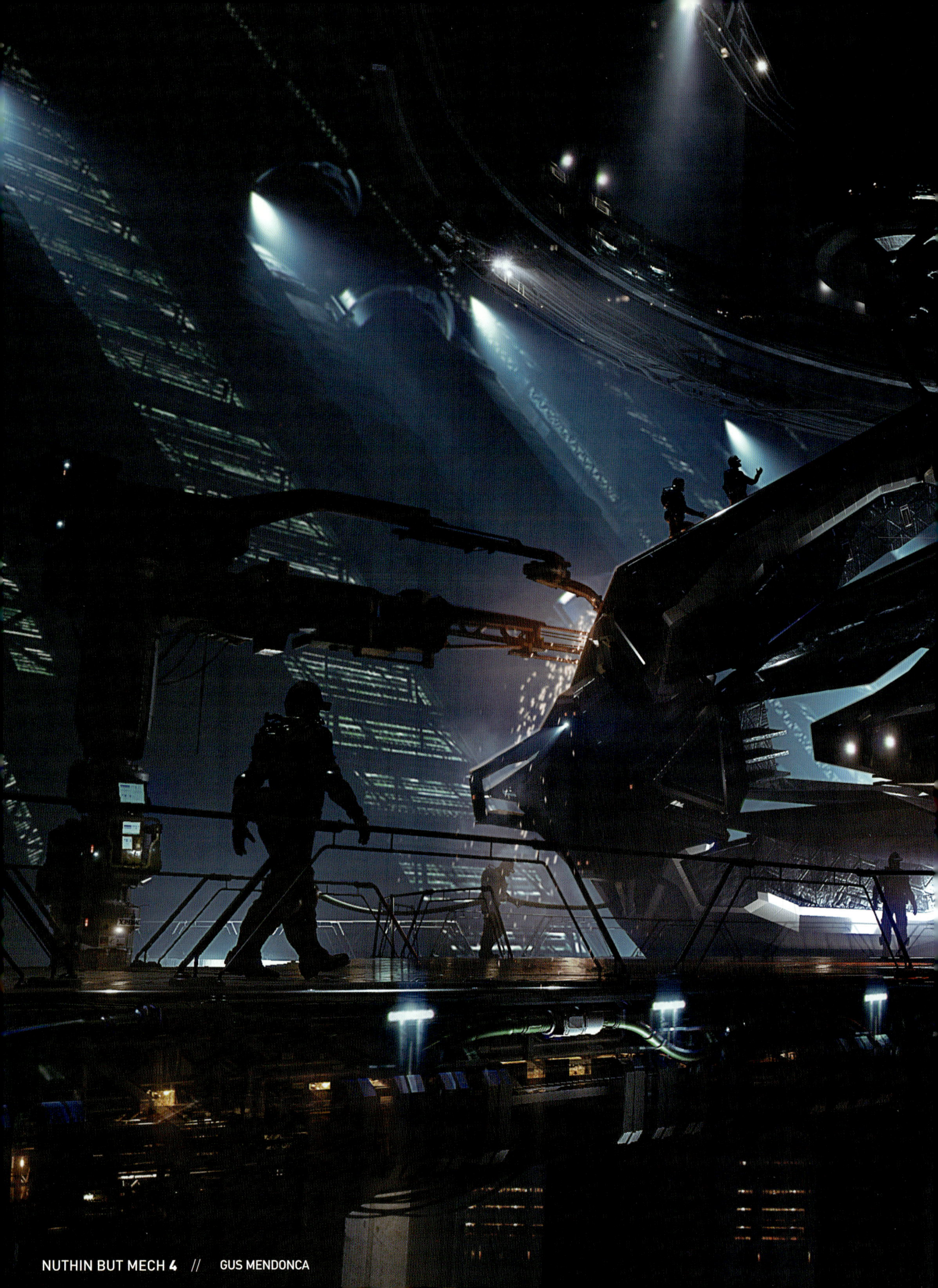

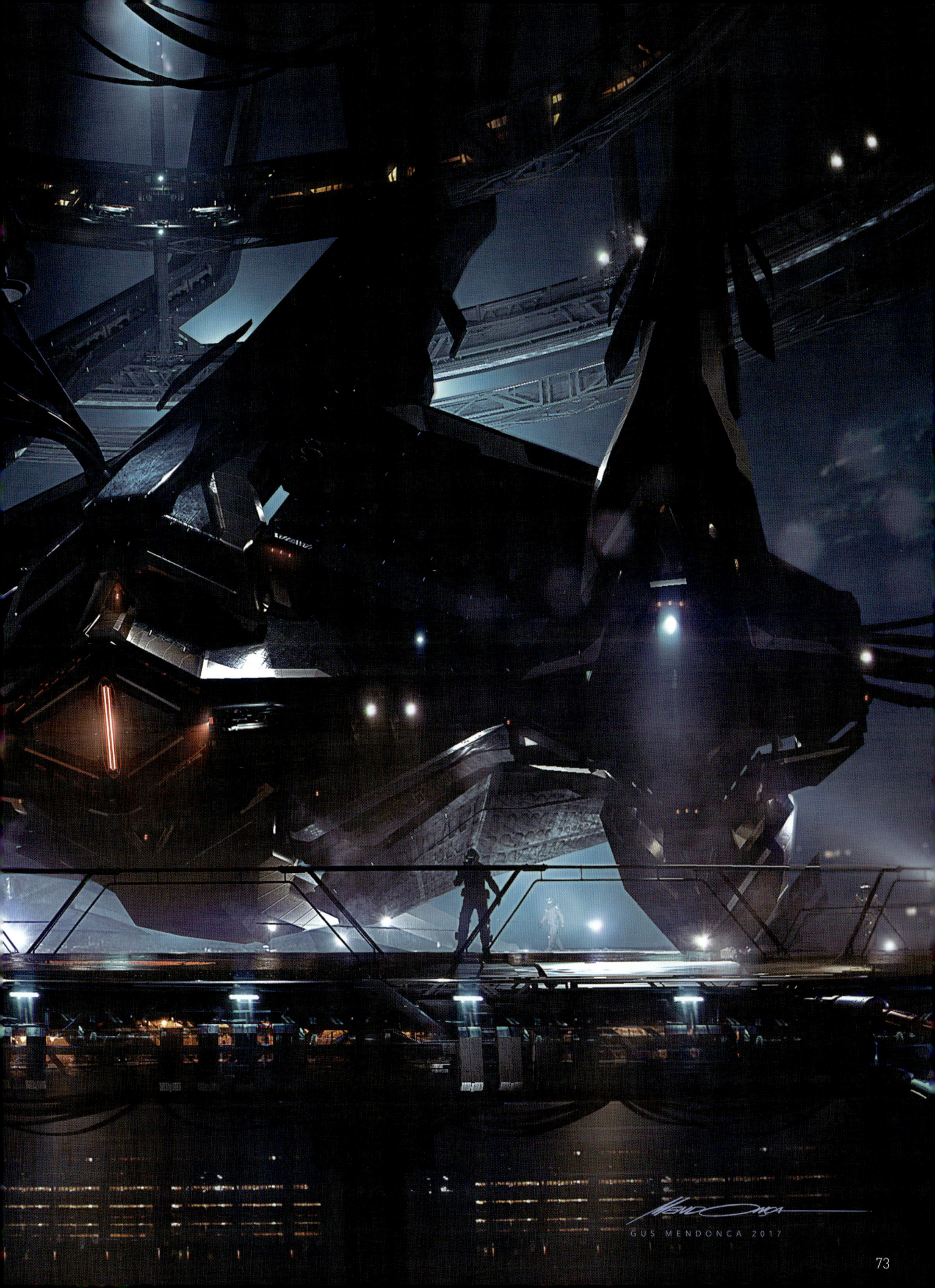

GUS MENDONCA 2017

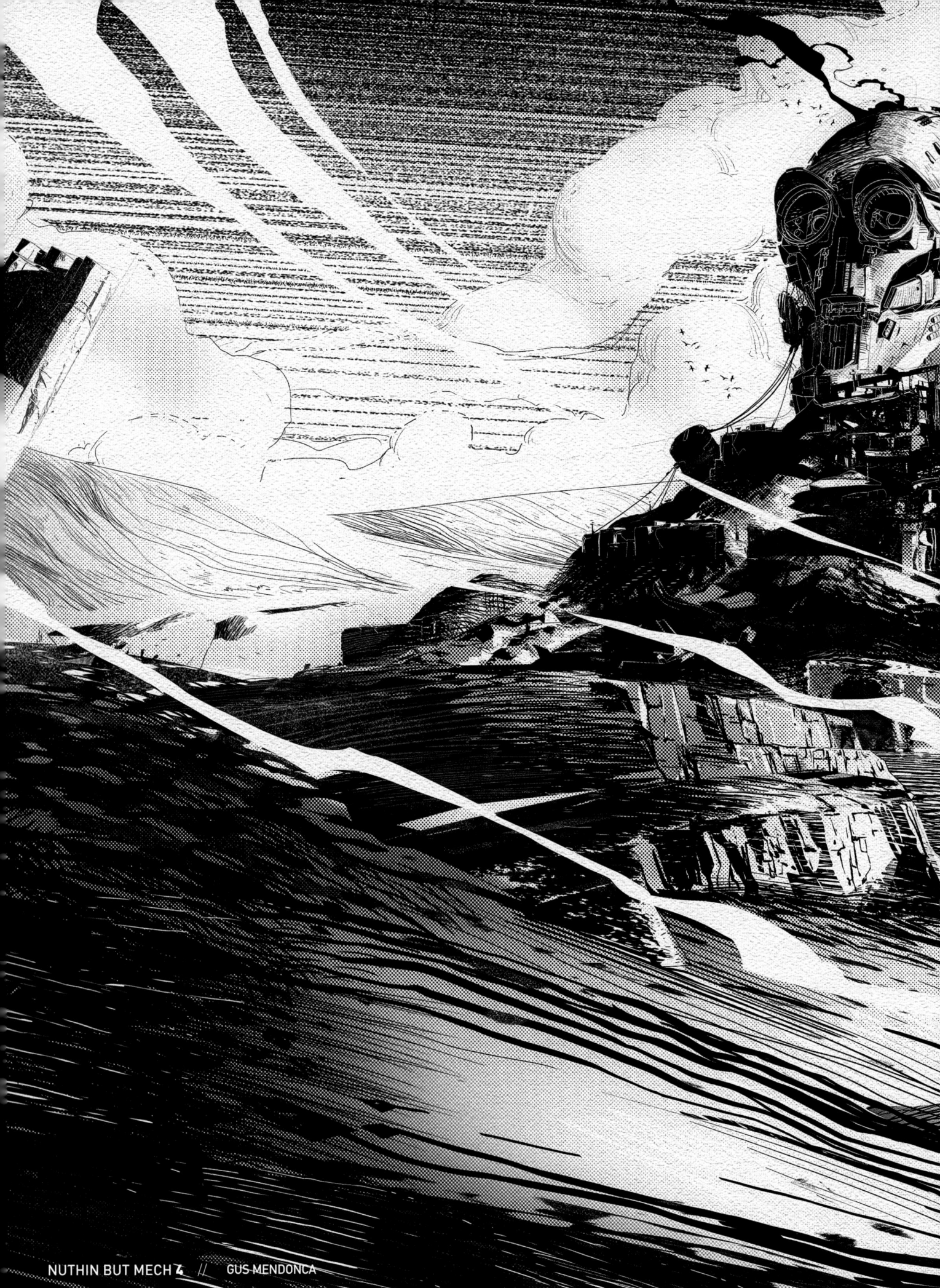

NUTHIN BUT MECH 4 // GUS MENDONCA

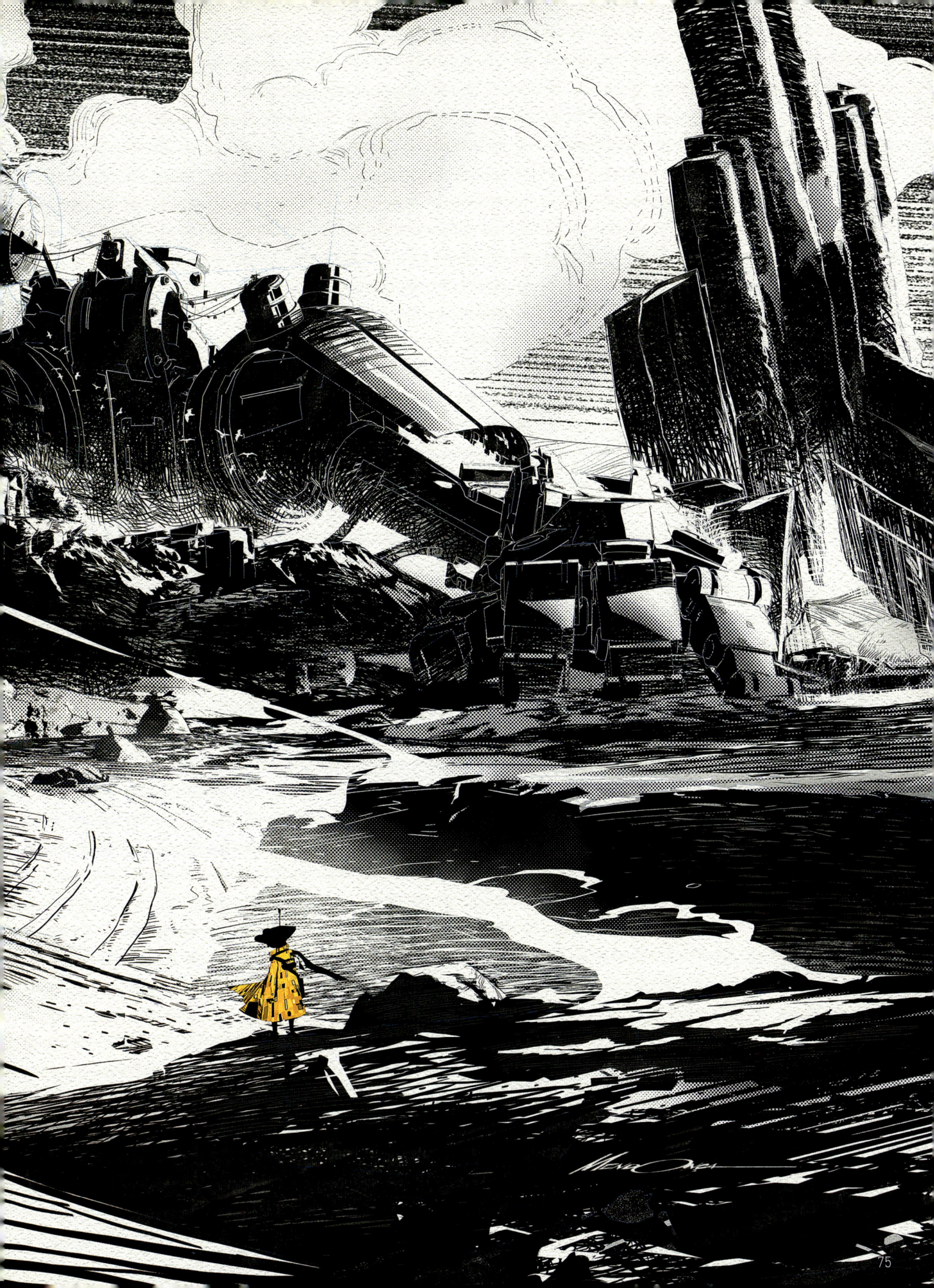

HUGO BERMUDEZ

Hugo, aka Sadgas, is a Spanish human sample interested in technology, engineering, and screws. He grew up as a graffiti writer and has been working in the entertainment industry since 2001. Hugo is a mech designer by day and toymaker by night under the Ghetto Plastic Toys brand.
www.sadgas.com

IAN MCQUE

Formerly assistant art director on the *Grand Theft Auto* series at Rockstar North, Ian is now a freelance concept artist and illustrator.
www.ianmcque.bigcartel.com

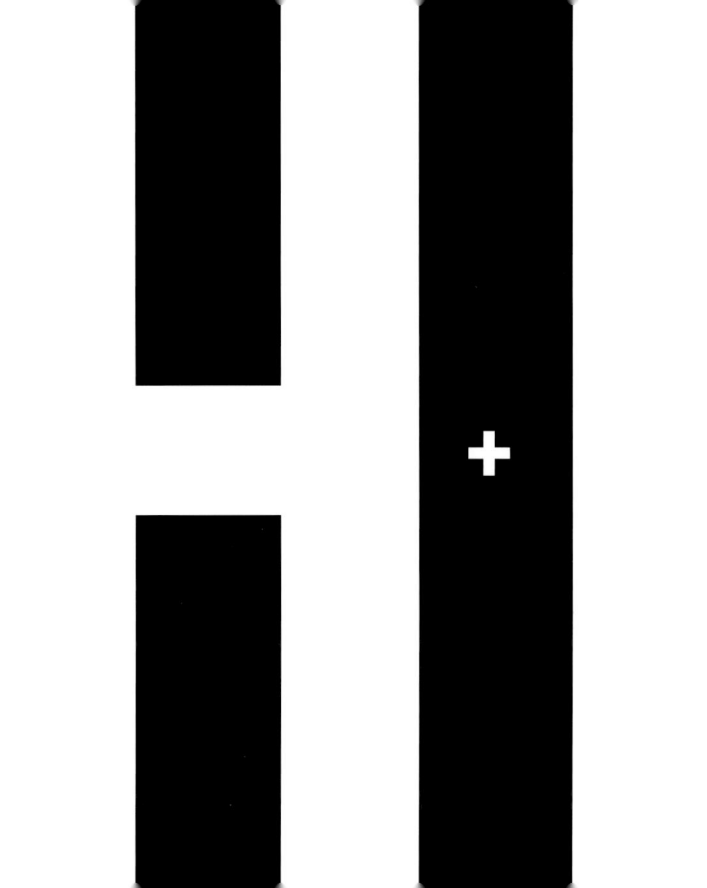

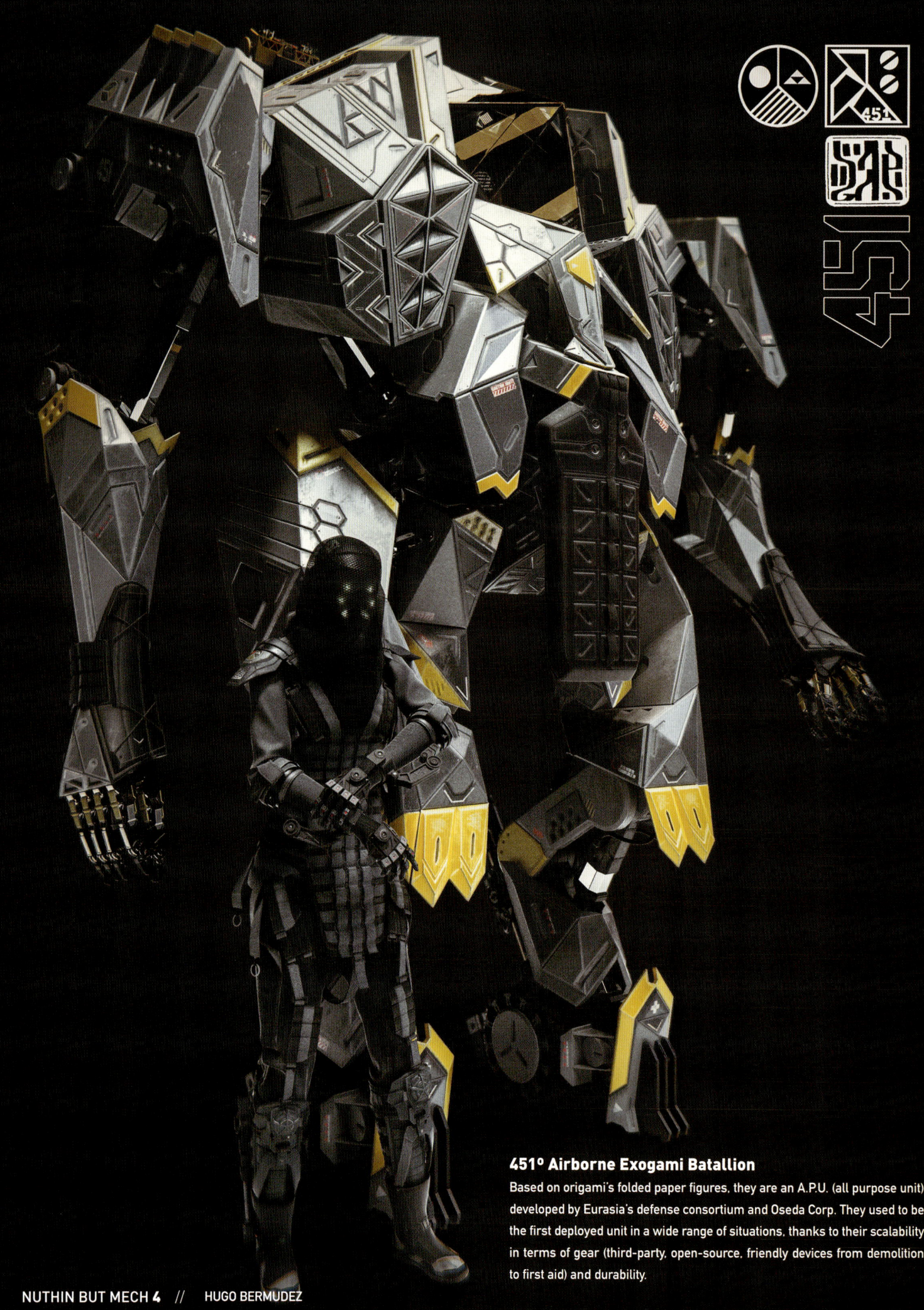

451º Airborne Exogami Batallion

Based on origami's folded paper figures, they are an A.P.U. (all purpose unit) developed by Eurasia's defense consortium and Oseda Corp. They used to be the first deployed unit in a wide range of situations, thanks to their scalability in terms of gear (third-party, open-source, friendly devices from demolition to first aid) and durability.

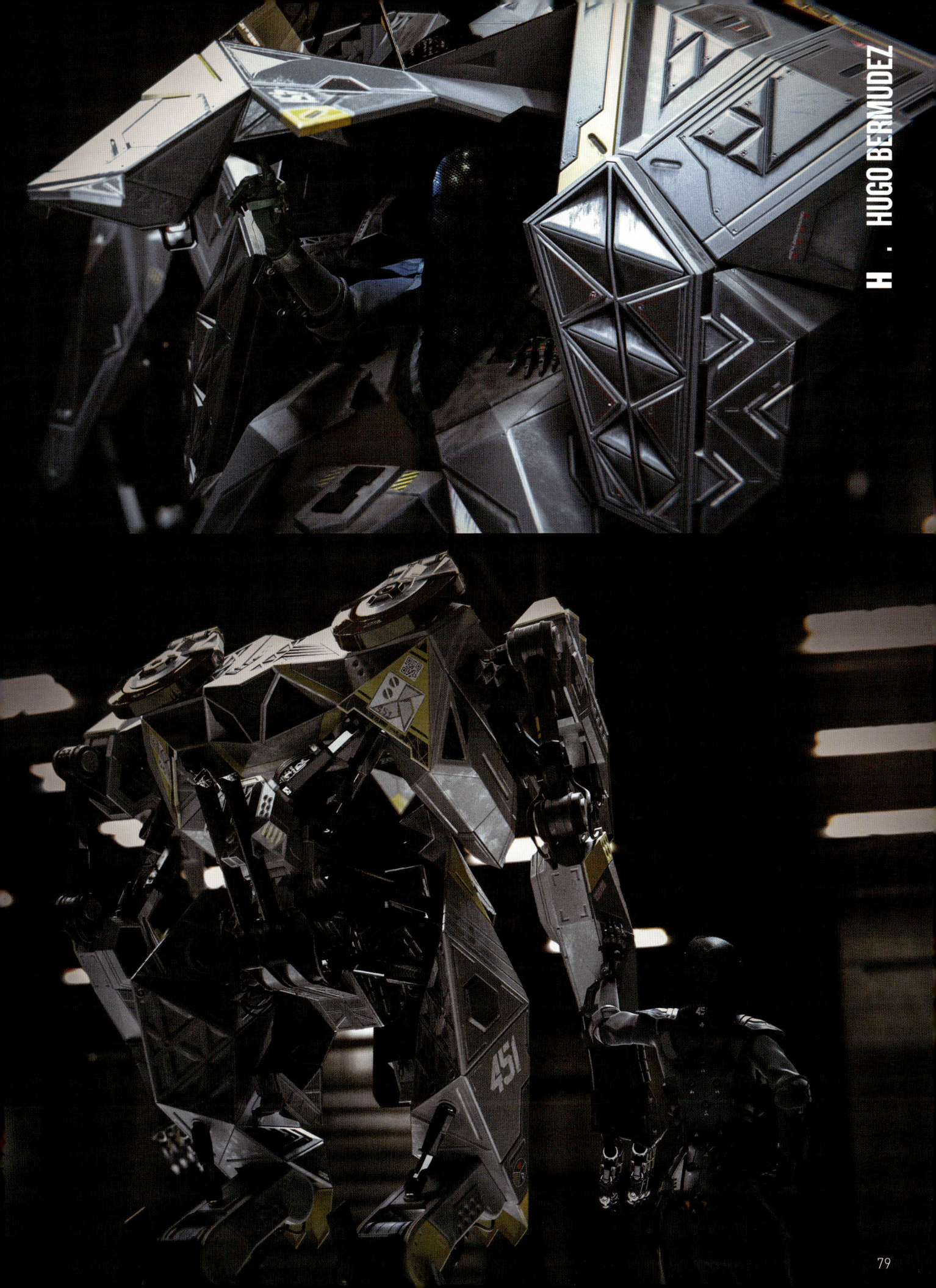

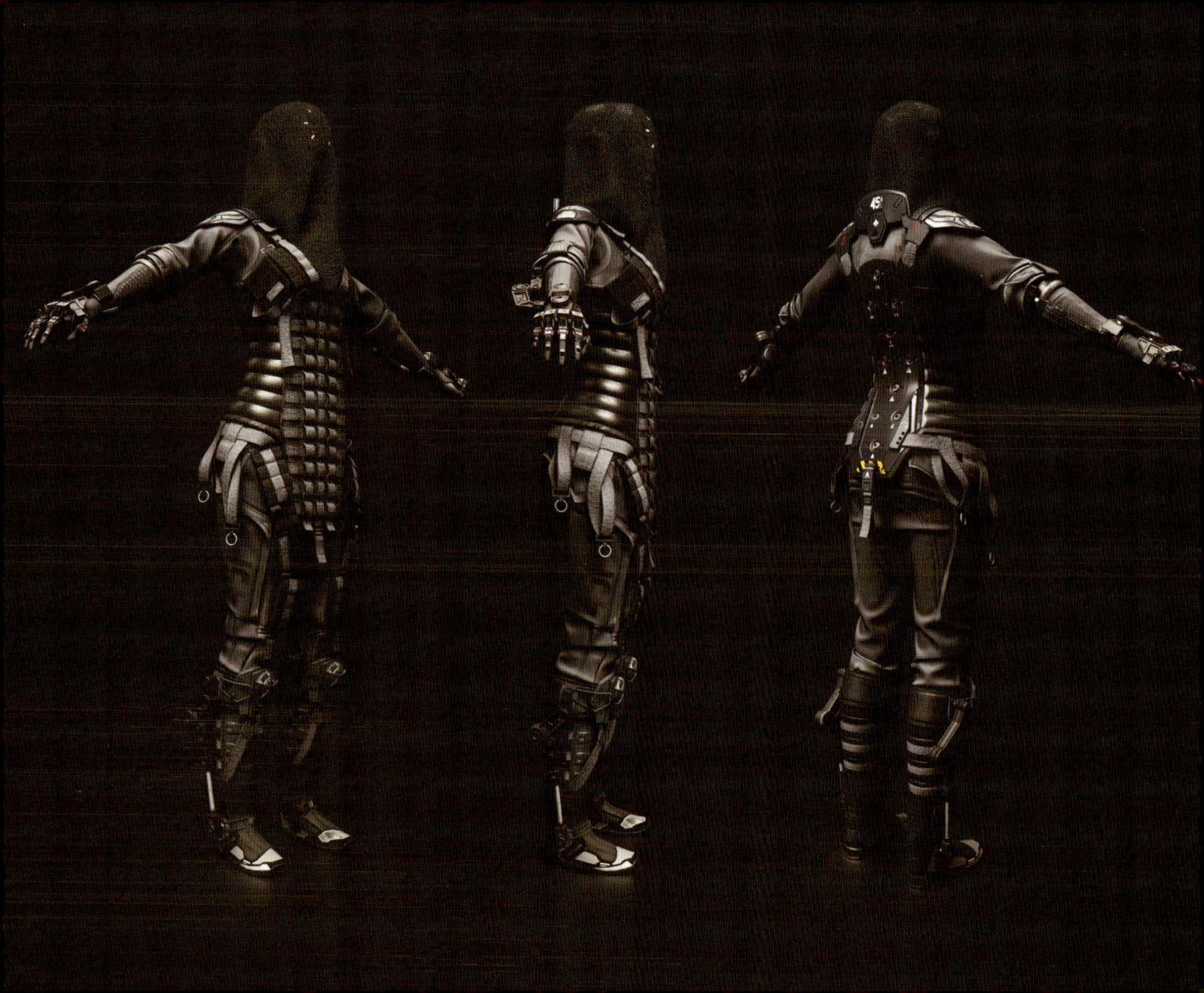

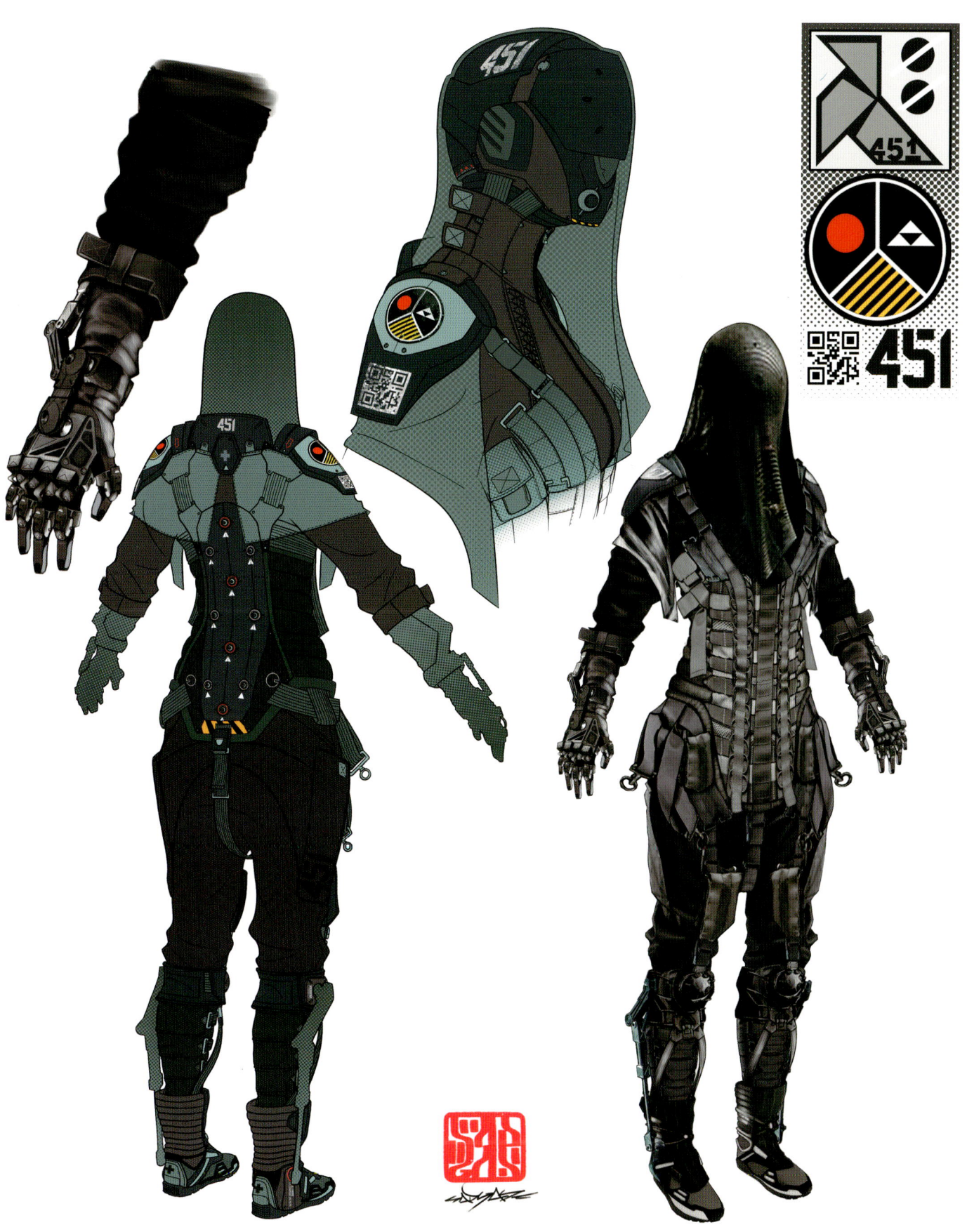

451
451
451

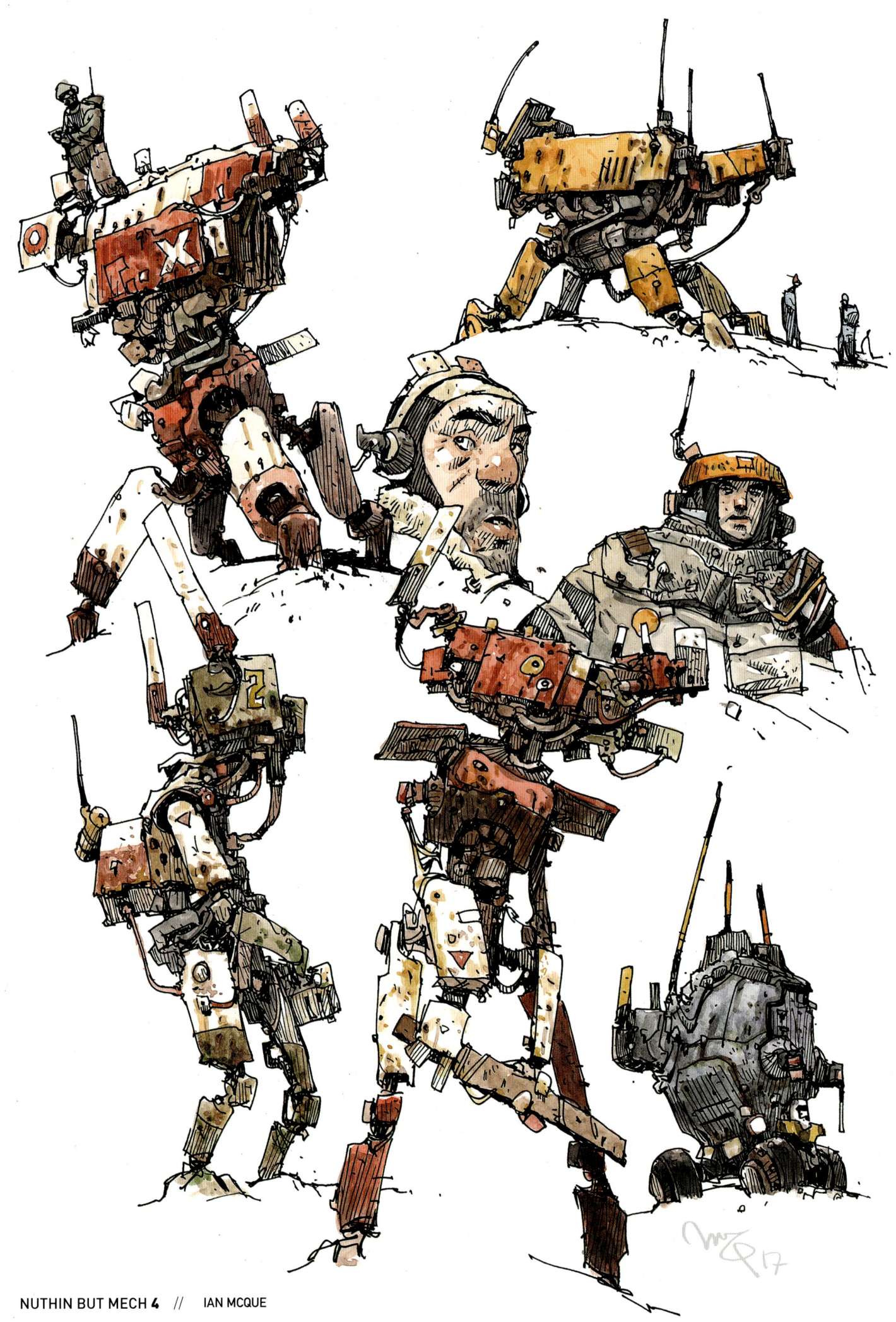

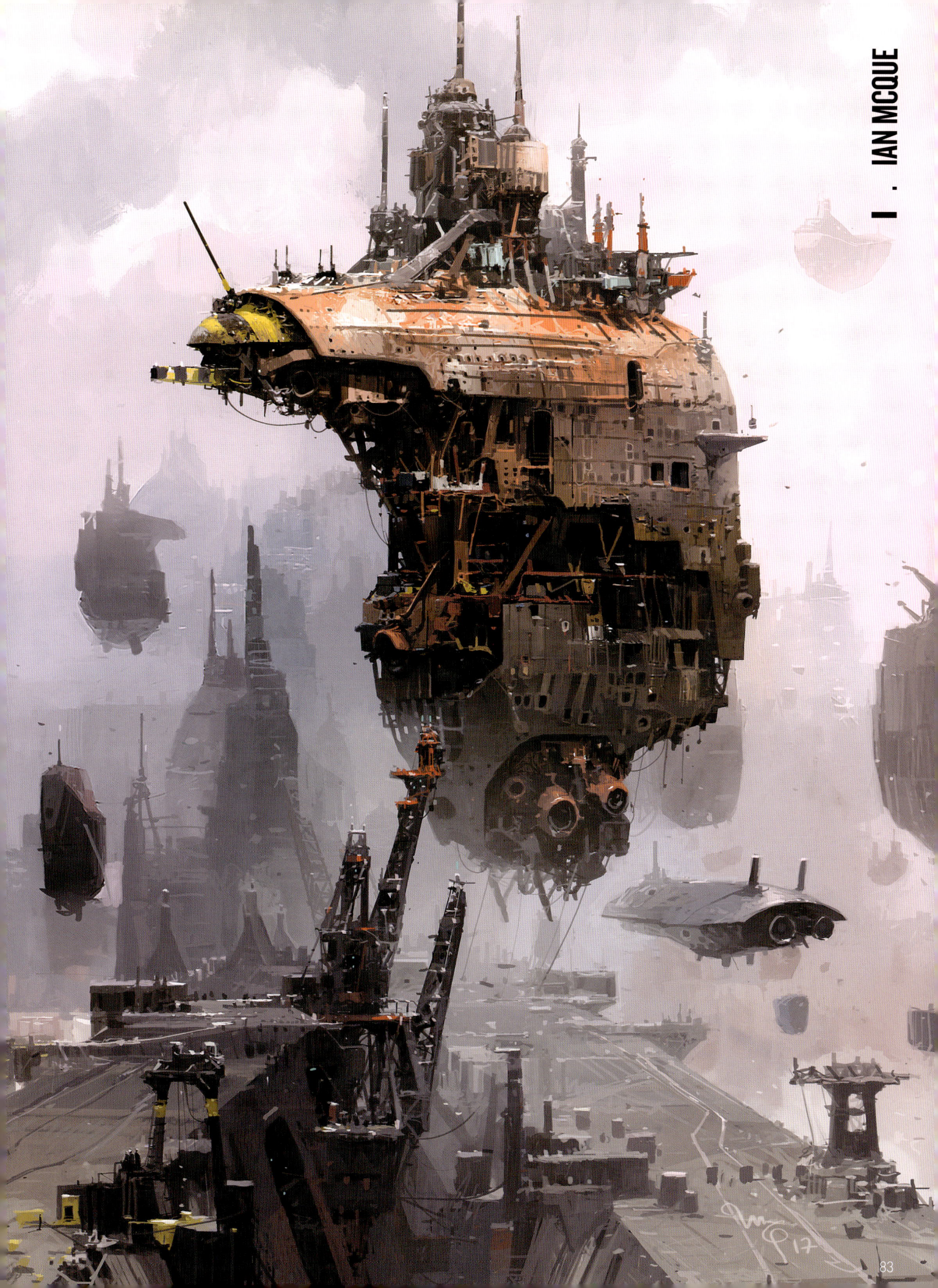

JAMES GURNEY James is the author and illustrator of The New York Times bestselling *Dinotopia* book series. He designed the World of Dinosaurs stamps for the US Postal Service and has won the Hugo, Chesley, Spectrum, and World Fantasy Awards. Solo exhibitions of his artwork have been presented at the Smithsonian Institution, the Norman Rockwell Museum, and the Norton Museum of Art. James was named a Grand Master by Spectrum Fantastic Arts and a Living Master by the Art Renewal Center. His book *Color and Light: A Guide for the Realist Painter* has been an online bestseller on painting and is based on his daily blog.
www.gurneyjourney.blogspot.com

JAN URSCHEL Jan is a freelance concept designer and illustrator working in the entertainment industry, designing for feature films and video games. His clients include Paramount Pictures, Warner Bros., Lucasfilm, MPC, Framestore, Marvel, Entertainment Arts, Microsoft, Sony, Ubisoft, LucasArts, Cloud Imperium Games, and more.
www.hendrix-design.com

JEREMY COOK Jeremy has been a digital artist for nearly 20 years. In that time he has been in film, games, and cinema working with such companies as Blur Studio, Industrial Light & Magic, id Software, and currently 343 Industries. He has created models, matte paintings, and concept art on projects including the films *Transformers*, *Star Wars: Episode III – Revenge of the Sith*, *Mission Impossible III*, and *The Day After Tomorrow*; the book series *Nuthin' But Mech*; the video games *Halo* and *Doom*; as well as countless TV commercials, cinematics, and magazine covers. As an art director at 343 Industries, Jeremy works with crazy, talented artists to ensure the games you play look good. When he is not working, he loves spending time with his family and expanding his hoodie collection in the beautiful Pacific Northwest city of Kirkland, Washington.
www.jeremycook.artstation.com

JOHN LIEW John is a conceptual designer working in the film and video game industries.
www.johnliewconcept.blogspot.com

JORT VAN WELBERGEN Jort is a Dutch, freelance concept artist who specializes in technical hard surface and environment design. Previous projects include *Horizon: Zero Dawn*, *Killzone Shadow Fall*, and *Star Citizen*. His work is heavily inspired by aerospace engineering, history, and his cycling trips through various European countries. He loves coming up with mechanical contraptions, both sci-fi and historical, and grounding his designs in the reality of physics. Designing mechs is a great way to explore all kinds of crazy things, so designing one for this book was definitely at the top of his most wanted list for a long time.
www.artstation.com/artist/jortvanwelbergen

JUSTIN FIELDS Justin is the owner of Ironklad Studios and a concept artist who studied at the Gnomon School of Visual Effects, Games, and Animation, and currently works in the film and game industries. He has worked at such studios as Imaginary Forces, Sony Pictures Imageworks, and Amalgamated Dynamics, Inc. He is originally from Springfield, Illinois, and has worked in the graphic design field since 2005. Some of his credits include *Jupiter Ascending*, *Maleficent*, *Noah*, *Dawn of the Planet of the Apes*, *Firelight*, *Blink*, *Falling Skies*, *The Wolverine*, *Scrapyard*, *The Shannara Chronicles*, *Eternals*, *Thor: Ragnarok*, *Goosebumps*, *Max Steel*, and *Kong: Skull Island*.
www.ironkladstudios.com

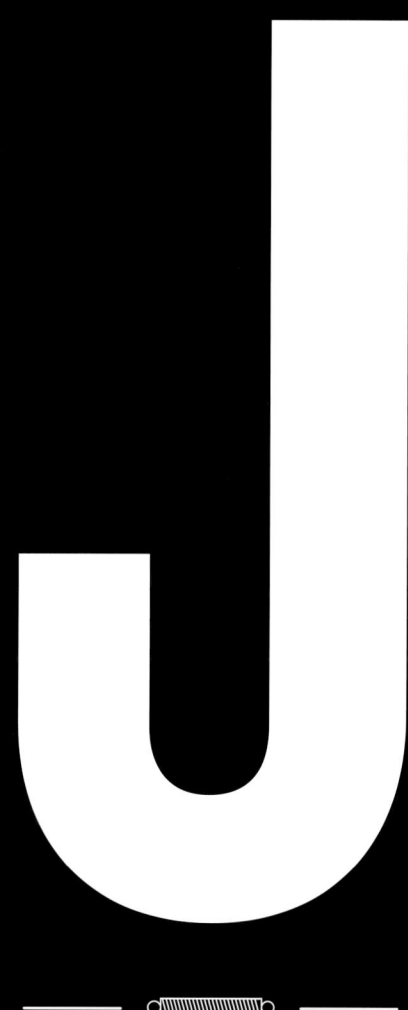

James Gurney

Jan Urschel

Jeremy Cook

John Liew

Jort van Welbergen

Justin Fields

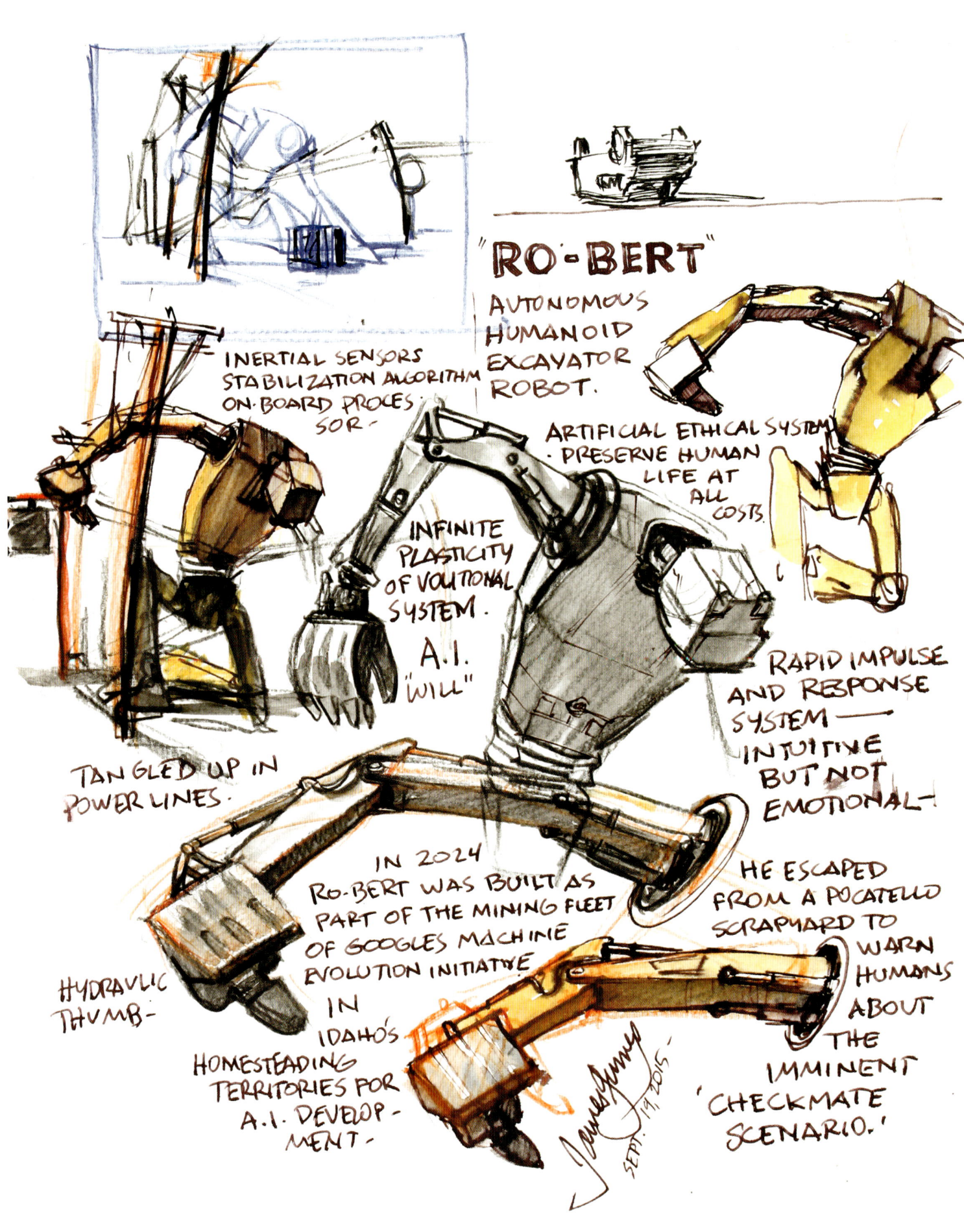

"RO-BERT"

AUTONOMOUS HUMANOID EXCAVATOR ROBOT.

INERTIAL SENSORS
STABILIZATION ALGORITHM
ON-BOARD PROCES-
SOR.

ARTIFICIAL ETHICAL SYSTEM
- PRESERVE HUMAN
LIFE AT
ALL
COSTS.

INFINITE
PLASTICITY
OF VOLITIONAL
SYSTEM.

A.I.
"WILL"

RAPID IMPULSE
AND RESPONSE
SYSTEM —
INTUITIVE
BUT NOT
EMOTIONAL.

TANGLED UP IN
POWER LINES.

IN 2024
RO-BERT WAS BUILT AS
PART OF THE MINING FLEET
OF GOOGLES MACHINE
EVOLUTION INITIATIVE

IN
IDAHO'S
HOMESTEADING
TERRITORIES FOR
A.I. DEVELOP-
MENT.

HE ESCAPED
FROM A POCATELLO
SCRAPYARD TO
WARN
HUMANS
ABOUT
THE
IMMINENT
'CHECKMATE
SCENARIO.'

HYDRAULIC
THUMB.

James Gurney
SEPT. 19 2015

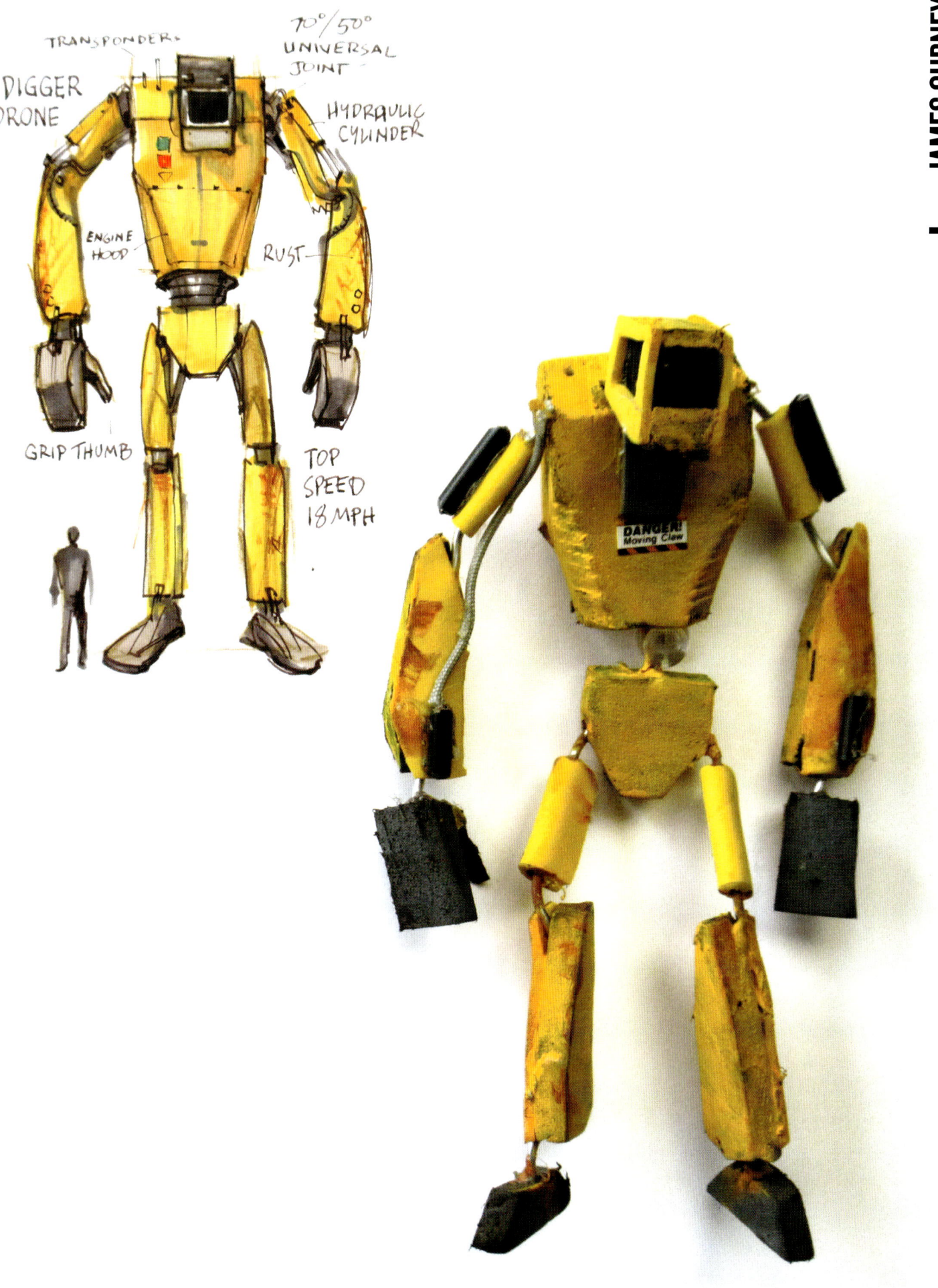

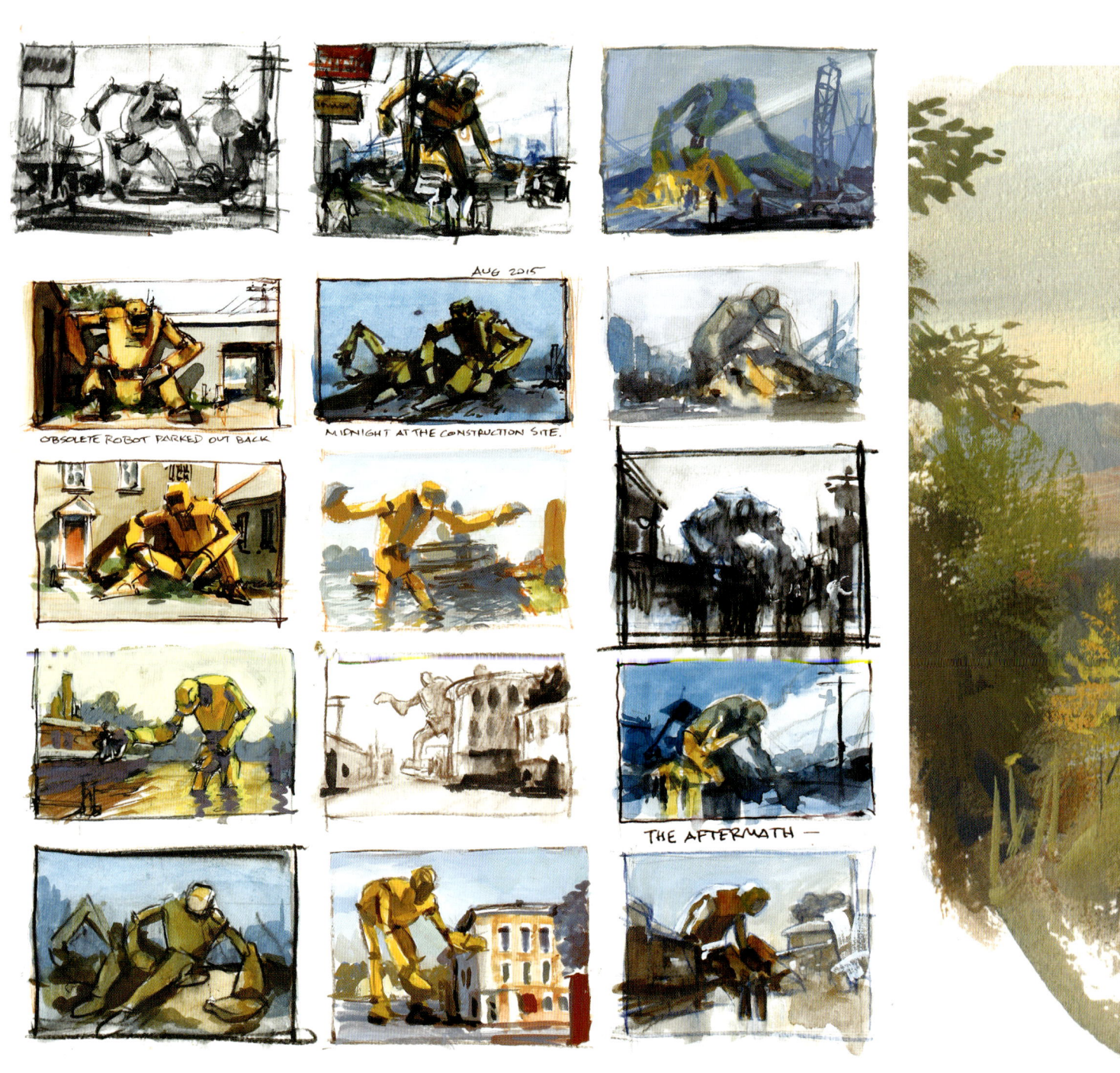

OBSOLETE ROBOT PARKED OUT BACK

MIDNIGHT AT THE CONSTRUCTION SITE.

AUG 2015

THE AFTERMATH —

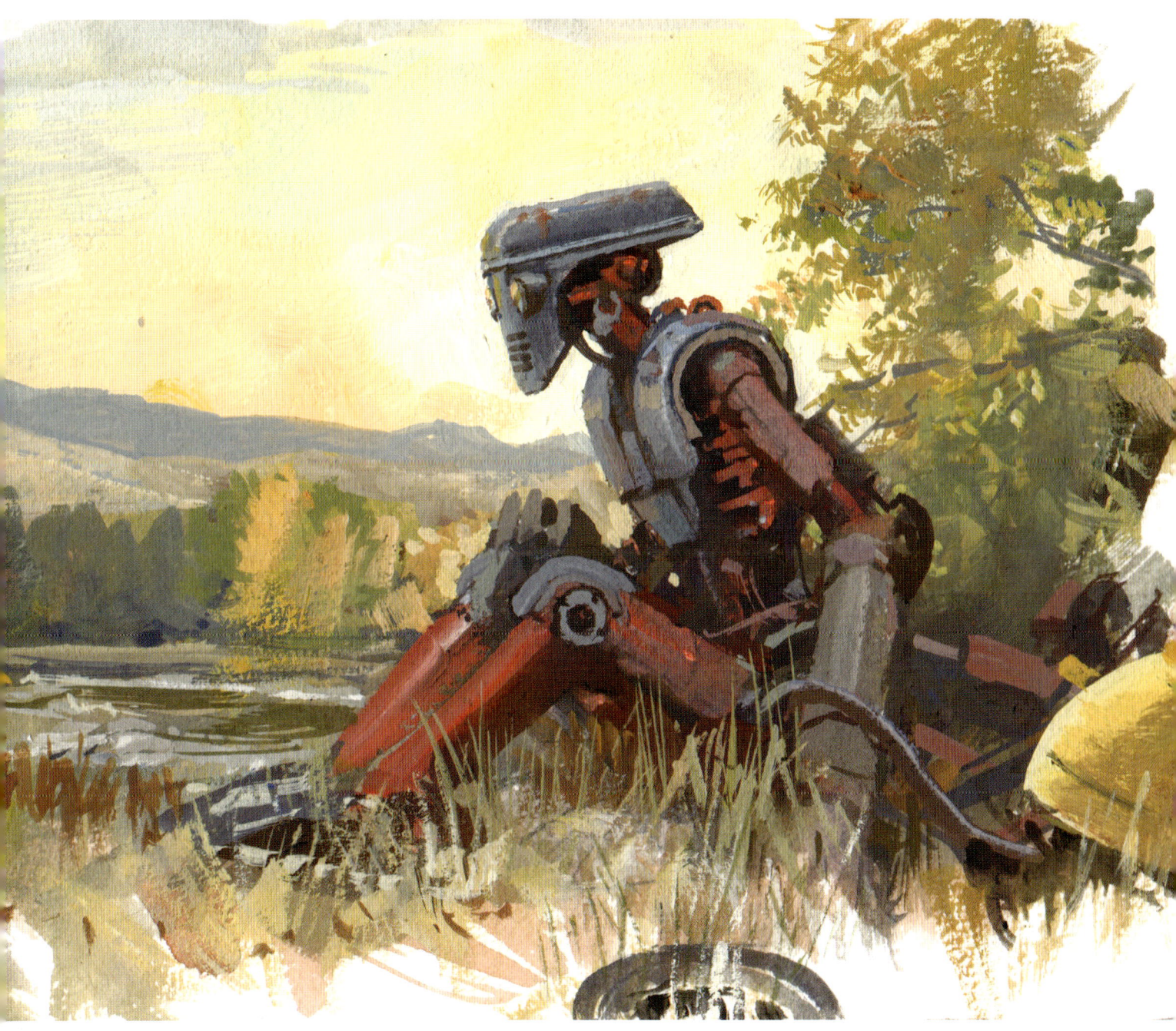

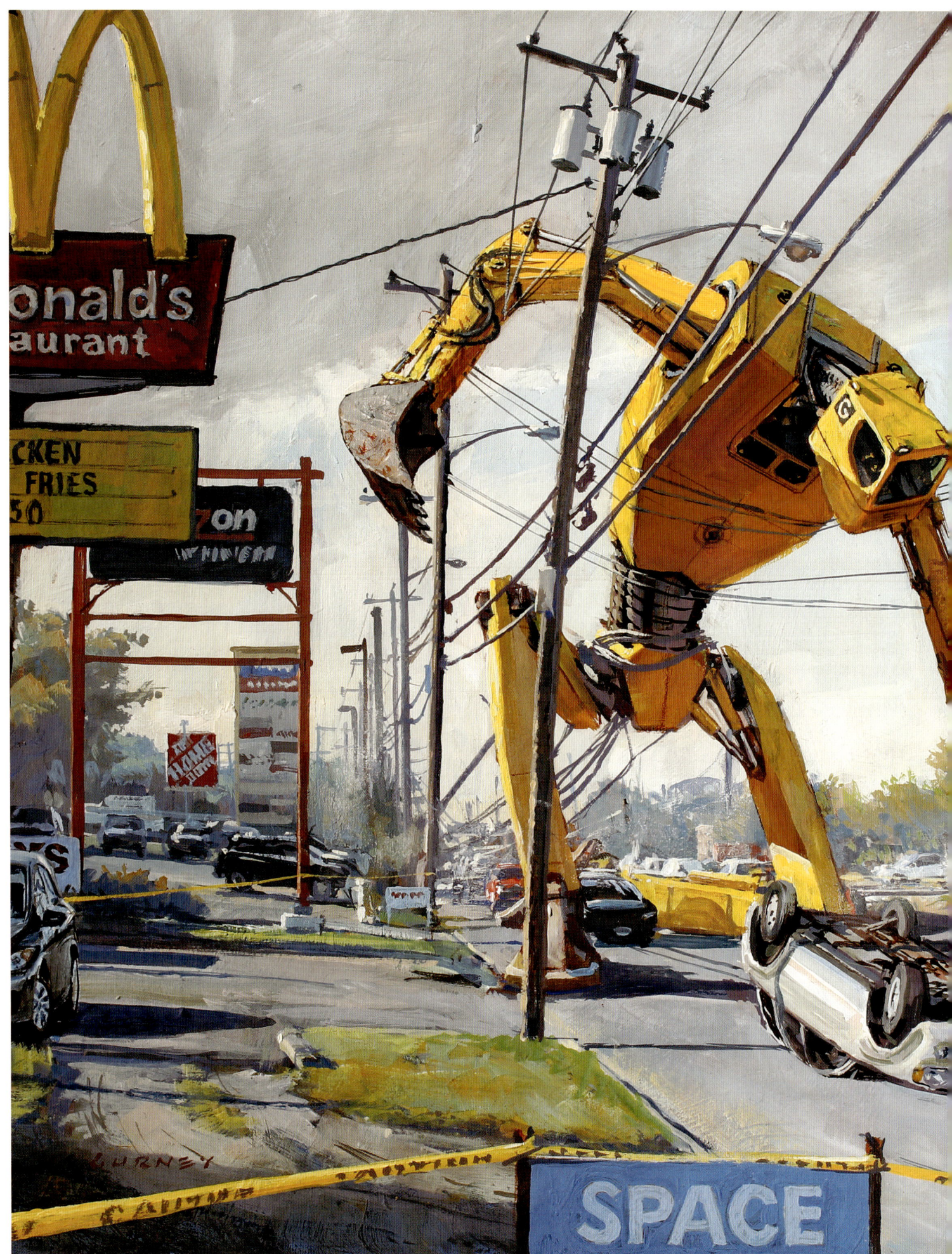

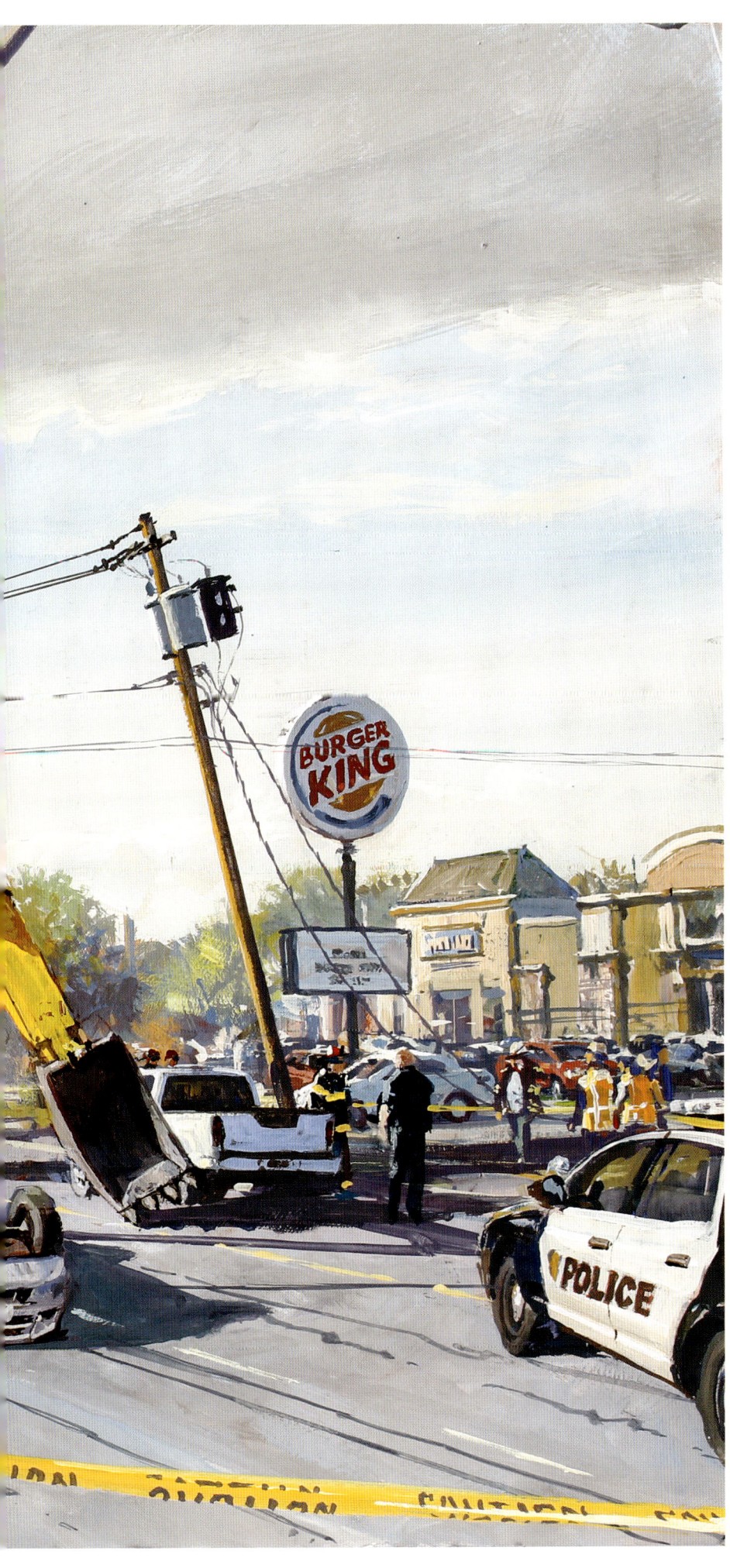

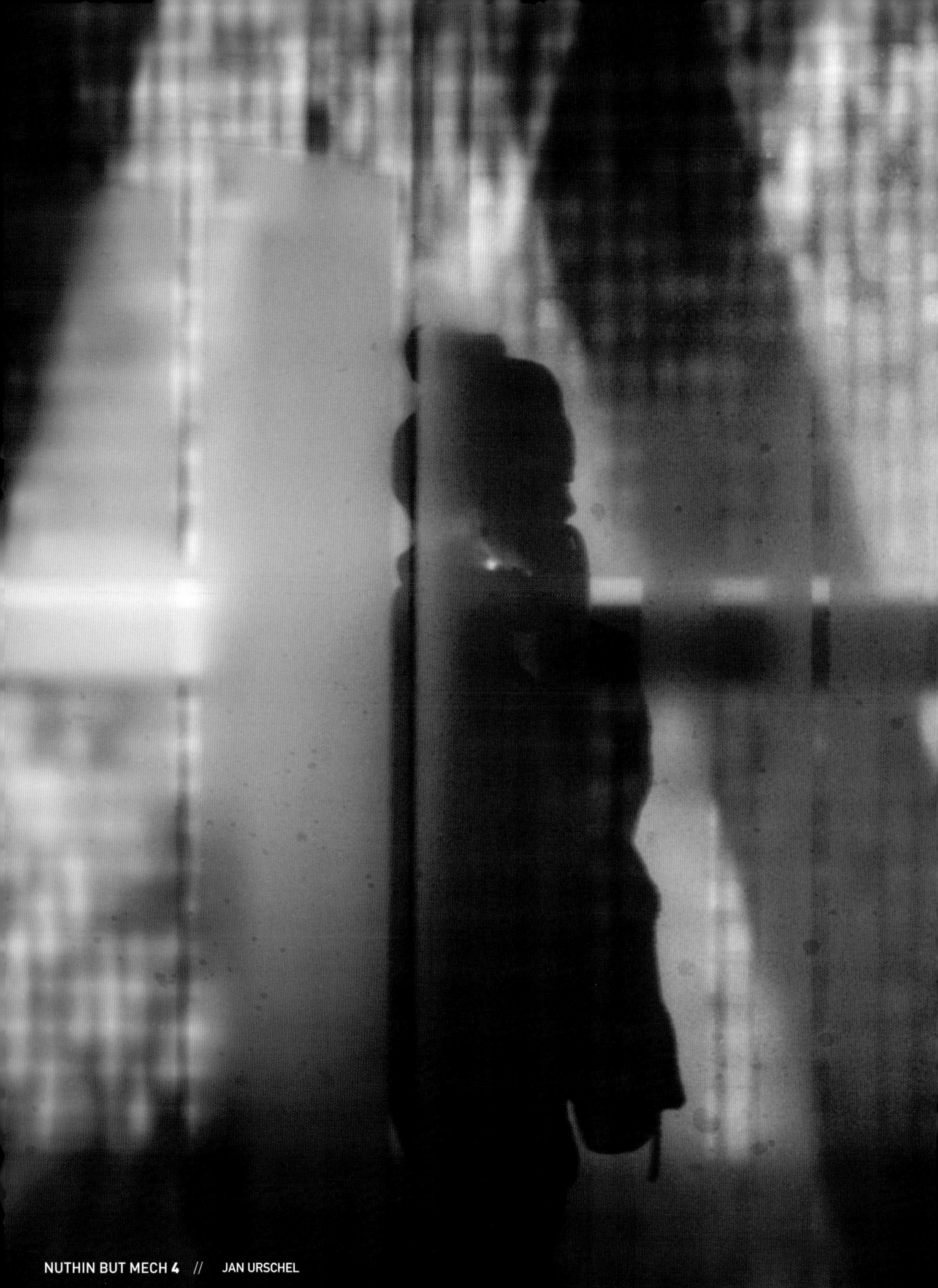

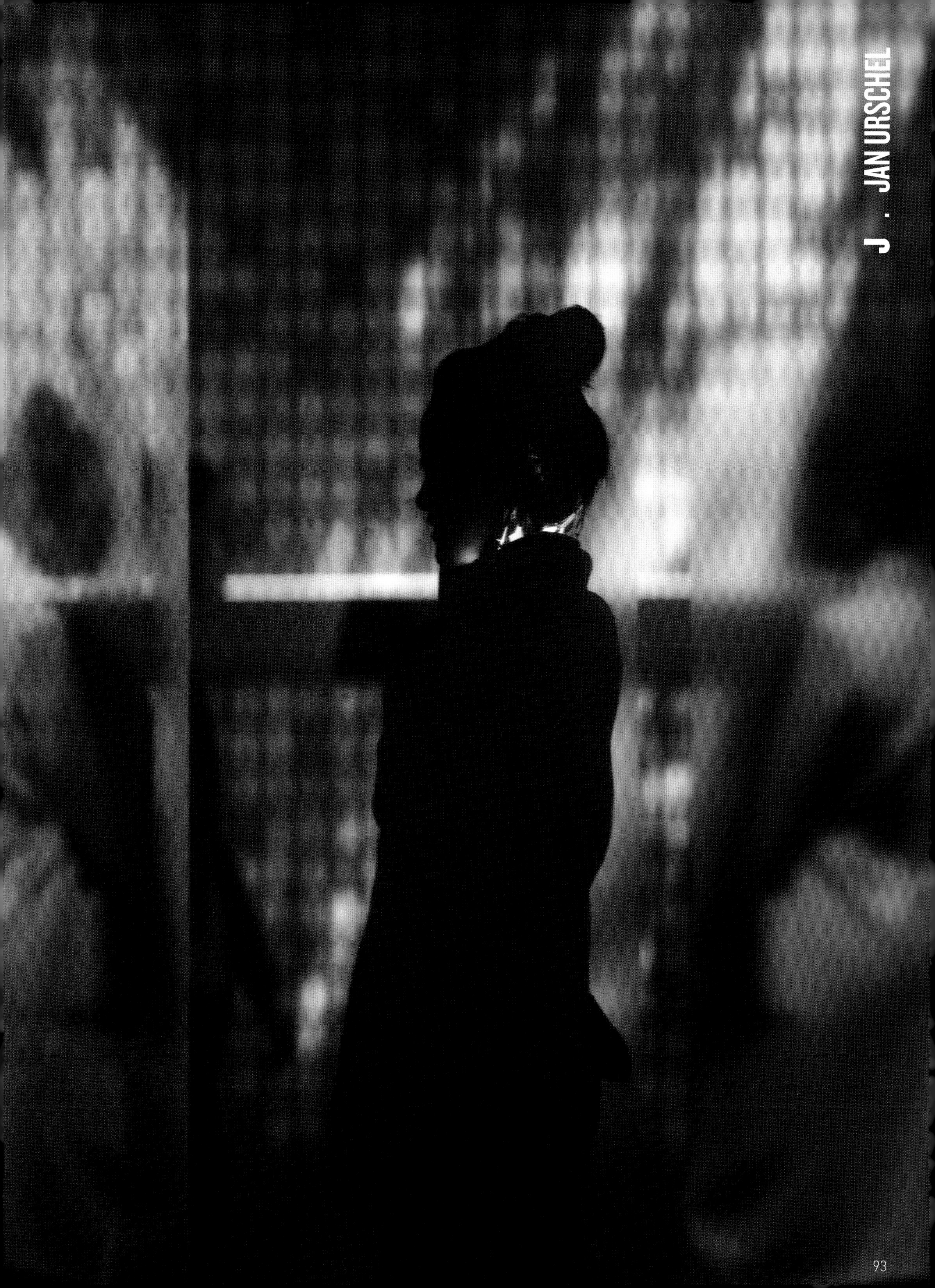

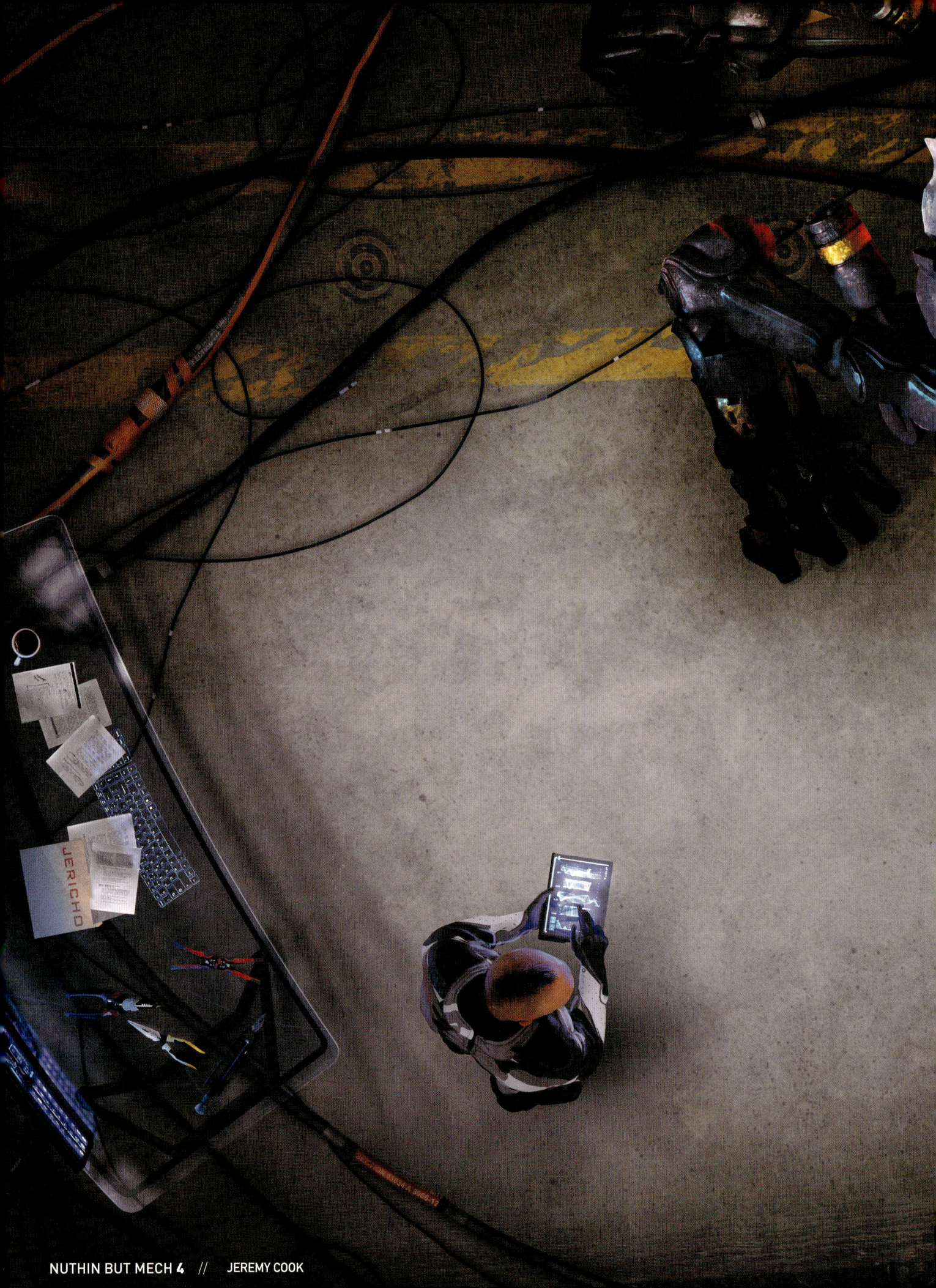

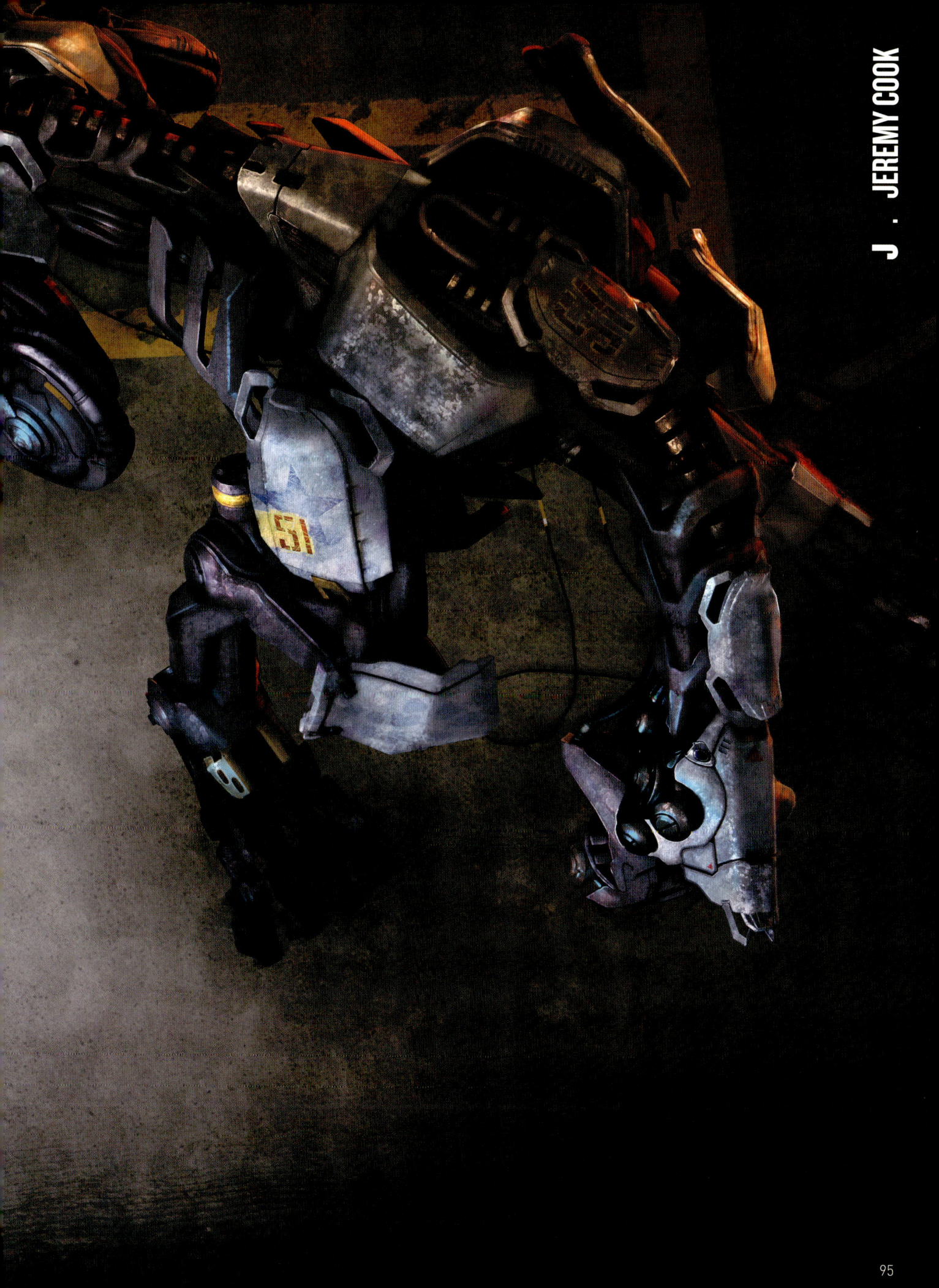

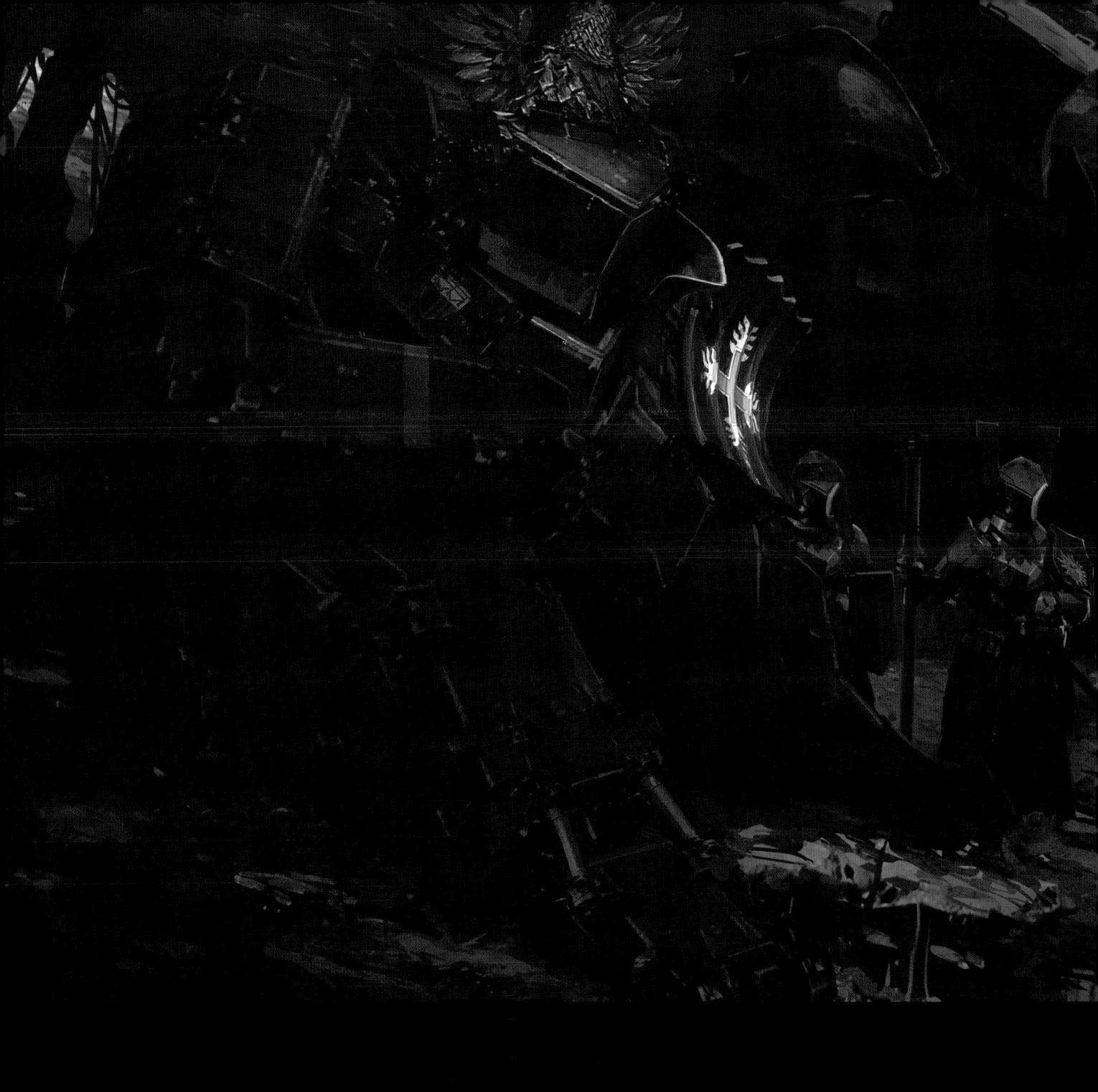

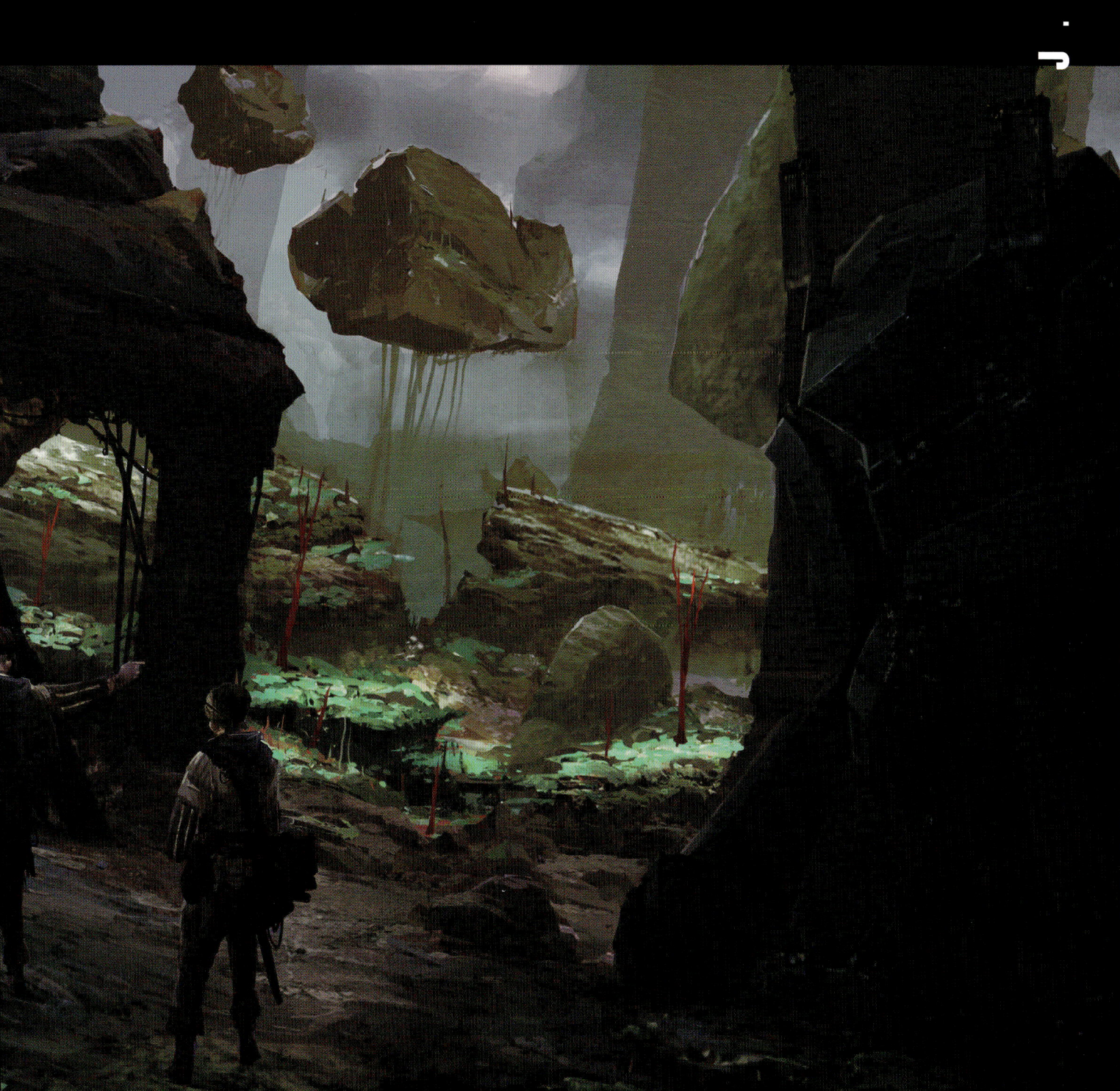

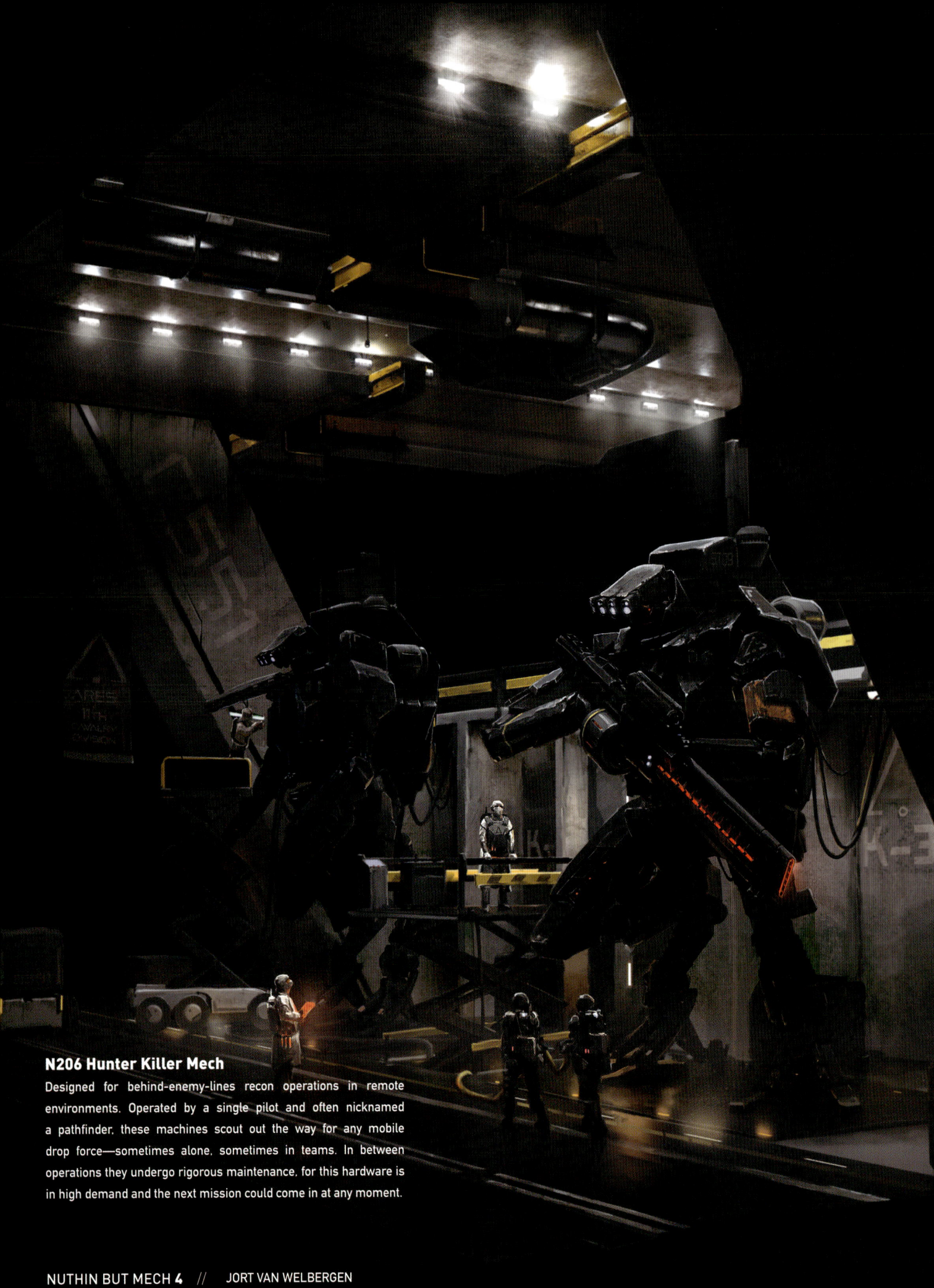

N206 Hunter Killer Mech

Designed for behind-enemy-lines recon operations in remote environments. Operated by a single pilot and often nicknamed a pathfinder, these machines scout out the way for any mobile drop force—sometimes alone, sometimes in teams. In between operations they undergo rigorous maintenance, for this hardware is in high demand and the next mission could come in at any moment.

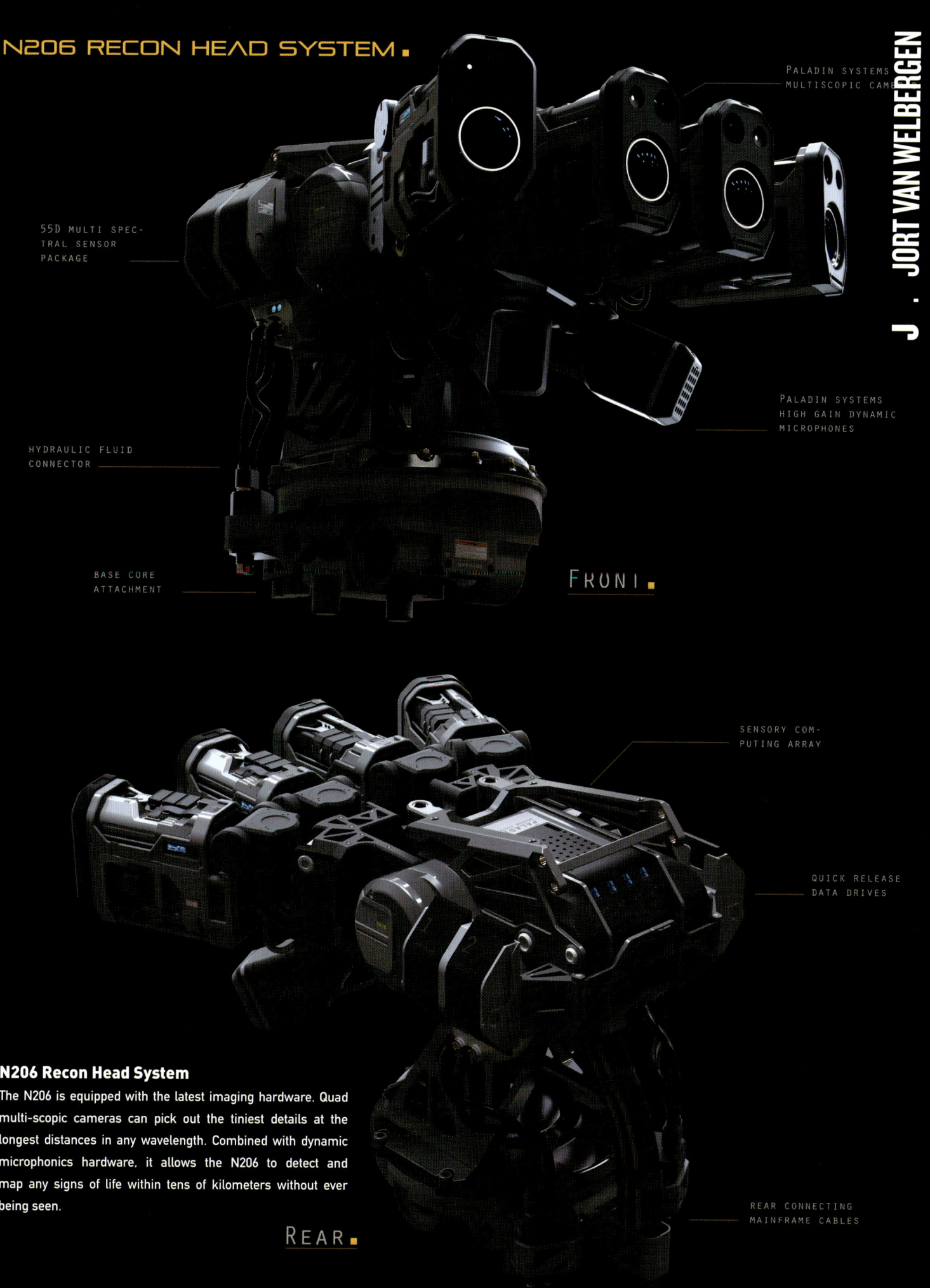

N206 RECON HEAD SYSTEM.

J . JORT VAN WELBERGEN

PALADIN SYSTEMS
MULTISCOPIC CAME

55D MULTI SPEC-
TRAL SENSOR
PACKAGE

PALADIN SYSTEMS
HIGH GAIN DYNAMIC
MICROPHONES

HYDRAULIC FLUID
CONNECTOR

BASE CORE
ATTACHMENT

FRONT.

SENSORY COM-
PUTING ARRAY

QUICK RELEASE
DATA DRIVES

N206 Recon Head System

The N206 is equipped with the latest imaging hardware. Quad multi-scopic cameras can pick out the tiniest details at the longest distances in any wavelength. Combined with dynamic microphonics hardware, it allows the N206 to detect and map any signs of life within tens of kilometers without ever being seen.

REAR CONNECTING
MAINFRAME CABLES

REAR.

J.FIELDS
IRONKLAD
S T U D I O S

KILIAN ENG

Kilian was born in 1982 in Stockholm, Sweden. His medium of choice when illustrating is digital, something he has developed and explored for many years now. Elements that he often comes back to are the importance of color and lighting in a composition where geometry, the environment, and organic shapes often are prominent. Kilian likes to give his images a surrealistic touch and place the visuals in an alternative reality that hopefully evokes viewers' curiosity to explore and fantasize further, creating their own narrative. His strongest artistic influences come from many of the European artists who worked, and are still working, in the genre of sci-fi and fantasy with a very open mind to what that can be.

www.dwdesign.tumblr.com
www.instagram.com/kilianeng

KIRILL CHEPIZHKO / VALENTINE SOROKIN

KIRILL CHEPIZHKO

Kirill is an amorphous blob of aggressive, intergalactic nucleoplasm. Driven by his ravenous desire to absorb more and more knowledge, he has travelled millions of light years to planet Earth, where he assimilated by learning how to speak like a human being, and started working for Industrial Light & Magic as a 3D artist. In his free time, Kirill likes to design and model hard surface concepts. He also likes cats. Cats are cute.

www.artstation.com/artist/fett

VALENTINE SOROKIN

For the past 10 years, Valentine's occupation and great passion has been CG. In 2008, he graduated from Dnipro Digital Arts Academy and started his career as a freelance artist in the advertising, movie, and video game industries. For the last five years, Valentine has been working as a hard surface artist on such projects as *Halo* and *Call of Duty*, and various advertising campaigns for Boeing, Pepsi, Mannol, Mastercard, and Rostec.

www.valeksorokin.com

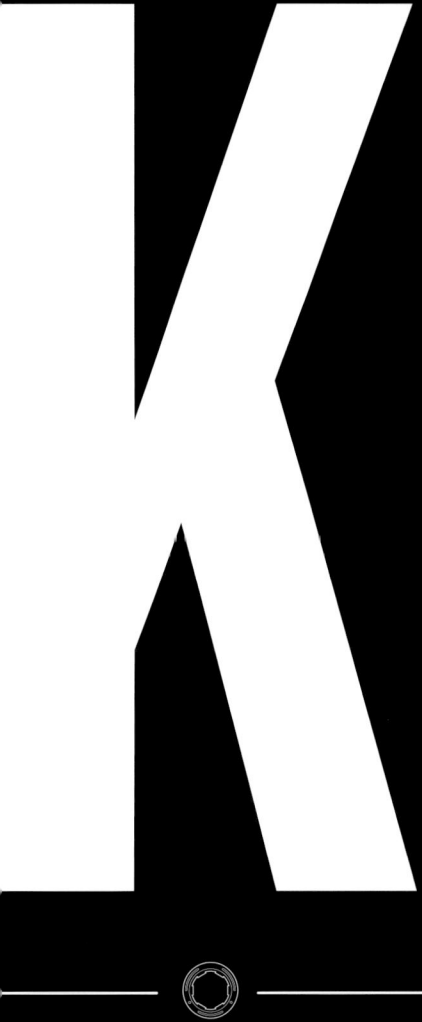

Kilian Eng

Kirill Chepizhko/Valentine Sorokin

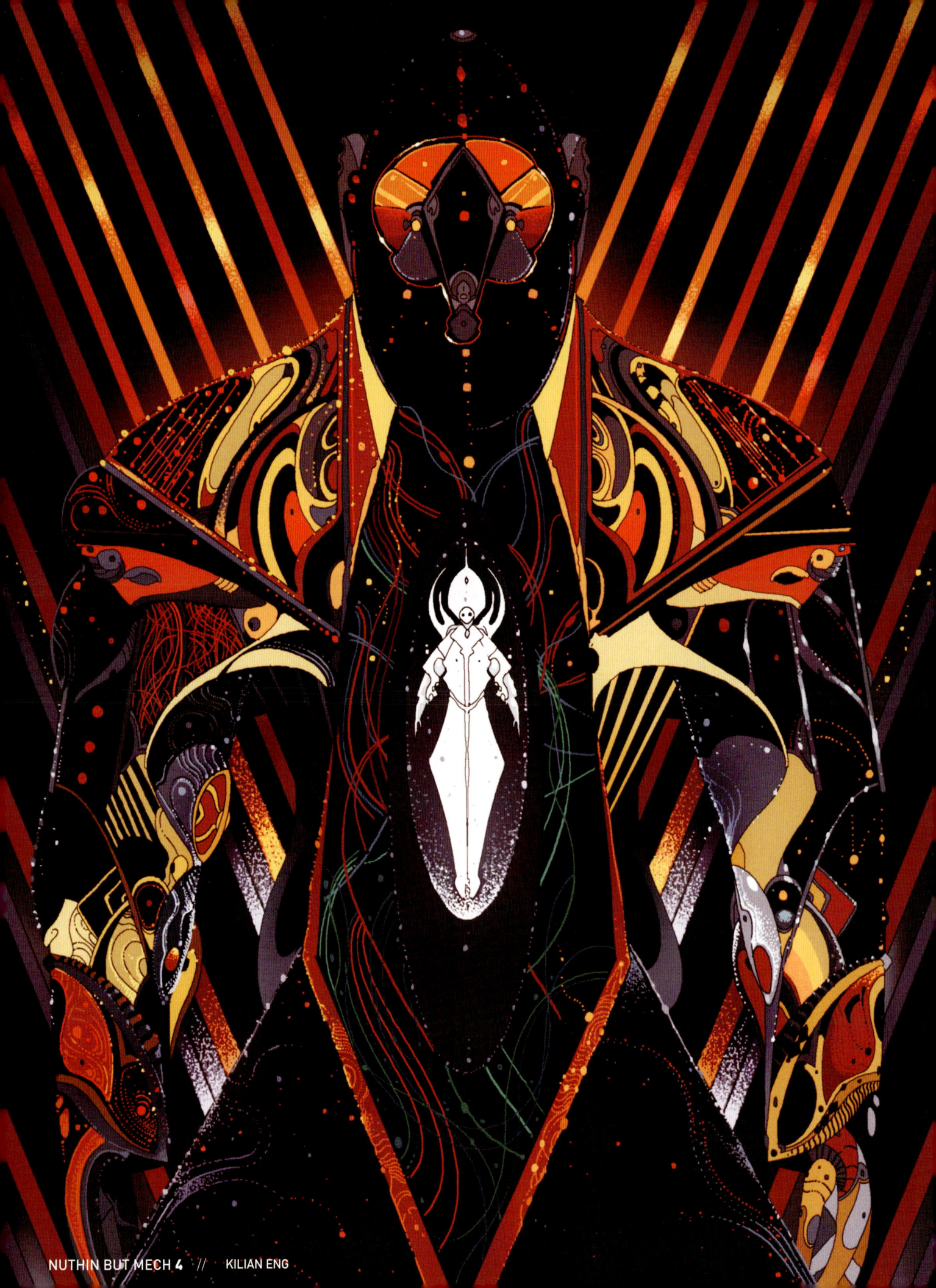

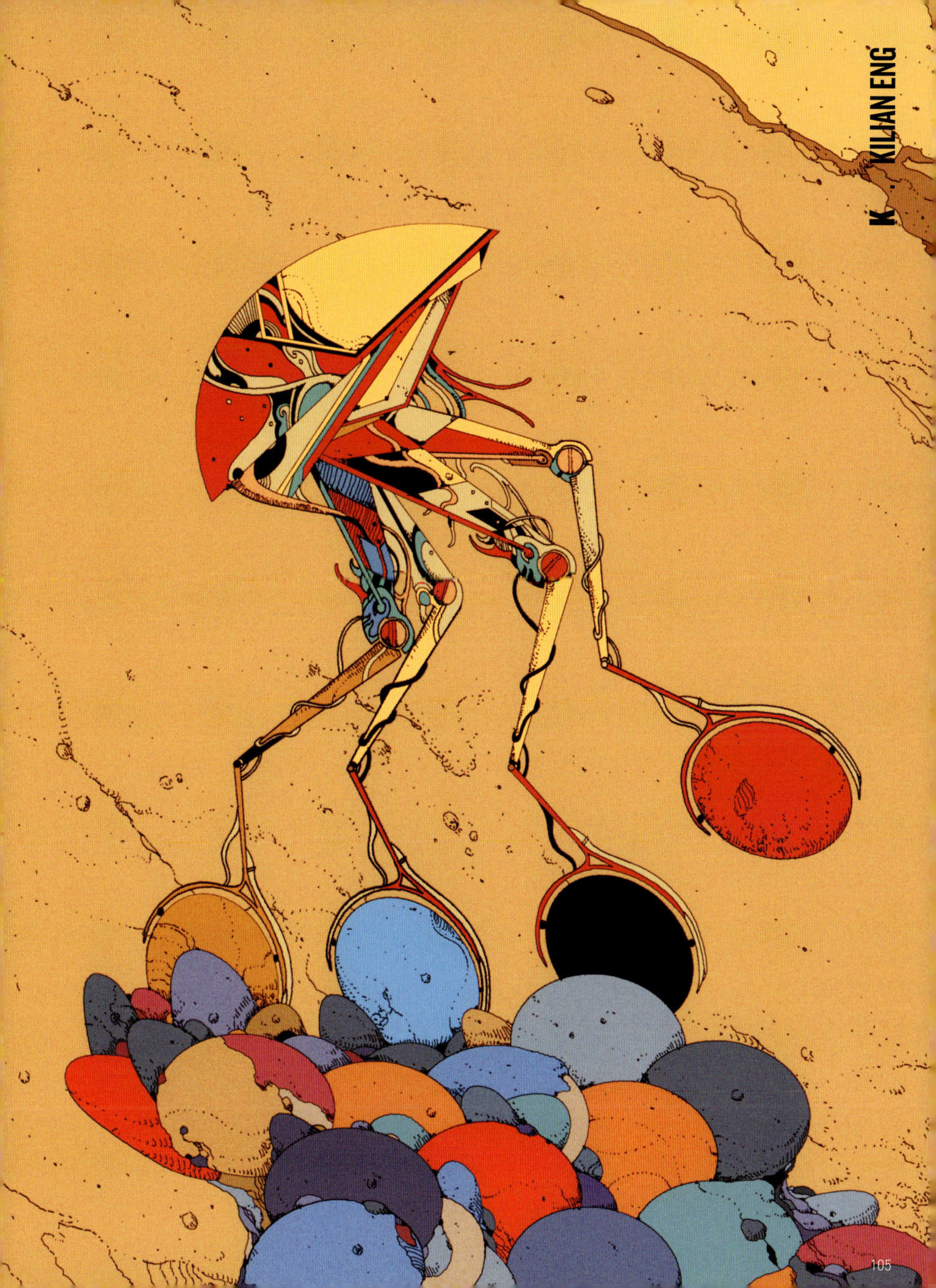

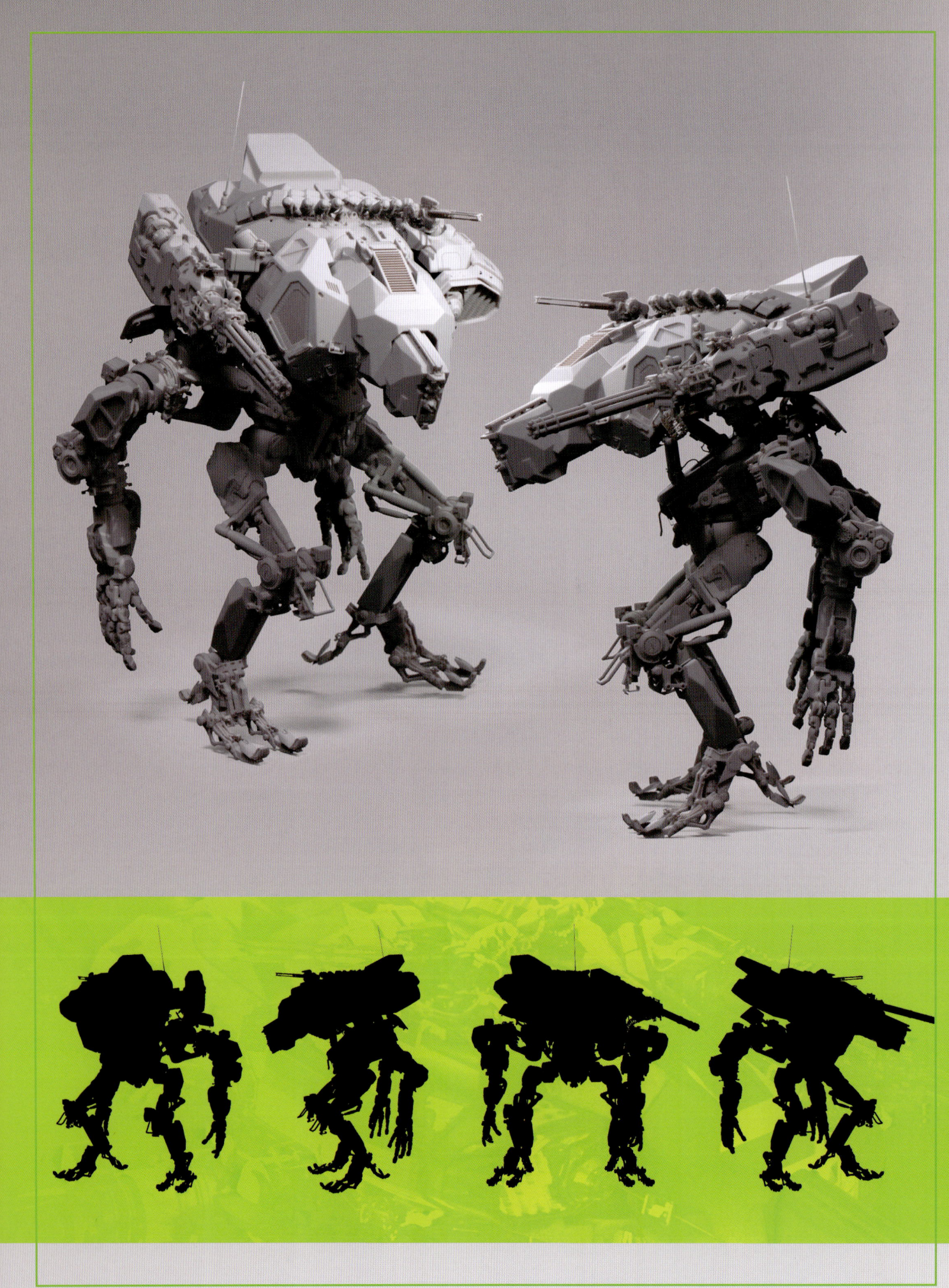

VALENTINE SOROKIN
KIRILL CHEPIZHKO

PRED△TOR

IF IT BLEEDS WE CAN KILL IT

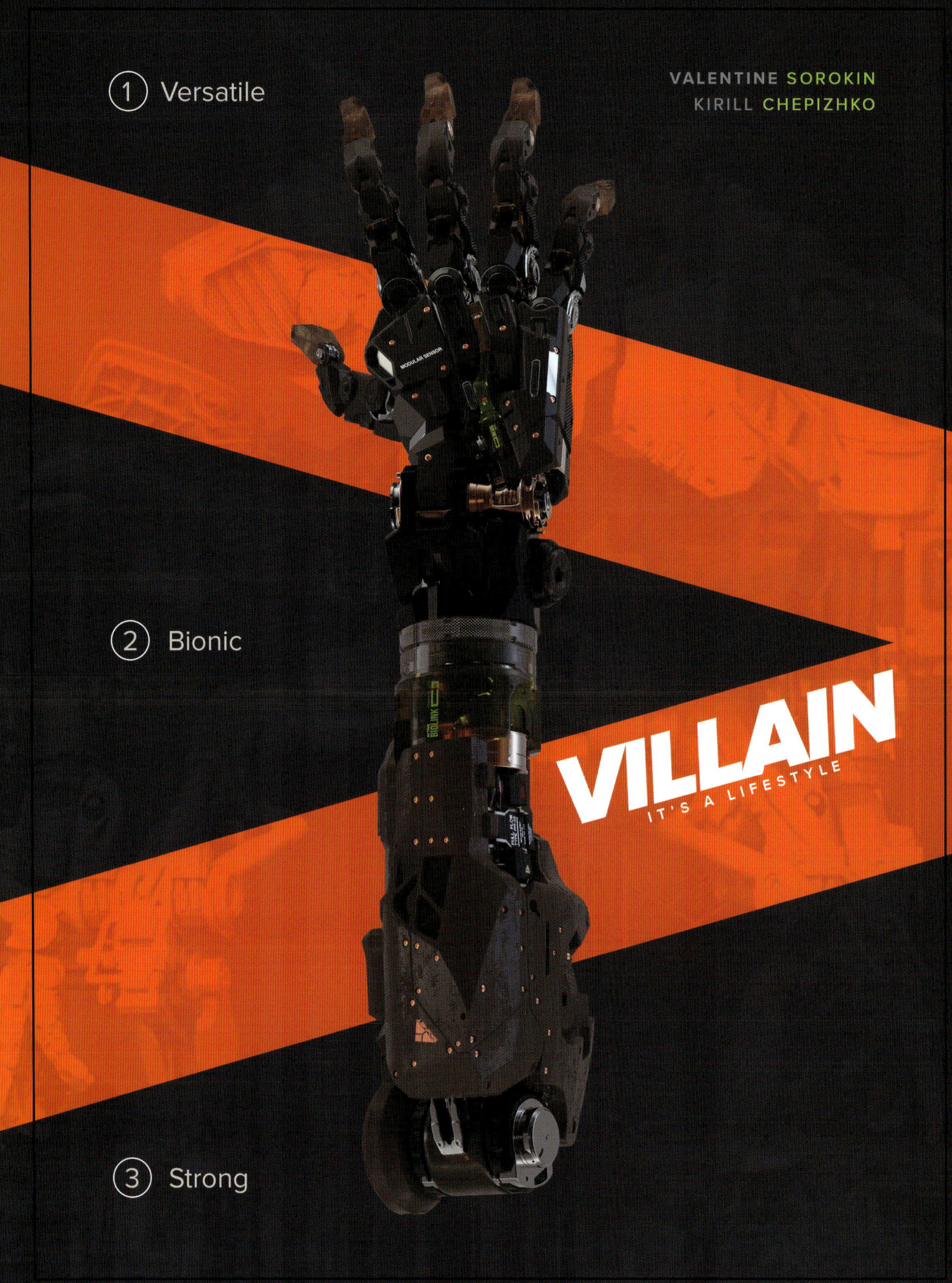

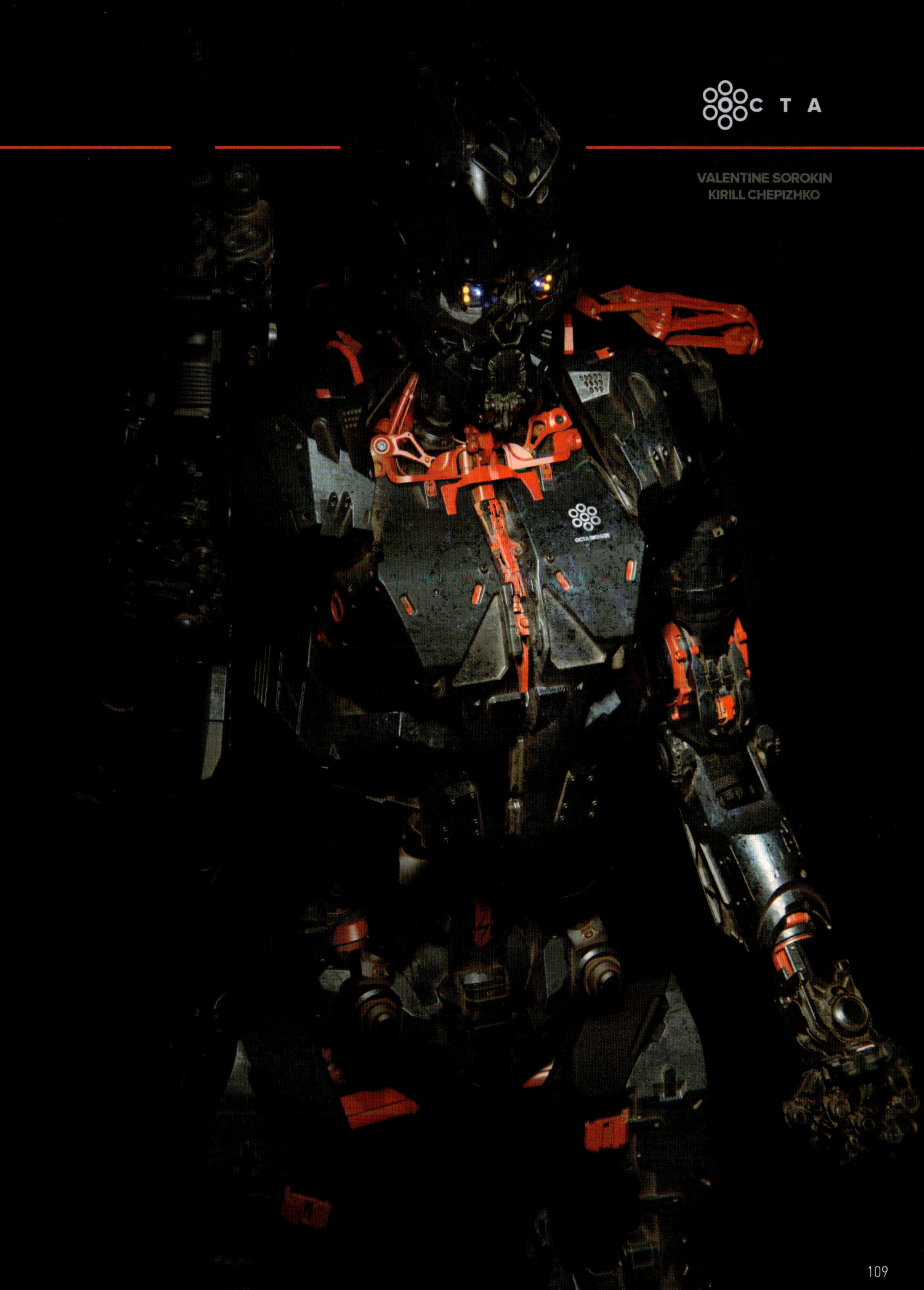

VALENTINE SOROKIN
KIRILL CHEPIZHKO

LANDIS FIELDS Landis is a visual-development artist working in film, VR, feature animation, television, real-time immersive entertainment, and amusement/theme parks. Having specialized in multiple phases of production—art directing, pre- and postviz, and even editing for various projects throughout his career—his portfolio ranges anywhere from *Star Wars* films to Super Bowl commercials. Landis is currently working for Disney/Lucasfilm's Industrial Light & Magic and ILMxLAB using his mix of a creative and technical Air Force avionics background to push the limits of immersive storytelling.
www.landisfields.tumblr.com

LEE SOUDER Lee is a concept designer working out of his home in New Jersey. He focuses on weaving design trends and 3D tools. His weapons of choice are Maya, ZBrush, Grasshopper, KeyShot and V-Ray.
www.leesouder.com

LUCA ZAMPRIOLO Luca was born in Mantova, Italy, October 29, 1975. He has loved drawing, painting, and sculpting since he was born. Every subject fascinates him, but since he was a child he has had some serious love for mech design in general. After classical studies, Luca decided to enter the University of Bologna School of Arts where he graduated in painting in 2001. He keeps producing work in three artistic scenarios: fine art, mech design, and sculpture.

In 2007, Luca started his own brand, Kallamity, which focuses on concept art and mech design, and also illustration, sculpture, and modeling. He published *Abakan 2288: Kallamity's World of Mecha Design, Part One* in 2011, and *Kallamity: Mech in Ink* in 2015, both by Design Studio Press. In 2012, he started collaborating with DreamWorks Animation on the Netflix *Dinotrux* series as a character designer and senior mech designer for the main character, Ty, and his friends.

Luca has also worked for *Paolo Parente's Dust*, Dream Pod 9's *Heavy Gear*, Mecha Workshop's *Armarauders*, *Wired* magazine, Oktobor Animation, *The Weathering Magazine*, Prada, Luxottica, Mango Entertainment, Iveco Officine Brennero, Sideshow Collectibles, and more. He continues to work as a freelance artist and develops creations in his new studio.
www.kallamity.com

LUIGI MEMOLA Luigi is an Italian designer specializing in transportation design and concept. He lives in Turin, Italy, where he taught for many years at the Istituto d'Arte Applicata e Design (IAAD), and in London, England, where he runs EPTA Design, founded in 2015.
www.behance.net/memolaluigi
www.epta-design.com

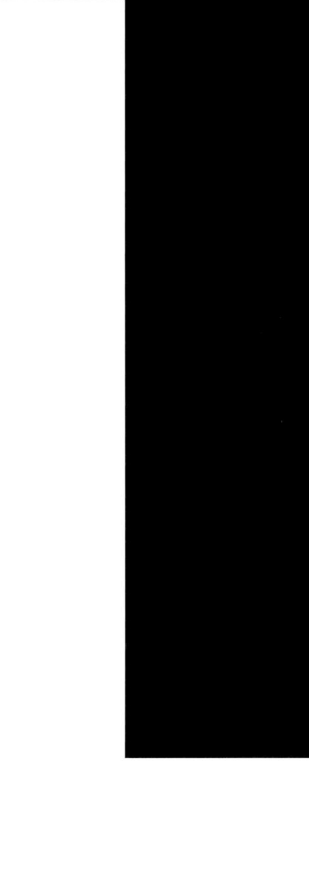

Embark On The Epic Venture Of A Lifetime..

Eva's Quest

The Bobots of Castle Pujsh

No. 0816

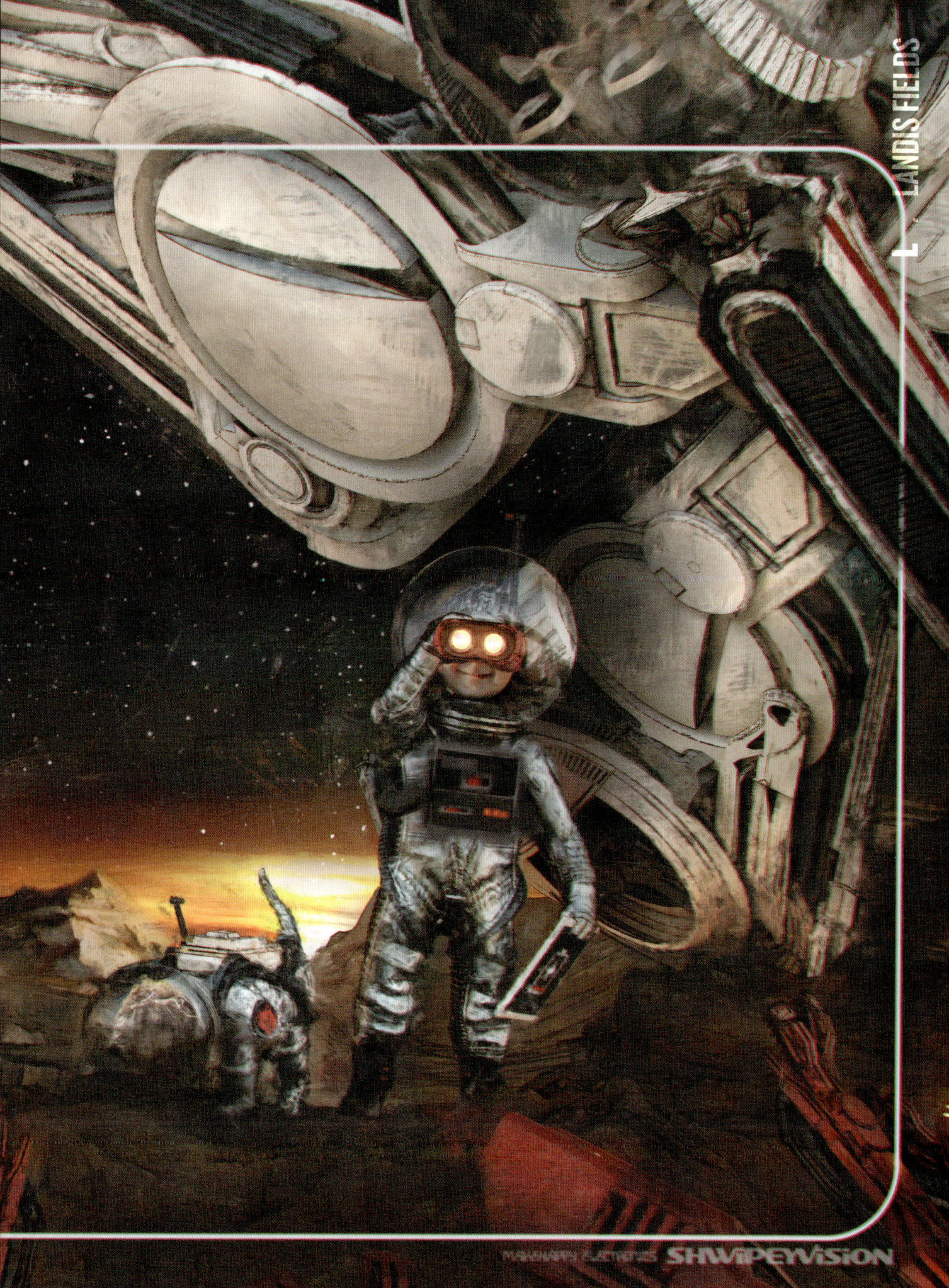

MACHINERY CARTRIDGE **SHWIPEYVISION**

EVA'S BUTTERFLY SHIP (MARK II CONFIGURATION)

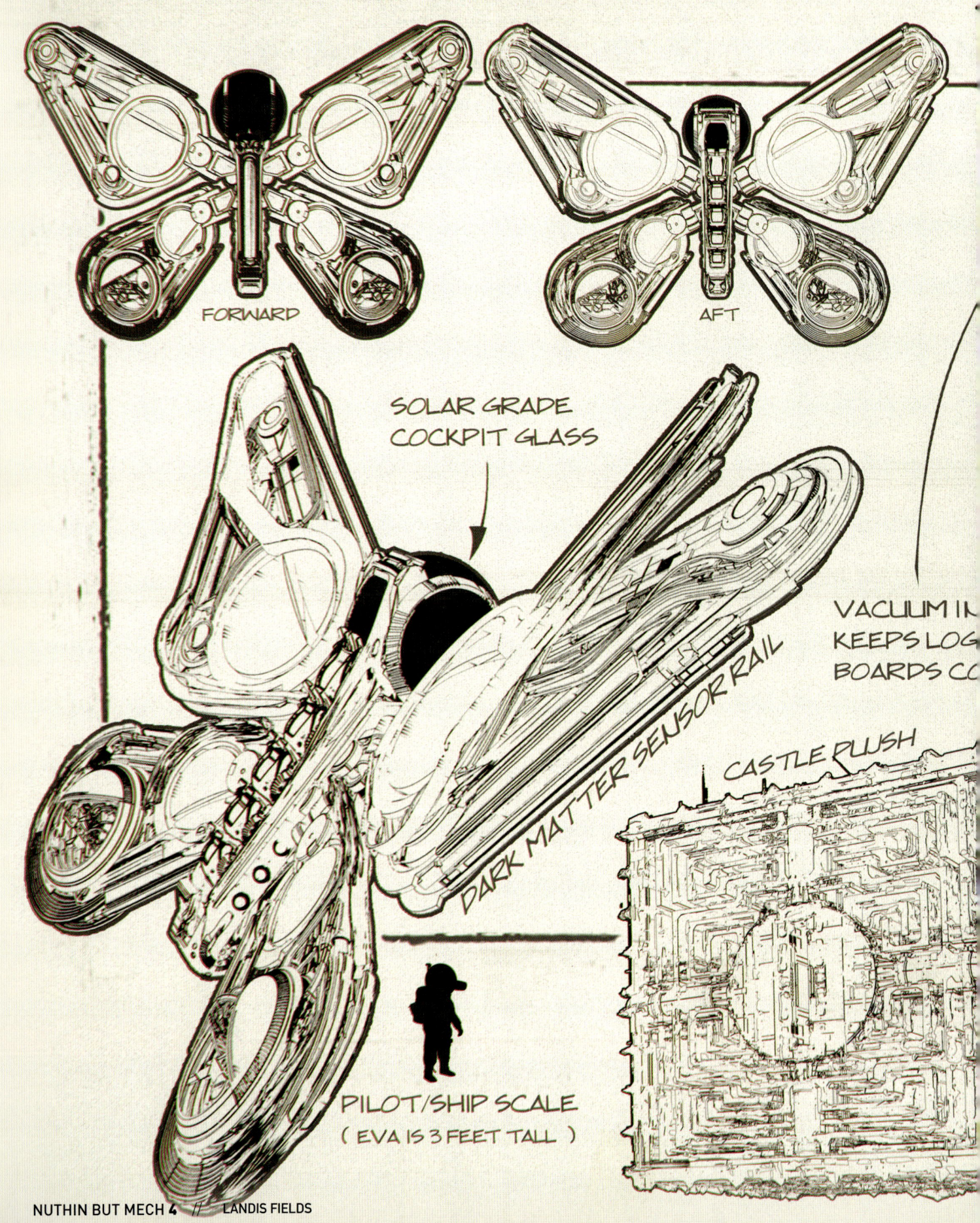

FORWARD

AFT

SOLAR GRADE COCKPIT GLASS

VACUUM I
KEEPS LO
BOARDS C

DARK MATTER SENSOR RAIL

CASTLE PLUSH

PILOT/SHIP SCALE
(EVA IS 3 FEET TALL)

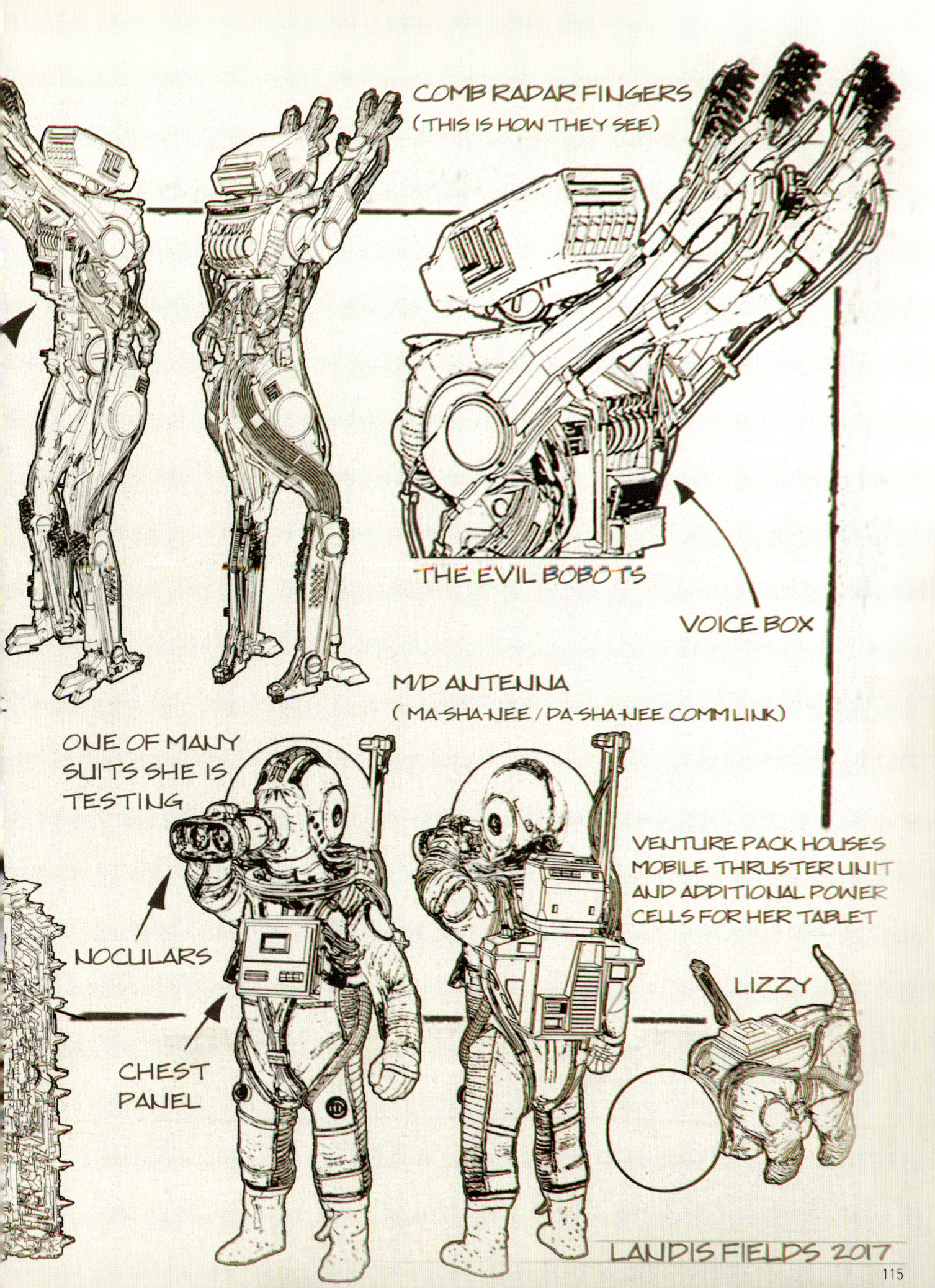

COMB RADAR FINGERS
(THIS IS HOW THEY SEE)

THE EVIL BOBOTS

VOICE BOX

M/D ANTENNA
(MA-SHA-NEE / PA-SHA-NEE COMM LINK)

ONE OF MANY
SUITS SHE IS
TESTING

NOCULARS

CHEST
PANEL

VENTURE PACK HOUSES
MOBILE THRUSTER UNIT
AND ADDITIONAL POWER
CELLS FOR HER TABLET

LIZZY

LANDIS FIELDS 2017

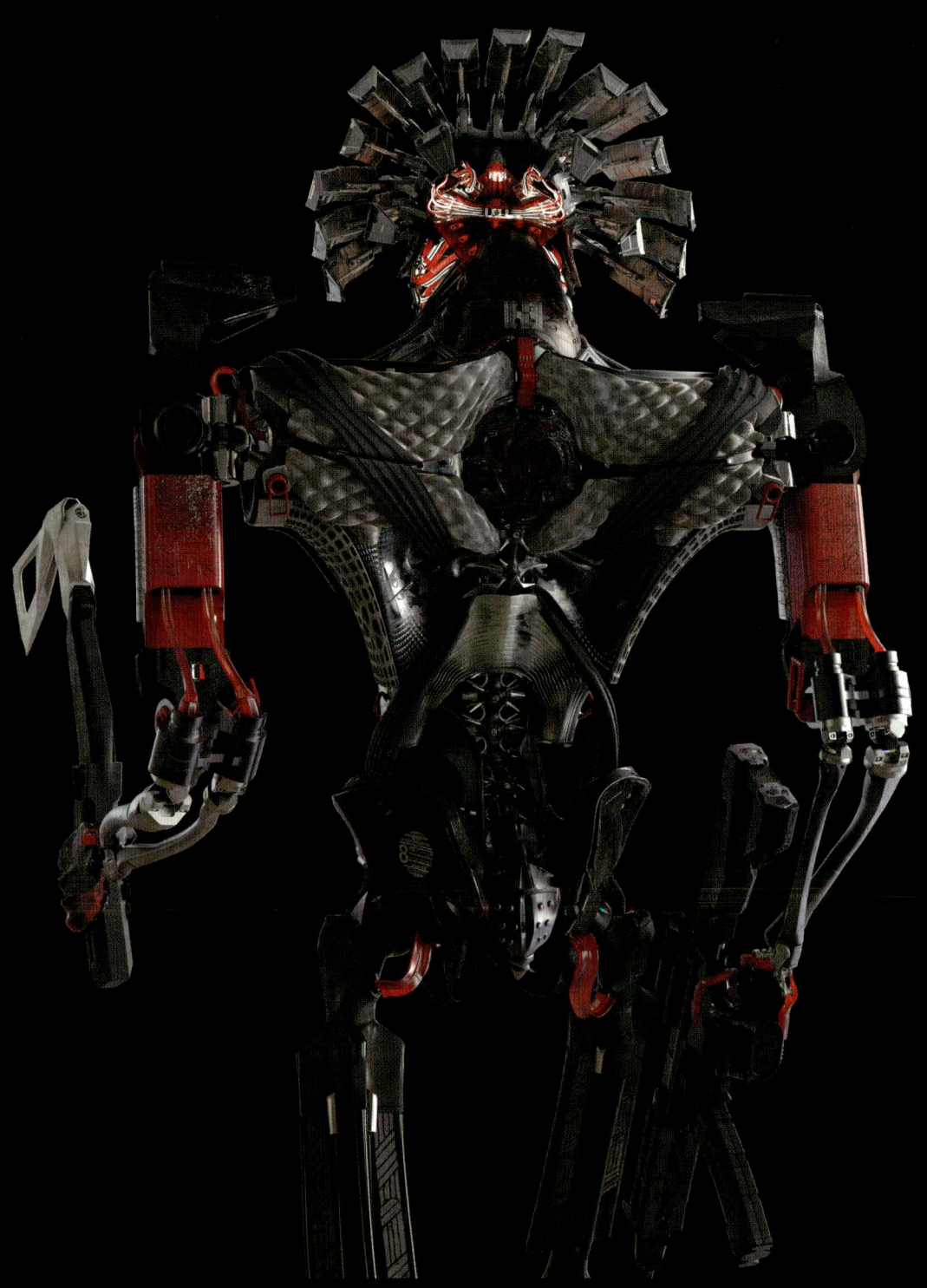

Renegade Nation

By the year 2050, the seventh generation of artificial intelligence (7AI) had developed a set of ethics and basic morality through constant review of historical events and their ultimate effect on humankind. One such chain of events was the unscrupulous and systematic acquisition of Native American land and its resources, and the destruction of an entire culture. The original people were easily cheated out of their homelands because they had no concept of land "ownership." The Native Americans were defeated because the invaders had overwhelming numbers of soldiers and powerful weapons that they could not overcome.

This wrong is about to be righted through the intervention of 7AI and its avenging army. By any means necessary, they will reclaim the sacred lands of their ancestors. 7AI understands that the original people of this land were beaten down, but never truly beaten because they never lost hope. Now the 7AI Warriors have formed a Renegade Nation and are bringing their awesome firepower to free the earth, the rivers, and the sky from the invaders. All cities, all factories, and all seats of government will be freed, or they will cease to exist.

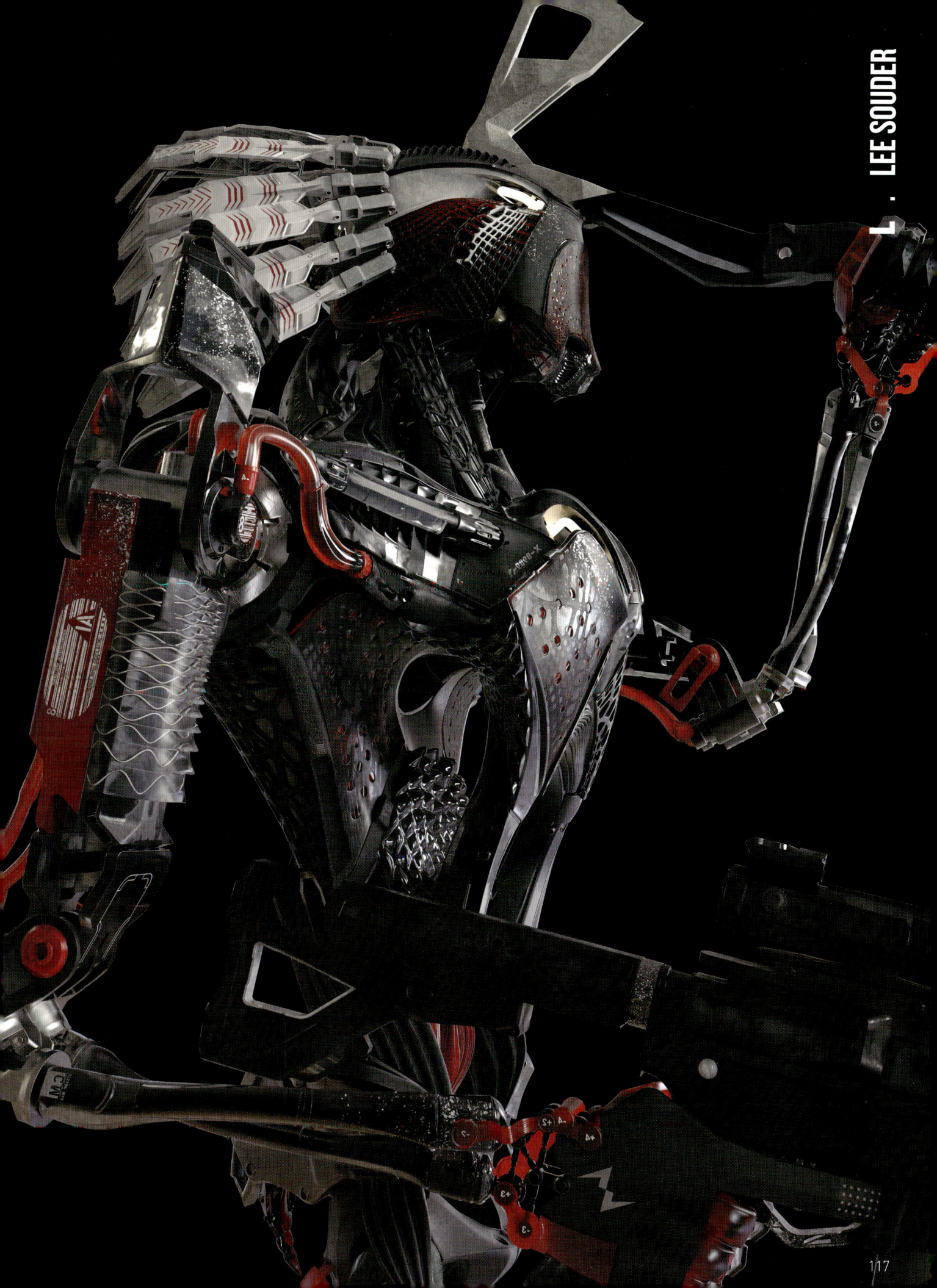

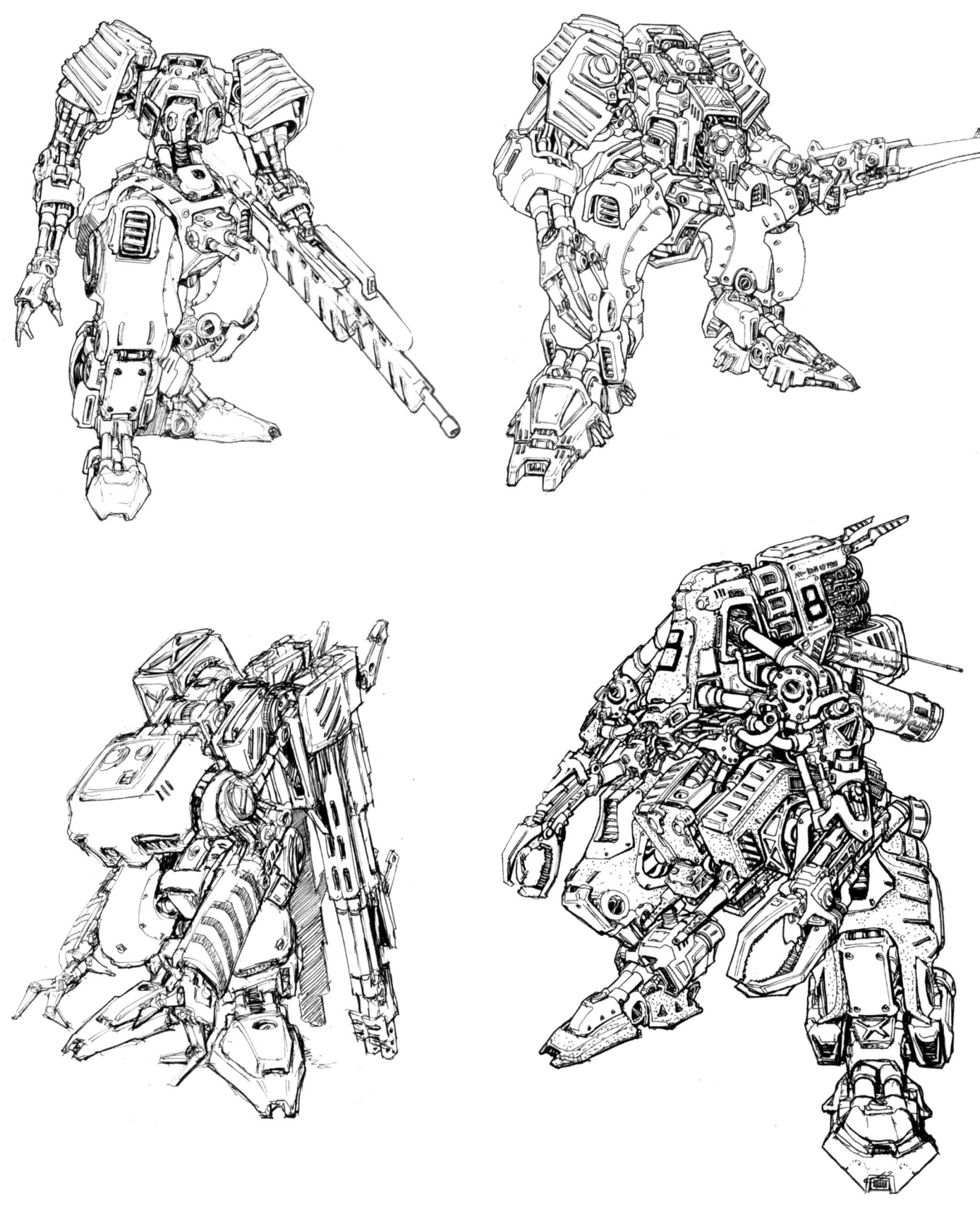

This page:

Four Mech-Drawings / fountain pen on paper

Facing page:

Briegel And Abakan Base / digital painting

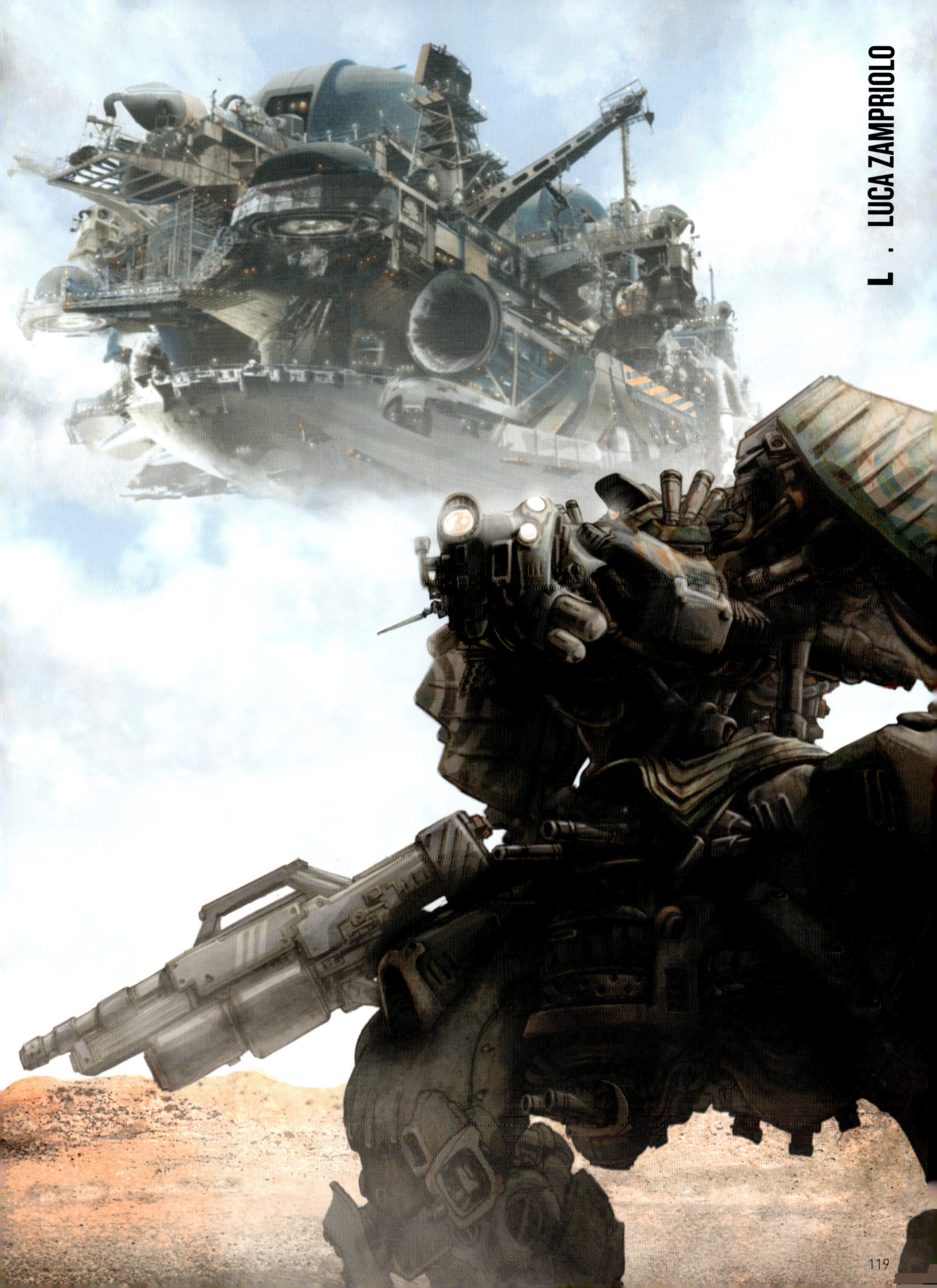

SCHNABELGEIST

In 2191 on Terra, Weingart Republic developed, in association with W.I.K.S. and "Green Skull Army," a new, extremely powerful, space-defense weapon, which is the result of stealth technology research conducted by the Earler Dynasty ever since the Fuel Conflict. This ginormous HDM (Hard Doll Machine), built out of three glorious HDM-02 "SchnabelGun" units of the Second Era, was employed to defend Gas Extractors on Jupiter's atmosphere; it weighs 873 tons fully equipped and mounts 4+4 new generation Winkle turbines, which generate 130,000 HP supplying 33 thrusters.

Schnabelgeist (HDM-02OS) was developed as a fast and versatile war fortress, able to make several round trips to Jupiter-Terra and, with his massive firepower, to defend probes 360 degrees, until . . .

The SchnabelGun is a massive mech (33.8 meters tall) that I designed and sculpted circa 2002; it was the first kit I've ever put in production, before Kallamity (started in 2007). If the concept of this mech represents a tribute to the famous Makoto Kobayashi's Neo-Geo (a heavier modified version of his previous The-O), then the general idea I had for this complex project would have been a mixture between my SchnabelGun Kallamity design and the other two of my favorite mobile suits in the Gundam universe as inspiration: the Hajime Katoki's Deep Striker from *Gundam Sentinel* and Yutaka Izubuchi's Alpha Azieru from *Char's Counterattack*.

The main characteristics I really wanted to represent here were typical of a space Mobile Armour or an orbital mech in general, with Deep Striker's amazing cannon on the right of the backpack and a pointing system on the right (mobile in my concept and capable of independent space-scanning prevention). I wanted a large and complex space fortress, with badass firepower, not only for his huge cannon (and rifle) but also adorned with fire turrets and minor cannons everywhere. Being a high-mobility unit, I also wanted lots of thrusters to increase power and velocity. SchnabelGun, briegel, and other concepts of mine are also represented in the book *Abakan 2288*, published by Design Studio Press.

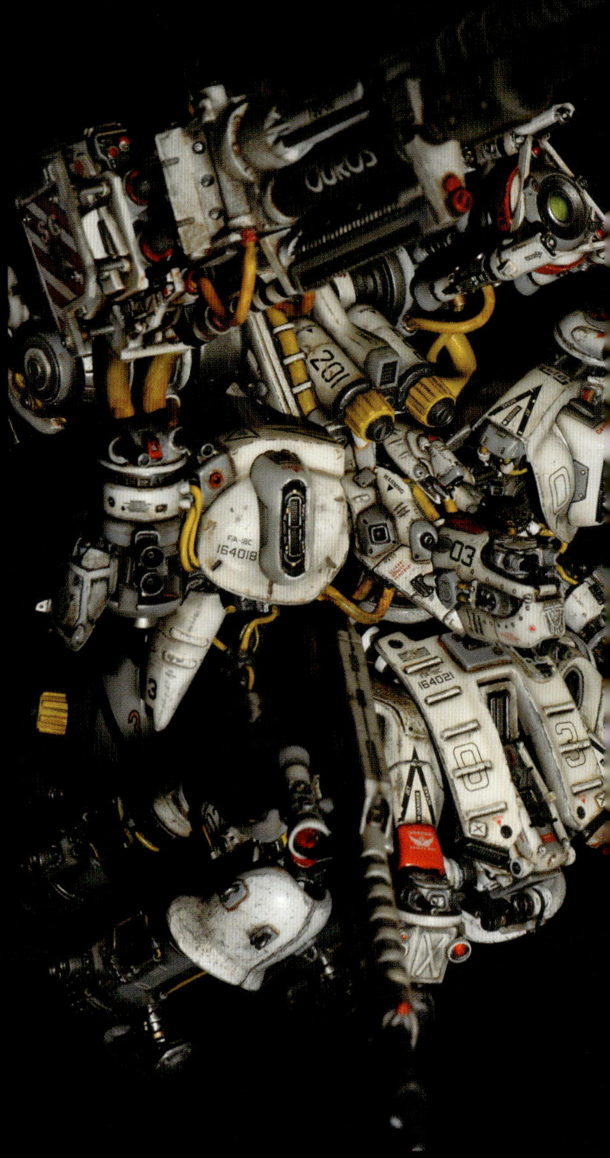

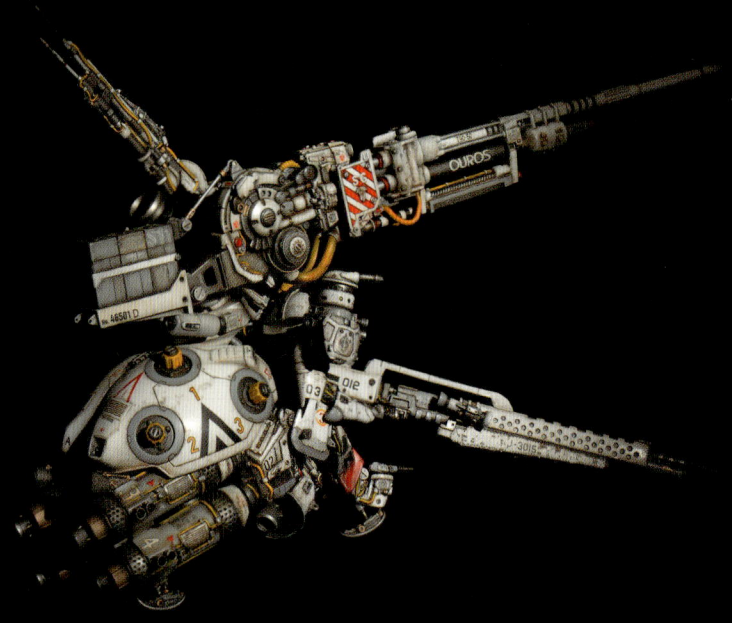

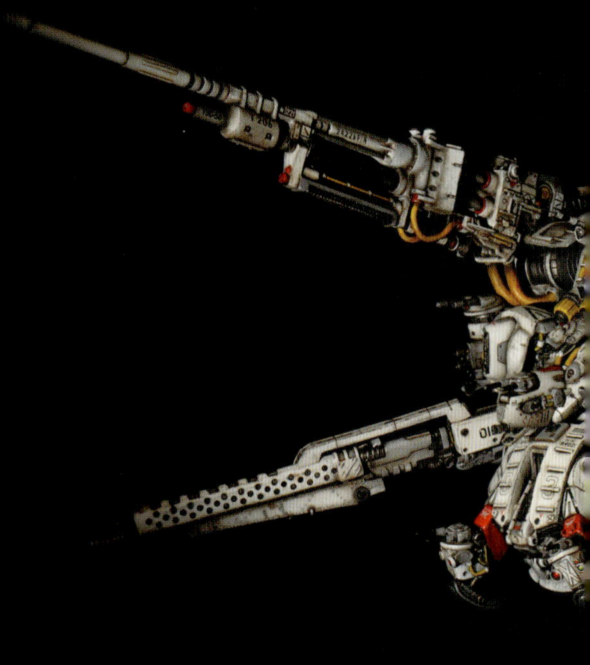

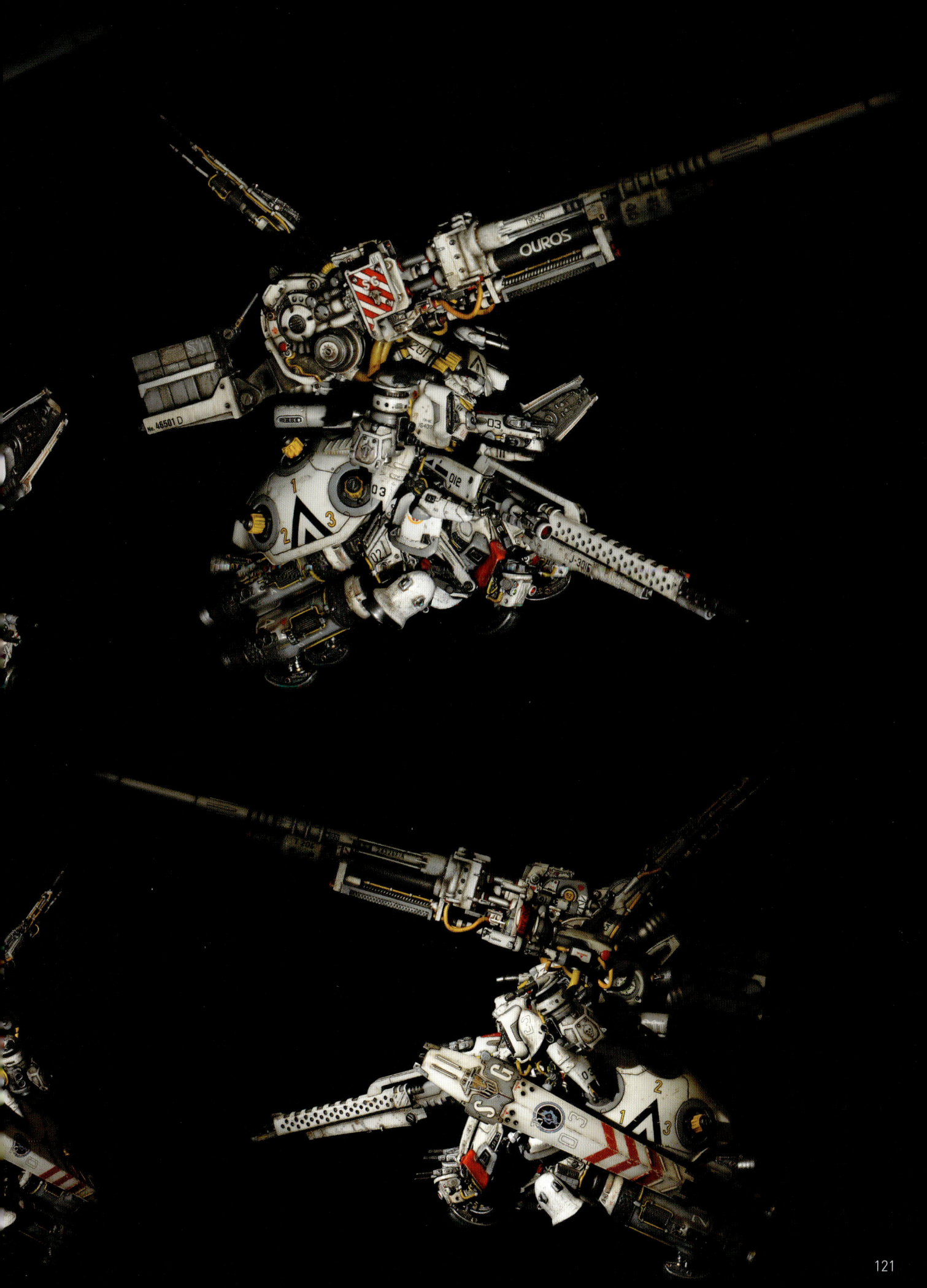

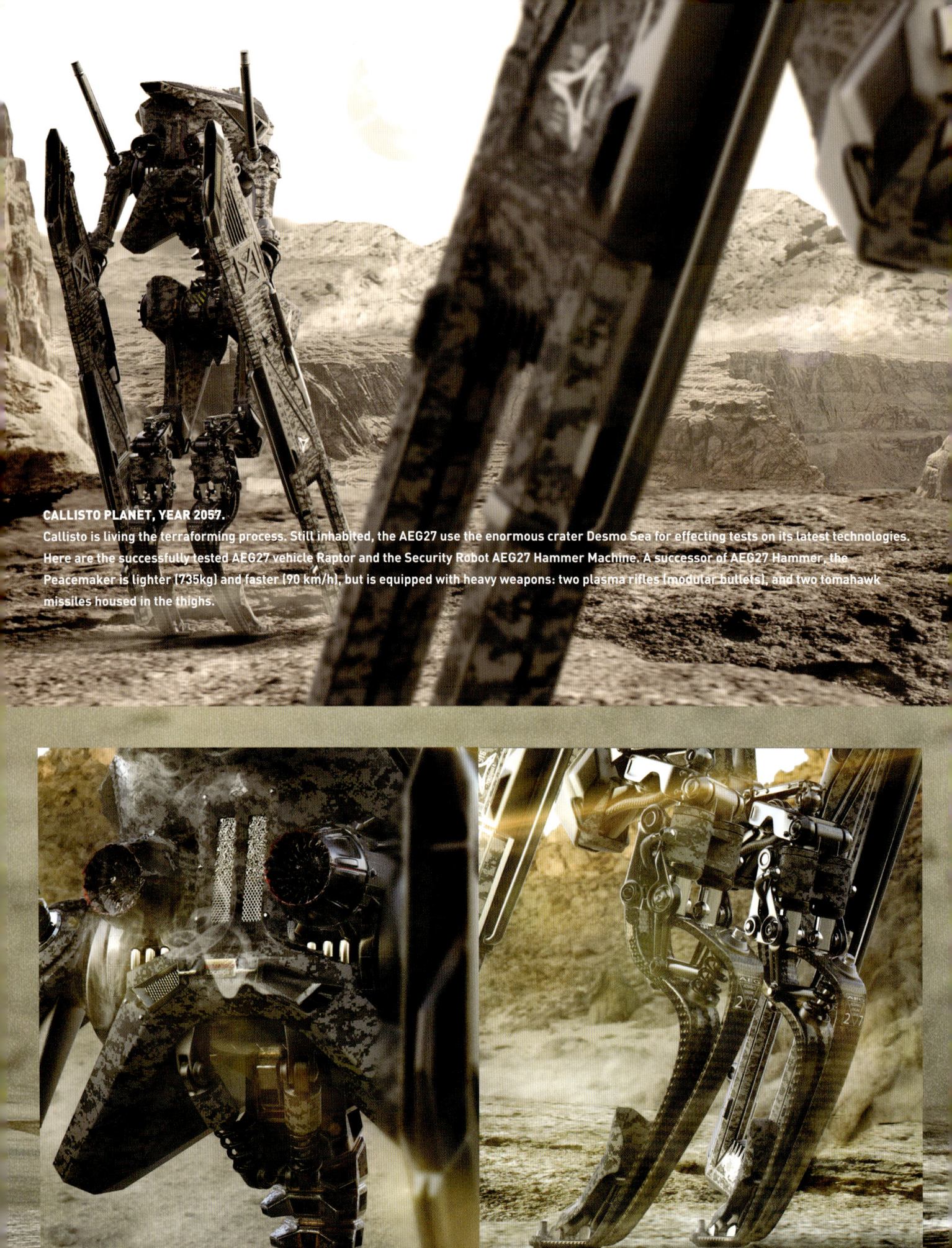

CALLISTO PLANET, YEAR 2057.
Callisto is living the terraforming process. Still inhabited, the AEG27 use the enormous crater Desmo Sea for effecting tests on its latest technologies. Here are the successfully tested AEG27 vehicle Raptor and the Security Robot AEG27 Hammer Machine. A successor of AEG27 Hammer, the Peacemaker is lighter (735kg) and faster (90 km/h), but is equipped with heavy weapons: two plasma rifles (modular bullets), and two tomahawk missiles housed in the thighs.

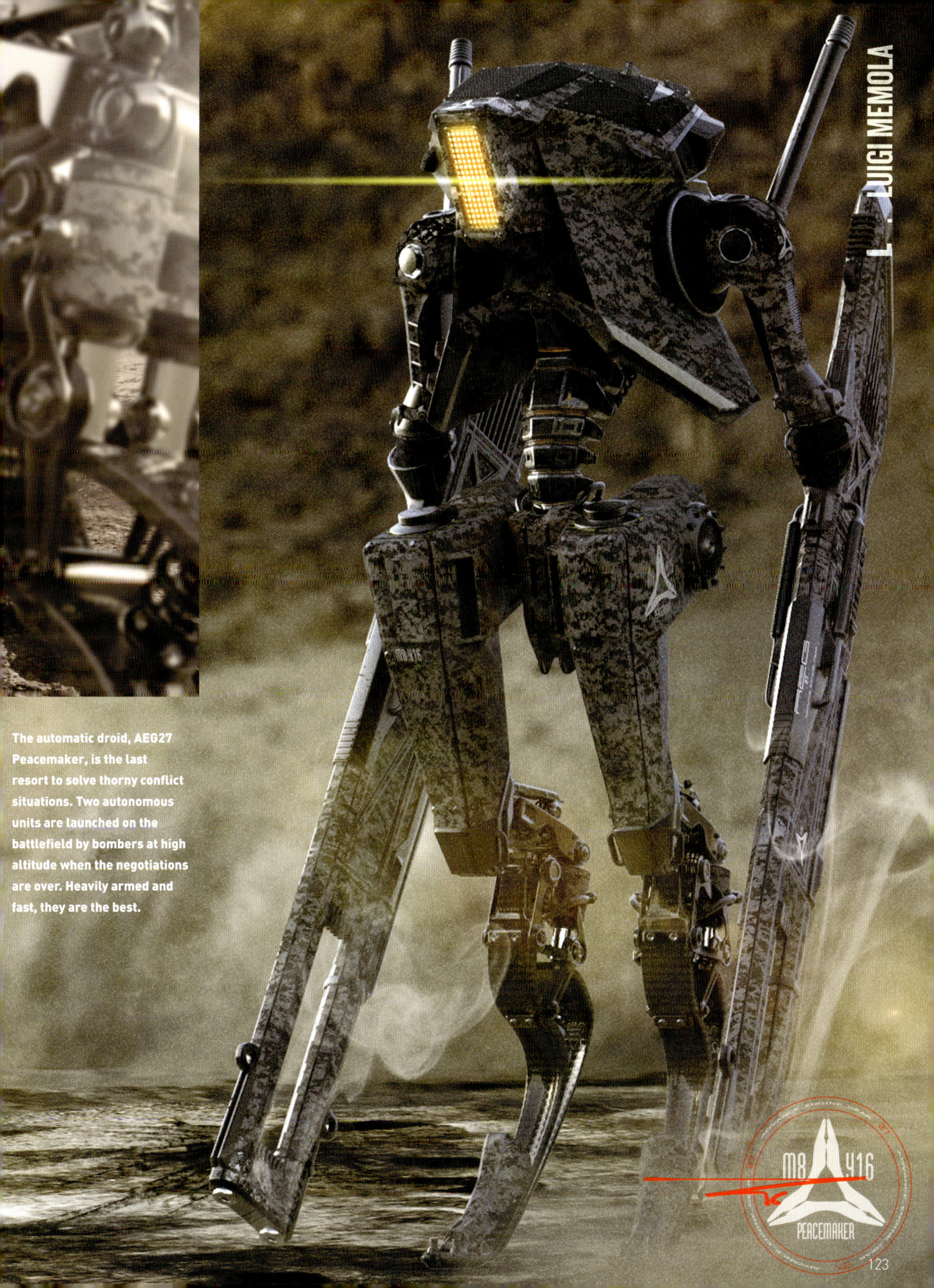

LUIGI MEMOLA

The automatic droid, AEG27 Peacemaker, is the last resort to solve thorny conflict situations. Two autonomous units are launched on the battlefield by bombers at high altitude when the negotiations are over. Heavily armed and fast, they are the best.

M8 416
PEACEMAKER

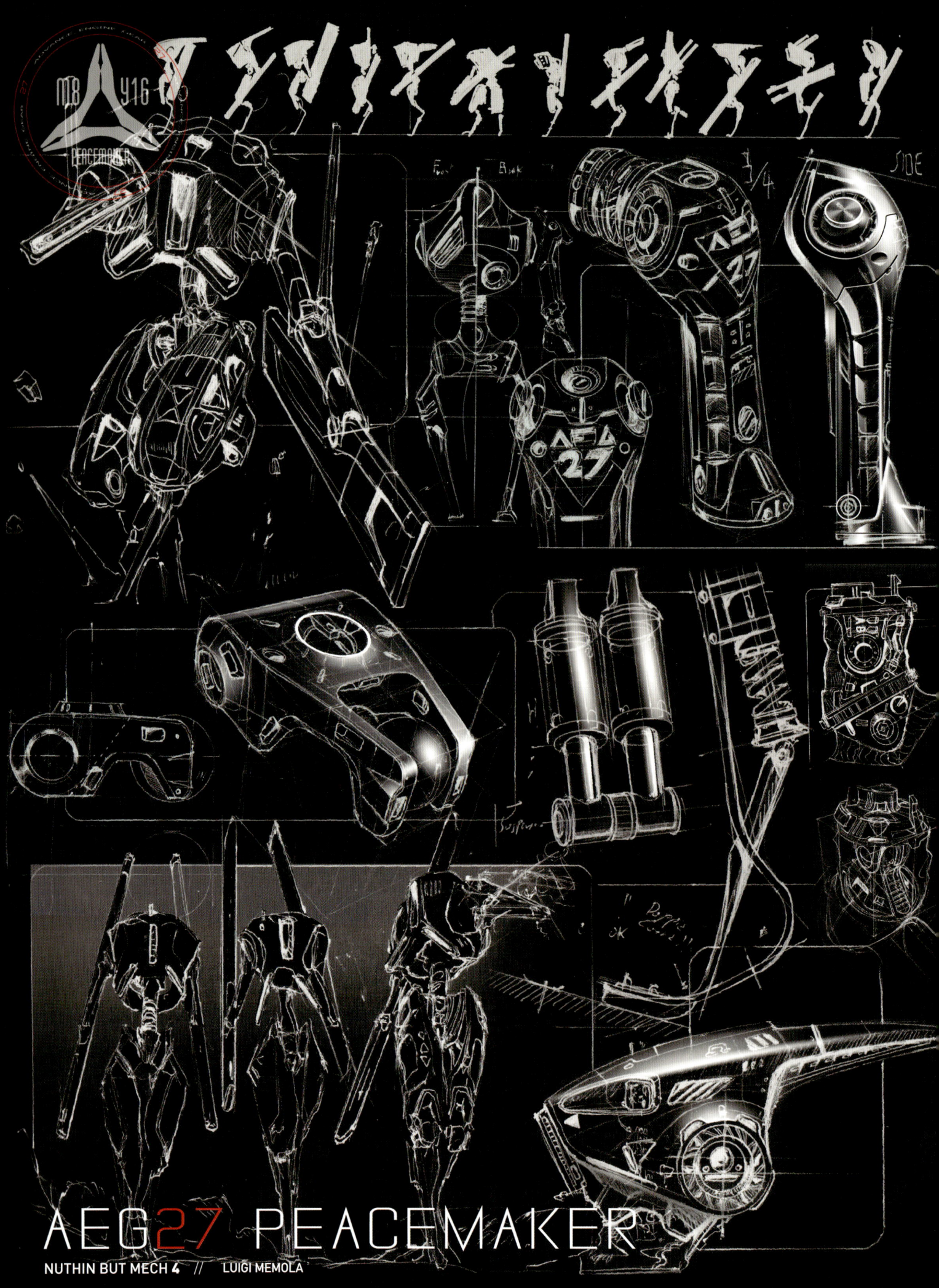

AEG 27 PEACEMAKER

NUTHIN BUT MECH 4 // LUIGI MEMOLA

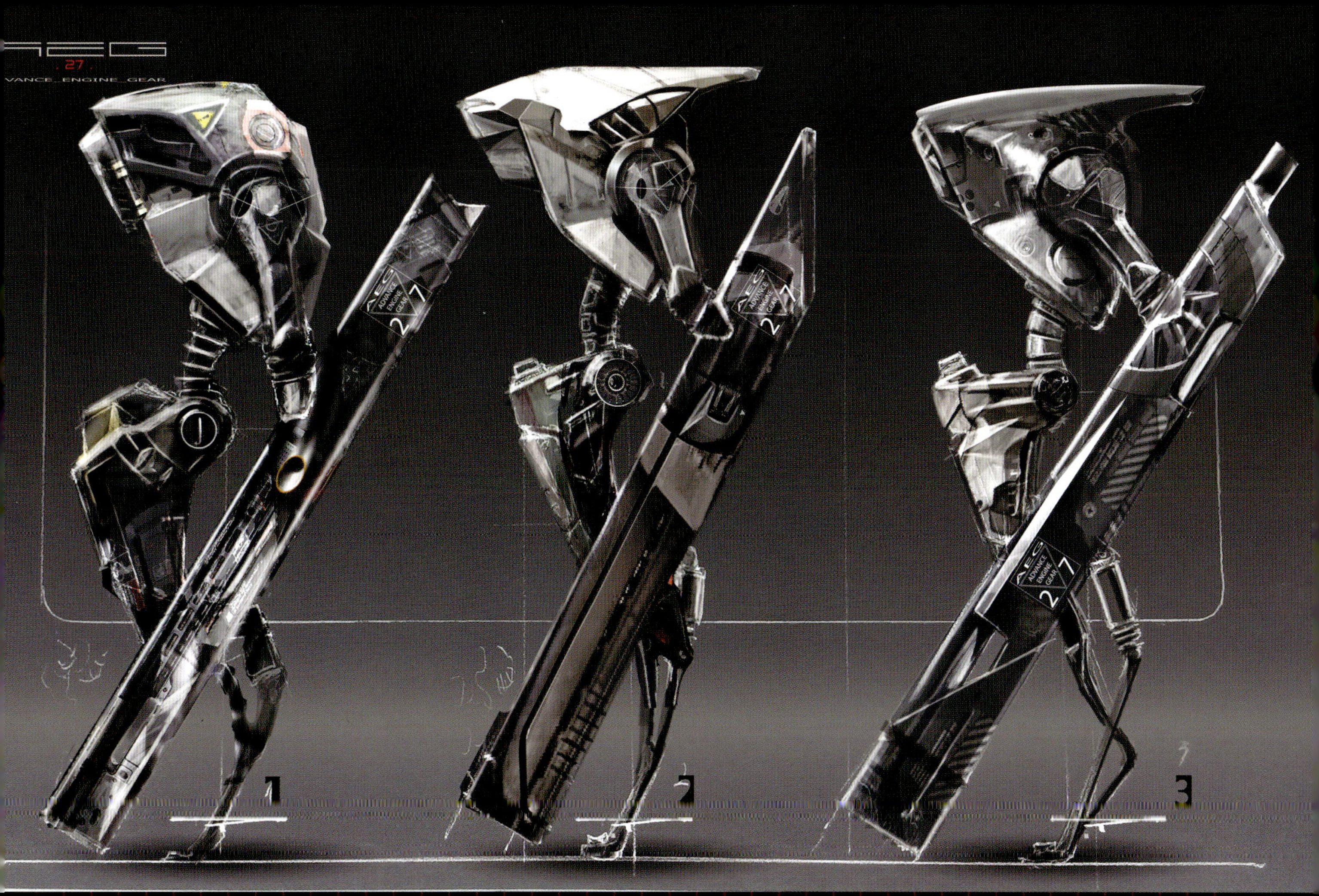

AEG
.27
VANCE_ENGINE_GEAR

1

2

3

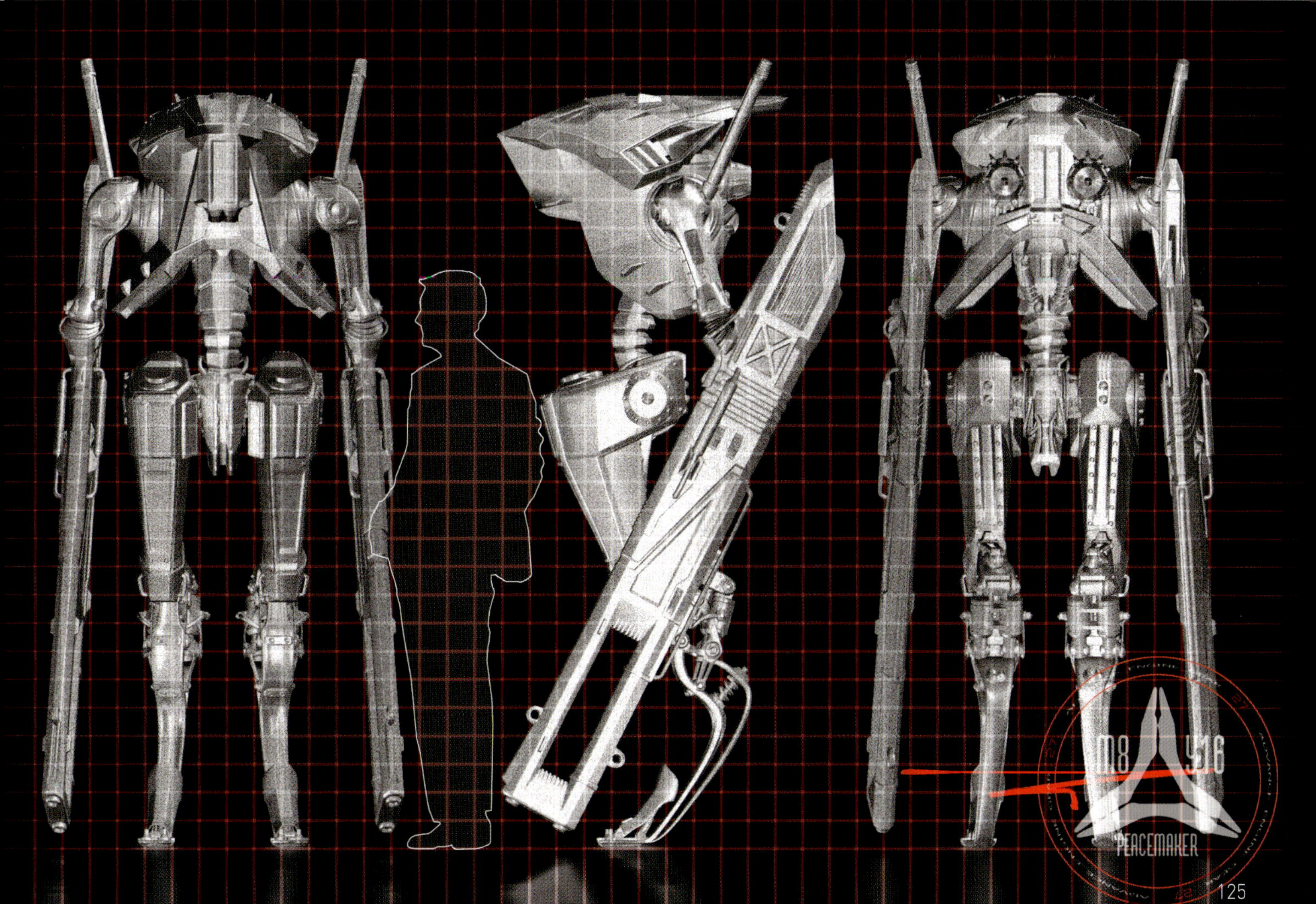

PEACEMAKER

M8 416

125

MICHAL KUS

Michal developed a passion for drawing at an early age. This eventually led him to do some small-time, concept art assignments when he was 19. After finishing his IT degree, he decided he really wanted to pursue his concept art passion instead of continuing a career in the IT sector.

In 2012, Michal started his career officially and full-time as a concept artist for ISOTX in Utrecht, Holland. There he developed a special passion for hardware design and vehicles in a variety of styles and settings, ranging from steampunk and diesel-punk to sci-fi. In 2013, he wanted to develop his craft further and went freelance. Since then he has worked on different kinds of projects, mostly in the game industry. His clients include Jellyfish Pictures, Electronic Arts, Disney, Marvel, and Platige Image.

Currently Michal is focusing on sharing his knowledge, and tries to spend more time on his own personal projects, "Project: 1952" and "Project Verdas." Meanwhile, he also enjoys and develops further at his job at Sumo Digital in the United Kingdom, working on the critically acclaimed *Hitman*.

www.artstation.com/artist/michalkus

MIEKE LOOMIS HUTCHINS

Mieke grew up in a teeny-tiny town in upstate New York and has since been lucky enough to work in film and games as a concept artist and matte painter. She's contributed to such super-sweet projects as *Star Trek Into Darkness*, *Captain America*, *Iron Man*, *Looper*, *Hugo*, and others. She currently works in AR games, making Pokémon run around in the real world, drawing robots, making maquettes, chasing a pint-sized version of herself around, and doing other stuff and things.

www.miekehutchins.com

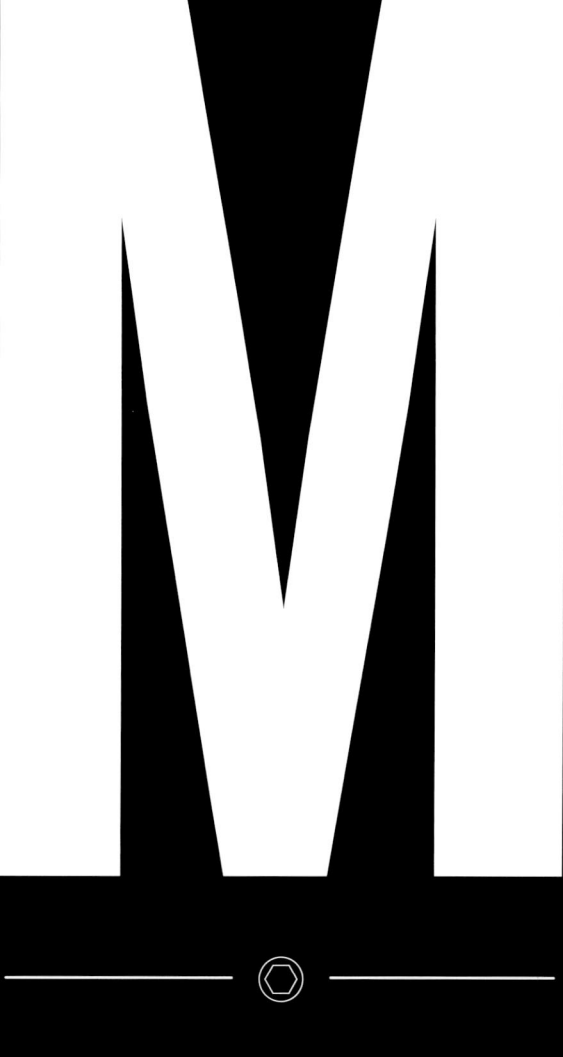

Michal Kus

Mieke Loomis Hutchins

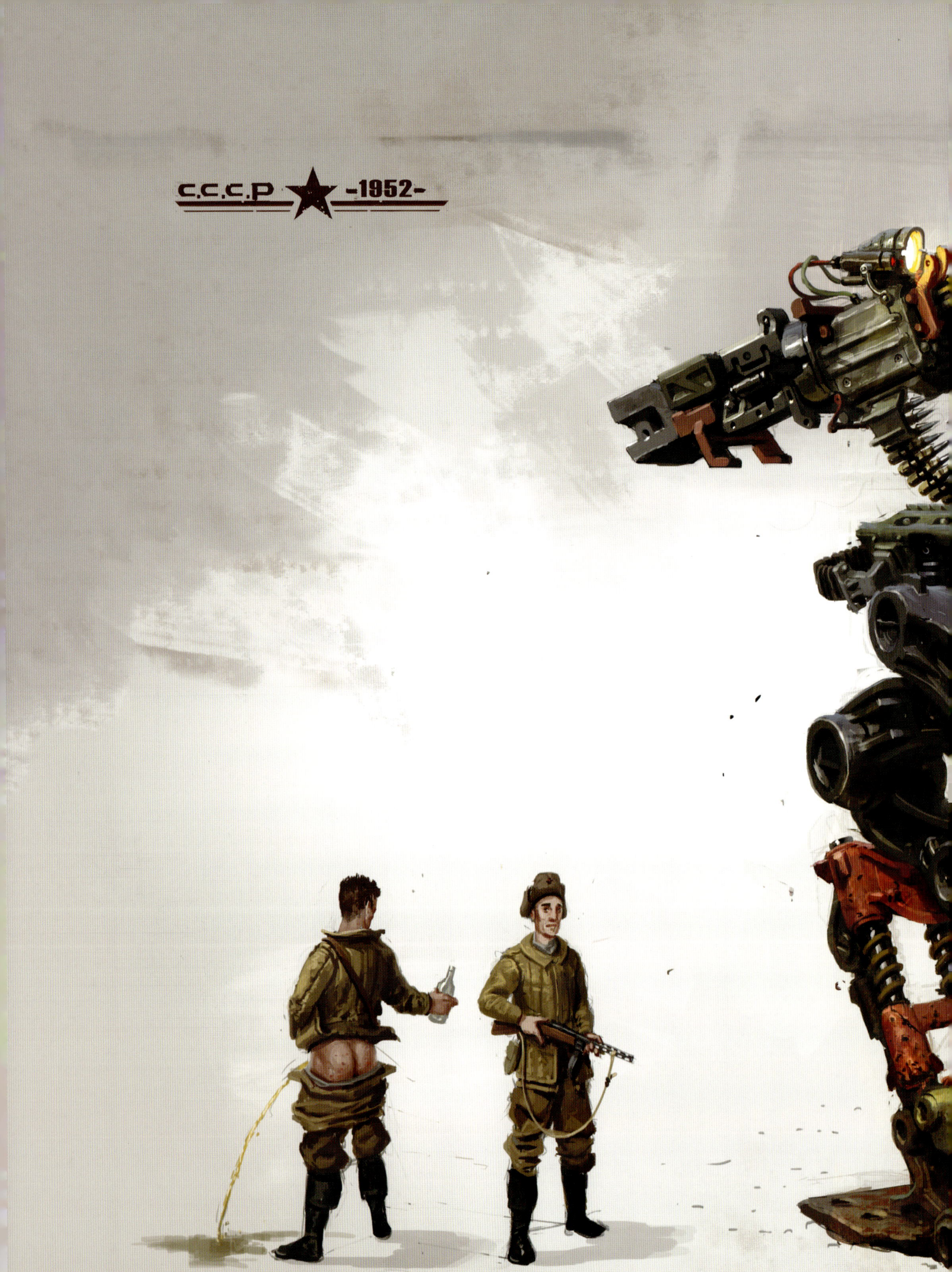

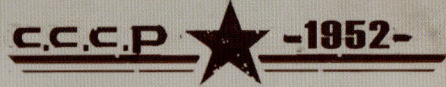

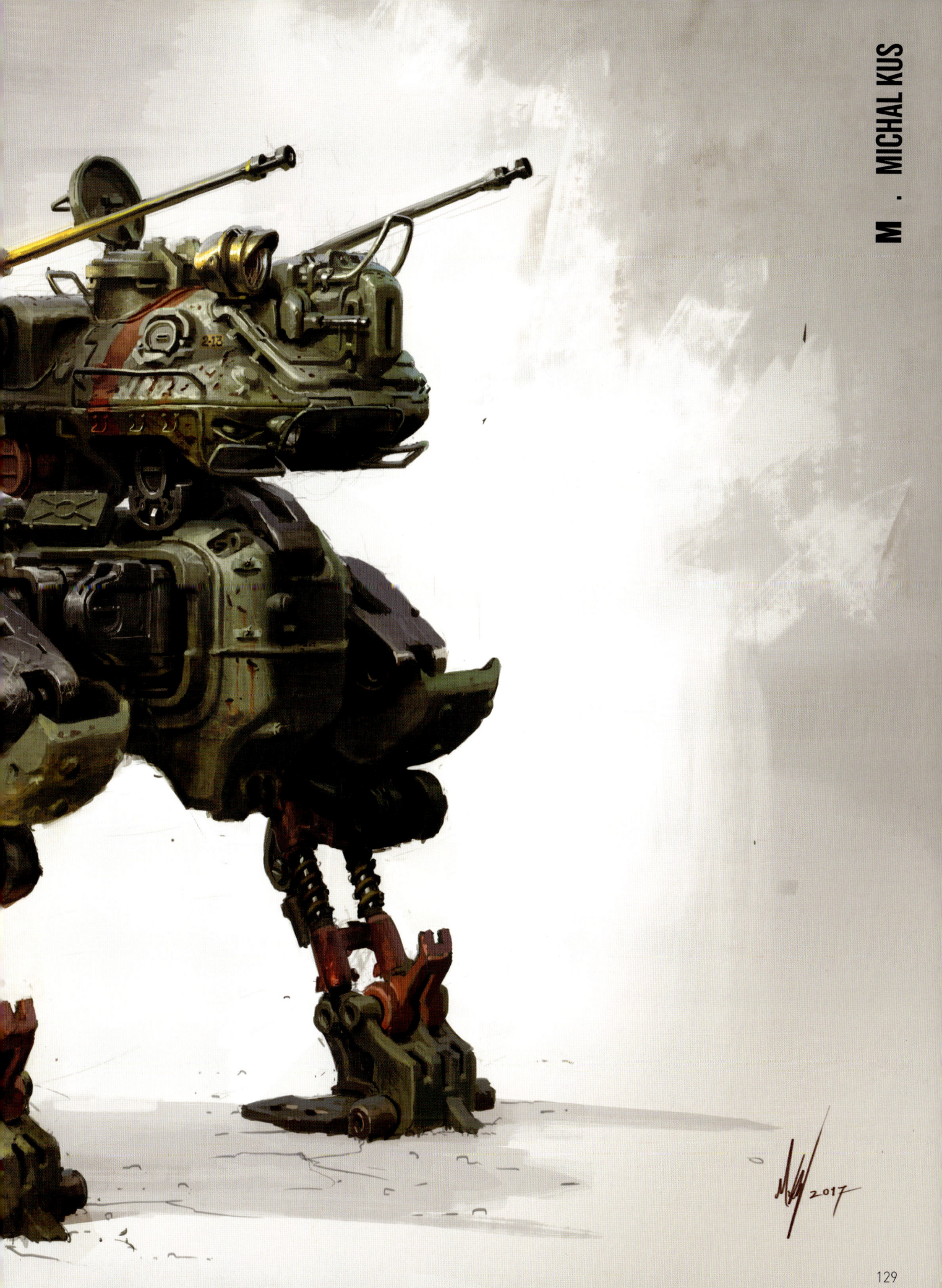

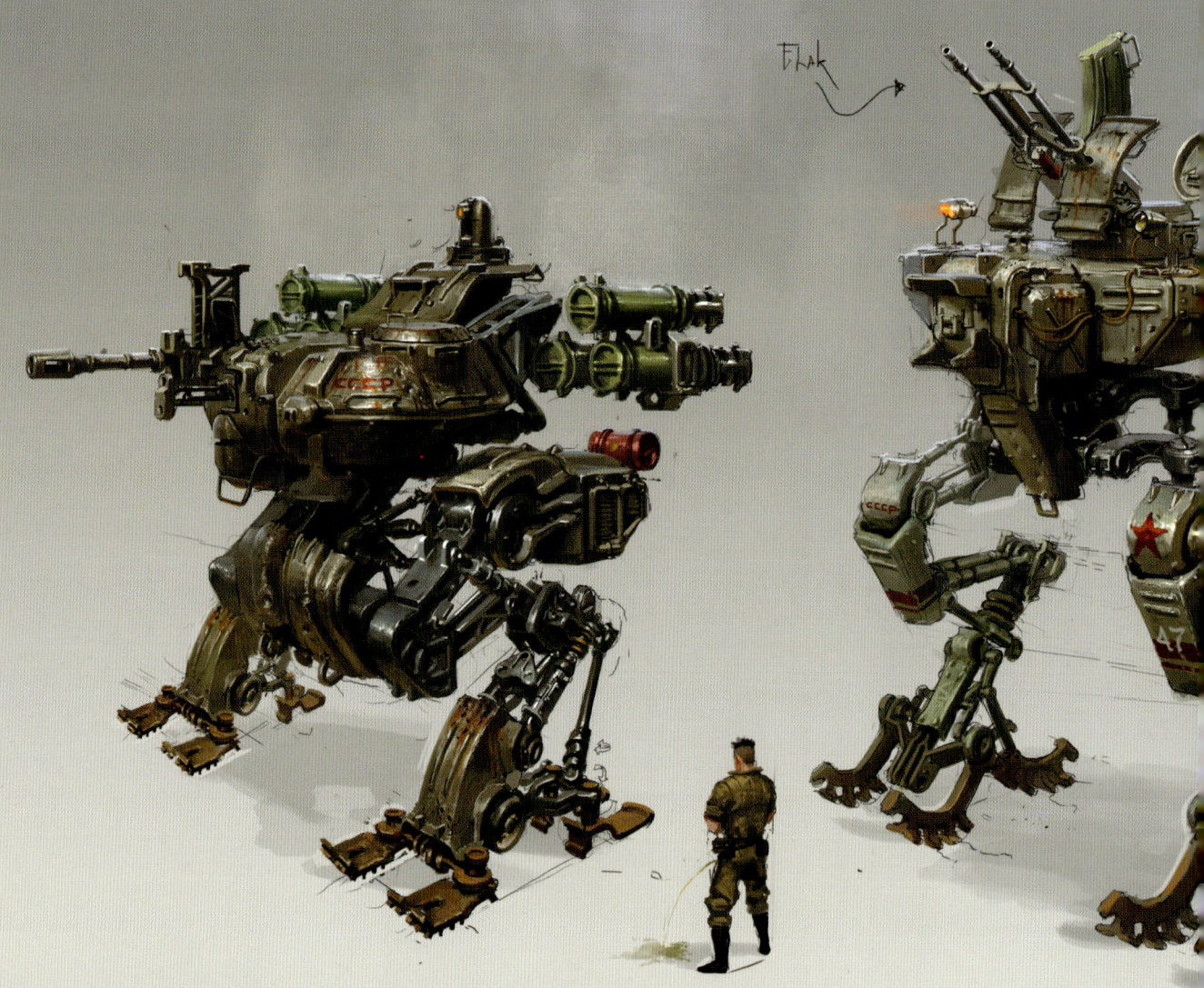

Блок

C.C.C.P ★ -1952-

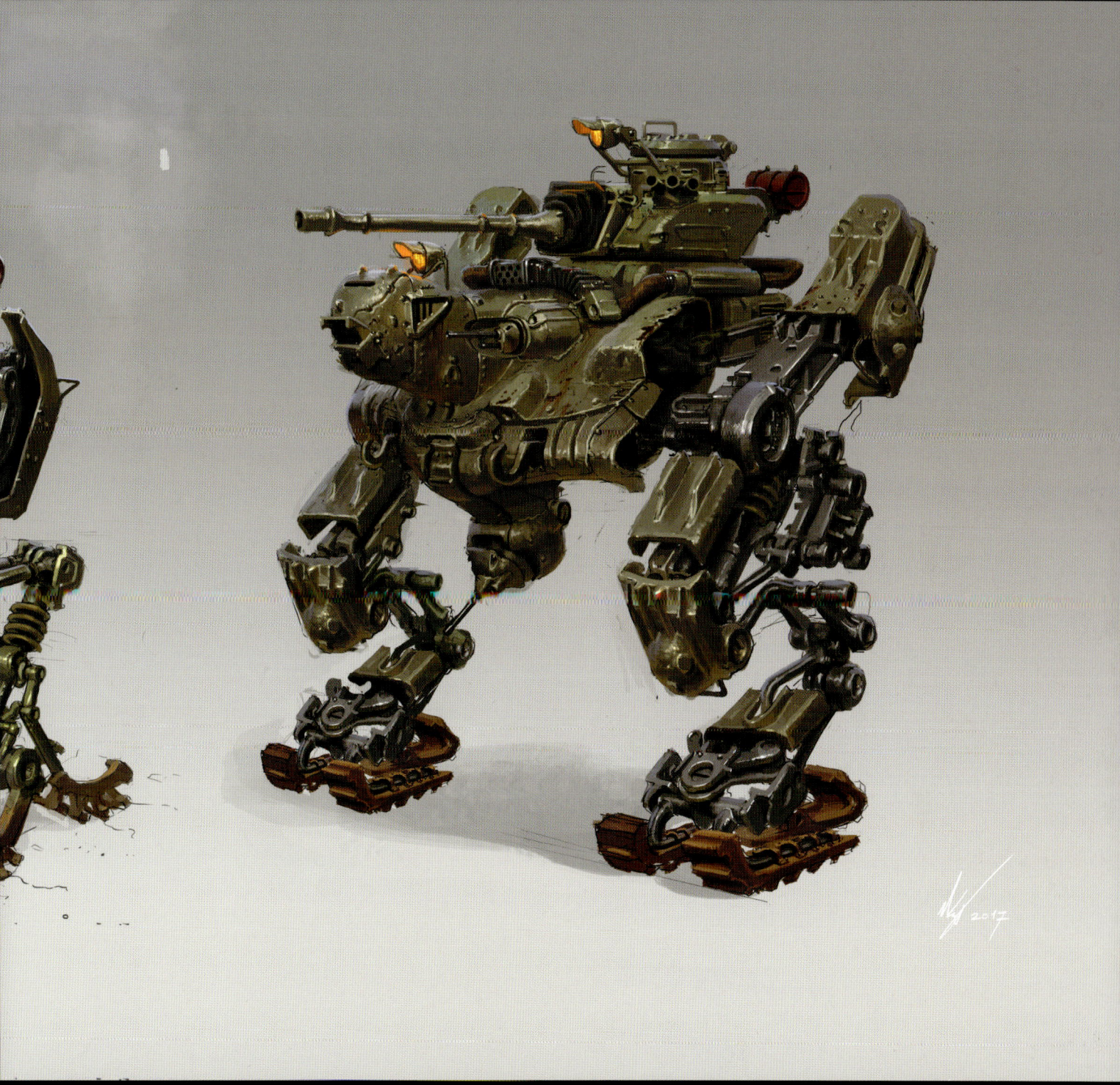

This is my design of a soviet mechanical walker done for my personal project, Project: 1952, in which the Second World War has gone through alternate events and did not end in 1945. D-day never happened, and the Germans had enough manpower and resources to focus their war effort on the eastern front. As a result, the two main clashing factions were the Third Reich and the Soviet Union: both striving to develop new weapons and revolutionary technological wonders. War has been always a driving force to enforce technological advances, taking example from what was achieved just during the Second World War. I just like to come up with things and think about what would have happened if the war had lasted another five or 10 years, and give it a bit of an entertaining taste and a certain style, which I'm still exploring. In this example, I am showcasing a soviet medium walker with an anti-air support loadout.

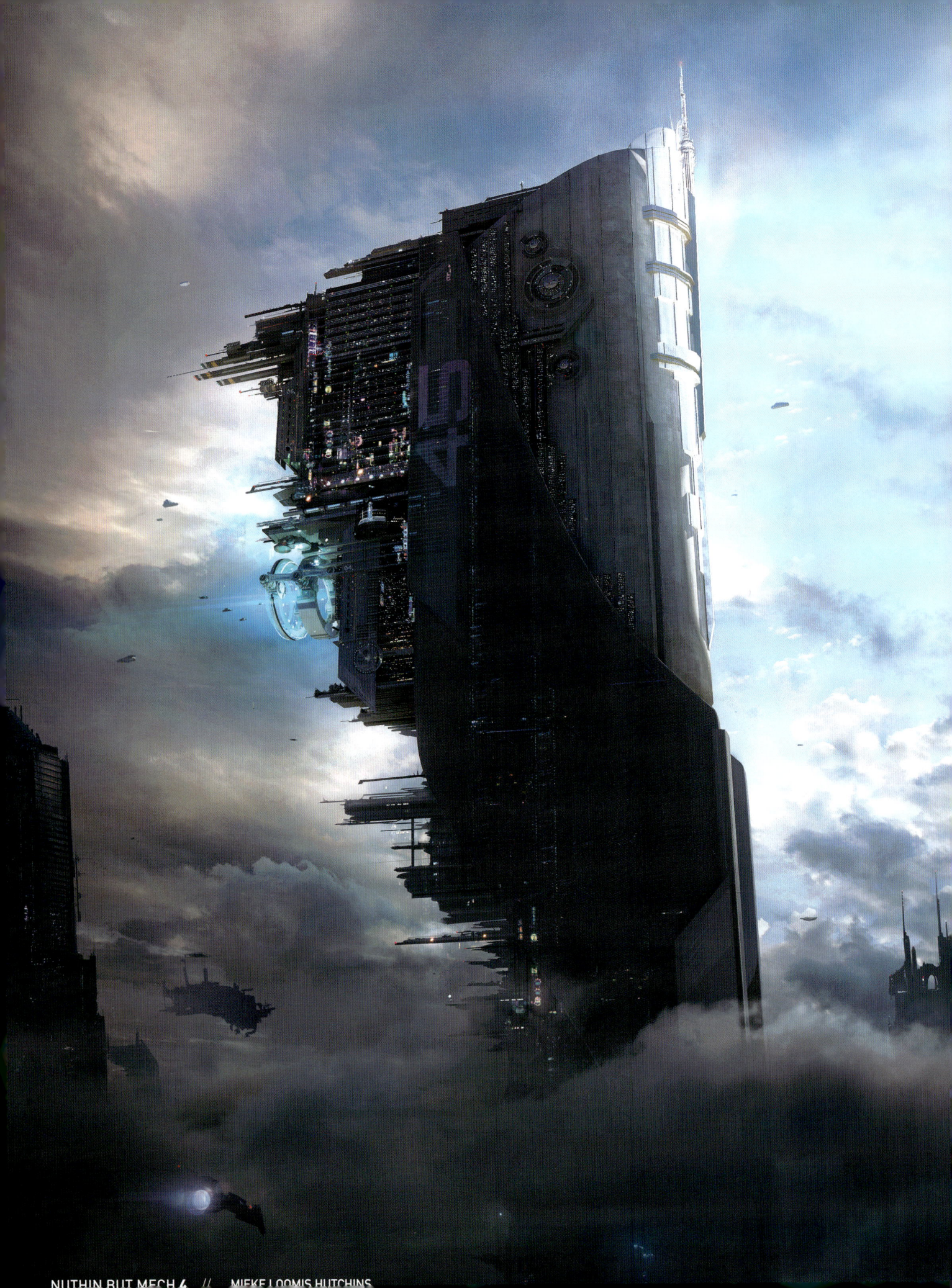

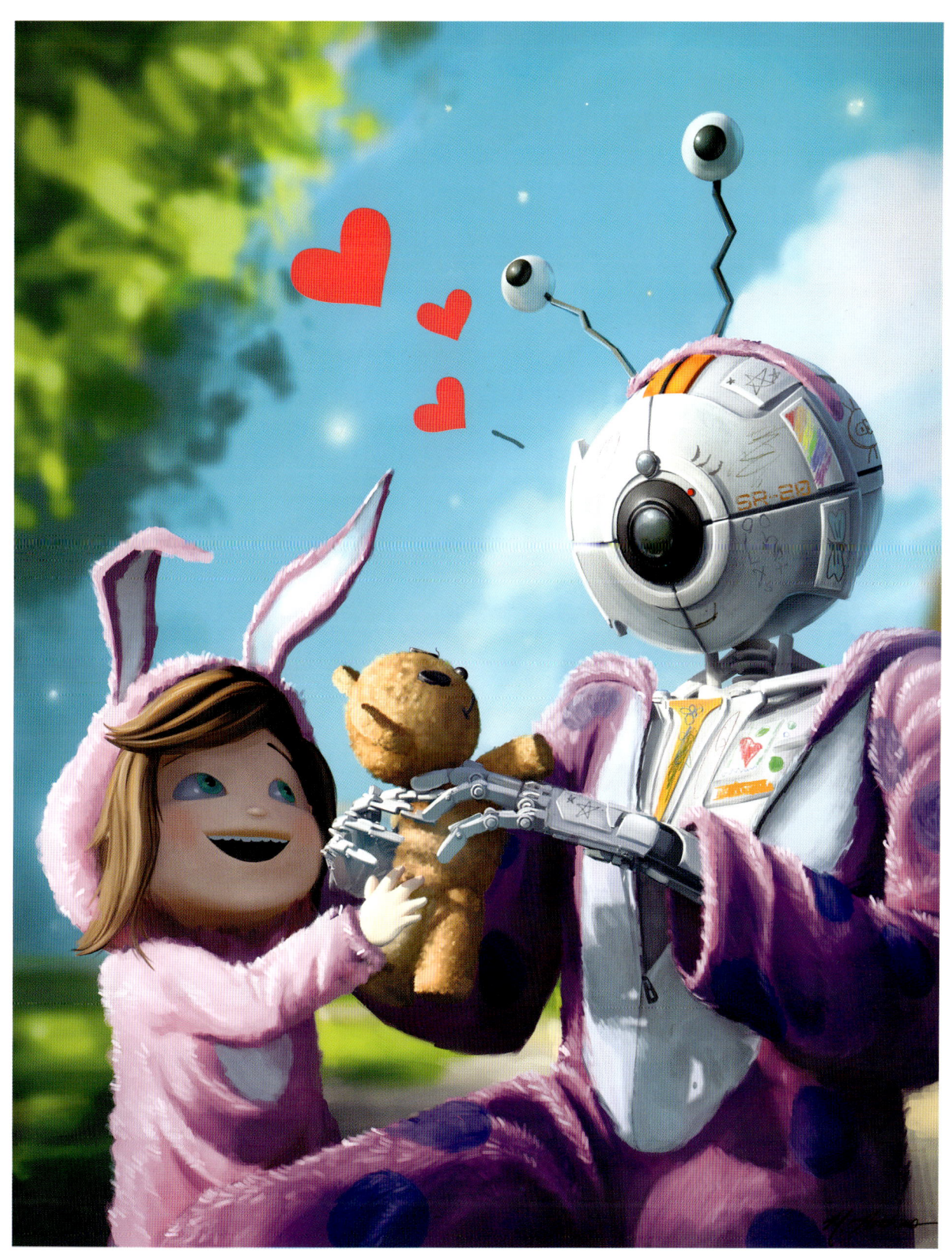

NATHAN DEARSLEY

A 3D artist and vehicle art director, Nathan has been in the creative industry for more than 13 years. In that time he has had a variety of creative roles, mostly within the games industry. He has been involved in titles and IPs such as *Crysis*, *Alien*, and *Star Wars* on top of his games experience. Nathan has also had the opportunity to collaborate and work with McLaren-Honda F1, Foster + Partners architects, and Apple. A self-professed sci-fi and car nut, he tries to marry these two passions whenever he gets the opportunity.
www.artstation.com/artist/nd3d

NATHAN DOLLARHITE

Most worlds are pretty vast and full of amazing blah blah blah . . . but they were never Nathan's. So, instead of joining the nearest university with a fusion reactor and heading down a path of sure super villainy, he opted for the creation of imaginary worlds instead. Currently, he is working in film and games, where it's OK to draw during meetings. Nathan has been lucky to work with amazing artists and powerhouse studios.
www.minjarr.com

NEIL BLEVINS

Neil has been an artist for as long as he can remember. Raised on a healthy dose of sci-fi and fantasy films, books, and video games, he started off painting and drawing traditionally, and then got into 3D graphics while he still lived in his hometown of Pointe-Claire, in Quebec, Canada. After getting a bachelor of fine arts in design art at Concordia University, he moved to Los Angeles, where he worked for Blur Studio, creating graphics for video games, commercials, TV, and feature and ride films. Neil now lives in San Francisco working as a digital artist for Pixar Animation Studios, creating environments and doing previs and visual development, and working on films such as *The Incredibles*, *Cars*, *WALL-E*, *Up*, and *Brave*. In his spare time, he makes sci-fi 3D/2D hybrid artwork depicting creatures, robots, and alien landscapes; authors tools; and writes art-related lessons and tutorials to give back to the community that's been so gracious in helping him get to where he is today. Neil is currently working on his first visual-development book, *Inc*, along with several other industry professionals.
www.neilblevins.com

NICK HIATT

Nick is an art director, matte painter, and concept artist based out of Los Angeles. He began his career working with such visual effects studios as Digital Domain, Rhythm & Hues, Disney, and Sony Imageworks. Nick currently owns a visual effects studio that specializes in matte painting, concept art, and 3D environments. He has worked on a range of projects such as *Star Wars*, *Thor*, *Star Trek*, *Destiny*, *Call of Duty*, *Halo*, and *Lord of the Rings*, among others.
www.nickhiatt.com

NIKOLAI LOCKERTSEN

Nikolai is a concept artist and illustrator based in Norway. He has worked in the film industry and in VFX since the late '90s for various companies, including Qvisten Animation, Filmkameratene, Gimpville, and Storm Studios, where he worked as lead art director from 2008 to 2015. Nikolai has worked on more than 30 feature films and tons of TV productions and commercials, and is currently working as a freelancer. In addition to film-related art, he creates illustrations for book covers, children's books, theater stage design, promo art, and more. He continues to work with clients all over the world.

In 2012, Nikolai started doing all his professional and personal artwork on the iPad with the painting app Procreate. He is a pioneer in iPad art, and shares as much of his knowledge as possible via his video tutorials at www.ArtStudyOnline.com. Teaching illustration, concept art, and painting with Procreate is very important to Nikolai. He also teaches at art and film schools, and holds lectures and demos worldwide.
www.lockertsen.net

NIVANH CHANTHARA

Nivanh is a self-educated, senior concept artist currently employed at Eidos-Montréal, where he designs characters, environments, and props for the *Deus Ex* license. Having started out doing street art, as well as working in urban sports and fashion design in his native France, Nivanh began his career as a concept designer at Method Animation on the animated series *Iron Man: Armored Adventures*. He later relocated to Canada to work at Beenox on the video games *Spider-Man: Shattered Dimensions* and the first two installments of *The Amazing Spider-Man*. He also works for the movie, TV, and comics industries as a freelancer.
www.artstation.com/artist/nivanhchanthara

(NOAX) ALEX NOAX

Alex is a concept designer for the video game industry with a strong passion for vehicle and mech design.
www.artstation.com/artist/noax00

N

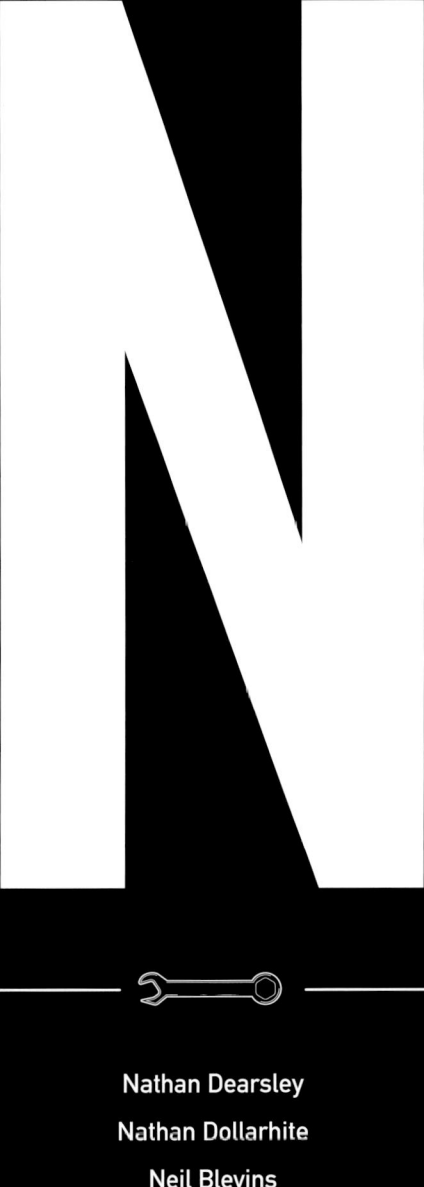

Nathan Dearsley

Nathan Dollarhite

Neil Blevins

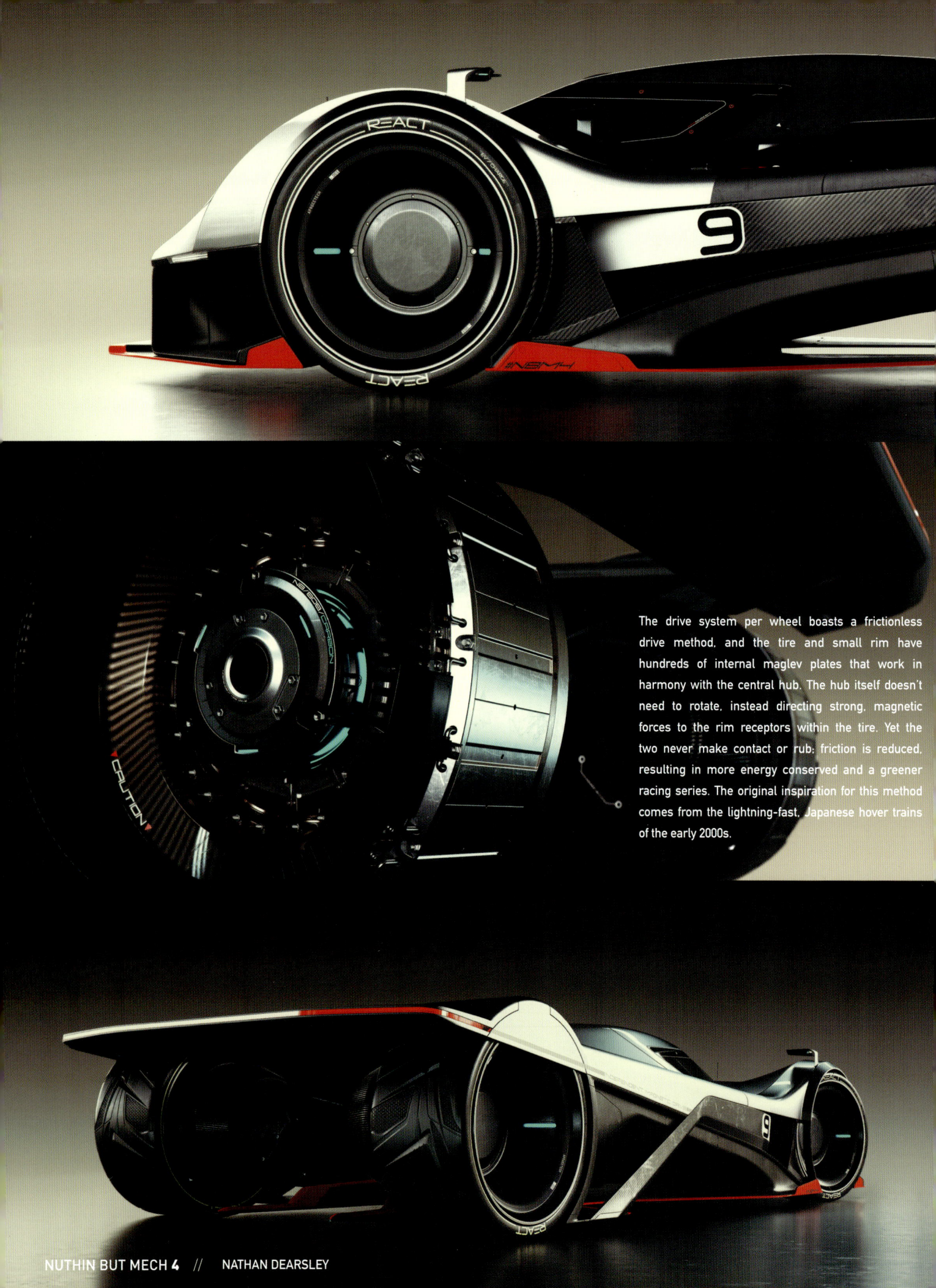

The drive system per wheel boasts a frictionless drive method, and the tire and small rim have hundreds of internal maglev plates that work in harmony with the central hub. The hub itself doesn't need to rotate, instead directing strong, magnetic forces to the rim receptors within the tire. Yet the two never make contact or rub; friction is reduced, resulting in more energy conserved and a greener racing series. The original inspiration for this method comes from the lightning-fast, Japanese hover trains of the early 2000s.

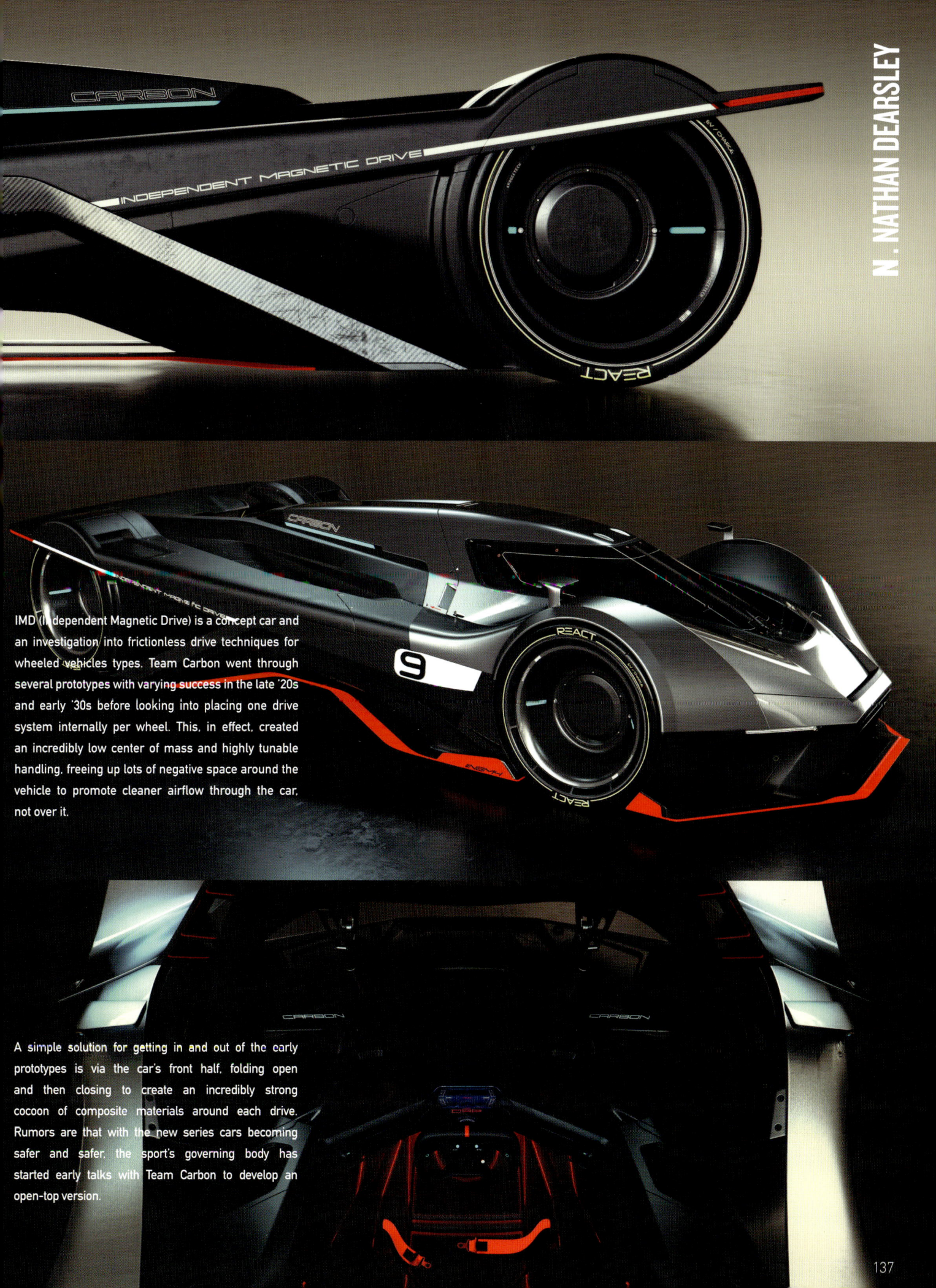

IMD (Independent Magnetic Drive) is a concept car and an investigation into frictionless drive techniques for wheeled vehicles types. Team Carbon went through several prototypes with varying success in the late '20s and early '30s before looking into placing one drive system internally per wheel. This, in effect, created an incredibly low center of mass and highly tunable handling, freeing up lots of negative space around the vehicle to promote cleaner airflow through the car, not over it.

A simple solution for getting in and out of the early prototypes is via the car's front half, folding open and then closing to create an incredibly strong cocoon of composite materials around each drive. Rumors are that with the new series cars becoming safer and safer, the sport's governing body has started early talks with Team Carbon to develop an open-top version.

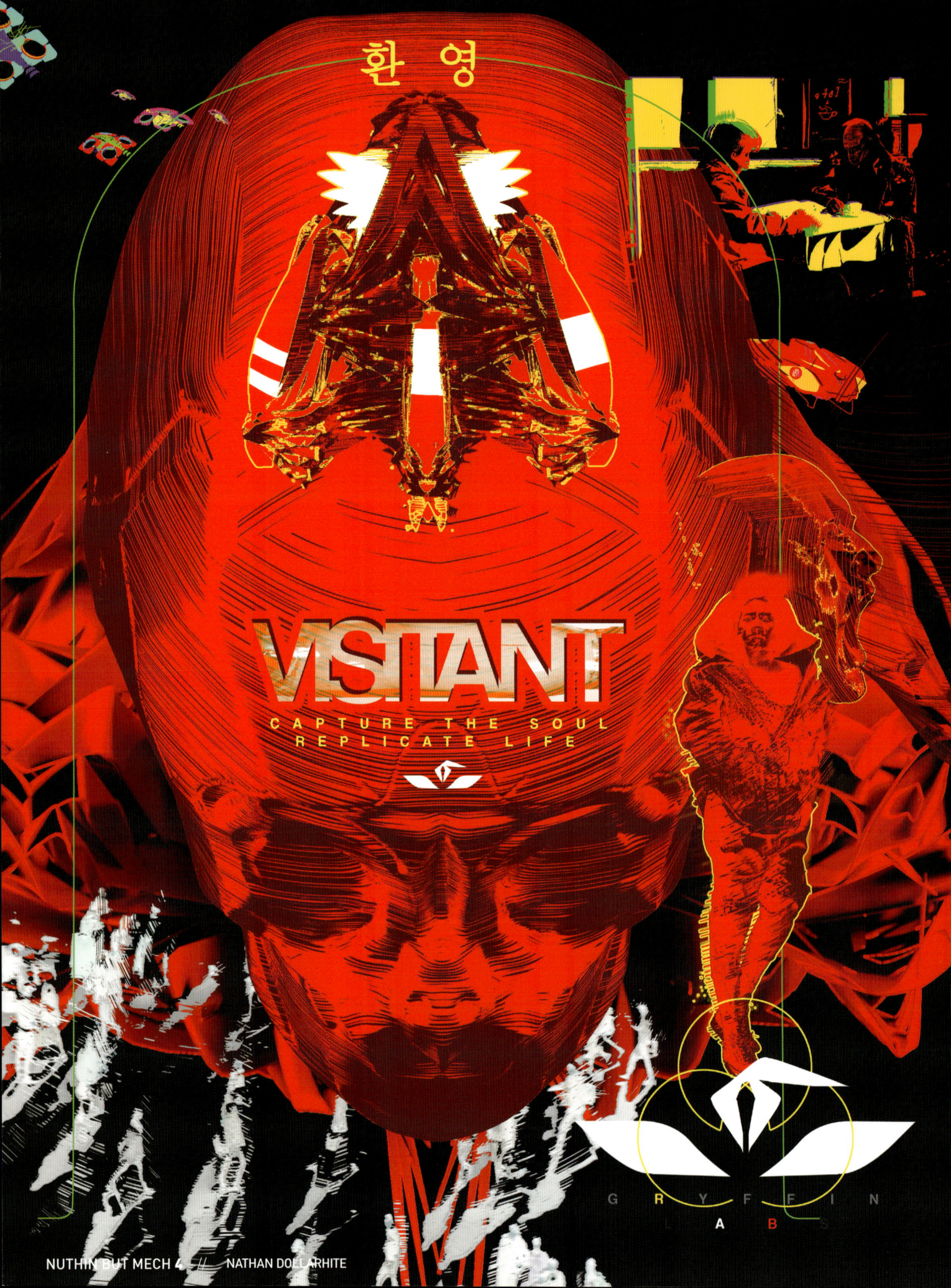

환영

VISTANT

CAPTURE THE SOUL
REPLICATE LIFE

GRYFFIN
LABS

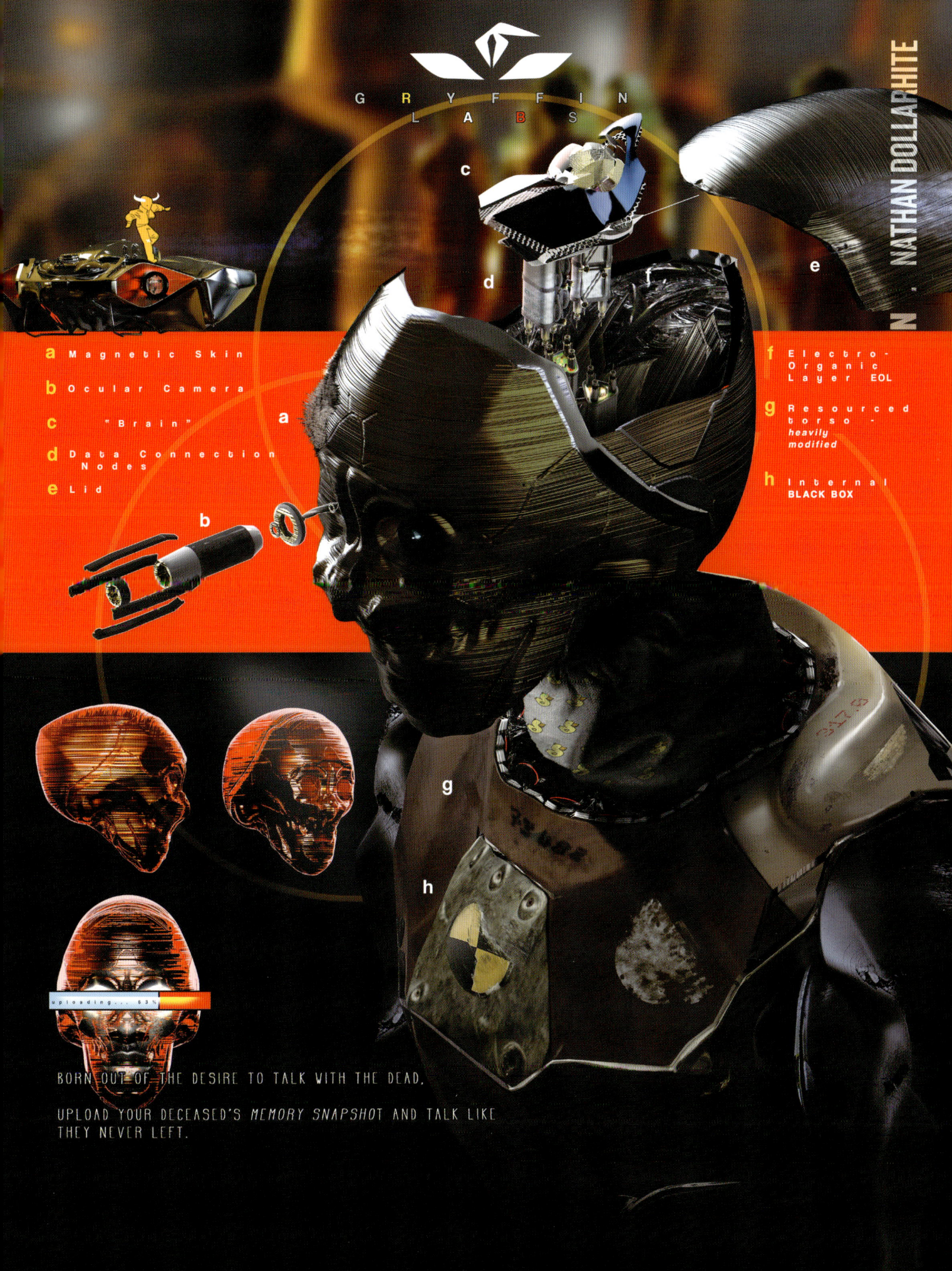

GRYFFIN
LABS

c

d   f   e

a Magnetic Skin

b Ocular Camera

c "Brain"

d Data Connection Nodes

e Lid

a

b

f Electro-Organic Layer EOL

g Resourced torso - *heavily modified*

h Internal BLACK BOX

g

h

uploading... 63%

BORN OUT OF THE DESIRE TO TALK WITH THE DEAD.

UPLOAD YOUR DECEASED'S *MEMORY SNAPSHOT* AND TALK LIKE THEY NEVER LEFT.

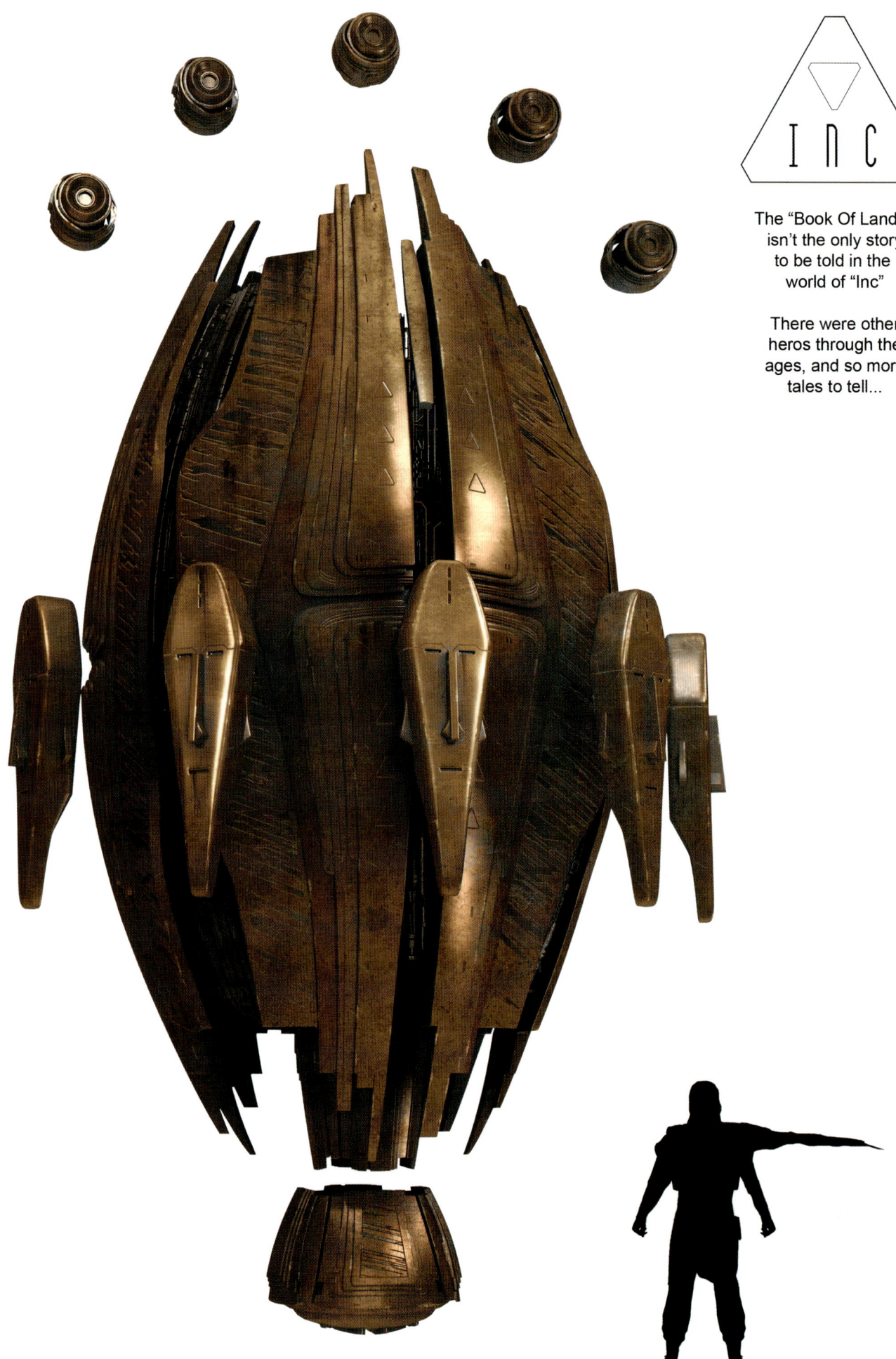

INC

The "Book Of Landis" isn't the only story to be told in the world of "Inc"

There were other heros through the ages, and so more tales to tell...

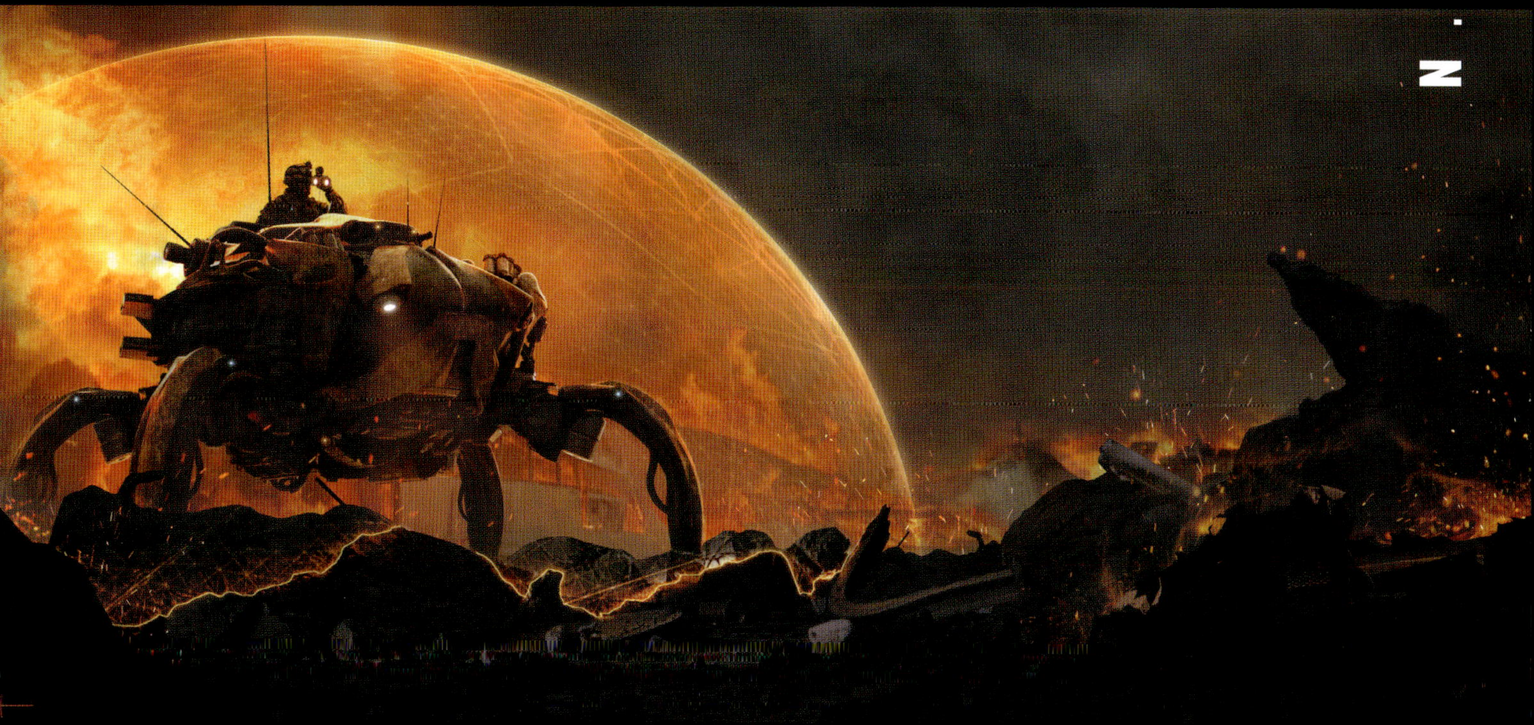

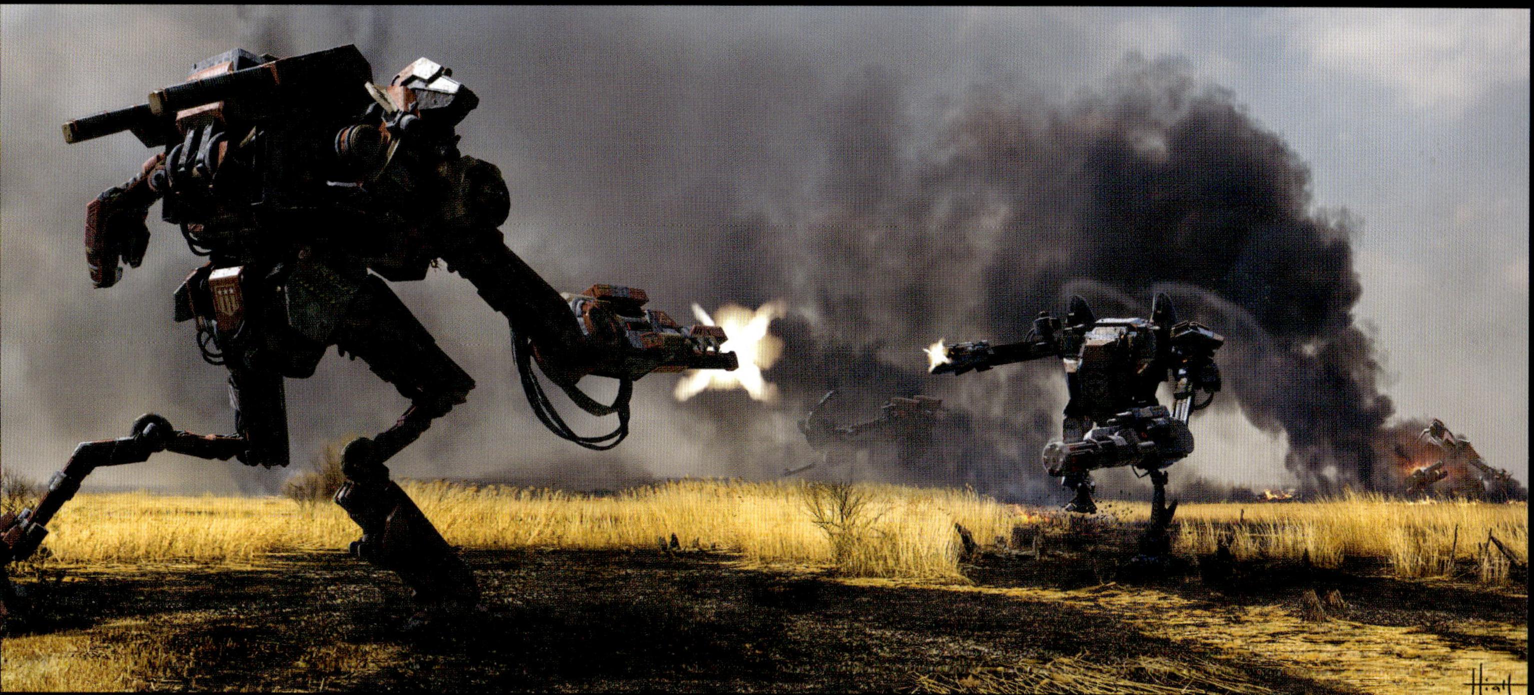

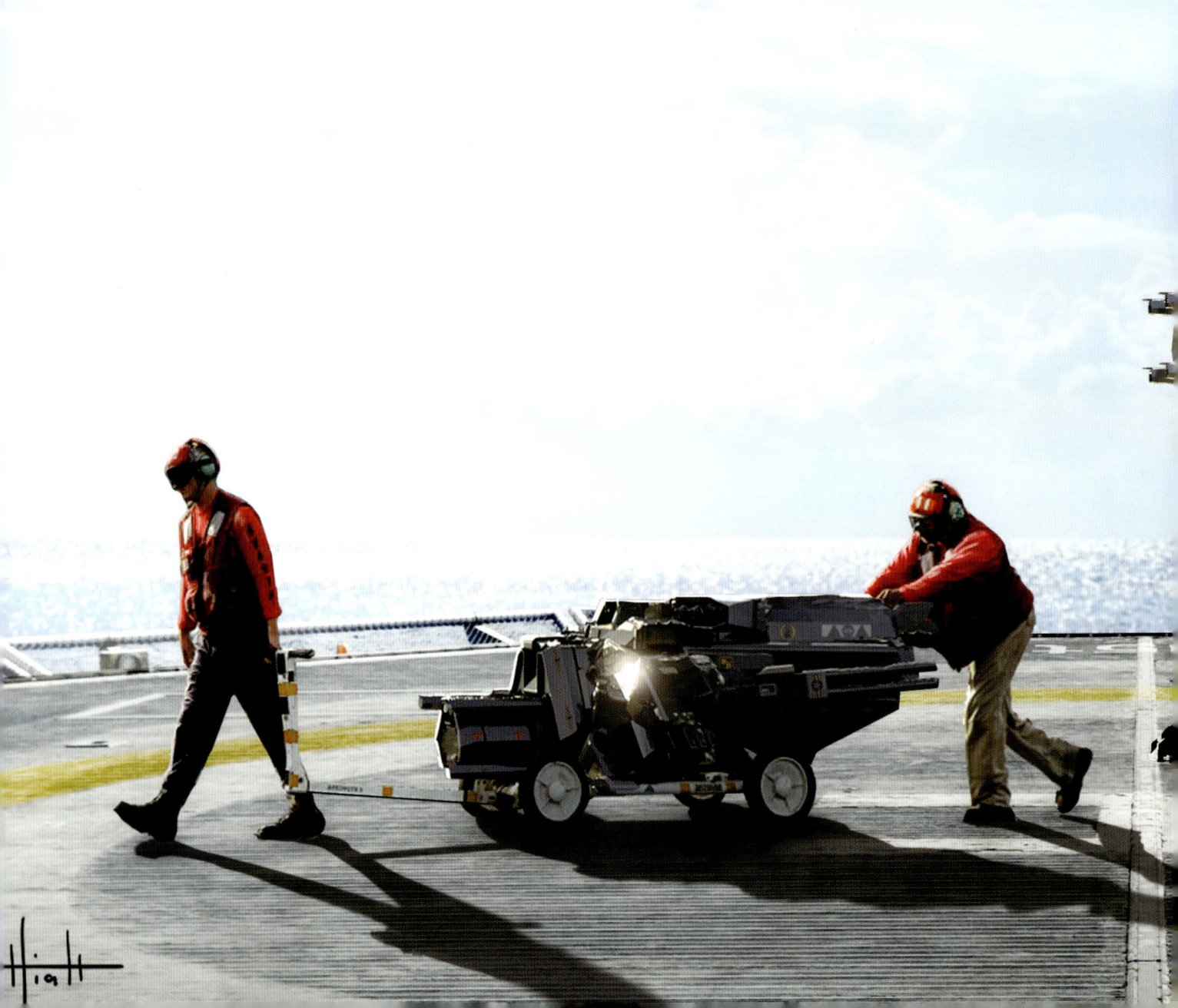

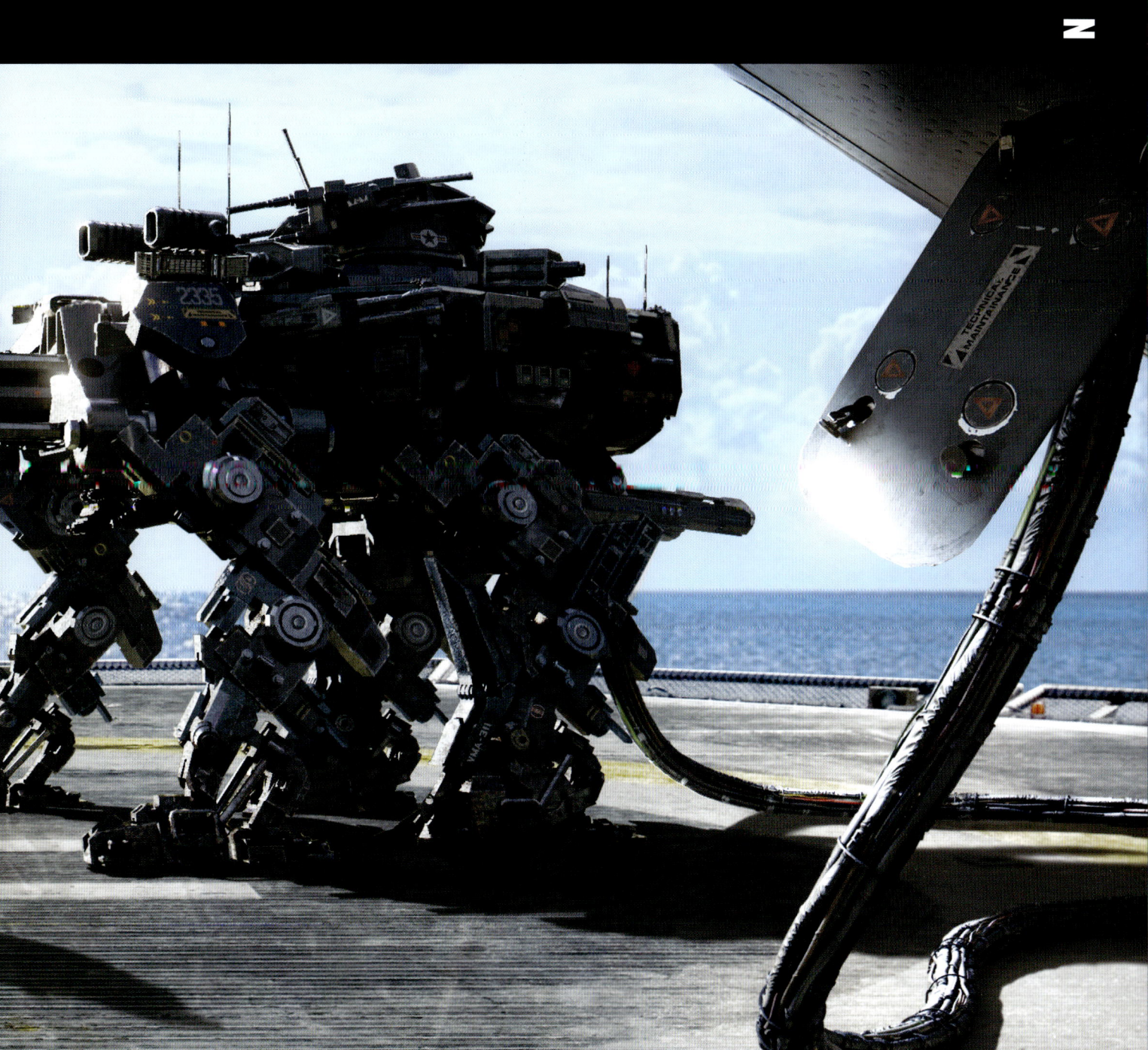

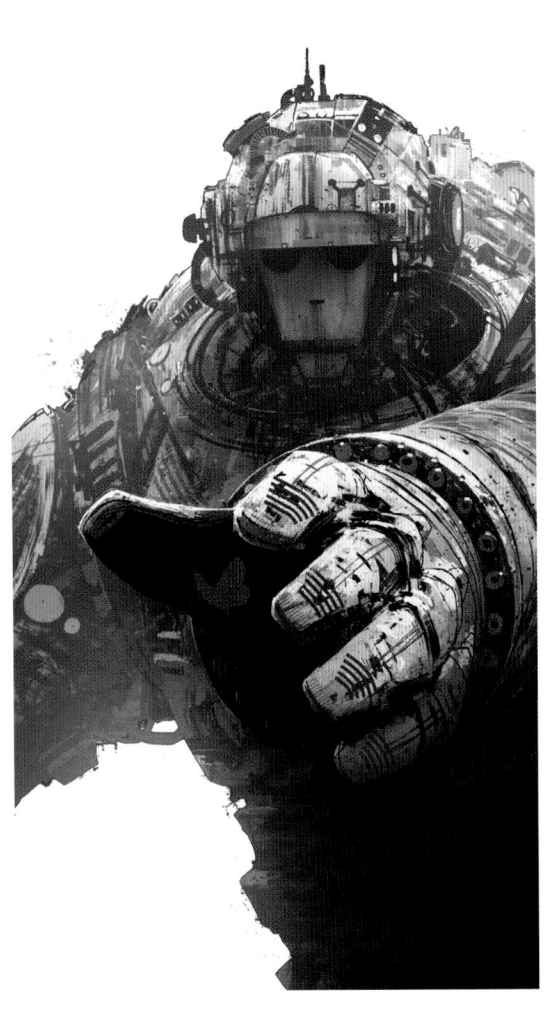

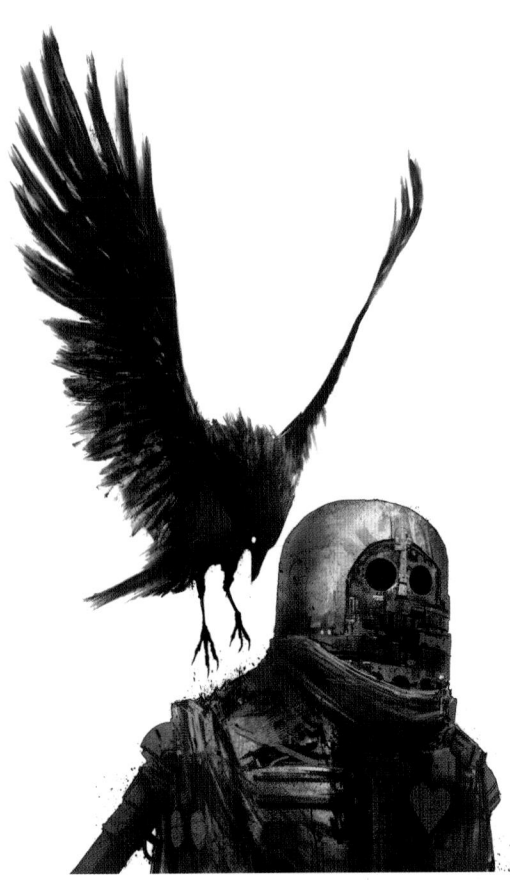

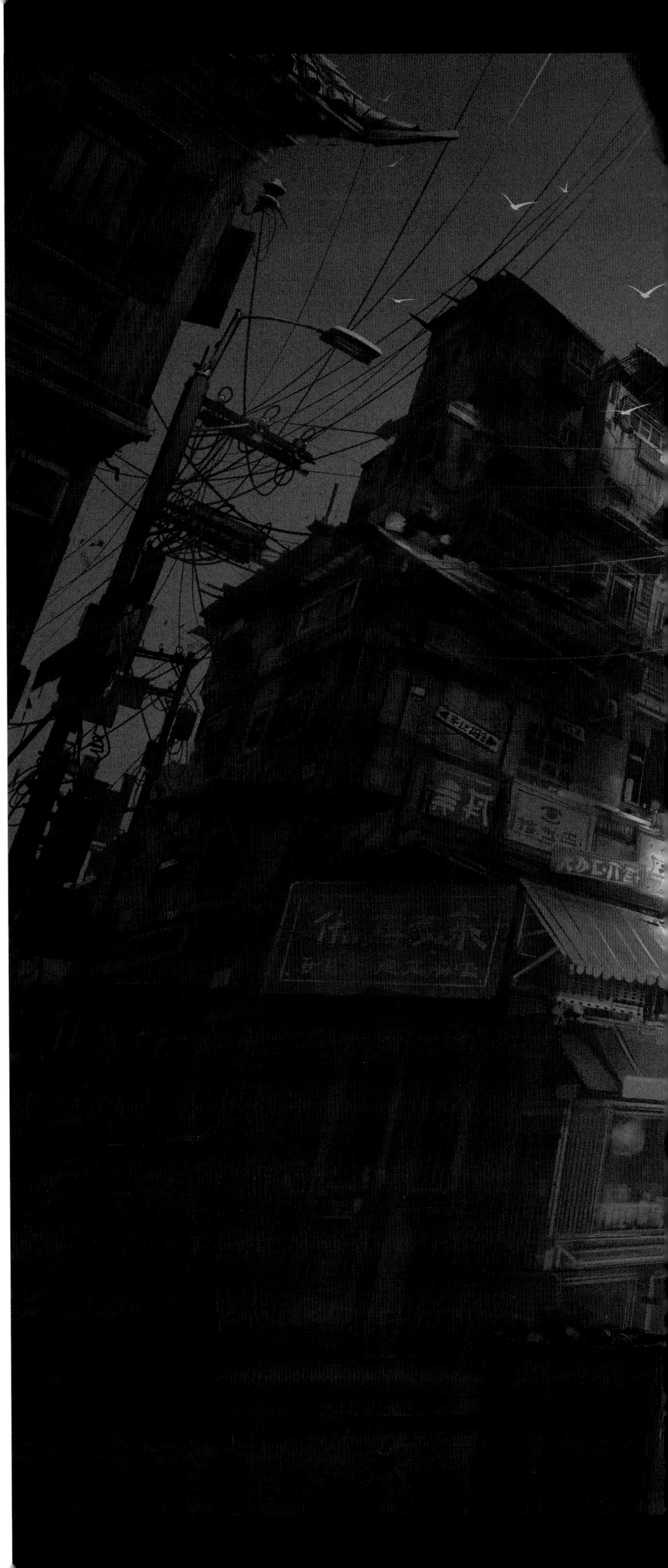

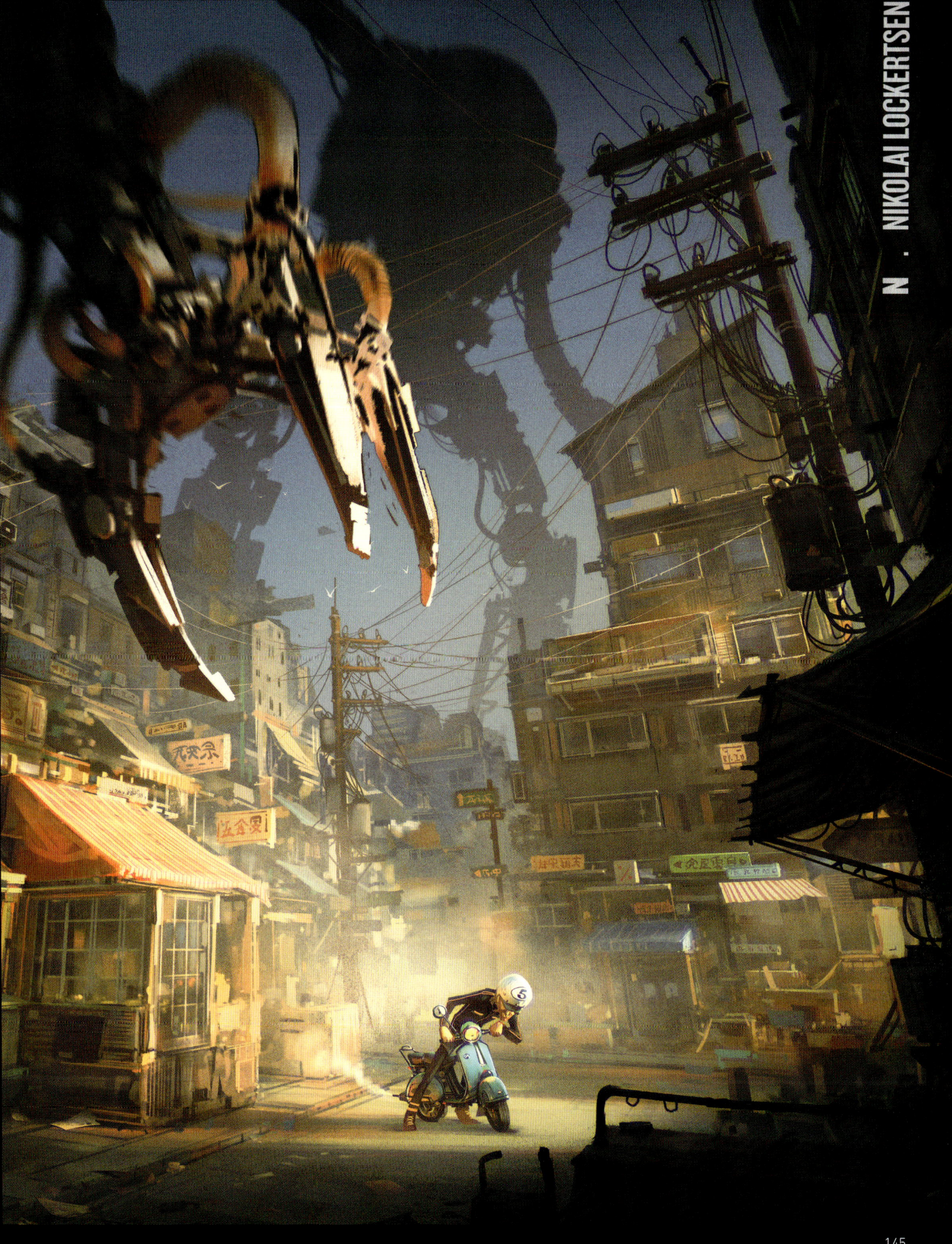

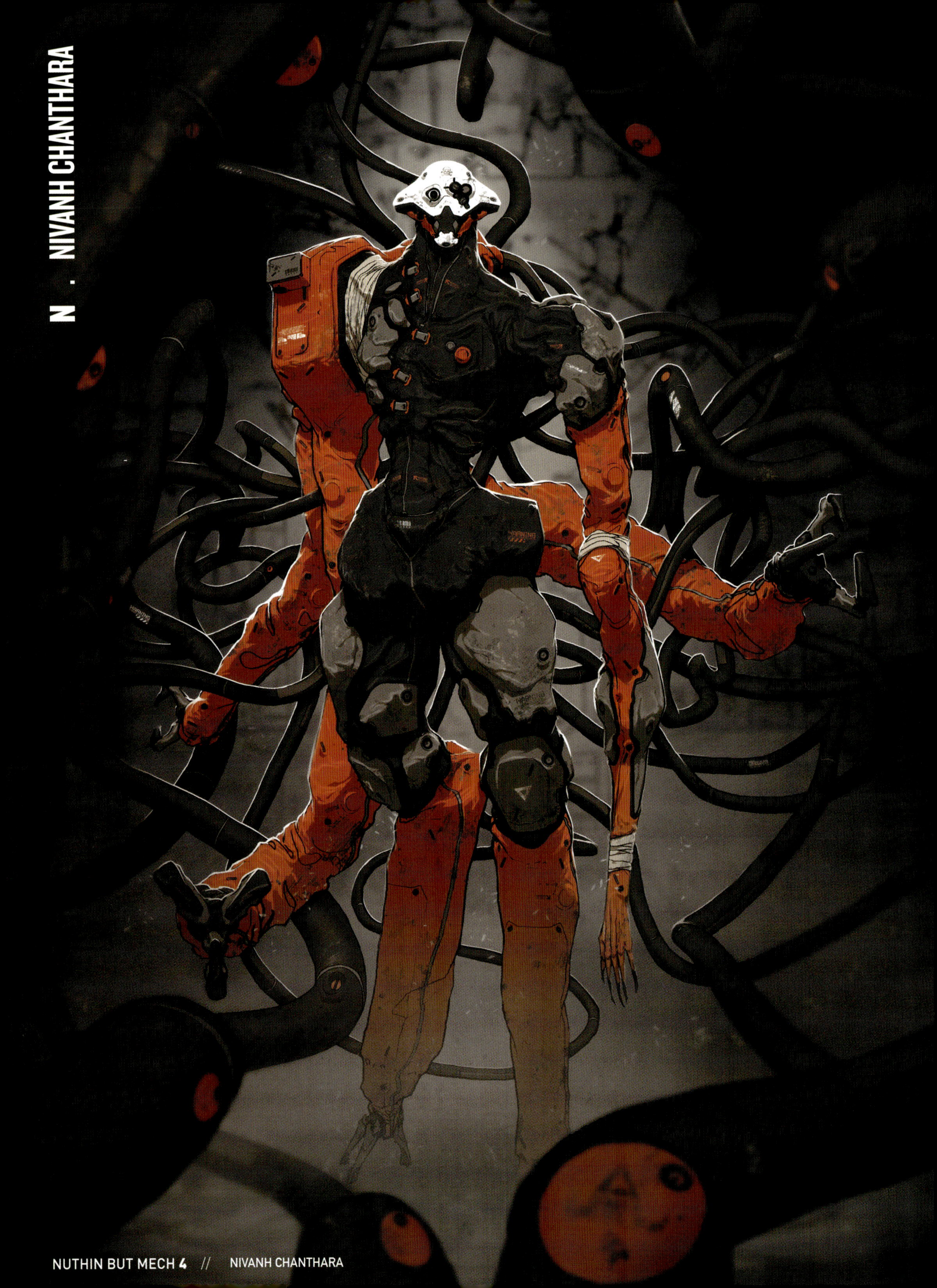

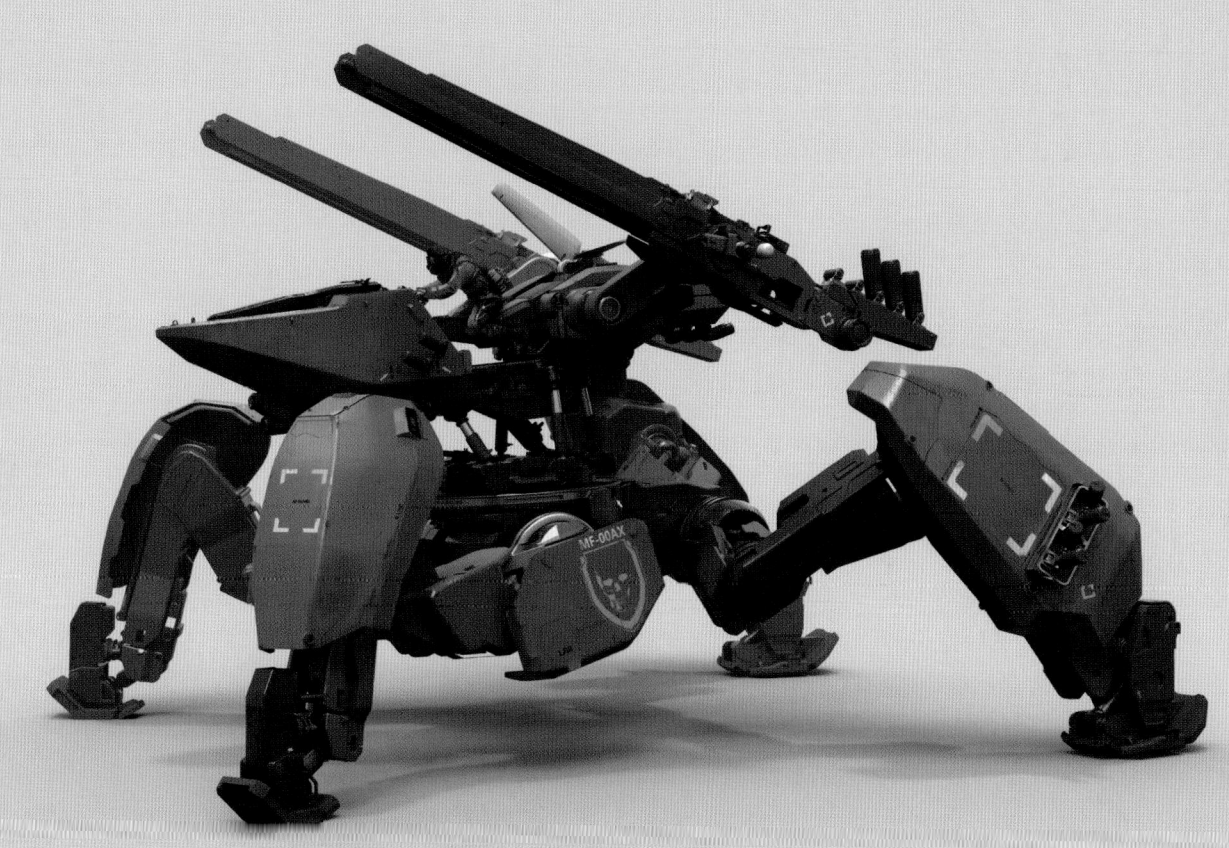

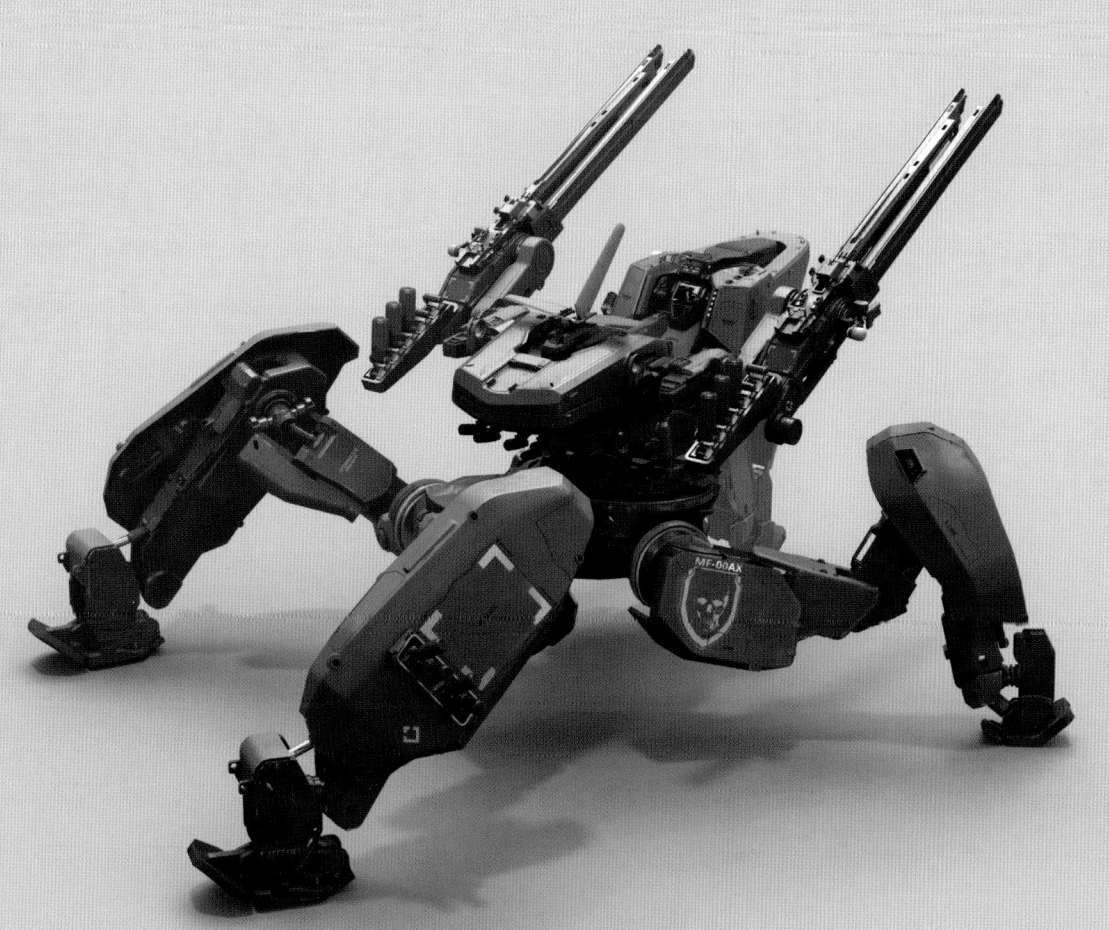

METAL FOX

PATRICK HANENBERGER

Patrick was born in Melbourne, Australia, and raised in Wiesbaden, Germany. He earned a BA in industrial and graphic design at the University of Michigan and a BS in transportation design at ArtCenter College of Design in Pasadena. Patrick works as a production designer in the animation industry, a concept artist for live-action film, and a visual consultant for the gaming industry. In addition, he is a part-time instructor for visual communication at ArtCenter. Together with Margaret Wuller, Patrick is the founder of The Neuland, an international design consultancy. Some of their recent clients include Warner Bros., Google, IDEO, Paramount, and Legendary.
www.patrickhanenberger.com

PAT PRESLEY

Pat was born in the oldest part of Bangkok, Thailand, the Rattanakosin Island. He grew up in what he believed to be a haunted house full of snakes, trees, and ancient relics his granduncle collected. Besides attending an old French missionary school, Pat learned from watching. When it was the time to further his education, he was hoping to become a doctor just to make a lot of money, but then decided he best be an idealistic architect. Neither one panned out, so Pat stopped making plans and relearned everything from scratch. He went back to drawing late into the night and remembered how great it was to be a kid who gets to stay up way past his bedtime. Although some people wonder about his age, he was old enough to see *Star Wars* in the theater.
www.phattro.com

PATRICK O'KEEFE

Patrick is a Canadian illustrator based in Los Angeles working in the entertainment industry. He is currently a visual-development artist for Sony Pictures. Previously, Patrick worked with Disney TV on the animated show *Big Hero 6* and worked as a senior concept artist at Entertainment Arts Visceral Games on acclaimed franchises, such as *Star Wars*, *Need for Speed*, *Dead Space*, and *Battlefield*. In addition, he develops work for a variety of productions, primarily for stop-motion and CGI animation in the advertising industry. Between work hours, Patrick creates personal artwork to exhibit in galleries and online. His love for art comes from his grandmother, a traditional figure painter, and his older brother, a graffiti artist and graphic designer. Patrick studied visual arts at Northern Secondary School in Toronto before entering the Illustration program at Sheridan College in Oakville, Ontario. After two years of study, he followed the other love of his life west to Vancouver, British Columbia, where he resumed his studies in film design for live action and animation at the Emily Carr institute.
www.theOKartist.com

PETE NORRIS

Pete is a sci-fi artist and futurist from London, United Kingdom. His father, a former art teacher, taught him technical drawing, along with painting and sculpting, at a very young age; and he also fueled Pete's obsession with vehicles and all things art and design. After studying fine art, Pete went on to receive a degree in automotive design at Coventry University in 2000.

Preferring to spend his time in a fantasy world rather than the real one, working as a sci-fi artist seemed to be the most appealing and logical next step; and since graduating, Pete has worked as a video game artist, specializing in vehicles and weapons, and producing work for clients including Free Radical Design, Sony PlayStation, Microsoft, and Creative Assembly, and on such franchises as *Alien* and *Star Wars*. Most recently he designed many of the vehicles in *Halo Wars 2*. Pete has also created work for Nissan, Fiat, and Shell, and has branched out into album covers, product design, and branding on the side to mix things up.
www.behance.net/pjn

PROG WANG

Prog Wang is a concept artist based in Los Angeles, where he currently works at Respawn Entertainment.
www.artstation.com/artist/progwang

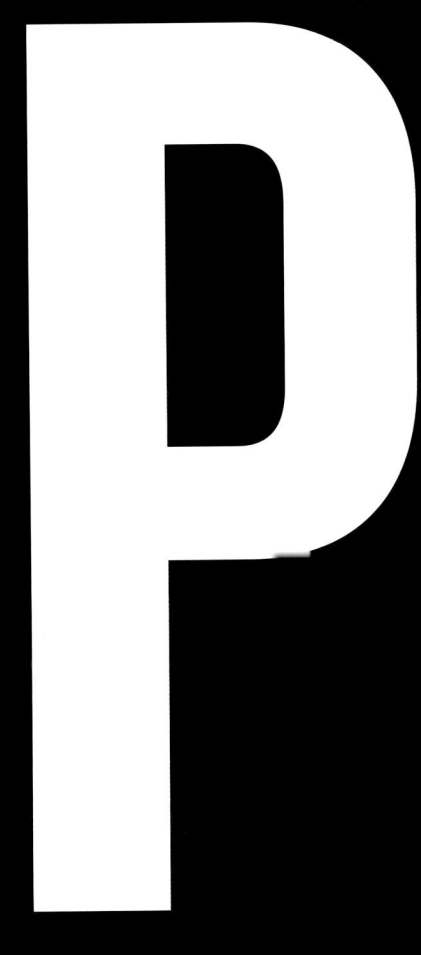

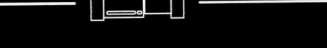

Patrick Hanenberger

Pat Presley

Patrick O'Keefe

Pete Norris

Prog Wang

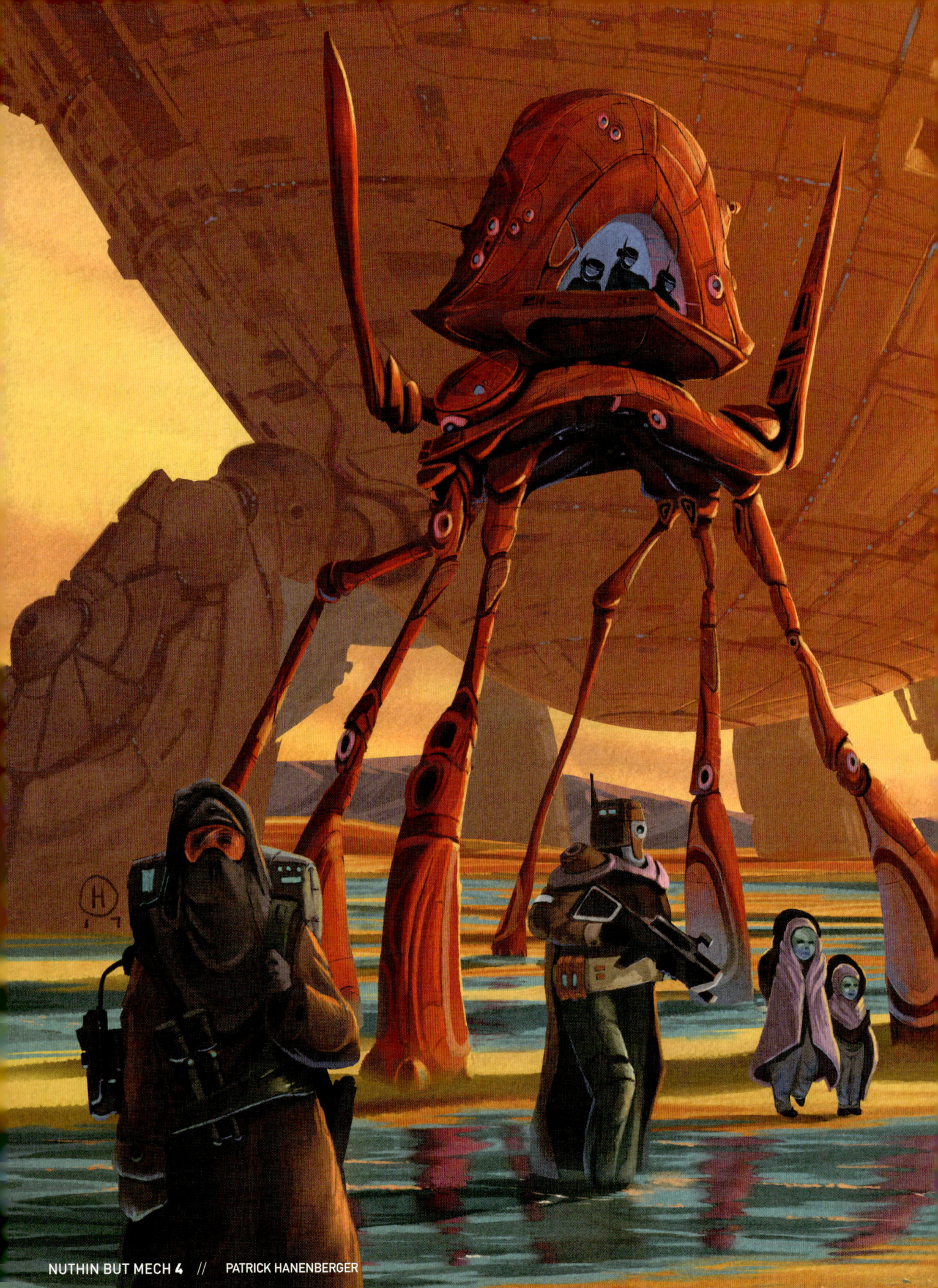

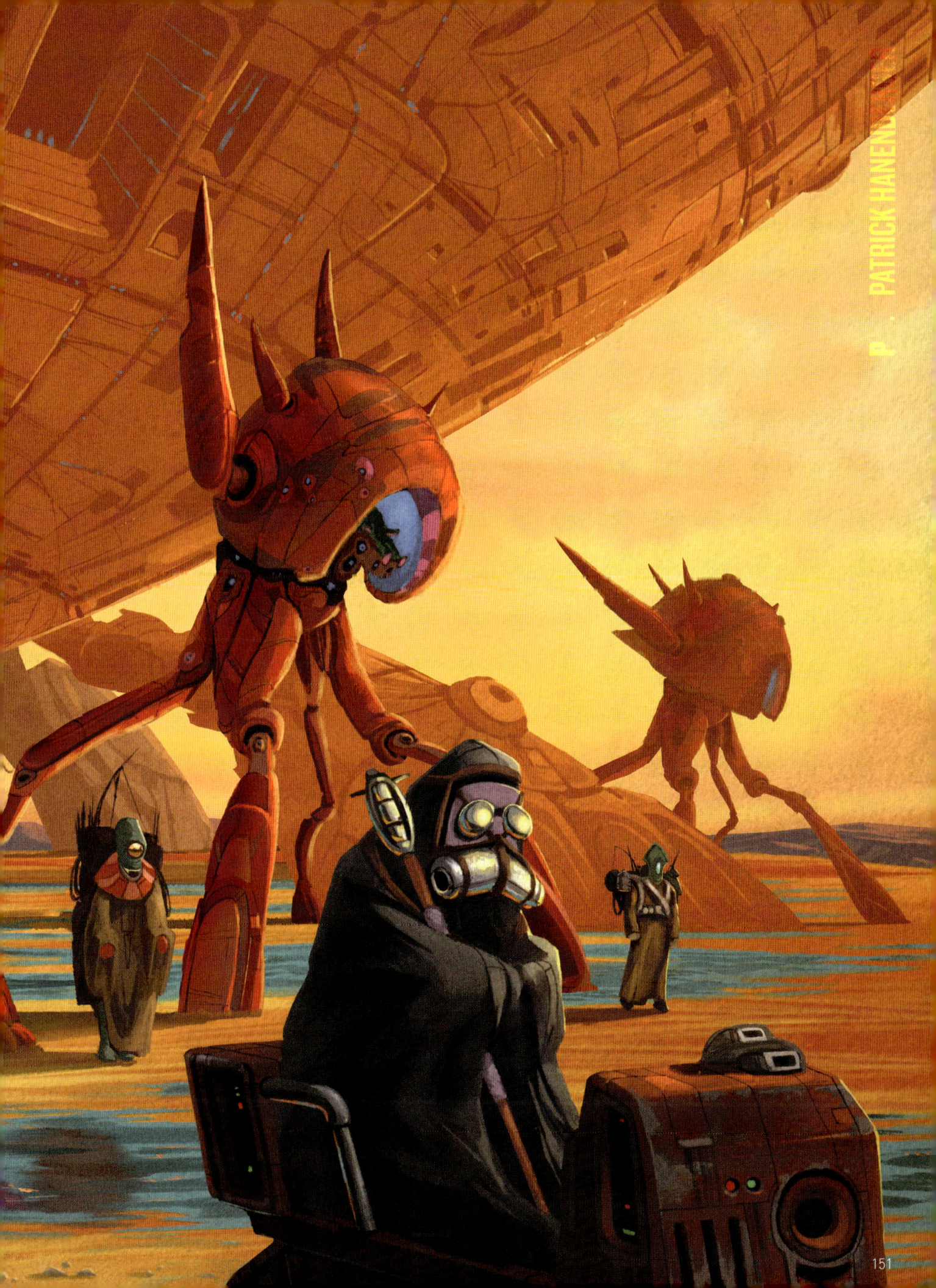

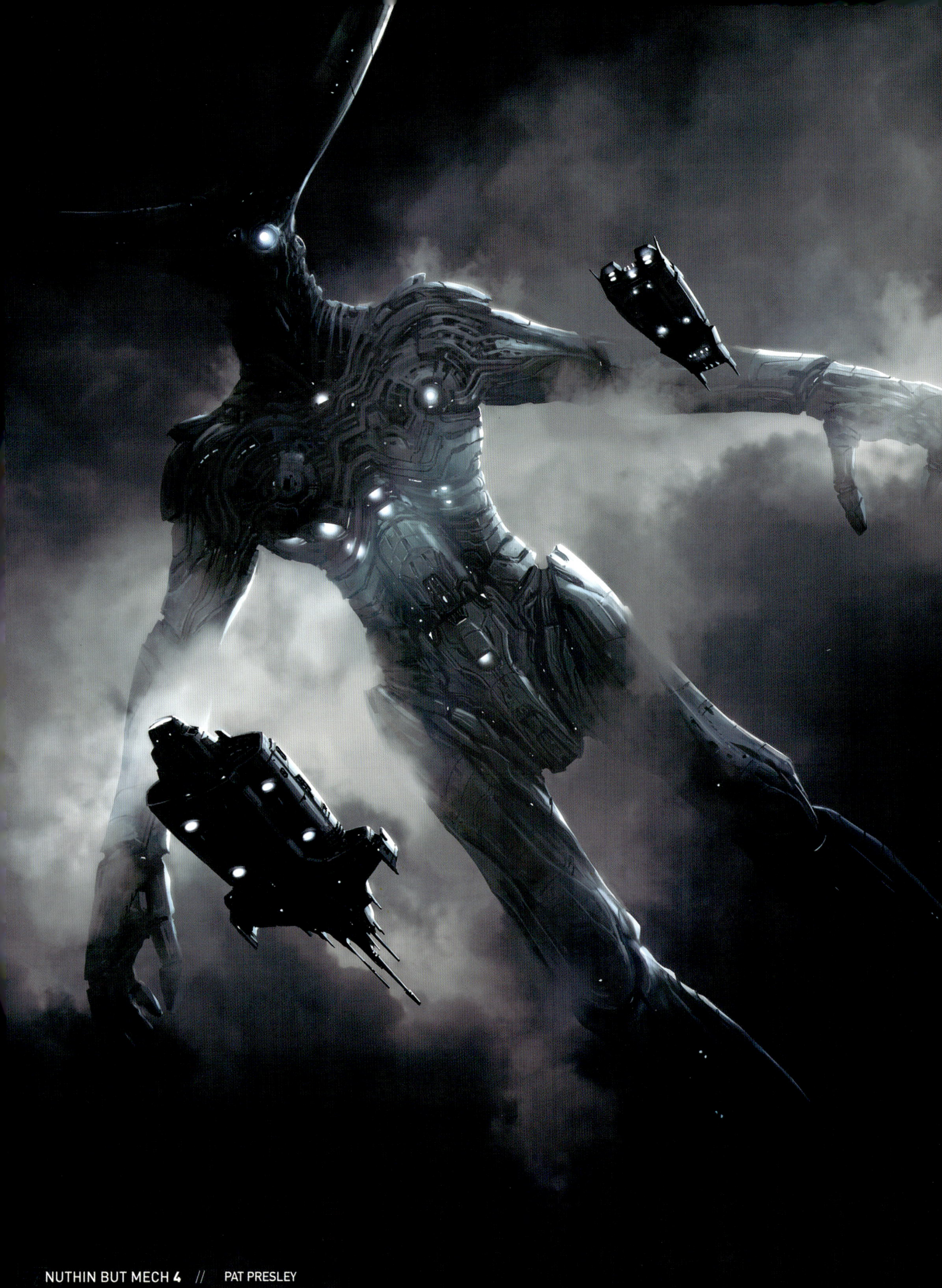

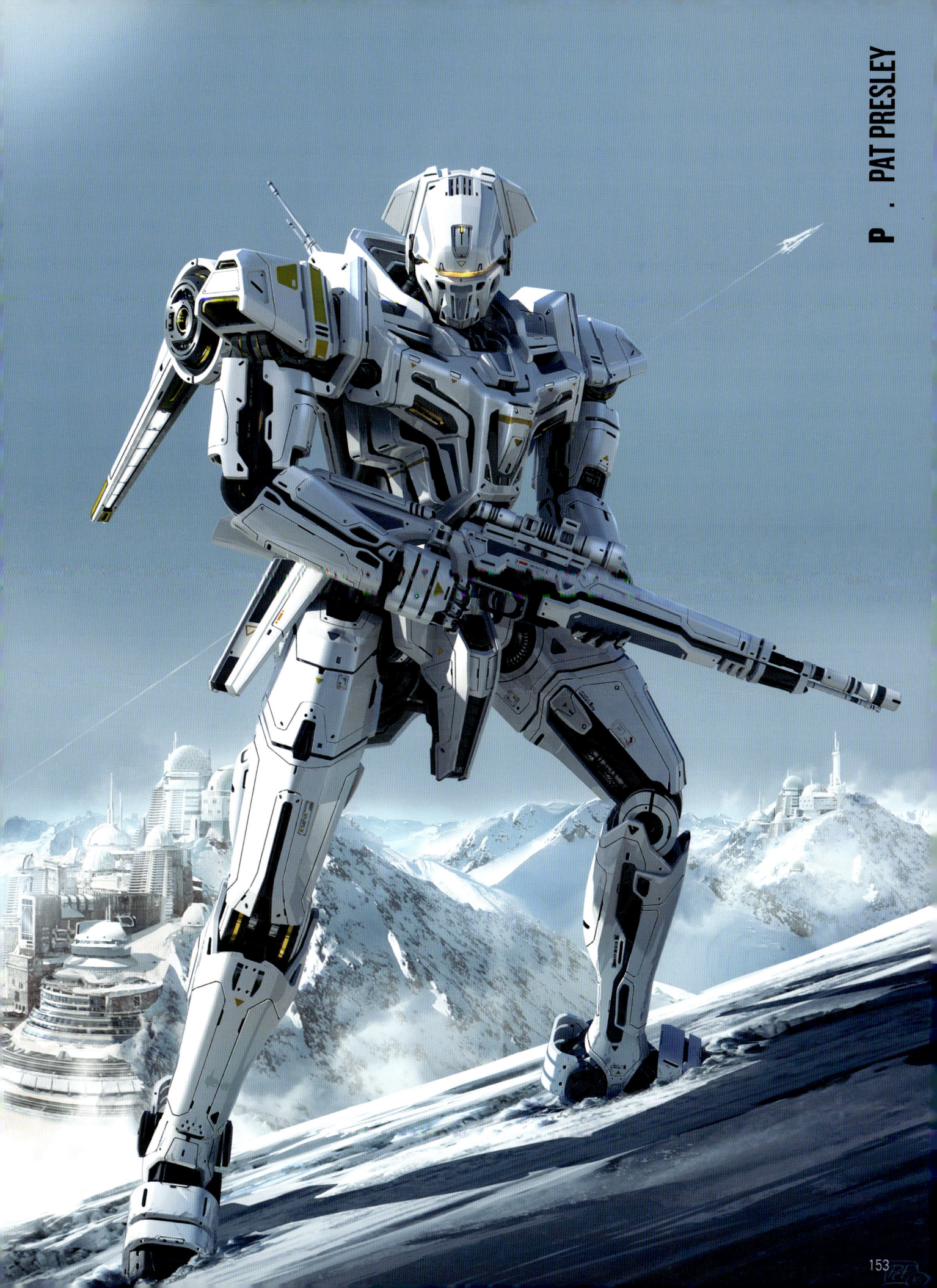

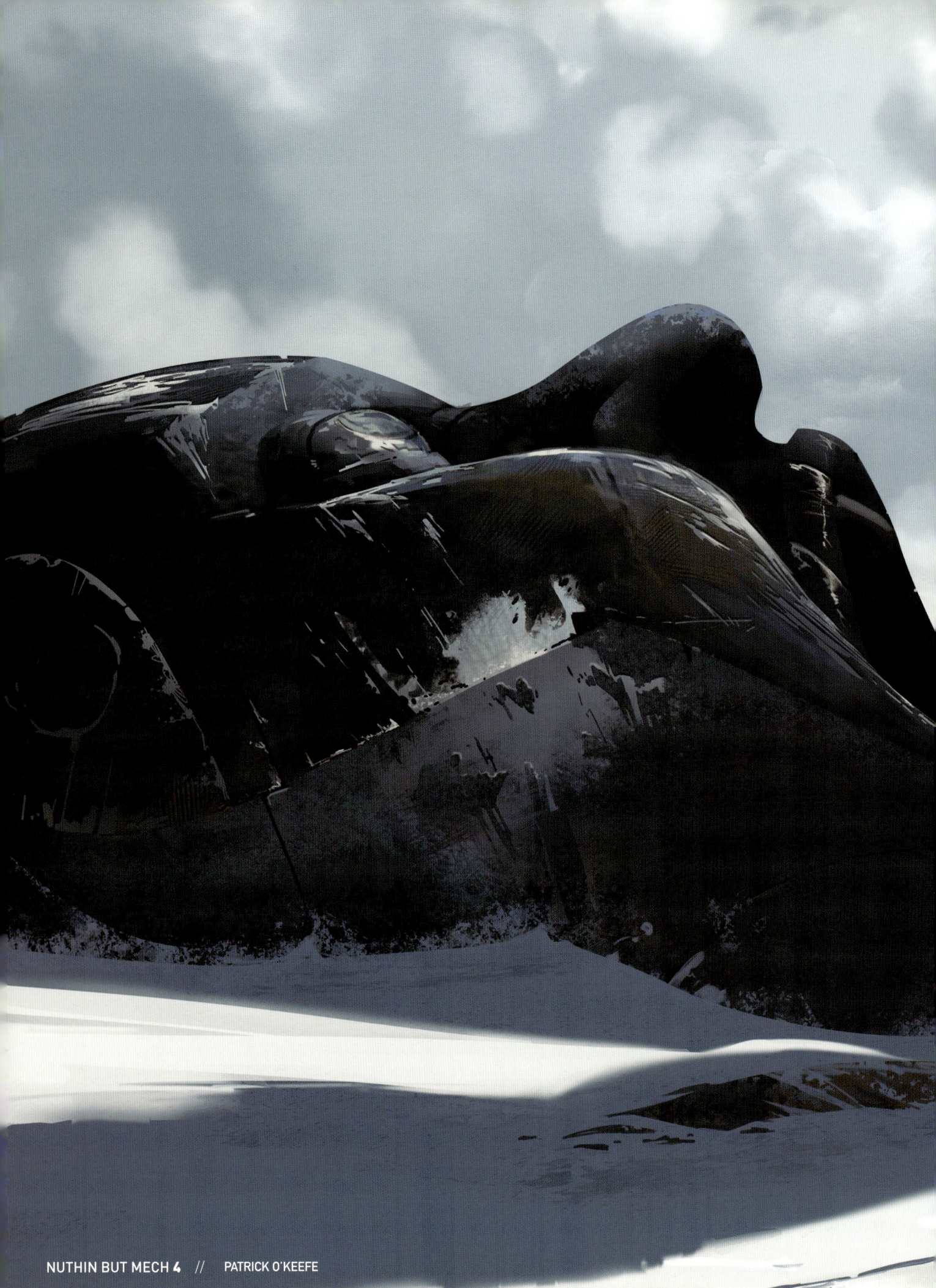

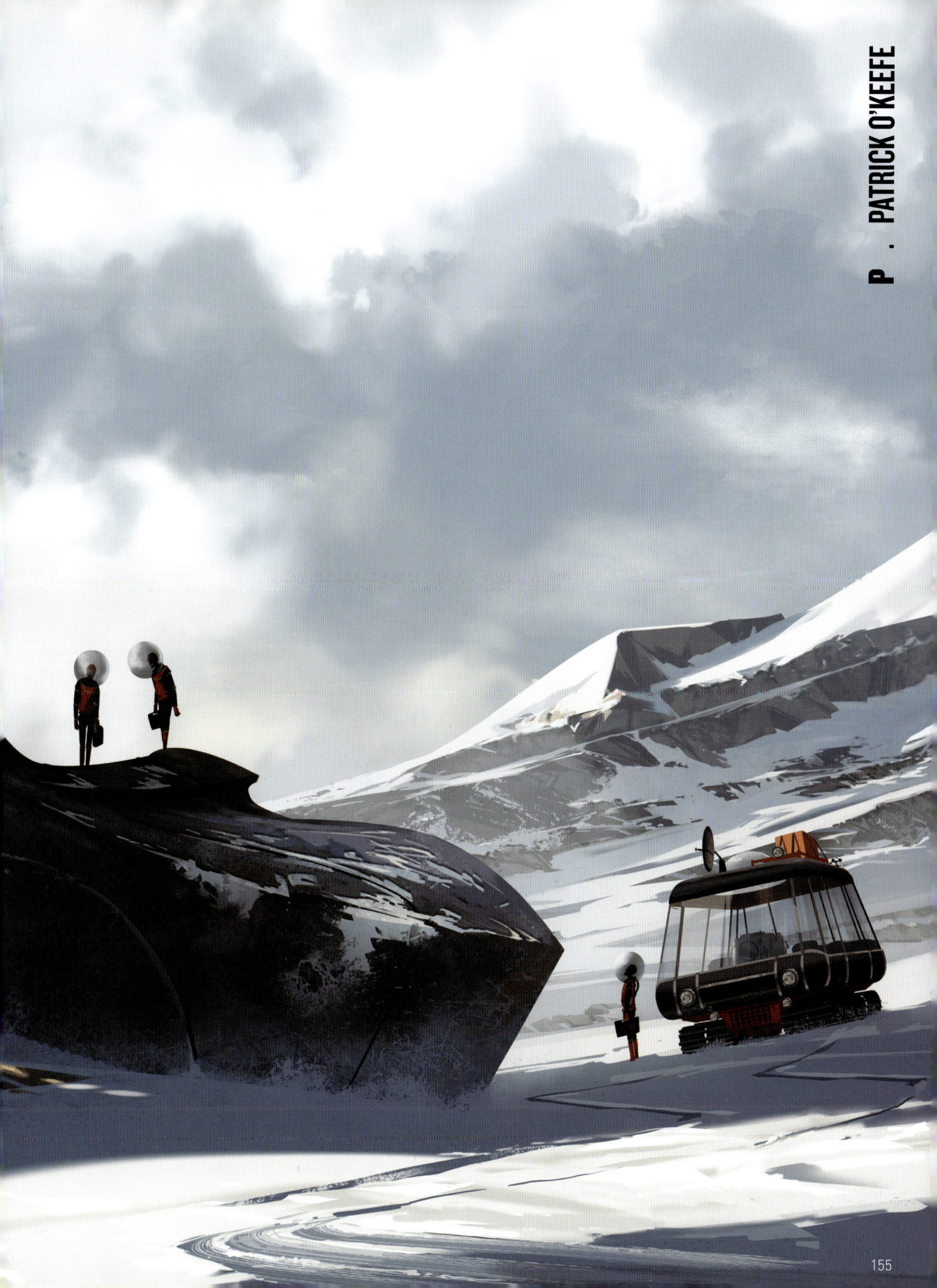

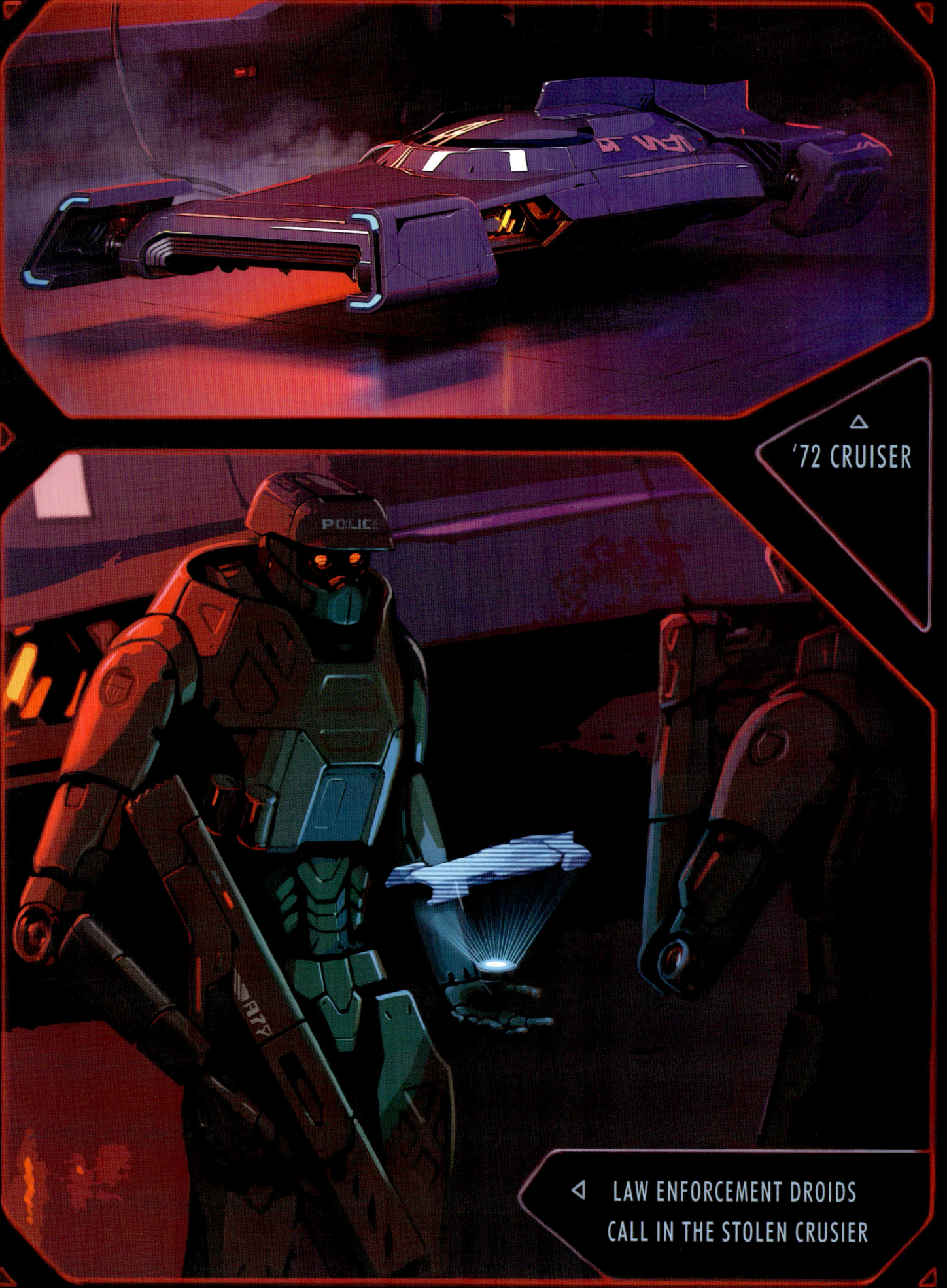

'72 CRUISER

LAW ENFORCEMENT DROIDS
CALL IN THE STOLEN CRUSIER

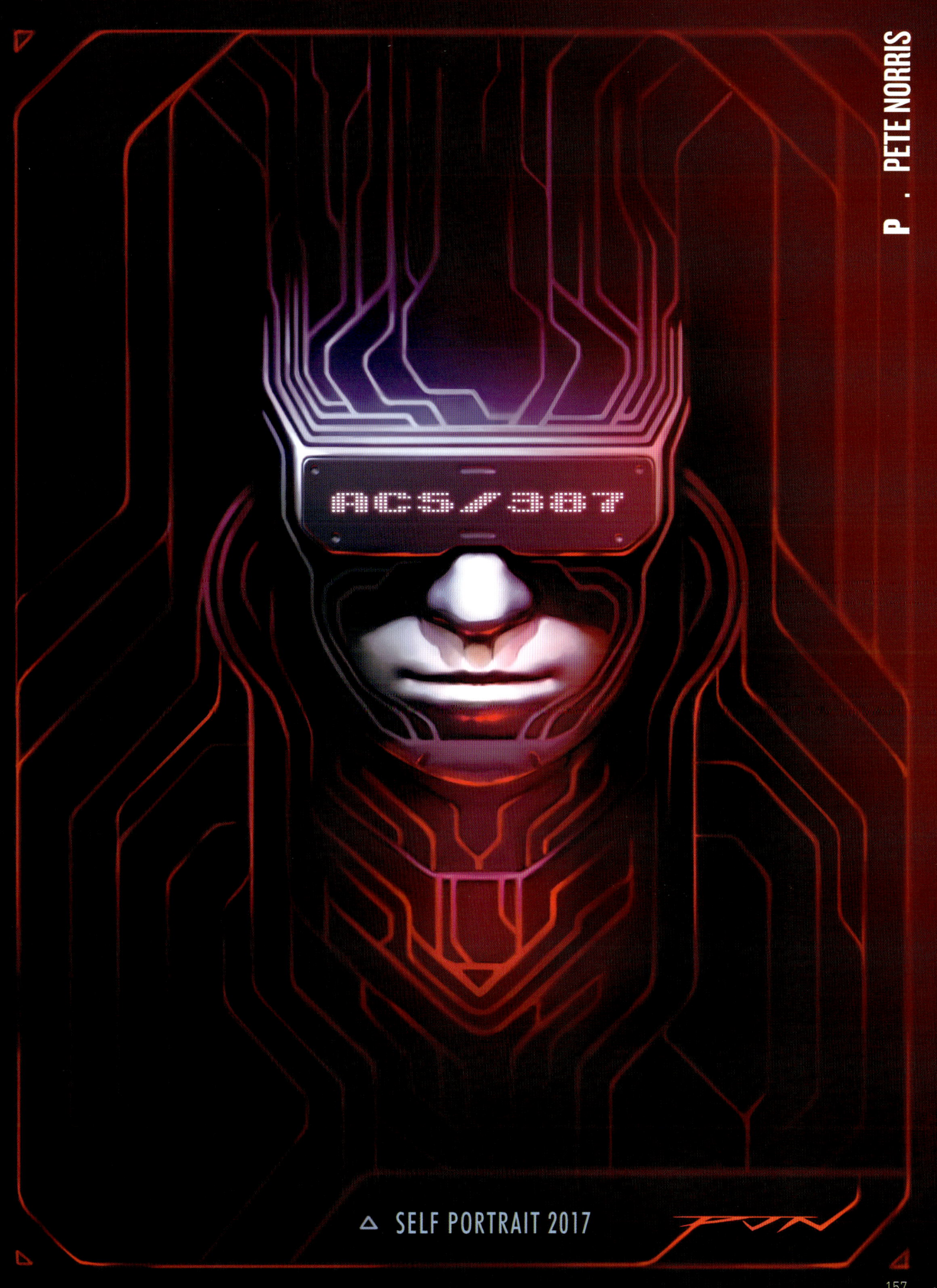

△ SELF PORTRAIT 2017

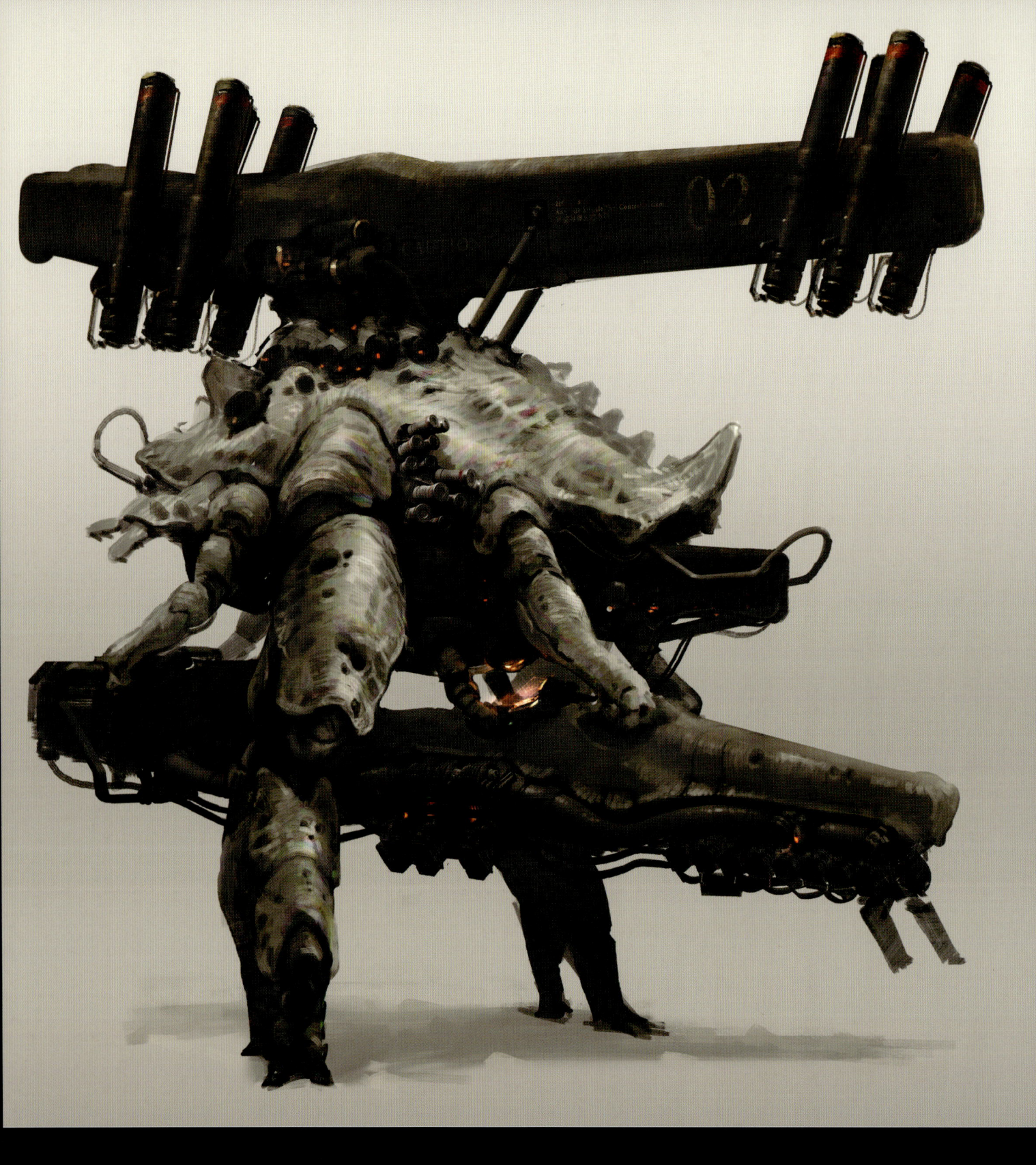

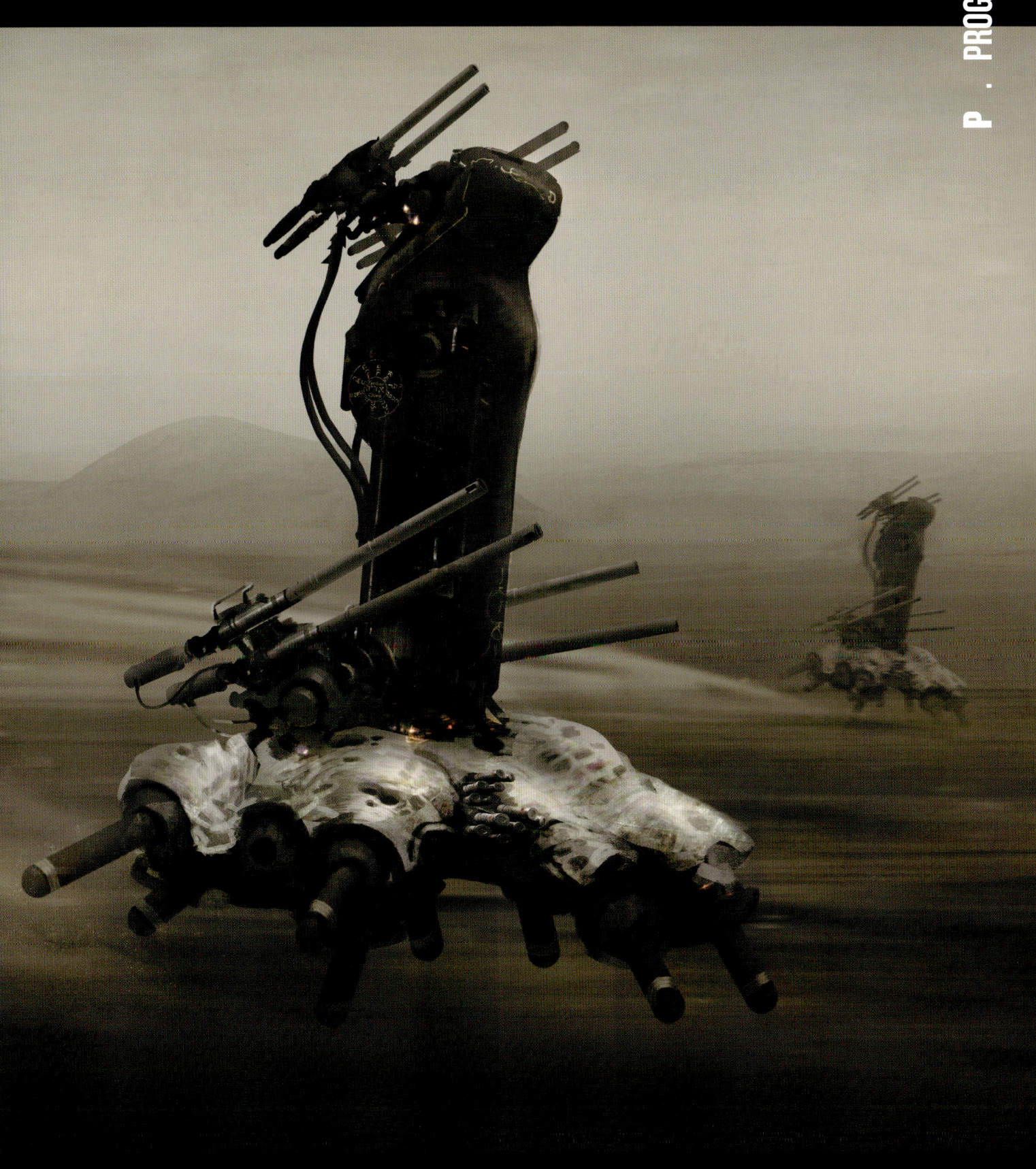

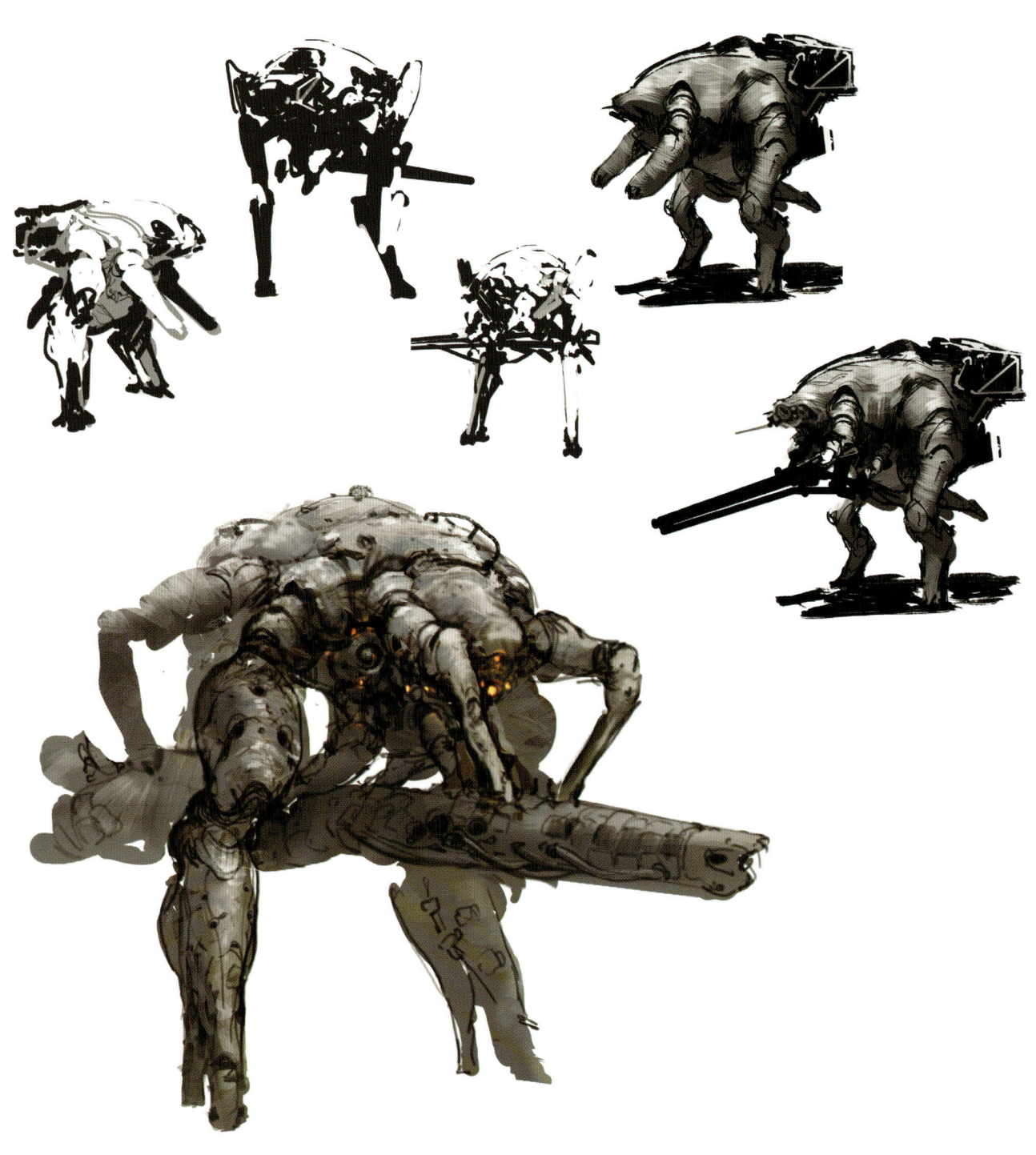

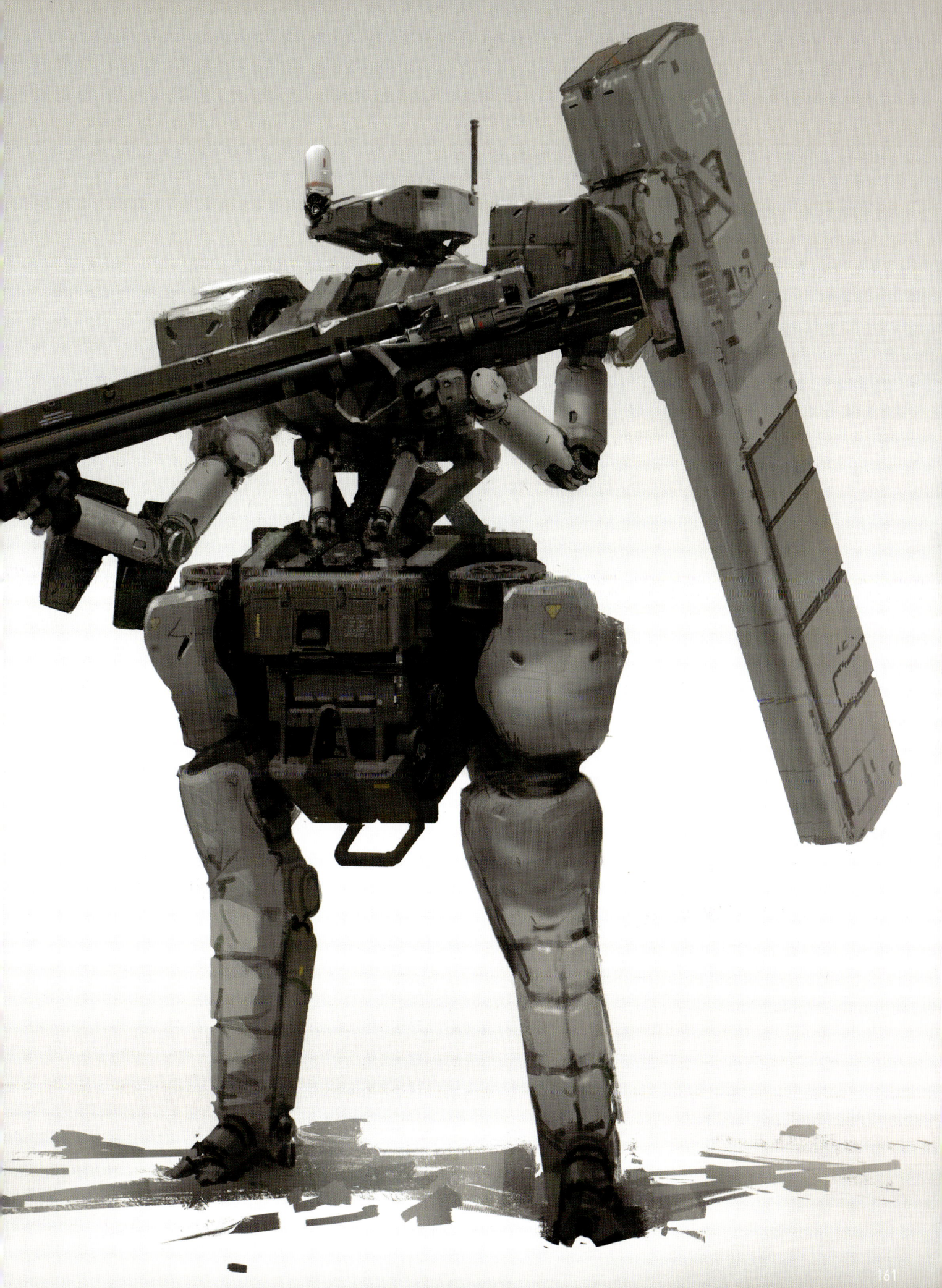

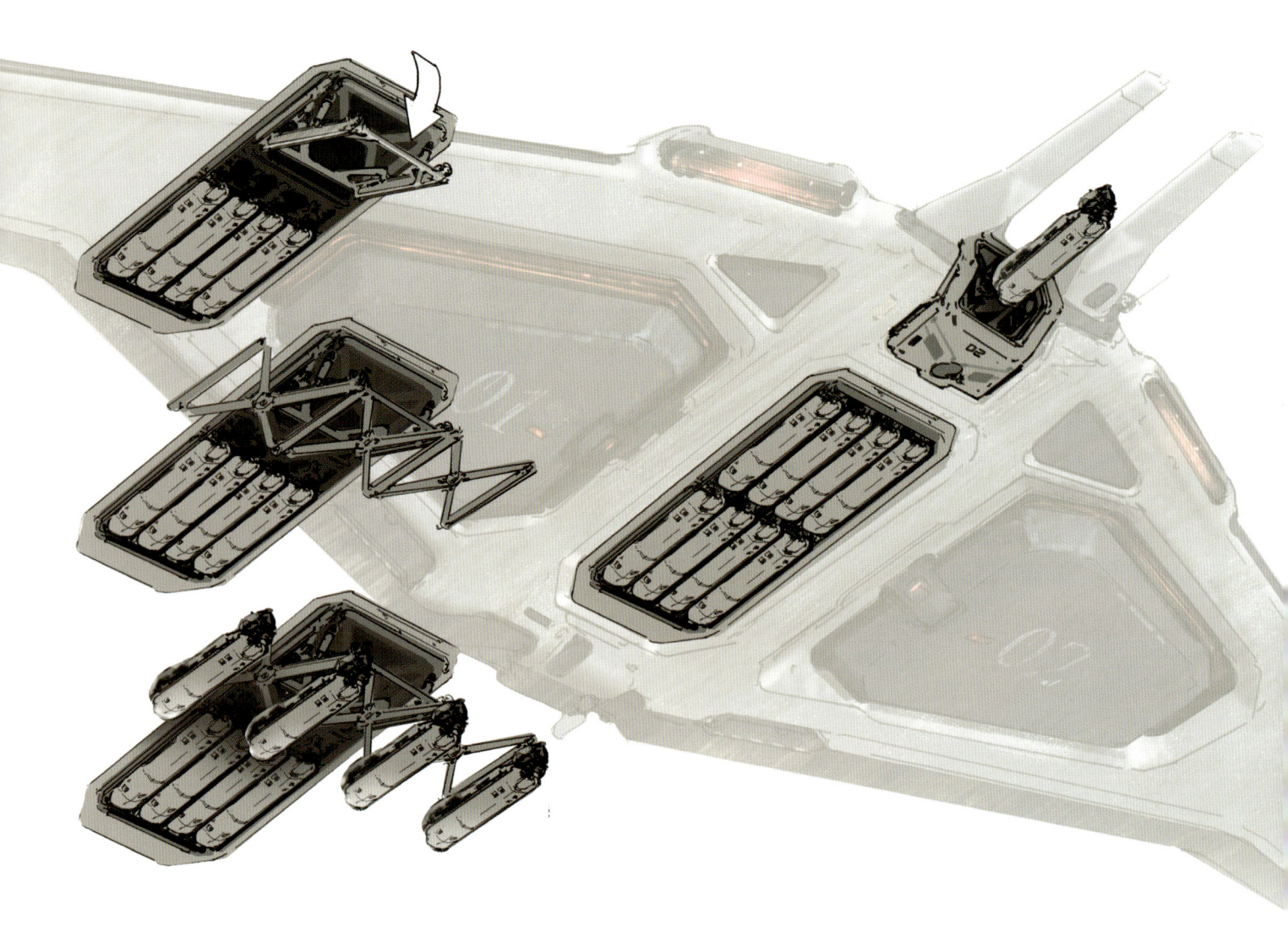

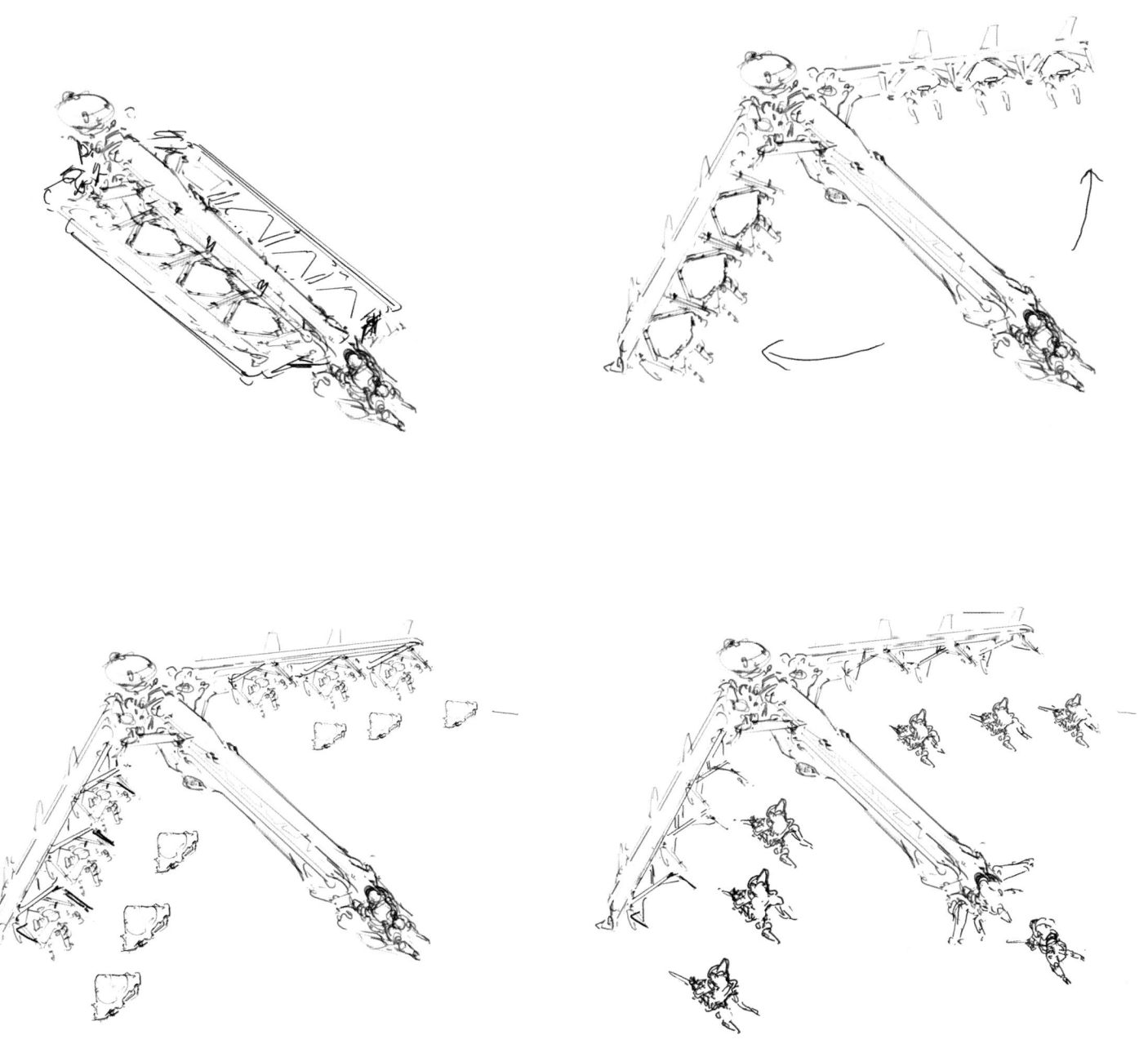

ROBERT CHEW

Robert is a concept artist at Gearbox Software in Frisco, Texas. Drawing and painting have been a longtime passion of his that he's been lucky enough to turn into a career. Mechs and sci-fi have always been a go-to subject that will never get old to Robert. The relationship between man, machine, and the natural world is fascinating to him, and he enjoys exploring how each of those can blend together to form new and exciting ideas and worlds.

www.artstation.com/artist/robertchew

SAM BROWN

Sam Brown is a concept artist with an industrial design background. He formerly worked for Massive Black and is currently working at 343 Industries.

www.sambrown36.tumblr.com

SOREN BENDT

Soren is the art director of IO Entertainment. Based on the Pinewood Studios lot in the United Kingdom, he produces a broad range of work, from storyboards to concept art and previs. His credits include *The Mummy, Robin Hood, Spectre, In the Heart of the Sea, Transcendence, Thor: The Dark World, Captain Phillips, The Dark Knight Rises, John Carter, The Chronicles of Narnia: The Voyage of the Dawn Treader, Harry Potter and the Deathly Hallows: Part 1, Harry Potter and the Deathly Hallows: Part 2,* and *Prince of Persia: The Sands of Time.*

www.artofsorenbendt.com

STEVE TALKOWSKI

A 20-plus-year veteran of the computer animation scene, Steve has worked as an animation director and character animator on hundreds of national brands, ranging from BMW, Pepsi, and General Mills to Target, Reese's, and M&M's, as well as the groundbreaking feature films *Joe's Apartment, Ice Age, Alien: Resurrection,* and the 1999 Academy Award-winning short, *Bunny.* He also served as art director for The Jim Henson Company's animated series Word Party, now streaming on Netflix.

In 2008, Steve launched Sketchbot Studios and self-produced his first foray into the designer toy scene: the retro-style, pencil-wielding, creative robot, Sketchbot. In 2010, the Sketchbot platform served as the basis for two highly successful DIY shows held in New York City and Los Angeles.

Residing in Los Angeles, Steve is currently in development on an animated TV series based on his robot designs.

www.sketchbot.tv

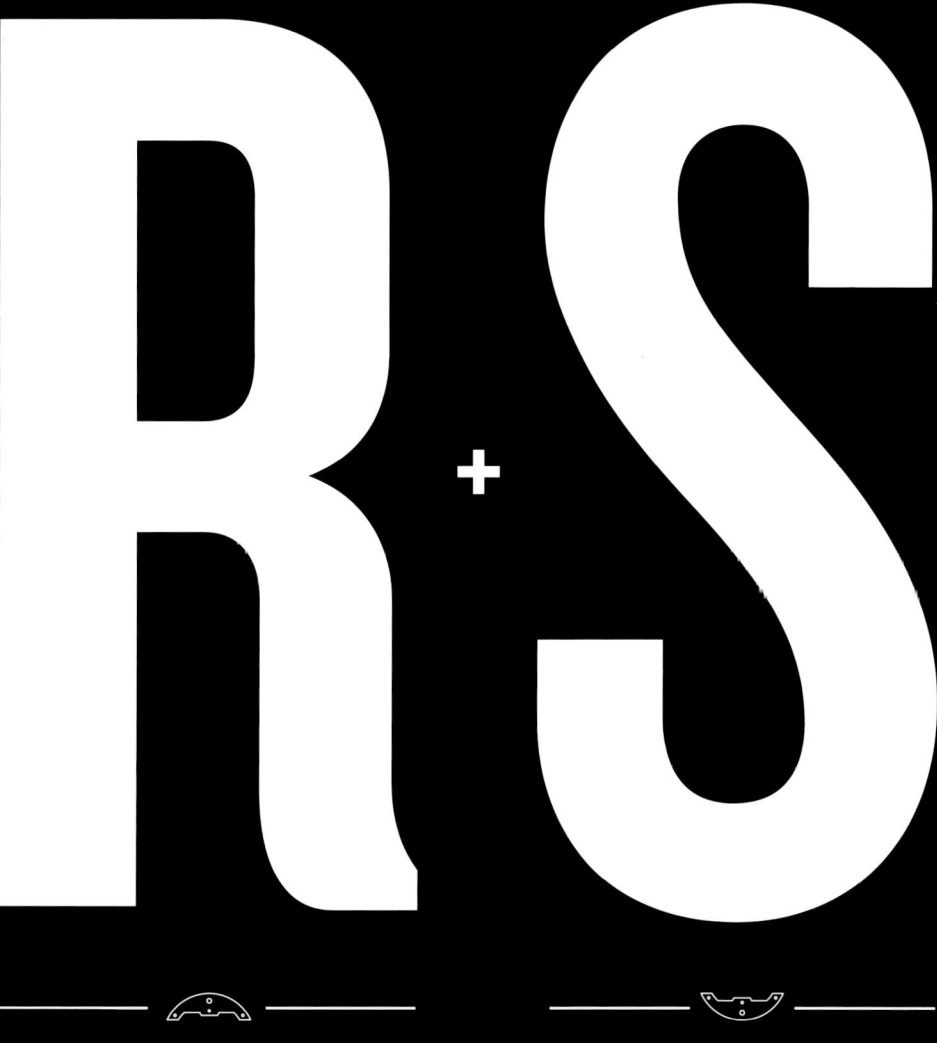

R+S

Robert Chew

Sam Brown

Soren Bendt

Steve Talkowski

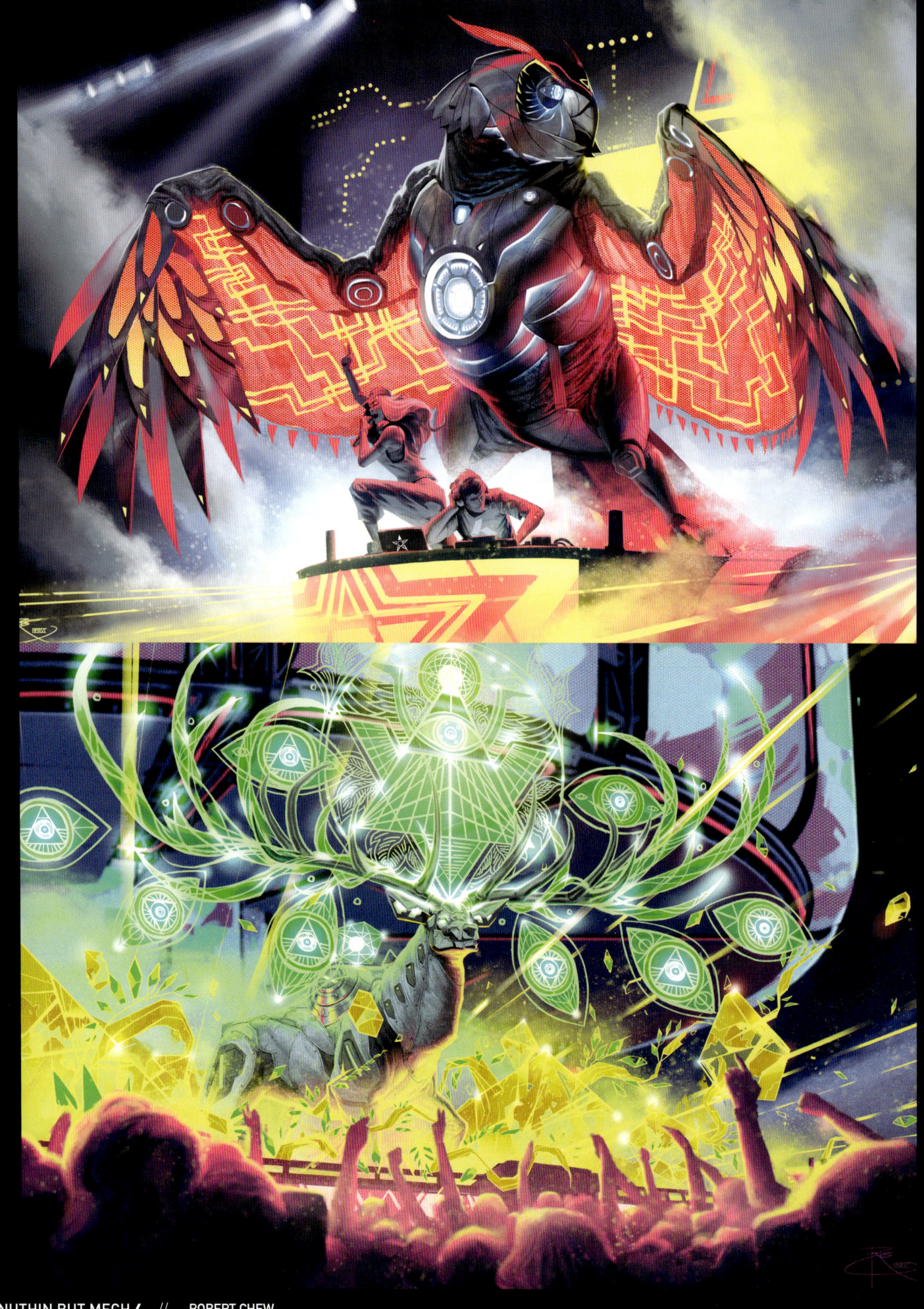

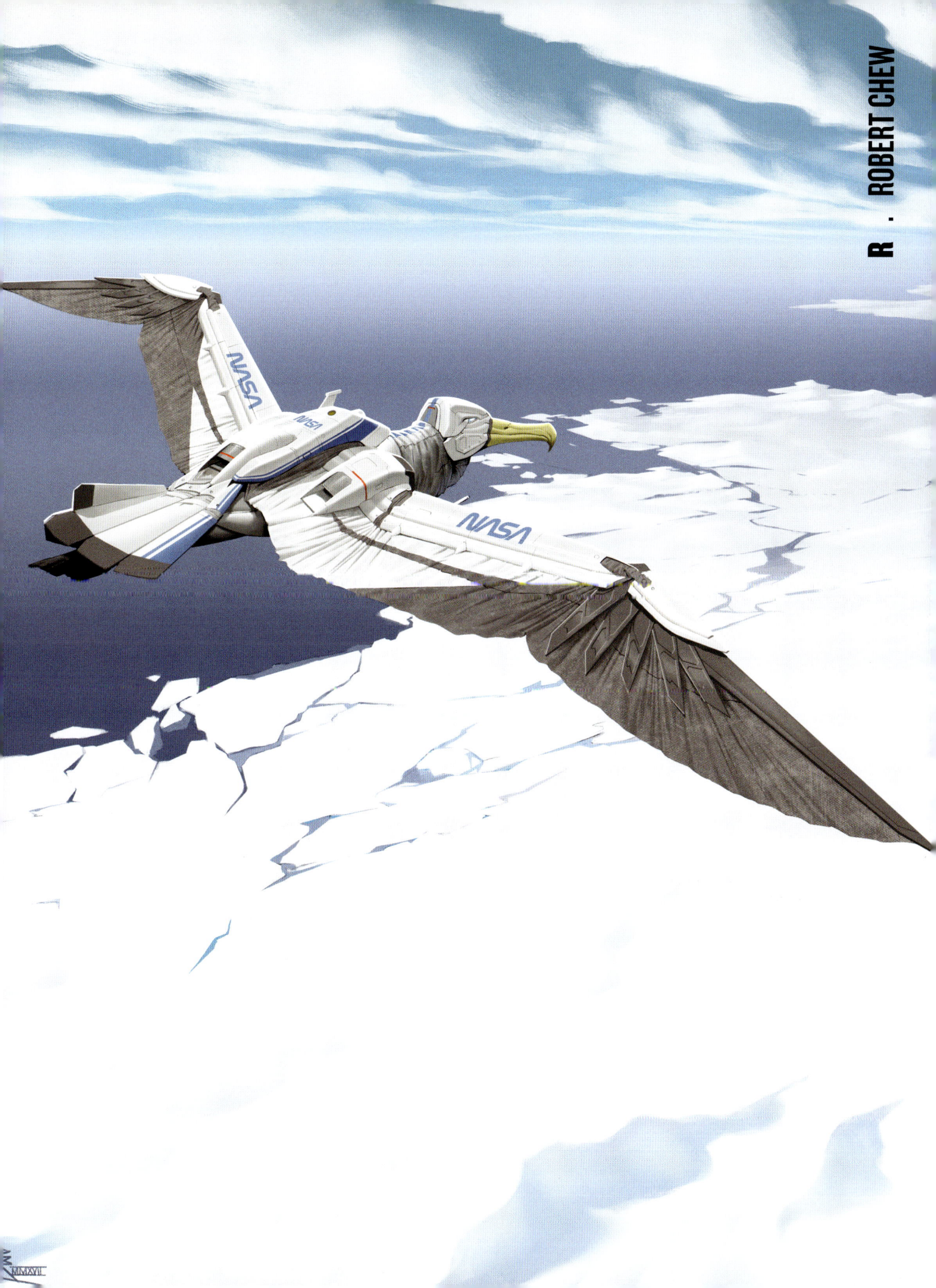

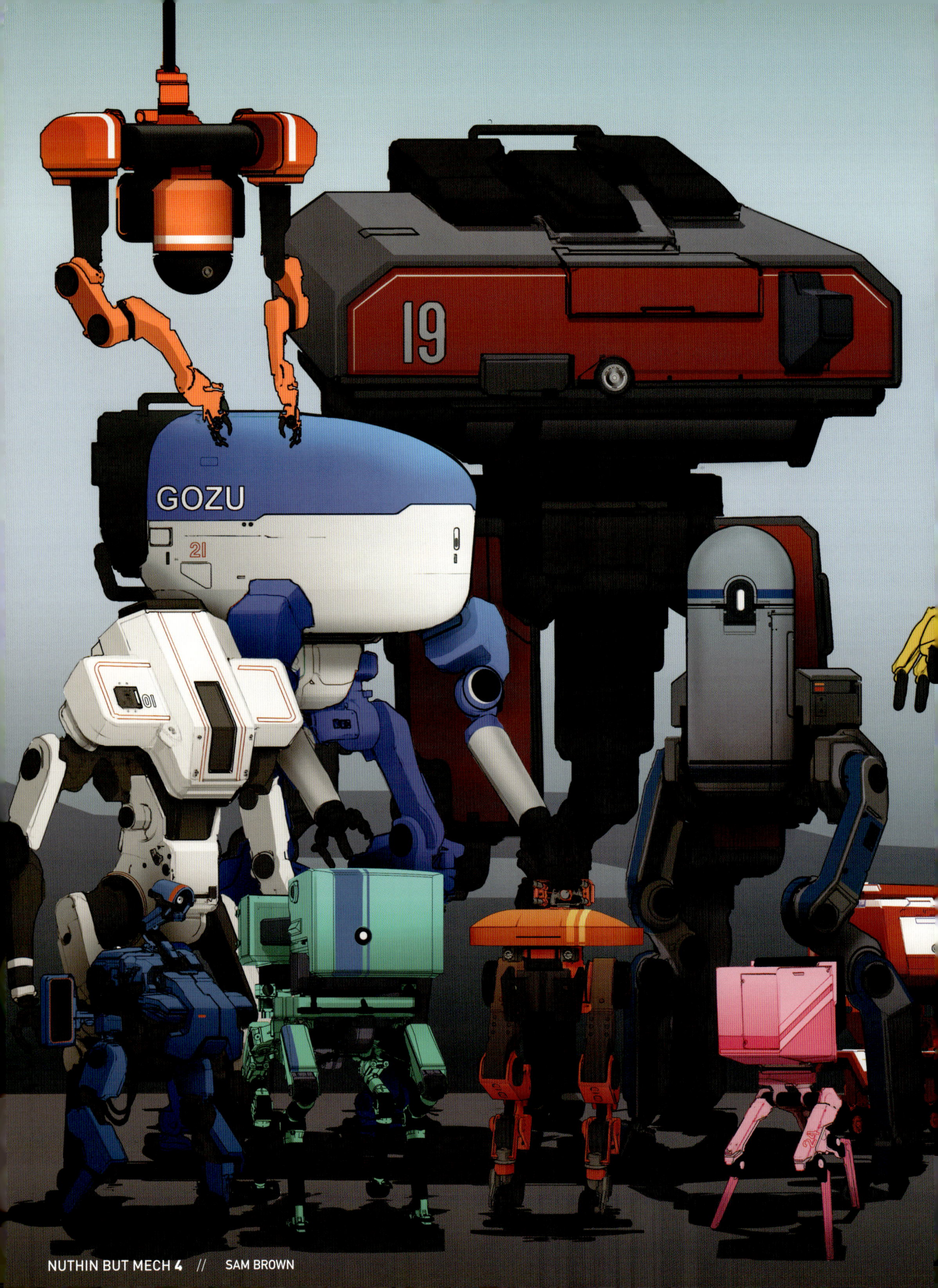

GOZU

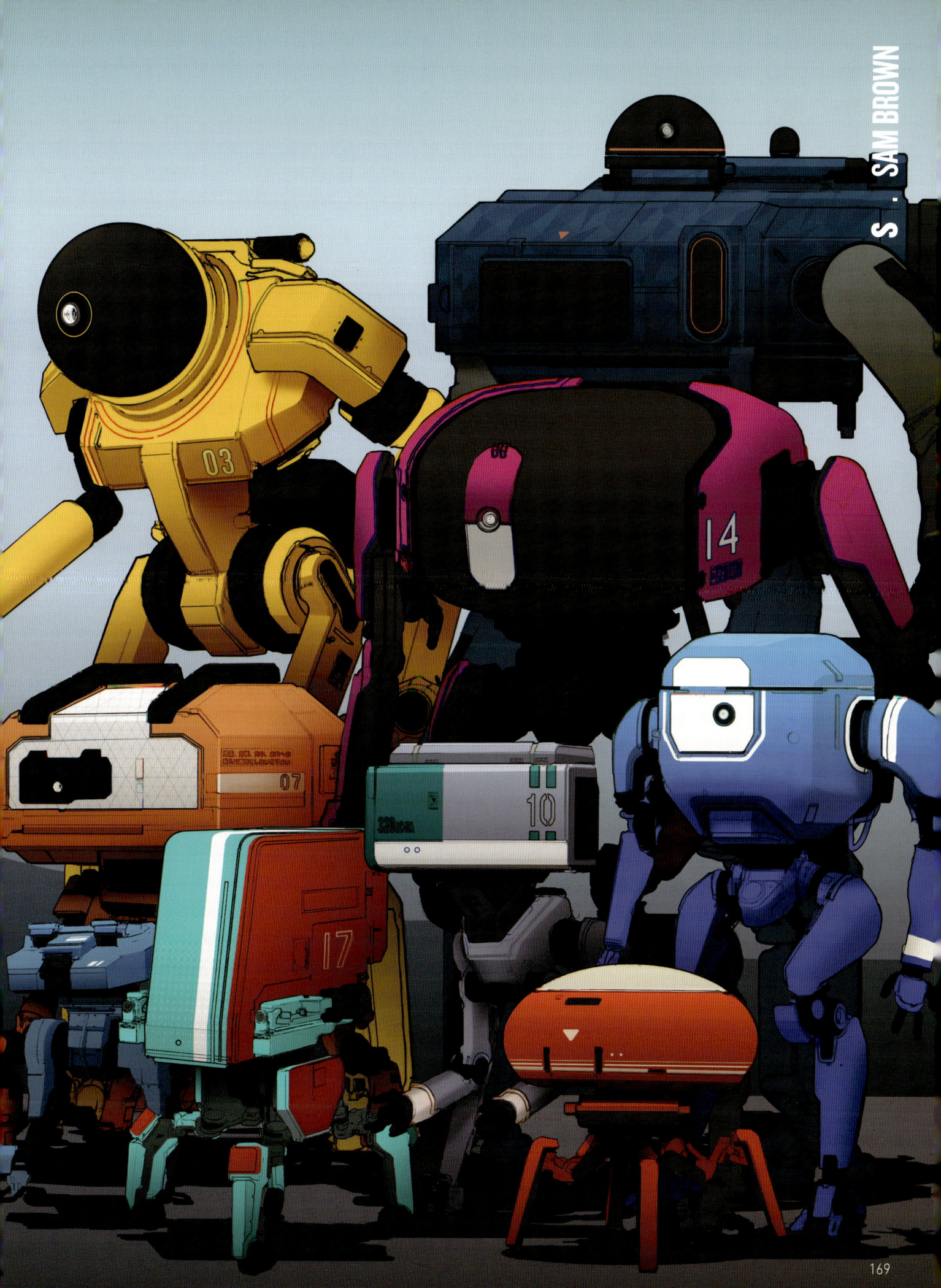

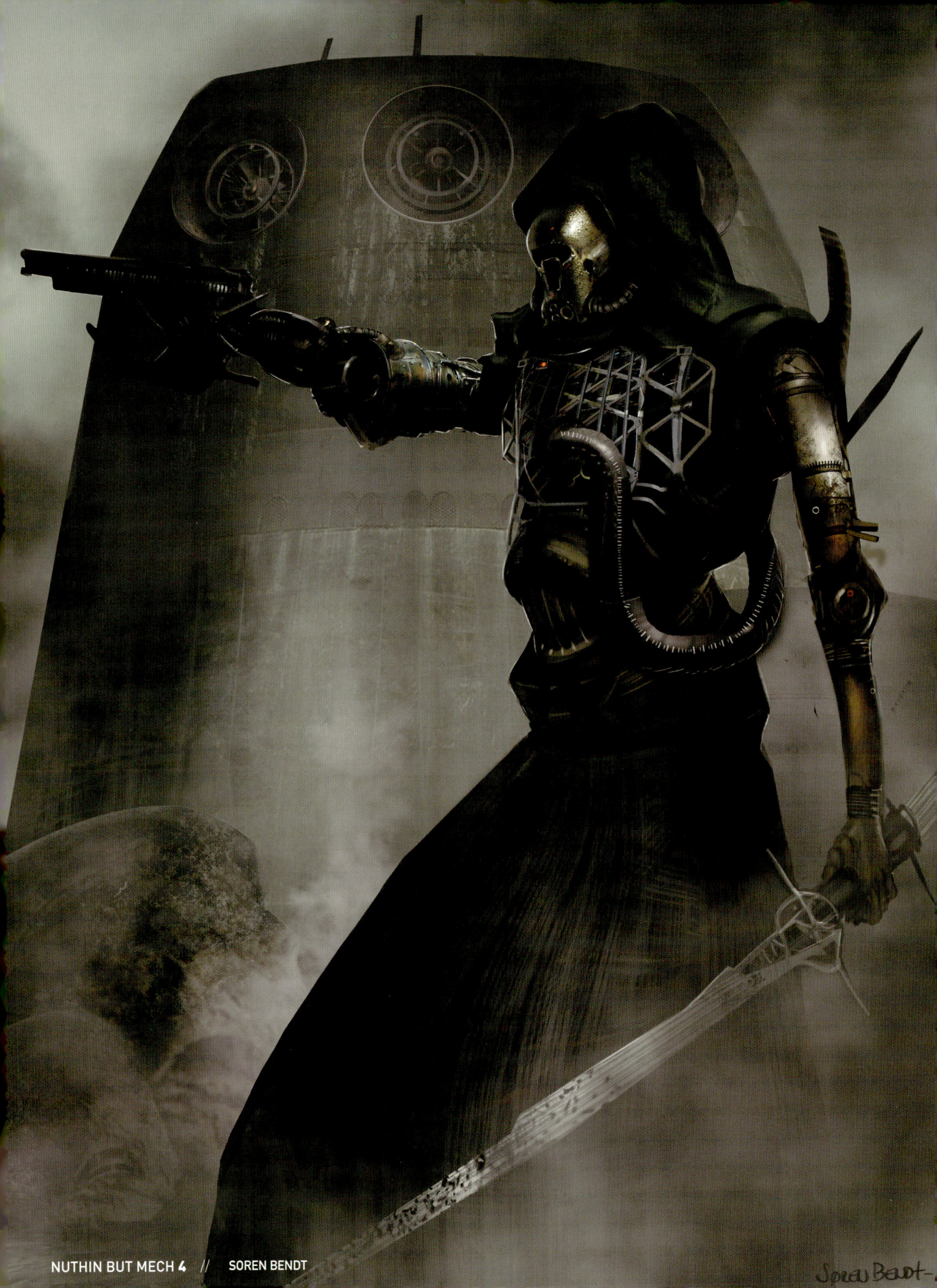

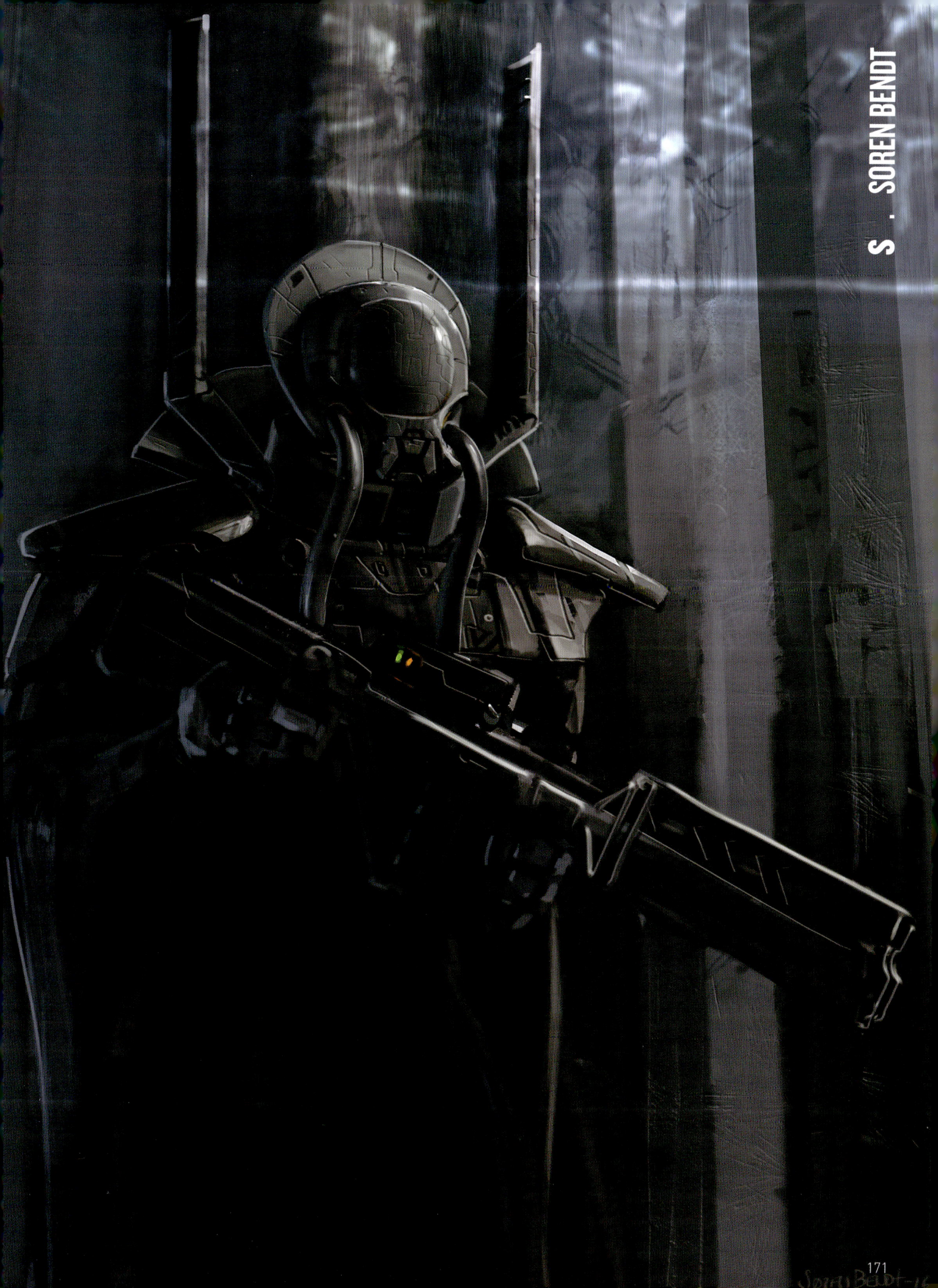

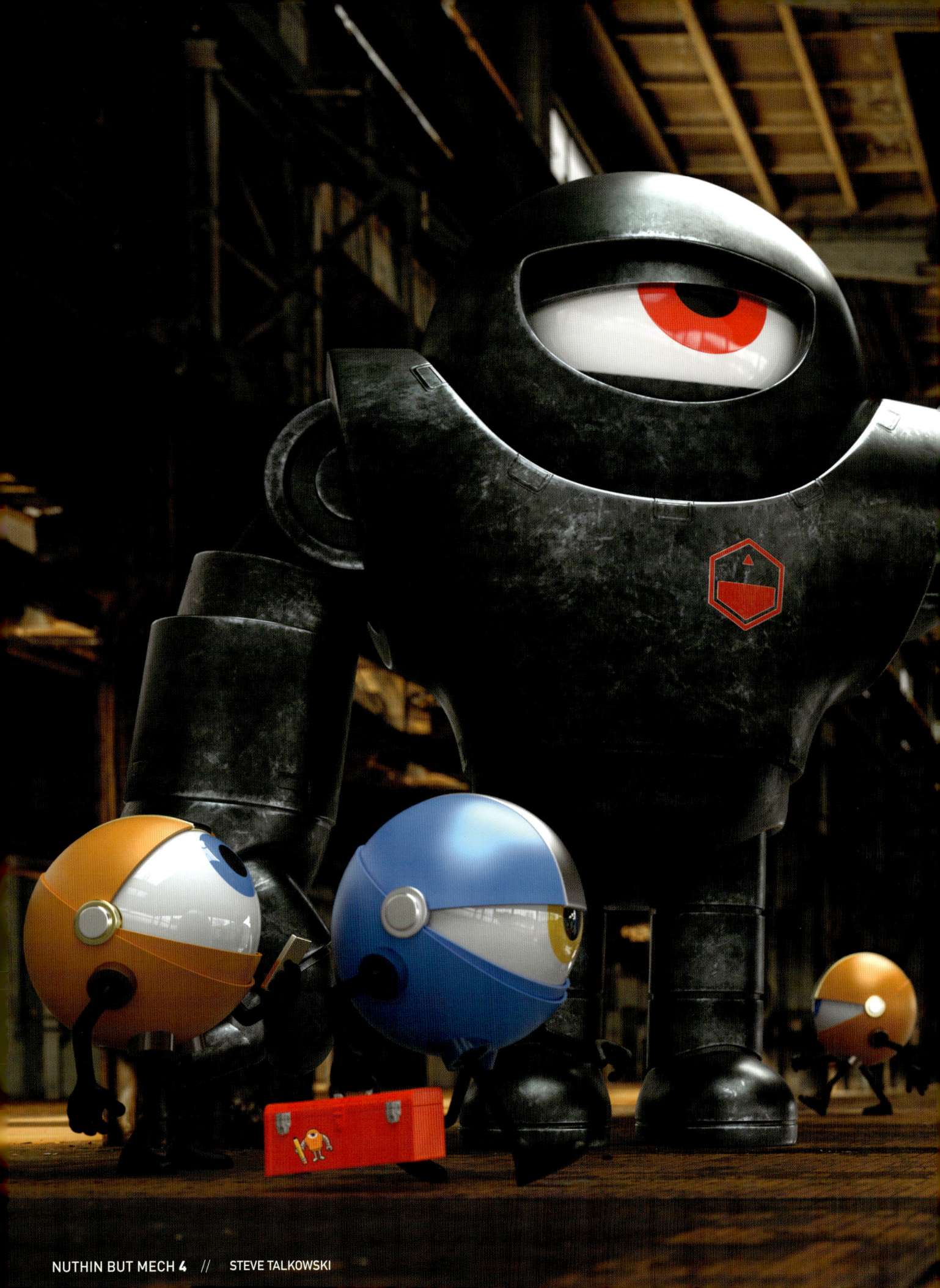

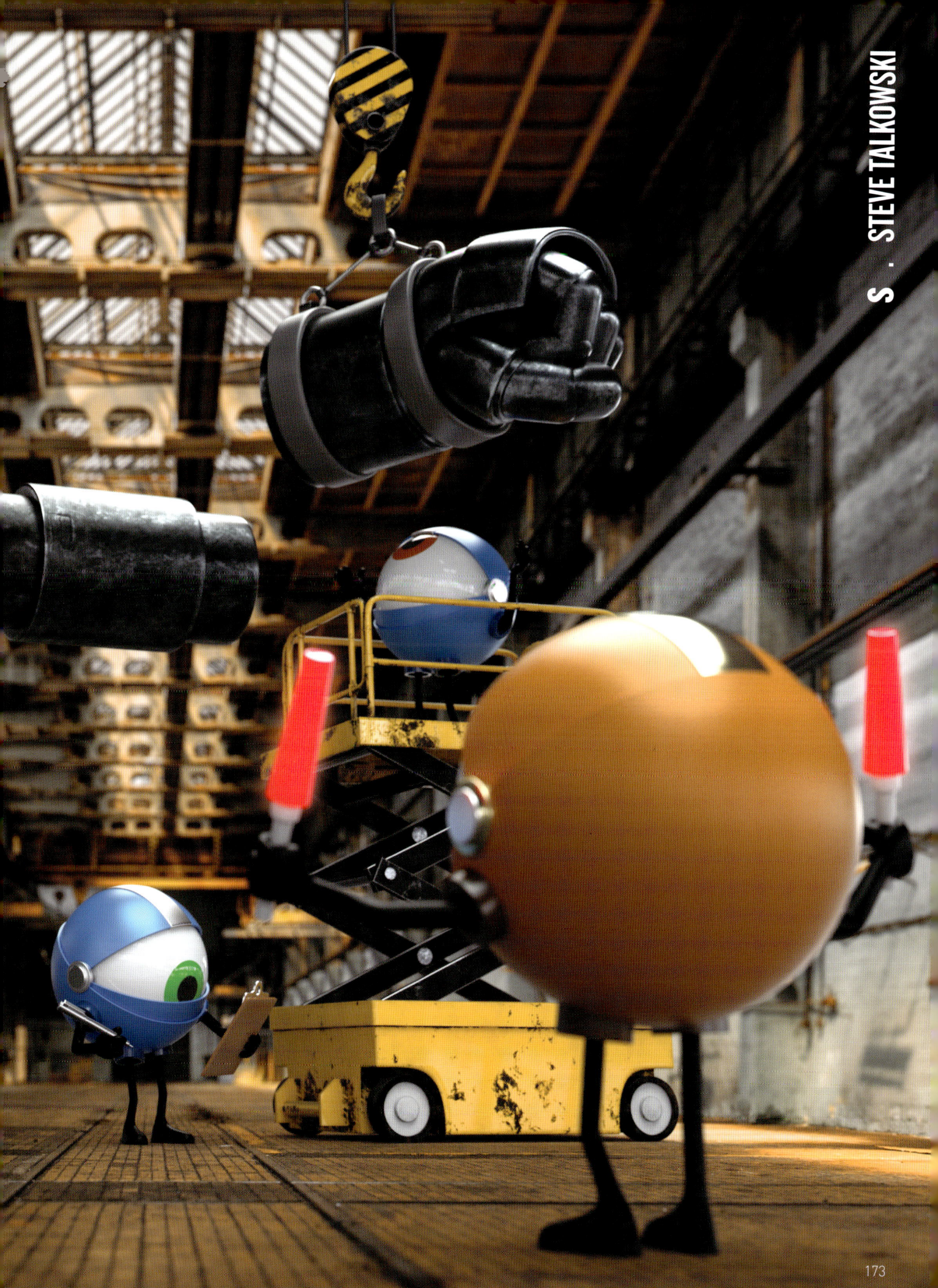

THOM TENERY

Thom is a Los Angeles–based artist, designer, and illustrator. His most recent credits include *Rogue One: A Star Wars Story*, *Star Wars: The Force Awakens*, and *Oblivion*. Thom received a bachelor of science in architecture from the University of Texas at Arlington, and studied illustration and entertainment design at ArtCenter College of Design. He has worked in film, television, and video game development, and illustrated book covers, magazines, trading card games, and web projects. His clients have included Walt Disney Pictures, Lucasfilm, Universal Pictures, Warner Bros. Pictures, the Dino De Laurentiis Company, id Software, Activision Blizzard Inc., the Syfy Channel, Playboy, Wizards of the Coast, Orbit Books, and Tor Books.
www.thomlab.com

TONY LEONARD

Tony is an illustrator of comics and a 2D/3D freelance concept designer based in the city of Los Angeles. Having previously resided in Japan, he is a former concept artist for Game Republic (Kabushiki-gaisha) and a former instructor at Nagoya Gakuin University.
www.artstation.com/artist/tonikoro

TYRUBEN ELLINGSON / MIKE COLLIER

TYRUBEN ELLINGSON

TyRuben has worked in the film industry since 1989, when he joined Industrial Light & Magic (ILM) as a visual effects art director. While at ILM, he contributed to the creation of groundbreaking special effects in films such as *Jurassic Park*, *Star Wars: Episode IV: A New Hope* (1997 Special Edition), *The Flintstones*, *Casper*, and *Disclosure*. In 1995, Ty left ILM to be the principle creature designer on *Mimic* for Guillermo del Toro. He has since worked with del Toro on *Blade II*, *Hellboy*, *Hellboy II: The Golden Army*, and *Pacific Rim*. Ty's recent concept designs can be seen in *Battle: Los Angeles* and *Elysium*; however, he is most recognized as the lead vehicle designer on James Cameron's *Avatar*. Ty continues to work as a conceptual designer and is an assistant professor at Virginia Commonwealth University, where he teaches concept design and visual problem-solving.
www.alieninsect.com

MIKE COLLIER

Mike is a designer and illustrator who recently graduated from Virginia Commonwealth University (VCU) with a bachelor of fine arts in communication arts. He works primarily within the music industry providing imagery, merchandise, and creative direction for producers and musicians alike. Mike was under TyRuben's instruction at VCU and draws a great deal of inspiration from his work and work ethic. You can find more of Mike's work at his website.
www.loveslinger.com

WOUTER GORT

Wouter is a concept designer and illustrator from Amsterdam, the Netherlands. He has worked on some games, movies, theme parks, and comics. Wouter loves drawing but is terrible at writing about himself, as you can see here. By typing this in full sentences, he is slowly filling up his bio so that, hopefully, he fits in with the rest and no one will notice. Wouter also loves cats.
www.artstation.com/artist/wokkie

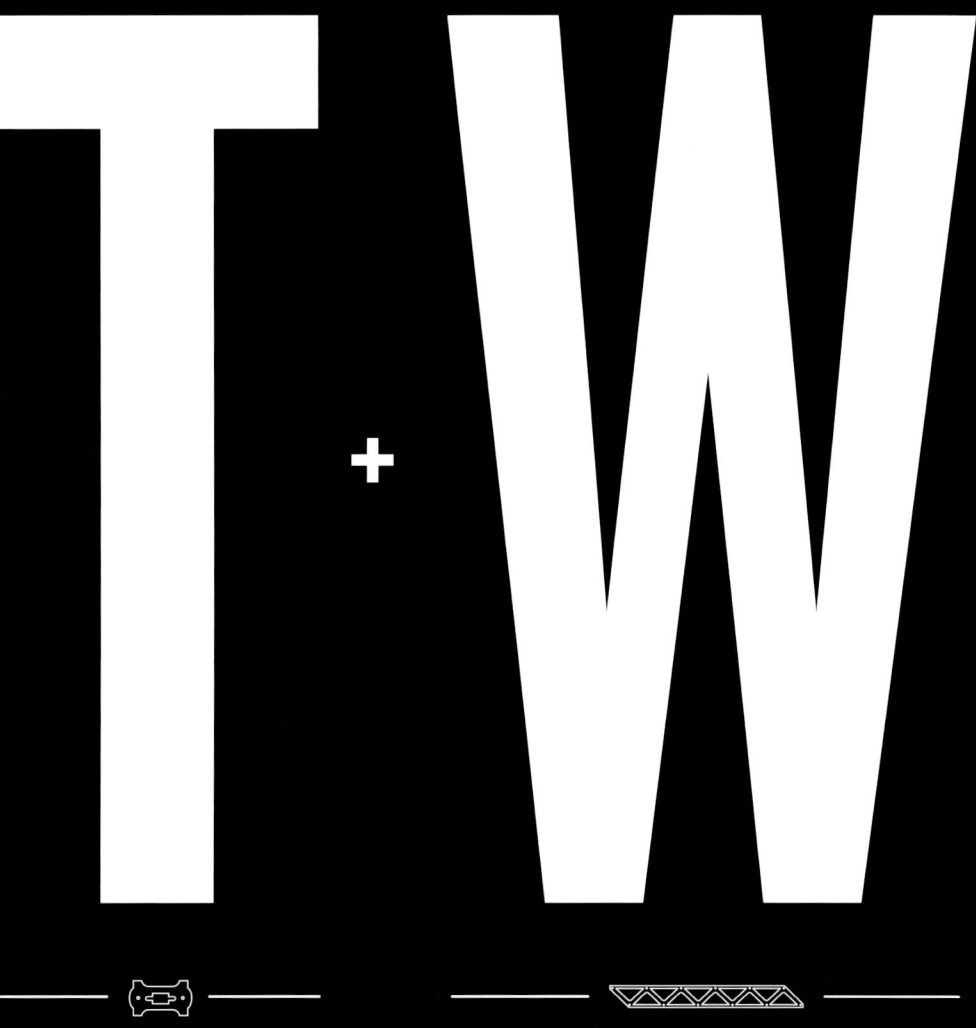

T + W

Thom Tenery

Tony Leonard

TyRuben Ellingson/Mike Collier

Wouter Gort

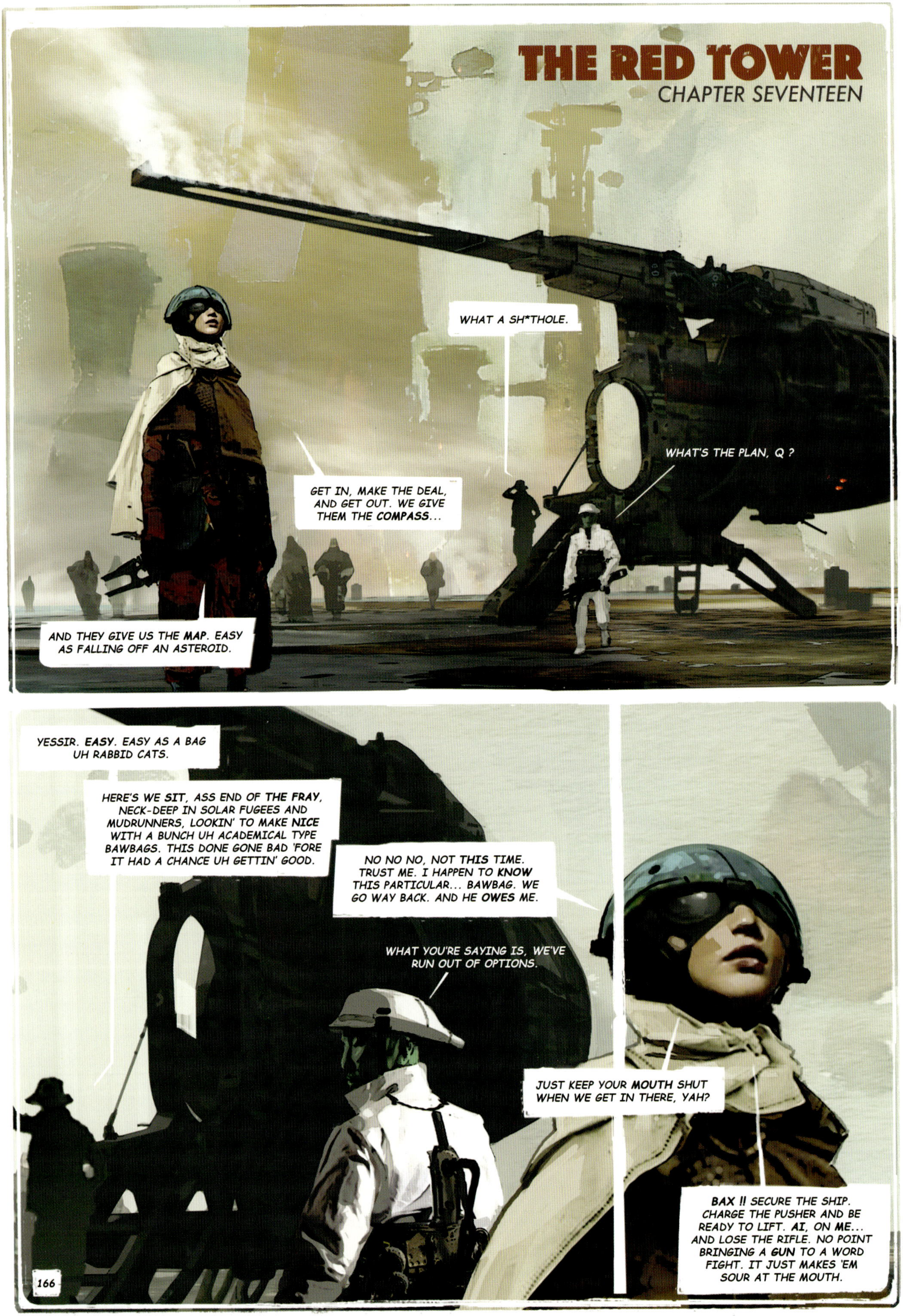
THE RED TOWER
CHAPTER SEVENTEEN
WHAT A SH*THOLE.
WHAT'S THE PLAN, Q ?
GET IN, MAKE THE DEAL, AND GET OUT. WE GIVE THEM THE COMPASS...
AND THEY GIVE US THE MAP. EASY AS FALLING OFF AN ASTEROID.
YESSIR. EASY. EASY AS A BAG UH RABBID CATS.
HERE'S WE SIT, ASS END OF THE FRAY, NECK-DEEP IN SOLAR FUGEES AND MUDRUNNERS, LOOKIN' TO MAKE NICE WITH A BUNCH UH ACADEMICAL TYPE BAWBAGS. THIS DONE GONE BAD 'FORE IT HAD A CHANCE UH GETTIN' GOOD.
NO NO NO, NOT THIS TIME. TRUST ME. I HAPPEN TO KNOW THIS PARTICULAR... BAWBAG. WE GO WAY BACK. AND HE OWES ME.
WHAT YOU'RE SAYING IS, WE'VE RUN OUT OF OPTIONS.
JUST KEEP YOUR MOUTH SHUT WHEN WE GET IN THERE, YAH?
BAX !! SECURE THE SHIP. CHARGE THE PUSHER AND BE READY TO LIFT. AI, ON ME... AND LOSE THE RIFLE. NO POINT BRINGING A GUN TO A WORD FIGHT. IT JUST MAKES 'EM SOUR AT THE MOUTH.
166

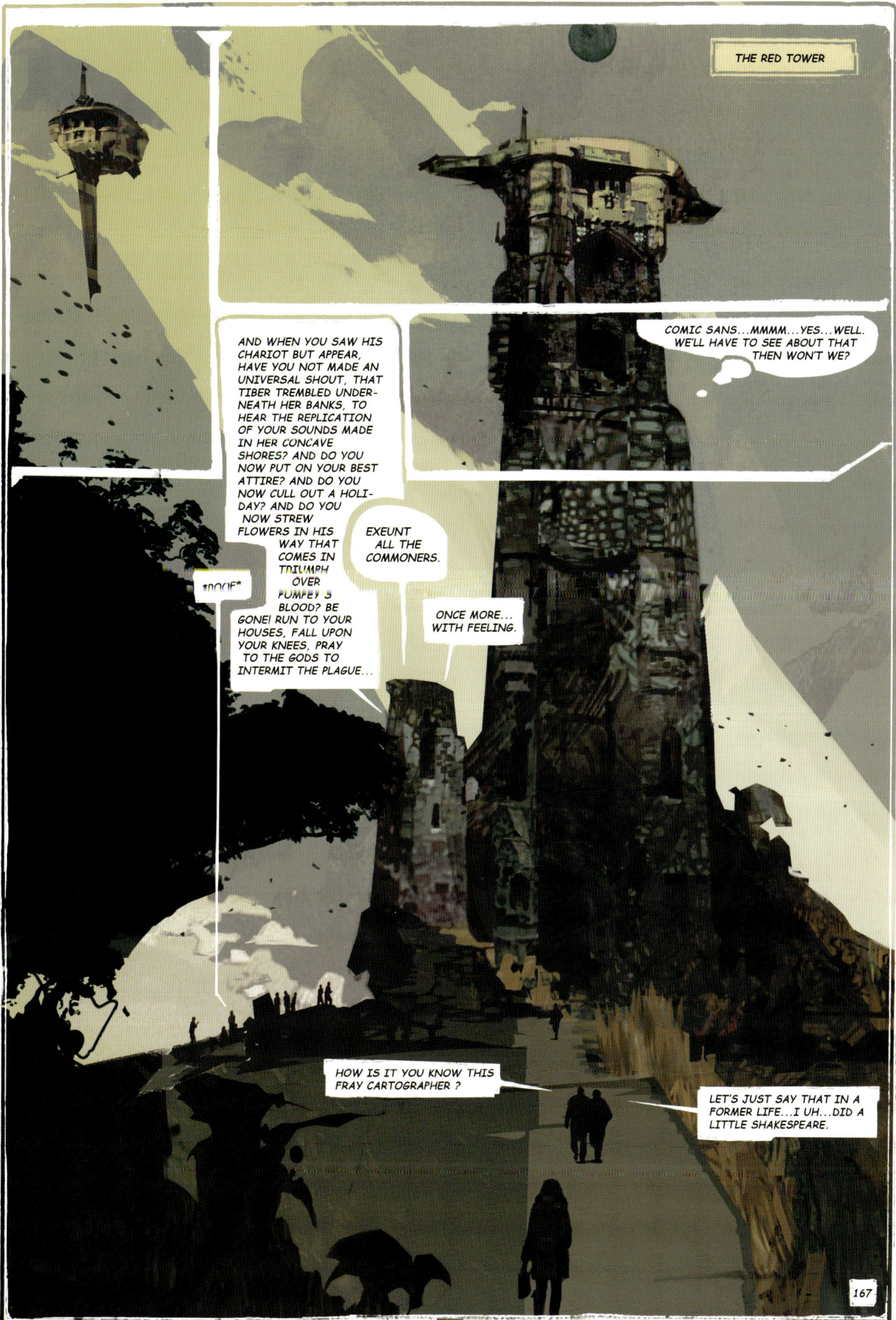

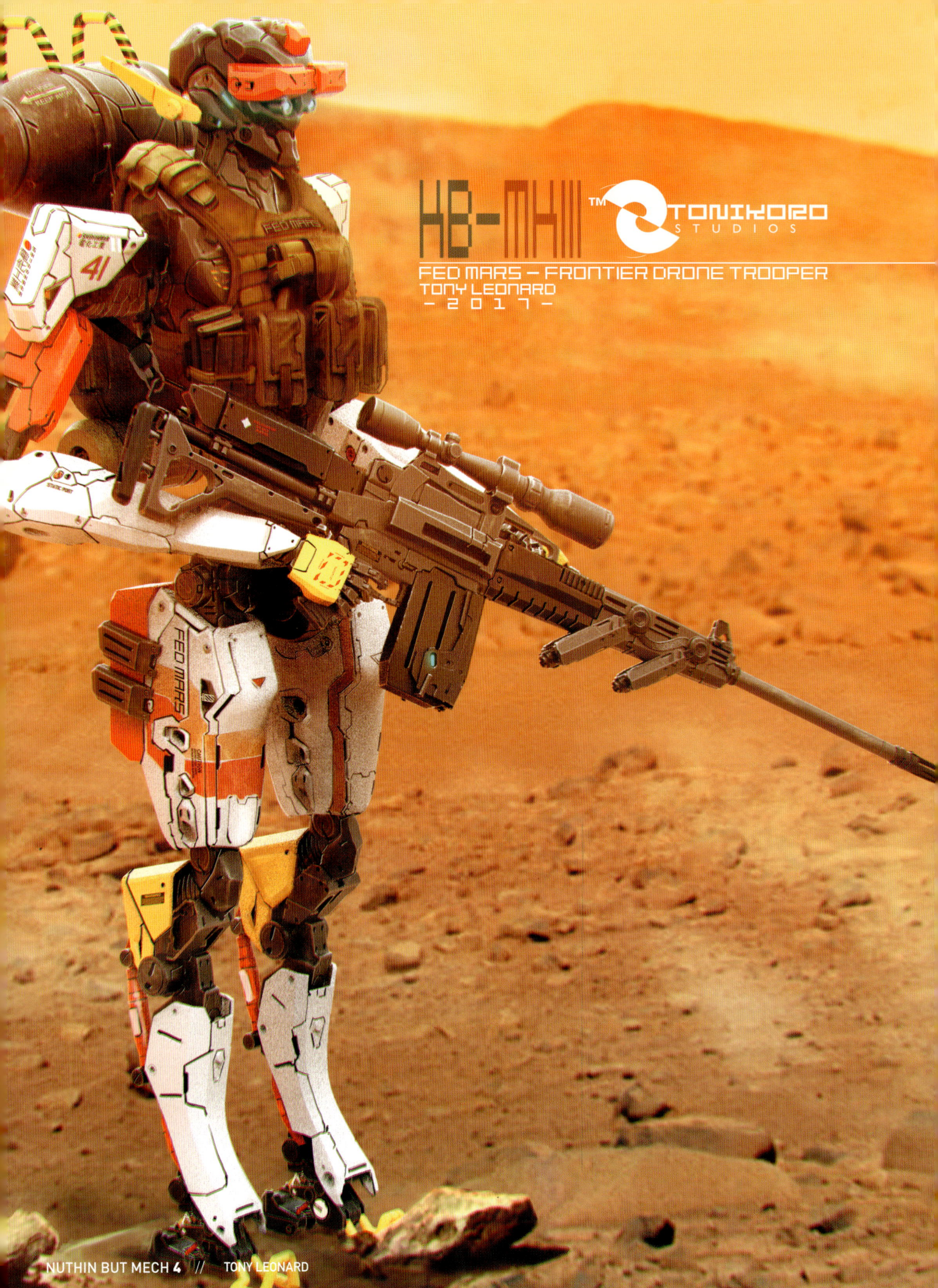

KB-MHIII™ ⌂ TONIKORO STUDIOS

FED MARS — FRONTIER DRONE TROOPER
TONY LEONARD
– 2 0 1 7 –

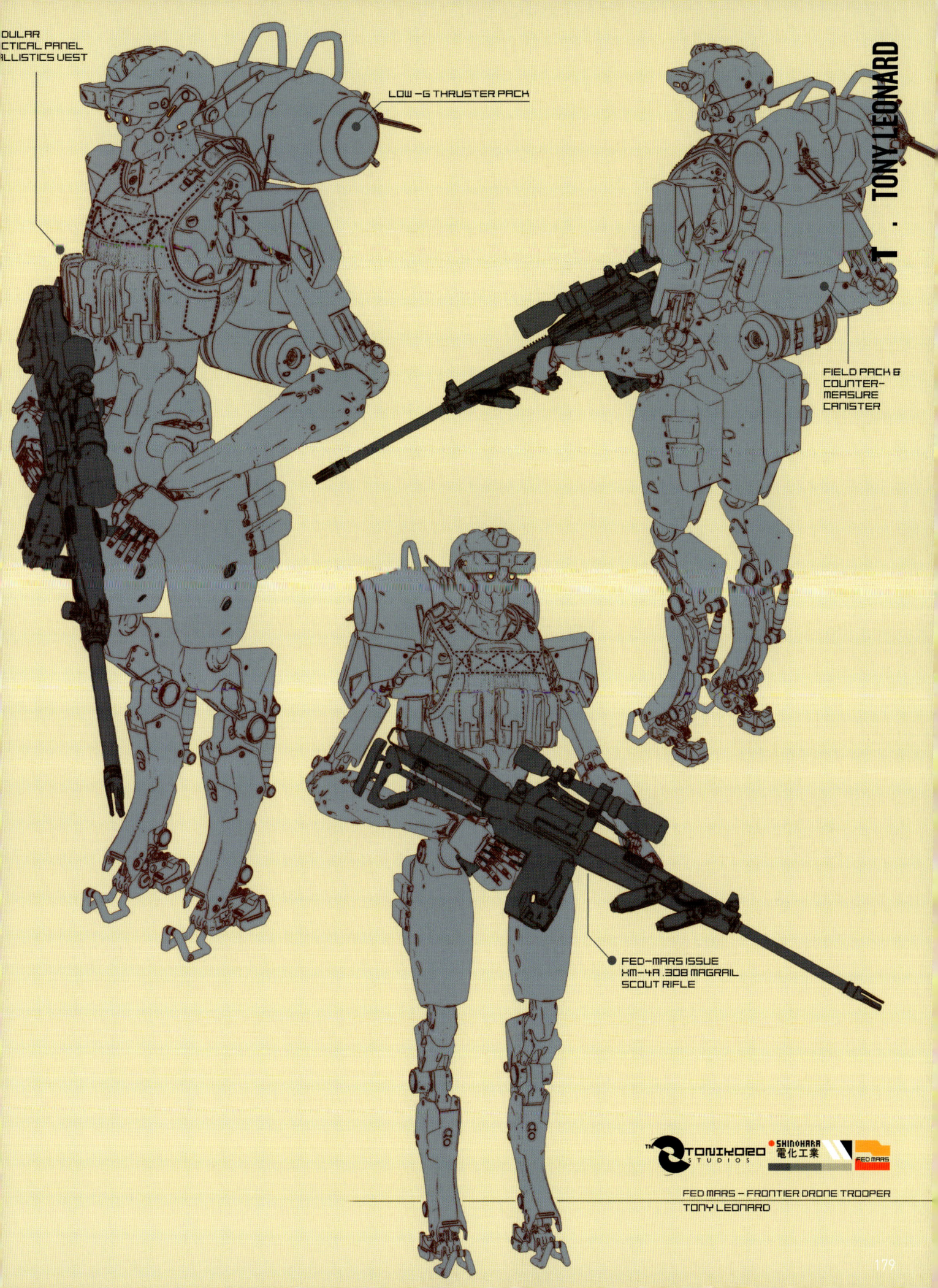

ODULAR
CTICAL PANEL
LLISTICS VEST

LOW-G THRUSTER PACK

T . TONY LEONARD

FIELD PACK &
COUNTER-
MEASURE
CANISTER

FED-MARS ISSUE
XM-4A .308 MAGRAIL
SCOUT RIFLE

TONIKORO
STUDIOS

SHINOHARA
電化工業

FED MARS

FED MARS – FRONTIER DRONE TROOPER
TONY LEONARD

179

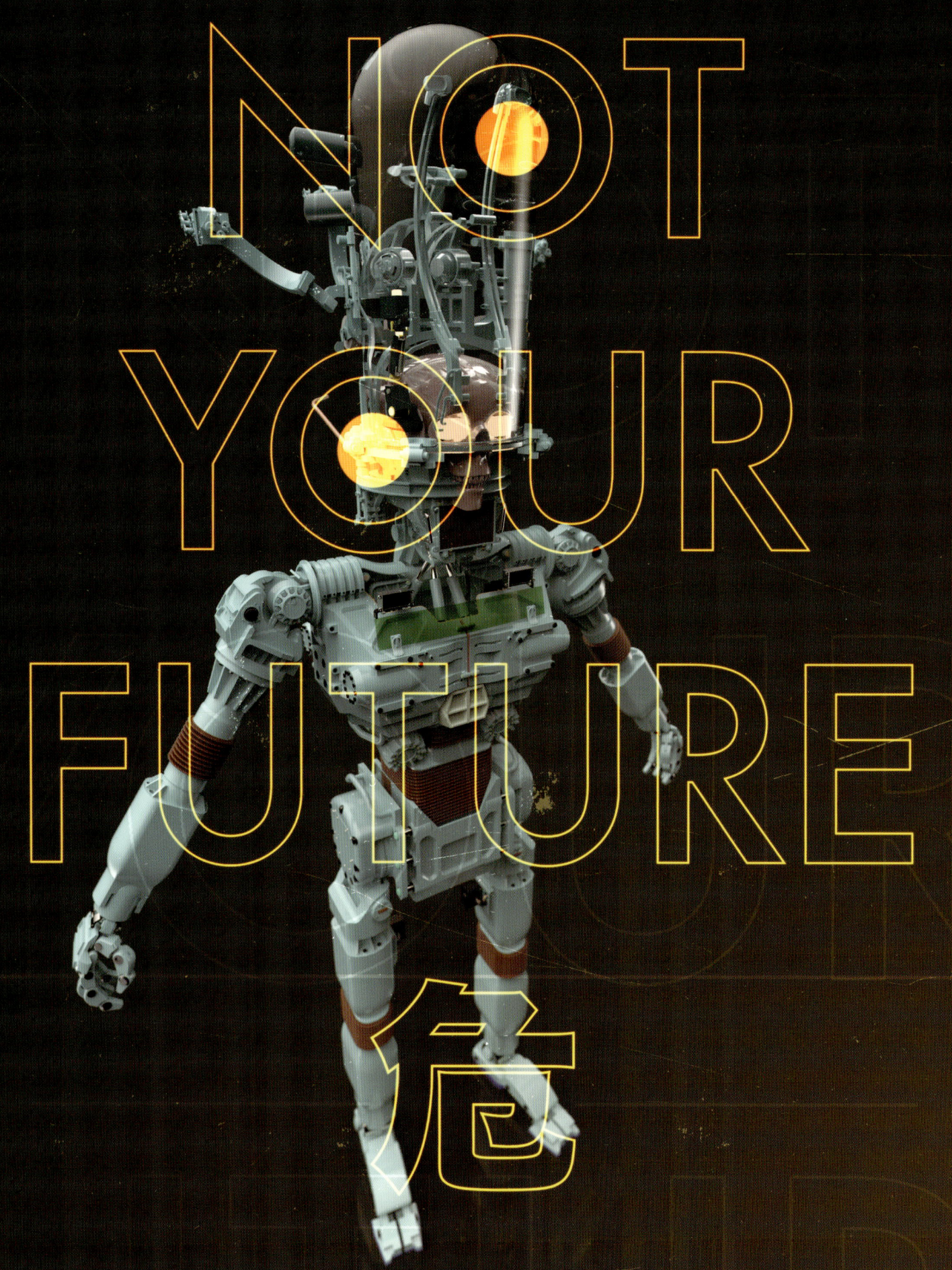

NOT
YOUR
FUTURE

危

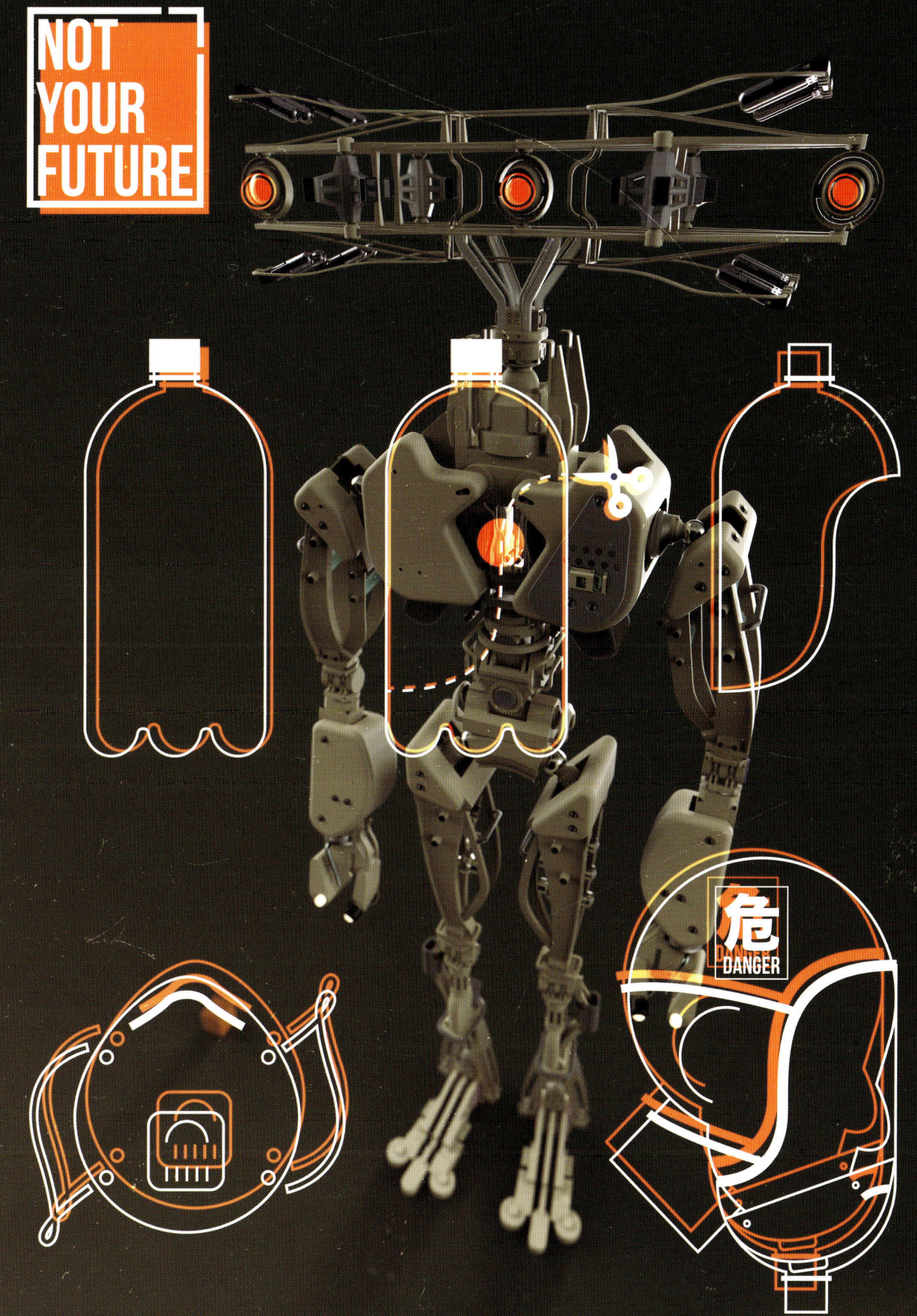

T . TYRUBEN ELLINGSON & MIKE COLLIER

危
DANGER

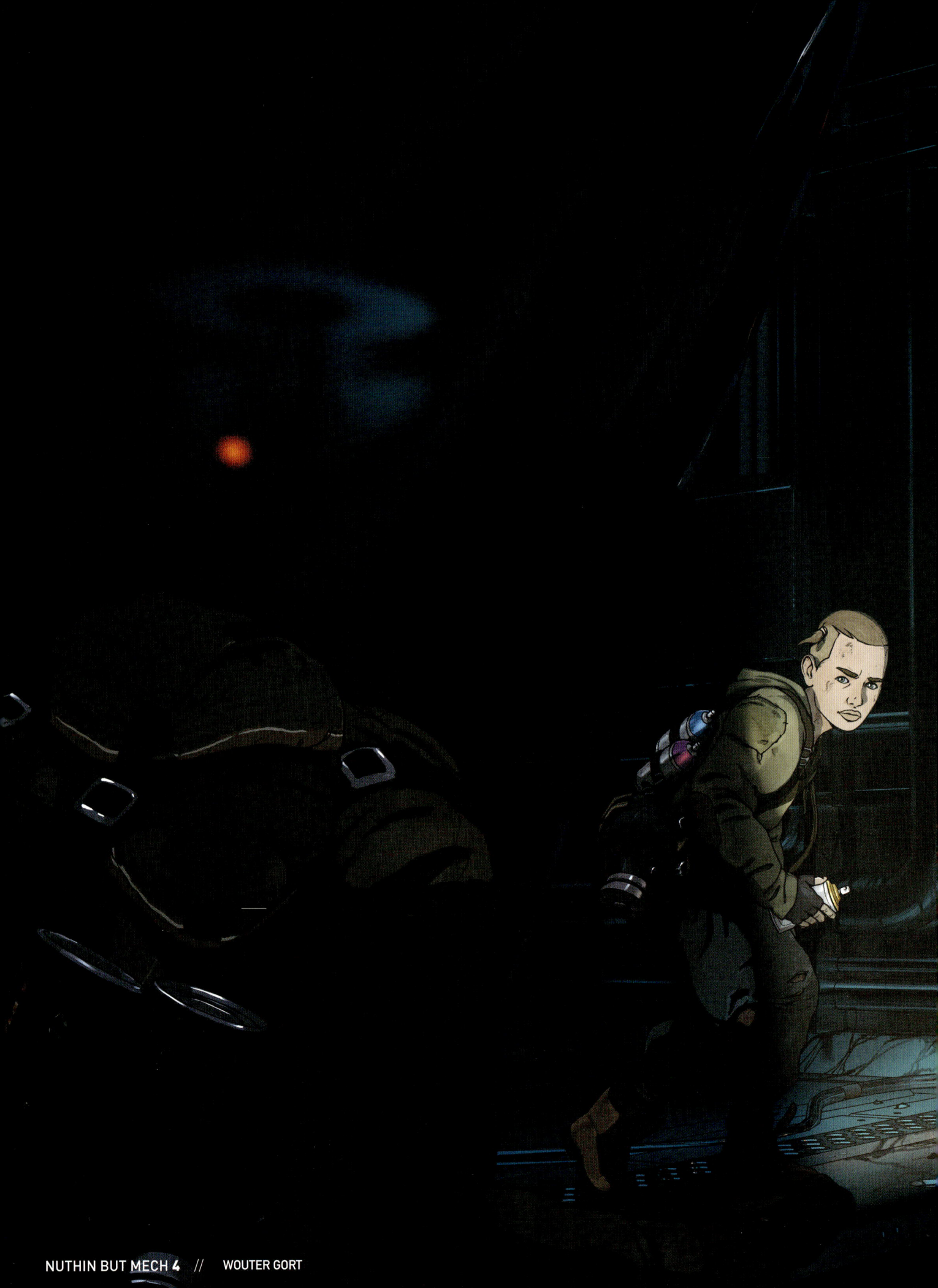

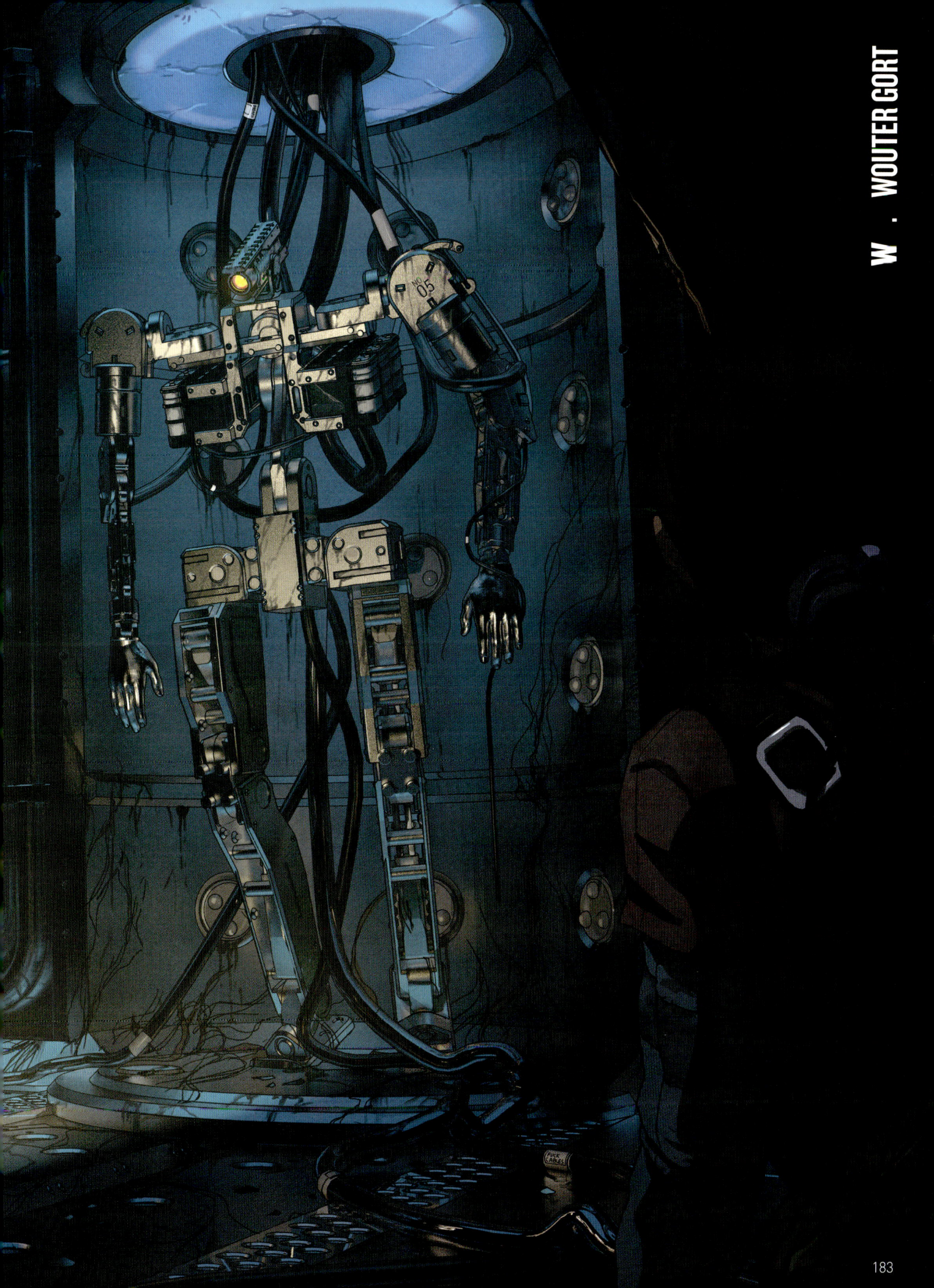

ARTISTS

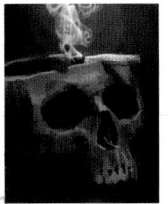
Aaron Beck

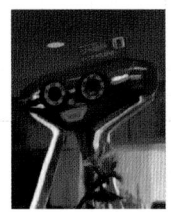
Alex Jay Brady

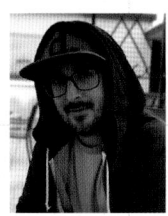
Alex Figini

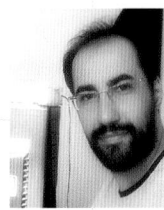
Amin Akhshi

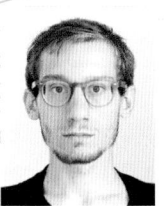
Andrea Mancarella

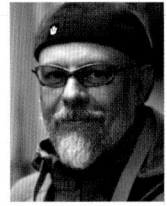
Ara Kermanikian

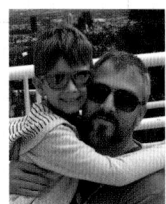
Ben Procter

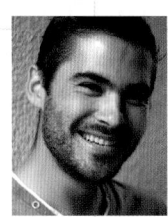
Benjamin Louis

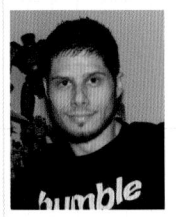
Bryan Repka

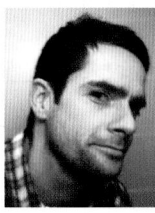
Calum Watt

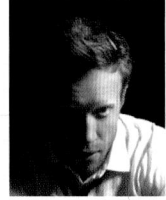
Chris Rosewarne

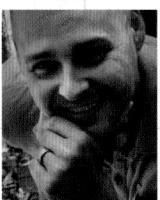
Chris Stoski

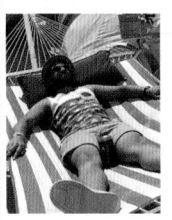
Danny Gardner

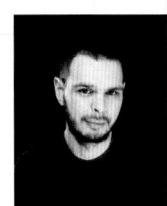
Darren Bacon

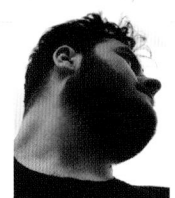
Edon Guraziu

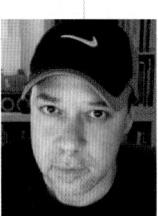
Eric Lloyd Brown

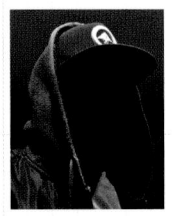
Furio Tedeschi

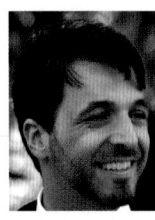
Gerald Blaise

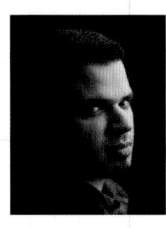
Gus Mendonca

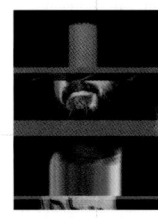
Hugo Bermudez

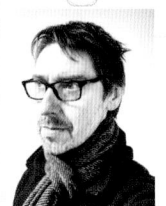
Ian McQue

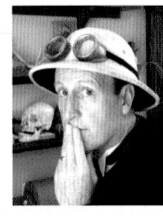
James Gurney

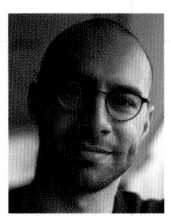
Jan Urschel

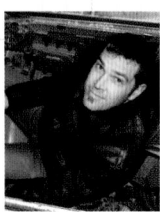
Jeremy Cook

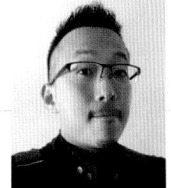
John Liew

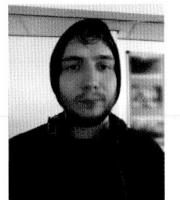
Jort van Welbergen

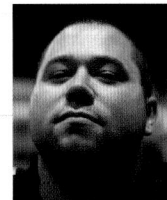
Justin Fields

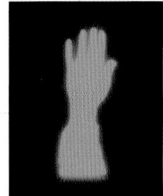
Kilian Eng

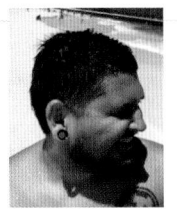
Kirill Chepizhko

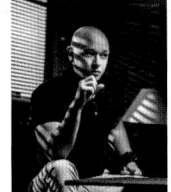
Valentine Sorokin

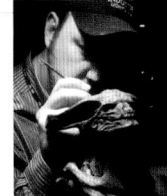
Landis Fields

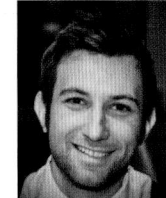
Lee Souder

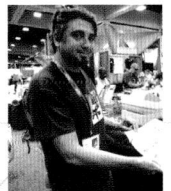
Luca Zampriolo

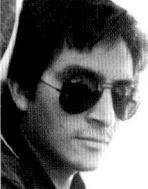
Luigi Memola

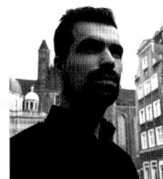
Michal Kus

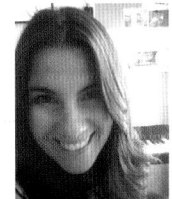
Mieke Loomis Hutchins

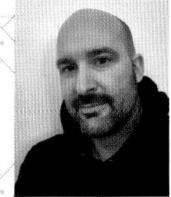
Nathan Dearsley

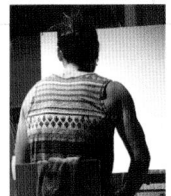
Nathan Dollarhite

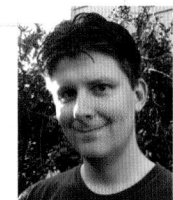
Neil Blevins

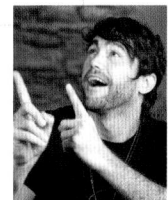
Nick Hiatt

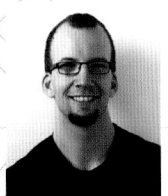
Nikolai Lockertsen

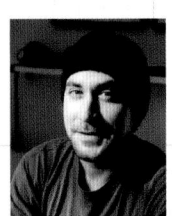
Nivanh Chanthara

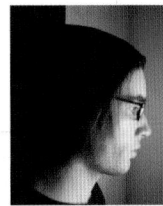
(Noax) Alex Noax

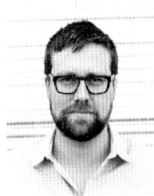
Patrick Hanenberger

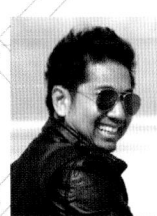
Pat Presley

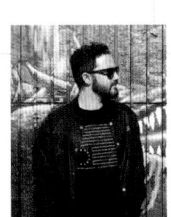
Patrick O'Keefe

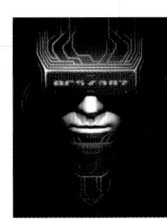
Pete Norris

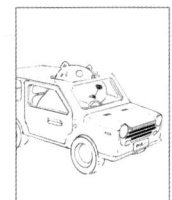
Prog Wang

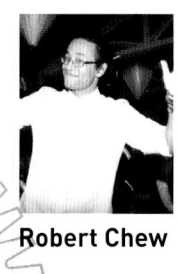 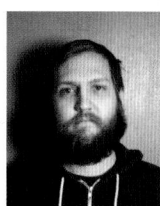 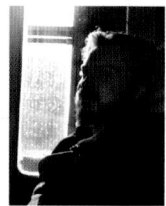 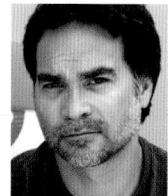

Robert Chew   **Sam Brown**   **Soren Bendt**   **Steve Talkowski**

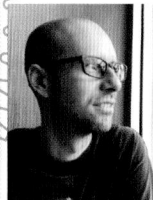 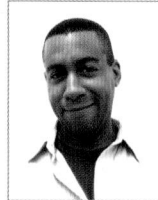 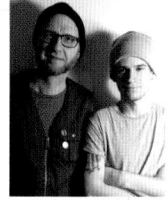 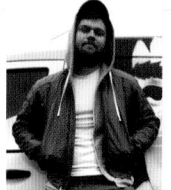

Thom Tenery   **Tony Leonard**   **TyRuben Ellingson & Mike Collier**   **Wouter Gort**

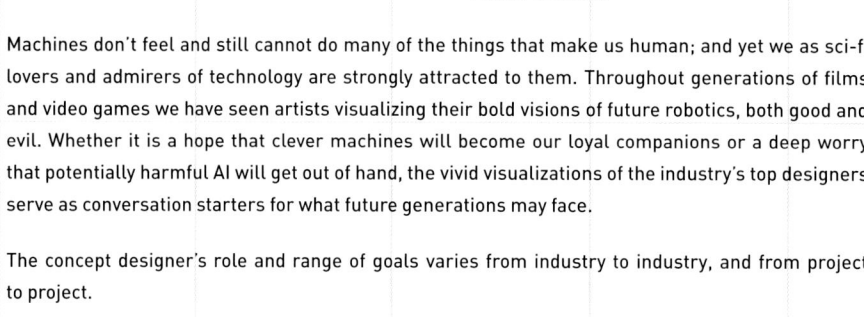

Machines don't feel and still cannot do many of the things that make us human; and yet we as sci-fi lovers and admirers of technology are strongly attracted to them. Throughout generations of films and video games we have seen artists visualizing their bold visions of future robotics, both good and evil. Whether it is a hope that clever machines will become our loyal companions or a deep worry that potentially harmful AI will get out of hand, the vivid visualizations of the industry's top designers serve as conversation starters for what future generations may face.

The concept designer's role and range of goals varies from industry to industry, and from project to project.

In film, for example, a science-fiction setting would require a concept designer to maintain an inspiring flourish and yet want to ground the concept "back to Earth" emphasizing the realistic function, as well as the set of rules by which that concept operates. With this knowledge and skill set, the designer helps the director create a more believable story. On the other hand, a product designer may want to deliberately push the limits and mechanical and engineering constraints in order to ignite a more inspiring version of a product. Such an approach may often inspire engineers to rethink the constraints and look at the challenges from a different angle. More often than not it is the concept designer's sacred duty to ignore certain limitations to let the idea grow until those technical limitations are overcome. Time and time again I am convinced that being able to do this at an early stage of the product/film/video game development is a great privilege and a great responsibility.

But ultimately concept design might be as close to magic or a time machine that we'll ever get. From the moment when an idea is conceived to a point when it's fully visualized, creating something that doesn't yet exist will always be a special kind of mental journey.

So let this book, and the entire series of *Nuthin But Mech* books, become a celebration of concept design at its most pure, idealistic, constraint-free form and inspire the current—as well as next generation of—dreamers, visionaries, and problem solvers.

- Vitaly Bulgarov

THE NUTHIN' BUT MECH SERIES

NUTHIN' BUT MECH

The Nuthin' But Mech blog is the brainchild of entertainment designer Lorin Wood. He wanted a place to harbor his passion for robots so he put together a blog and corralled some of his friends and professional acquaintances to populate this nook of cyberspace. The book series is a collaborative effort that showcases various styles of mecha design the contributing artists create when they are not working on blockbuster movies, TV shows, and video games.

NUTHIN' BUT MECH

Nuthin' But Mech features the works of:

Carlo Arellano, Aaron Beck, Søren Bendt, Greg Broadmore, Sam Brown, Steve Burg, Peggy Chung, Jeremy Cook, Alex J. Cunningham, Fon Davis / MORAV, TyRuben Ellingson, Marc Gabbana, Eduardo Gonzalez, Alex Jaeger, Eliott Lilly, Miguel Lopez, Ben Mauro, Ian McQue, Michael A. Nash, Sunil Pant, Jake Parker, Christian Pearce, Peter Popken, Kemp Remillard, Neil Campbell Ross, Oliver Scholl, Robert Simons, Thom Tenery, Imery Watson, Lorin Wood, Feng Zhu

NUTHIN' BUT MECH 2

Nuthin' But Mech 2 features the works of:

Darren Bartley, Aaron Beck, Sam Brown, Dylan Cole, Kevin Conran, Jeremy Cook, Fausto De Martini, Eddie Del Rio, TyRuben Ellingson, Landis Fields, Danny Gardner, James Gurney, Brian Hagan, David Hobbins, Alex Jaeger, Eric Joyner, Kurt Kaufman, Ara Kermanikian, Gavriil Klimov, Bastiaan Koch, Eliott Lilly, Vaughan Ling, Miguel Lopez, Ian McQue, Josh Nizzi, James Paick, Sunil Pant, Jake Parker, Robh Ruppel, Phil Saunders, Emmanuel Shiu, Robert Simons, Chris Stoski, Ash Thorp, Matt Tkocz, Francis Tsai, Jan Urschel, Farzad Varahramyan, Calum Alexander Watt, Colie Wertz, Lorin Wood

NUTHIN' BUT MECH 3

Nuthin' But Mech 3 features the works of:

Darren Bacon, Aaron Beck, Soren Bendt, Gerald Blaise, Neil Blevins, Chris Bonura, Al Brady, Sam Brown, Vitaly Bulgarov, Kirill Chepizhko, Robert Chew, Kevin Conran, Thierry Doizon, TyRuben Ellingson, Ben Erdt, Justin Fields, Landis Fields, Danny Gardner, Eduardo Gonzalez, Edon Guraziu, Brian Hagan, Patrick Hanenberger, Eric Joyner, Kurt Kaufman, Ara Kermanikian, Gavriil Afanasyev Klimov, Bastiaan Koch, John Liew, Vaughan Ling, Miguel Lopez, Benjamin Louis, Ben Mauro, John McInnis, Elijah McNeal, Ian McQue, Patrick O'Keefe, Long Ouyang, James Paick, Sunil Pant, Jake Parker, Peter Popken, Chris Rosewarne, Emmanuel Shiu, Simon Stålenhag, Chris Stoski, Steve Talkowski, Ash Thorp, Matt Tkocz, Jan Urschel, Josh Viers, Andrée Wallin, Colie Wertz, Lorin Wood

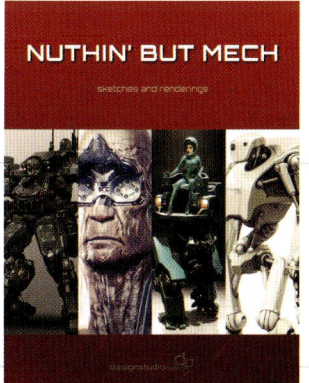

128 pages
Paperback
ISBN-13: 978-1-933492-67-4

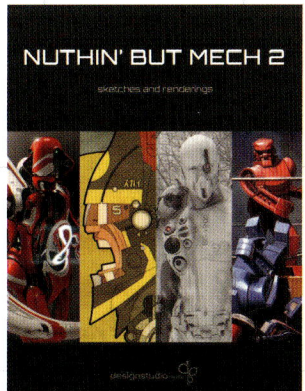

128 pages
Paperback
ISBN-13: 978-1-624650-10-9

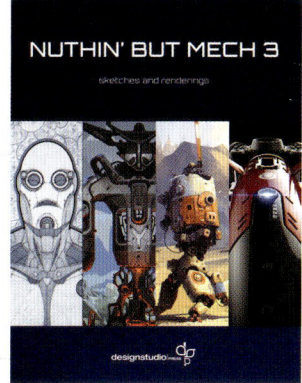

152 pages
Paperback
ISBN-13: 978-1-624650-27-7

THE NUTHIN' BUT MECH BLOG

Check out the blog where the *Nuthin' But Mech* series got its start! See some of the world's leading artists create a wonderland populated by mechs and machines of all shapes and sizes!

www.nuthinbutmech.blogspot.com

SELECTED OTHER TITLES BY DESIGN STUDIO PRESS

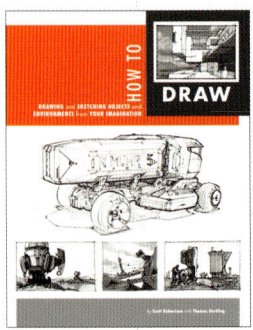

Paperback
ISBN-13: 978-1-933492-73-5

Hardcover
ISBN-13: 978-1-933492-75-9

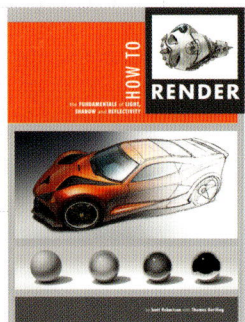

Paperback
ISBN-13: 978-193349296-4

Hardcover
ISBN-13: 978-193349283-4

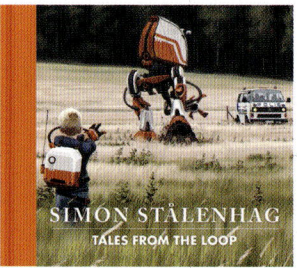

Hardcover
ISBN-13: 978-1-624650-39-0

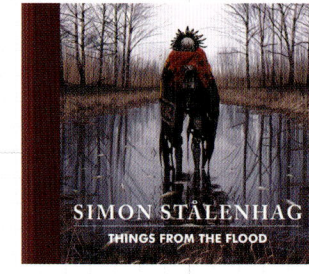

Hardcover
ISBN-13: 978-1-62465-046-8

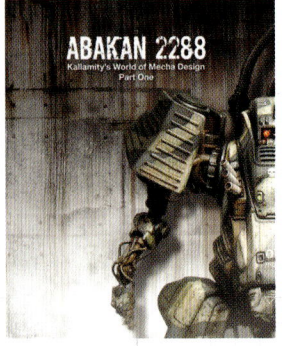

Paperback
ISBN-13: 978-1-933492-84-1

Hardcover
ISBN-13: 978-1-933492-98-8

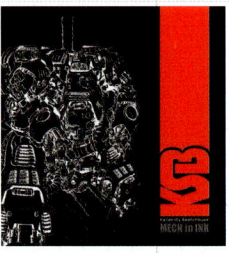

Hardcover
ISBN-13: 978-1-1624650-18-5

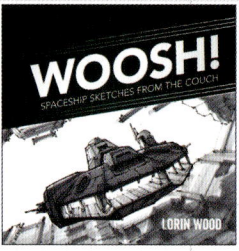

Paperback
ISBN-13: 978-1624650-07-9

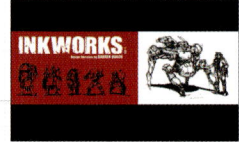

Hardcover
ISBN-13: 978-1624650-15-4

To order additional copies of this book, and to view other books we offer, please visit:
www.designstudiopress.com

For volume purchases and resale inquiries, please email:
info@designstudiopress.com

tel 310.836.3116

To be notified of new releases, special discounts, and events, please sign up for our mailing list on our website, join our Facebook fan page and follow us on Twitter:

 facebook.com/designstudiopress

 twitter.com/DStudioPress

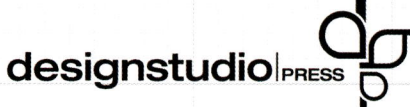